The Tursky tannery, Krynki, c.1912. Courtesy of Randy Kepecs. Kusiel (Yekutiel) Tursky, 19, in dark suit at center. His brother Shimon stands to his left; his sister Chuma looks through window at right. The tannery was owned by Shumel Lieb Tursky, their father.

Memorial Book of Krynki
(Krynki, Poland)

Translation of
Pinkas Krynki

Original Book Edited by: D. Rabin

Originally published in Tel Aviv by
Former Residents of Krynki
in Israel and the Diaspora, 1970

A Publication of JewishGen, INC
Edmond J. Safra Plaza, 36 Battery Place, New York, NY 10280
646.494.5972 | info@JewishGen.org | www.jewishgen.org

Memorial Book of Krynki (Krynki, Poland)
Translation of *Pinkas Krynki*

Editor of Original Yizkor Book: D. Rabin
Project Coordinator: Michael Palmer
Layout and Name Indexing: Jonathan Wind
Reproduction of Photographs: Sondra Ettlinger
Cover Design: Nina Schwartz

Printed in the United States of America by Lightning Source, Inc.

Library of Congress Control Number (LCCN): 2022934809

ISBN: 978-1-954176-45-4 (hard cover: 426 pages, alk. paper)

About JewishGen.org

JewishGen, an affiliate of the Museum of Jewish Heritage - A Living Memorial to the Holocaust, serves as the global home for Jewish genealogy.

Featuring unparalleled access to 30+ million records, it offers unique search tools, along with opportunities for researchers to connect with others who share similar interests. Award winning resources such as the Family Finder, Discussion Groups, and ViewMate, are relied upon by thousands each day.

In addition, JewishGen's extensive informational, educational and historical offerings, such as the Jewish Communities Database, Yizkor Book translations, InfoFiles, Family Tree of the Jewish People, and KehilaLinks, provide critical insights, first-hand accounts, and context about Jewish communal and familial life throughout the world.

Offered as a free resource, JewishGen.org has facilitated thousands of family connections and success stories, and is currently engaged in an intensive expansion effort that will bring many more records, tools, and resources to its collections.

Please visit https://www.jewishgen.org/ to learn more.

Executive Director: Avraham Groll

About the JewishGen Yizkor Book Project

Yizkor Books (Memorial Books) were traditionally written to memorialize the names of departed family and martyrs during holiday services in the synagogue (a practice that still exists in many synagogues today).

Over the centuries, as a result of countless persecutions and horrific atrocities committed against the Jews, Yizkor Books (Sefer Zikaron in Hebrew) were expanded to include more historical information, such as biographical sketches of famous personalities and descriptions of daily town life.

Following the Holocaust, the idea of remembrance and learning took on an urgent and crucial importance. Survivors of the Holocaust sought out other surviving residents of their former towns to memorialize and document the names and way of life of those who were ruthlessly murdered by the Nazis. These remembrances were documented in Yizkor Books, hundreds of which were published in the first decades after the Holocaust.

Most of these books were published privately, or through landsmanshaftn (social organizations comprised of members originating from the same European town or region) that still existed, and were often distributed free of charge. Sadly, the languages used to document these crucial histories and links to our past, Yiddish and Hebrew, are no longer commonly understood by a significant percentage of Jews today. As a result, JewishGen has undertaken the sacred responsibility of translating these books into English so that the culture and way of life of these communities will be preserved and transmitted to future generations.

In 1986, a group of farsighted JewishGenners started a project to pool their efforts together in groups based upon their ancestors from each town and donate money to get the Yizkor books of their ancestral towns translated into English. As the translated material became available, it was made accessible for free at www.JewishGen.org/Yizkor. Hardcover copies can be purchased by visiting https://www.jewishgen.org/Yizkor/ybip.html (see below).

It is our hope that the translation of these books into English (and other languages) will assist the countless Jewish family researchers who are so desperately seeking to forge a connection with their heritage.

Director of JewishGen Yizkor Book Project: Lance Ackerfeld

About JewishGen Press

JewishGen Press (formerly the Yizkor Books-in-Print Project) is the publishing division of JewishGen.org, and provides a venue for the publication of non-fiction books pertaining to Jewish genealogy, history, culture, and heritage.

In addition to the Yizkor Book category, publications in the Other Non-Fiction category include Shoah memoirs and research, genealogical research, collections of genealogical and historical materials, biographies, diaries and letters, studies of Jewish experience and cultural life in the past, academic theses, and other books of interest to the Jewish community.

Please visit https://www.jewishgen.org/Yizkor/ybip.html to learn more.

Director of JewishGen Press: Joel Alpert
Managing Editor - Jessica Feinstein
Publications Manager - Susan Rosin

Notes to the Reader

The images in the original book were reproduced from photographs from the time of the first edition. These reproductions were already of poor quality, being pre-war and at least 30 or more years old. As a result the images in the book are not very good and the best achievable.

A reader can view the original scans of the book on the websites listed below.

The original book can be seen online at the Yiddish Book Center website:

https://www.yiddishbookcenter.org/collections/yizkor-books/yzk-nybc313837/pinkas-krinki

or

at the New York Public Library Digital Collections website:

https://digitalcollections.nypl.org/items/30129f40-7525-0133-6825-00505686d14e#/?uuid=306aeee0-7525-0133-d60d-00505686d14e

To obtain a list of Shoah victims from Krynki (Krynki, Poland) the reader should access the Yad Vashem web site listed below; one can also search for specific family names using family name option. These lists are continually updated by Yad Vashem, so it is worthwhile to periodically search these lists.

There is more valuable information (including the Pages of Testimony, etc.) available on this website: https://yvng.yadvashem.org/

A list of all books available from JewishGen Press along with prices is available at: https://www.jewishgen.org/Yizkor/ybip.html

Acknowledgements And Dedication

Over twenty years ago, I began coordinating the translation of Pinkas Krynki, a Yizkor book. Little did I know then how much time it would take and how many people would be involved in this project. After many starts and stops, ups and downs – the book you're holding is now an unabridged English edition.

Yizkor books were written with great pain for the terrible loss of people, culture and tradition. The language in this book can be far from perfect, as is true for most Yizkor books.

There are so many people to thank for this accomplishment – all the folks at JewishGen and the JewishGen Press. Special thanks to Lance Ackerfeld., who kept the project on track through the years.

I also want to thank the many translators: Dora Rytman, Sara Mages, Eszter Andor, Hadas Eyal, Gloria Berkenstat Freund, Hadassah Goldberg, Judie Goldstein, Benjamin Kamm, Jerrold Landau, Danny Rubinoff, and Jim Yarin, with special thanks to Jerrold Landau for getting us through all the remaining Hebrew sections and preparing the book for this publication.

Last, but not least, I wish to thank everyone who contributed financially to make this English translation possible.

The book is dedicated to my Wolf family from Krynki, especially my great grandmother, Cherney Wolf (see picture below). Plus those who survived World War II, and sadly, the many who did not. Our cousins, Feivel Wolf, Lola Wolf-Resnick, and Samuel Wolf were among the survivors who wrote about their experiences and accounts of the War for this book

Michael Palmer, Project Coordinator

Cherney Wolf. Photo taken about 1900 in Krynki. Not in original book; Courtesy of Michael Palmer

Credits and Captions for Book Cover

Front cover

Top: *View toward St. Anne's Church from Kavkaz district, June 2014.* Photo by Tomek Wisniewski (Bagnowka-Bialystok). Kavkaz synagogue, right, is now the Communal Cultural Center in Krynki.

Bottom:
Wedding guests, Krynki, December 1937. Courtesy of Helen Abeles.

Back cover

Right: *First Girls' Hebrew School in Krynki, 1903.* Middle row, sixth and eighth from the left, founders Sima and Malka Grossman. Between them, student Hindke Nisht. Courtesy of Hadassah Goldberg, John Gorfinkel, and the Former Residents of Krynki in Israel.

Lower left: *Couple poses in front of the Kavkaz (Jewish and tannery) district, 1938.* Courtesy of the Communal Cultural Center in Krynki and Bob Silverstein.

Lower right: *Bryna Itta Shushan, Krynki,* February 12, 1922. Courtesy of Rosalind Finkelstein. From a photo postcard sent to her cousin in America.

Geopolitical Information

Krynki, Poland is located at 53°16' N 23°47' E and 136 miles ENE of Warszawa

	Town	District	Province	Country
Before WWI (c. 1900):	Krynki	Grodno	Grodno	Russian Empire
Between the wars (c. 1930):	Krynki	Grodno	Białystok	Poland
After WWII (c. 1950):	Krynki			Poland
Today (c. 2000):	Krynki			Poland

Alternate Names for the Town:

Krynki [Pol, Rus], Krinek [Yid], Krienek, Krinki, Krinok

Nearby Jewish Communities:

Odelsk, Belarus 9 miles N

Kolonia Izaaka, Belarus 9 miles N

Vyalikaya Byerastavitsa, Belarus 11 miles ESE

Gródek 12 miles SSW

Indura, Belarus 13 miles NNE

Sokółka 16 miles NW

Michałowo 18 miles SSW

Jałówka 18 miles SSE

Kuźnica 18 miles NNW

Supraśl 18 miles W

Svislach, Belarus 21 miles SE

Mstibovo, Belarus 22 miles ESE

Lunna, Belarus 24 miles ENE

Wasilków 24 miles WSW

Sidra 25 miles NW

Zabłudów 25 miles SW

Volpa, Belarus 25 miles ENE

Ros, Belarus 26 miles E

Golobudy, Belarus 26 miles SE

Janów Sokolski 27 miles WNW

Narew 27 miles SSW

Nowy Dwór 27 miles NNW

Białystok 28 miles WSW

Vawkavysk, Belarus 29 miles ESE

Hrodna, Belarus 29 miles N

Skidel, Belarus 29 miles NE

Narewka 30 miles S

Jewish Population: 3,542 (in 1900)

Map of Poland with **Krynki** indicated

TABLE OF CONTENTS

Krynki Rabbinate

In the flourishing years of Krynki (1897 - 1915)

The Tannery Town of Krynki in creativity and struggle

The First World War

Jewish Krynki between the Two World Wars (May 1919 – September 1939)

Under the Renewed Polish Reign (May 1919 - September 1939)

The Jewish Public Life

Krinik in the Past: From the Distant Past

Descriptions and memories

Destruction and Heroism

After the Holocaust

Supplementary Material

Name Index

Memorial Book of Krynki

(Krynki, Poland)

53°16' / 23°47'

Translation of *Pinkas Krynki*

Edited by: D. Rabin

Published in Tel Aviv by Former Residents of Krynki
in Israel and the Diaspora, 1970

Acknowledgments

Project Coordinator:

Michael Palmer

**Our sincere appreciation to Chaim Sheinberg, for Former Residents of Krynki in Israel,
for permission to put this material on the JewishGen web site.**

Thanks to Monica Reiss for her help in planning the translation project.

This is a translation from: *Pinkas Krynki*; Memorial Book of Krynki, ed. D. Rabin, Tel Aviv: Former residents of Krynki in
Israel and the Diaspora, 1970

[Page 7 - Yiddish] [Page 5 - Hebrew]

To You, Krinek

By Baruch Niv (Bendet Nisht)

Translated from the Yiddish by Judie Goldstein

Krinek, our hometown, is now for us, former residents of Krinker throughout the world and *Yad Vashem* [a memorial of names], only a written gravestone for the generations. The *"Pinkas Krynki"* is a community book of our glorious community that was mowed down. – A remembrance of our nearest and dearest. This is for our fathers and mothers, sisters and brothers, comrades and relatives who were so cruelly tortured, murdered and gassed together with the millions of our people by the German Nazi animals and their bestial assistants, Polish and Ukrainian murderers of Israel.

***

Our Jewish Krinek, a small but important ring in the glorious chain of Lithuanian-Polish Jewry, inherited and possessed a variety of peculiar traits. During the last generation of its existence, Krinek bubbled with initiative and energy, economical diligence, and had an energetic and full-blooded social life. It sprouted from struggling laborers and young people who brought liberation and revival to the Jewish community and risked their lives as pioneers.

A community rooted in studies and Judaism, imbued with the tradition of religious law and good deeds, our Krinek in it last fifty years represented a multicolored image. There were rich manufacturers, middle-class merchants and respected citizens, artisans and storekeepers, laborers of all kinds and the principal, tannery workers – a Jewish industrial proletariat!

On the religious side were learned *misnagdim* [opponents of Hasidism] and scholars, *musarniks* [ethics movement] and fervent Hasidim. There were yeshiva boys and young men as well as young married men who sit studying Torah and *Ein Jankev* [collection of stories from the Talmud] and Talmud as well as ordinary religious Jews. On the other side were free, worldly enlightened men, intellectuals and young Socialists and workers. And as far as the community was concerned – inspired followers of various efforts according to their taste, from *"Sholom Emuni Israel"* to fervent anarchists at the beginning of the 20th century and through Communists in the 1910's.

And according to *"Ani Mamin"* there were those who were certain of the Messiah's coming, even though he was late in coming and further believed in a world redeemer who would ransom the Jewish people. And from the other side – there were Zionist pioneers who dreamt about returning to Zion and dedicating their lives to establishing their people in a new and independent country, Israel.

The Krinek community, although small, competed with many bigger ones and even large Jewish centers. The rabbinical chair was occupied by great Torah scholars of their generation, prominent personalities - virtuous men. The Krinek Jewish revolutionaries were extremely militant – the Krinek bitter tannery strike at the end of the 19th century established them in the Jewish labor world. Our "sisters and brothers" carried out a surprise victory driving out the local Tsarist government and for several days ruled the shtetl. Three Krinek freedom fighters were occupied in a number of revolutionary acts in other Russian cities, including Peterburg [St.Petersburg, Leningrad].

But Krinek was especially distinguished by competing in the realm of education. Our small community built a substantial modern school system for religious education, Jewish secular in Yiddish, and Zionist pioneer in Hebrew. And for parents, even the oppressed, it was not difficult to work and take classes.

Krinek was involved in all other activities: culture, self and mutual aid, social work. It was rich in content and spiritual – a shtetl and city!

And as the terrible, unfortunate decline moved closer – Krynki's Jewish youth were the first in the area to participate in the last battle against the Nazi King of the Demons. This was for the honor of the people of Israel and in order to rescue, although few, those who would have to tell the world and the children's children what happened to our people and to the martyred Krinek Jewish community as a whole.

* * *

Our "*Pinkas Krynki*" is dedicated to the martyred community Krinek that was and is no more – its history, life, creation, struggle, battle and mass death.

A Yiddish letter from Bendet Nisht to the Krynki landsleit. Tel Aviv, July 1969

[Page 11 - Yiddish] [Page 9 - Hebrew]

The "Pinkas Krynki"

By the Editorial Board

Translated from the Yiddish by Judie Goldstein

Our martyred brothers who were tortured by the Nazi King of Demons were not favored with a burial in a Jewish cemetery. The gassed bodies were burned and even their ashes were spread over the unclean Polish fields, without even a stone over them as a marker, by the disgusting beasts.

A world of destruction led by "the bearers of human culture" their mouths silent and their ears deaf to the screams for help from a people, our Jewish people. Our people were condemned, laughed at by them and tortured with uncommon cunning. Not even a Satan of all Satans could have brought this about. Also, at present, old and new enemies lie in wait to annihilate our remnant. Every Jewish individual and of course every Jewish community, wherever you are, G-d forbid that you should ever forget, and not remember, every day!

"*Pinkas Krynki*" – is an eternal memorial to our martyrs – and a reminder to you. The "*Pinkas*" is their monument – one written with a pen – one that will last for generations! It is a monument that stands on its own. It is not even necessary to go to or travel to the cemeteries of which nothing remains. Our remembrance "stone" needs to find a place where there is still a Jewish community, a Jewish school, a synagogue, a library or institution somewhere in the world – and with every person from Krynki or with descendants of Krynki families. Let our "*Pinkas Krynki*" call out from every bookcase daily, always, every hour and every moment and remember to cry out "do not forget!"

And the book also represents, for our children, those we lost– the ordinary, shining, productive Jewish people of Eastern Europe, the ancestors of our people spread throughout the world, of which our Krynki community was an important ring.

We, the editorial board of the "*Pinkas,*" had as our assignment the reconstruction, before our eyes, of the image of our Jewish community in Krynki, and to fashion a mirror from which it would shine, as far and as complete as possible. We endeavored to bring forth the history pages of our martyred community and the events that took place from its founding, industrial power, struggles, fights and revolts. We maintained the vital outline of the generations to examine the way of life in Krynki and of its energetic, bubbling Jewish organized society and above all – to uncover the glorious character of the people of this society who shone in the hearts of our "people," the ordinary simple people.

And so we searched to bring out the high ideals and aspirations, to salvage what dominated our shtetl as well as the devotion to their own family and also to the community as a whole. They were prepared to pay with their lives in troubled times.

We put all of this together, whatever was left, in a story of the generations for our future generations so that they should be able to learn and know about their origins and the sources and roots from which their ancestors made a living and grew.

* * *

The small history section in our "*Pinkas*", whether the distant or recent past or the holocaust period – we based it on documentary support or reports by witnesses that were investigated. In cases where we did not have any other evidence, we went to various comparable alternatives, and therefore it was not possible to avoid certain repetitions.

In the Krynki community chronicles and documents that were gathered (such as the "*Pinkas HaKahal*" [the Community Record] records from Burial Society, for example) unfortunately, no trace remained. In this case we only have certain chapters and events. Everything was put together and composed of scattered authentic sources and there is no disputed information.

The "*Pinkas Krynki*" is, in general and in for the most part – a collective book, a work of our fellow townspeople who with love and devotion wrote a great treasure of treatises, and warm images. The book is full of memories about our shtetl Krynki, its Jews and their life. Some was written while Jewish Krynki still existed. The remainder was written with broken hearts soon after the destruction.

A special affection is deserved of the survivors of the destruction who with courage managed to write for the whole world and for us, their lamentable stories of the suffering and extermination of our city and people. They should receive our highest praise.

The book was written in both languages used by Krynki Jews, Hebrew and Yiddish. We have chapters and treatises, overviews and lists translated from one language to the other.

We have enriched the "*Pinkas*" with photographs of Jewish Krynki institutions, organizations, personalities and figures – to fix them in our memories. Therefore the entire Yizkor Book is dedicated to those who are no longer among us. We have refrained from putting in biographies of living people.

We have included maps and several drawings of the holocaust period done by Noteh Kozlovski, a Krynki friend. And in memory of the people we have included a list of the Jewish residents and families in Krynki before the outbreak of the destructive war.

* * *

With reverence we present this "*Pinkas Krynki*" to our fellow townspeople throughout the world and readers who are interested in the history and fate of our people.

May the *Pinkas Krynki* be received and kept for generation in each Krynki family, and for Jews everywhere in the world, and be placed in Jewish schools, yeshivas and institutions of high learning; in the synagogues and "Temples", reading rooms, libraries and archives wherever there are Jews.

May the "*Pinkas*" serve as a permanent remembrance of the six millions Jewish martyrs, among them our Krynki community, that our enemies murdered, cutting short their lives.

Remember this and never forget it!

Editorial colleagues and workers of the Yizkor Book

Sitting from the right: Benjamin Weinstein, Mashka Rokhkin, Boruch Gib, Bendet Nisht, Sheyme Kaplan, Yerachmiel Vine
Standing: Efrim Efrimson, Chava Yarushevski z"l, Shmuel Geler, Chaim Steinberg, Yenta Kaplan, Ida Sheyma Lider

[Page 14 - Yiddish & Hebrew]

We Express Our Deep Thanks

By the Association of Former Krynkers in Israel

Translated from the Yiddish by Judie Goldstein

To all our fellow townspeople and corporations that provided financing and material for the preparation and publishing our Yizkor Book for our community and its martyrs and above all:

The Krynki *landsmanshaftn* [associations of former residents] in New York, Los Angeles and Chicago in the United States; the Krynki Union in Uruguay and Argentina; the individual in Porto Alegra and in Rio de Janeiro, Brazil; the small Krynki settlement in Mexico – Sisi; and the Krynki in Melbourne, Australia.

And to all the dedicated volunteers from our *landsmanshaft* in Israel and in general to everyone who helped.

***

[Page 15 - Yiddish & Hebrew]

"Thanks to the Initiators who Made this Possible"

By the Editor

Translated from the Yiddish by Judie Goldstein

This writing immortalizes the memory of our people in Europe, our murdered brothers, in a Yizkor Book especially based on documents that until now embraced only a part of the destroyed communities. Many communities with their long, rich histories have until now not written their histories. Their *landsmanshaft* [association of former residents] and comrades are still considering how to undertake such a difficult task of remembrance.

Certain *landsmanshaftn* got together years ago and created "Yizkor Book Committees" and " editorial boards" and evenpublished their names and those of the volunteers. But of their work, nothing is heard. Other *landsmanshaftn* have called for "active collection" of documents, photographs and other material necessary for the projected Yizkor Books and gathered a lot but are still far from the mark. It is no surprise for those who are well versed in the difficulties of preparing and putting out a true written memorial.

The Krynki *landsleit* [former residents] recognized that they had chosen to take on the work and get it done! Certainly people were impatient to see the "*Pinkas Krynki*" finished and published. It takes considerable time to produce any worthwhile Yizkor Book, as the road contains obstacles (the Krynki book is not alone), either unforeseen or from heaven and not every difficulty can be overcome.

It is necessary to coordinate colleagues' activities and the editing in order to be successful. Certainly deserving of our praise is the tireless, initiator, the person who was central to the creation of "*Pinkas Krynki*," – my good friend for many, many years Boruch-Bendet Niv-Nisht. From the time he took on the task and until the "*Pinkas*" was published, all those years he faithfully watched over the creation of this work, even during his travels and during difficult personal circumstances, which he put aside, he never turned away from the preparation and publishing of the Yizkor Book or from trying to speed up the publication of the "*Pinkas*" until it was finished.

He deserves a separate thank you from all Krynkers for this beautiful publication.

[Page 23]

Note!

Translated by Jerrold Landau

We have added an index of topics at the end of the book, to make it easier for those interested to find incidental topics – which are of great interest to the public, but were not collected into their own chapters or sections, or were not given their own headings, and are not listed in the table of contents.

Articles which do not note the name of the author, or are noted with any pseudonym, were written by the editor. He was also the translator from language to language – Yiddish or Hebrew, and he prepared the index of topics.

The translation of the quote from Psalms on page 261 is from Yehoash.

Anything noted in the text in square brackets [] – is an addition by the editor.

[Page 24]

Krynki Map

Prepared by Paul Ogden

From the history of the Jews in Krynki

[Page 31 - Yiddish] [Page 25 - Hebrew]

The History of the Jews in Krynki up to the 1890's

Dov Rabin

Translated from the Yiddish by Danny Rubinoff

Translator's Note: The Hebrew sections on pages 25-30 are equivalent with the Yiddish sectionon pages 31-37, although the headings do not match exactly.

From the distant past in Krynki

Krynki (Krynyk, Krynek) was founded at the White Russian–Polish crossroads, approximately forty-nine kilometers south of Grodno. Like other settlements in the area, Krynki inherited its name from a tributary which flows near the town and deposits its water into the nearby Svisloc River, itself a tributary of the Neman River. Krynki is situated in a hilly and fertile area. Not far from Krynki from toward the west is found the ancient Krynki "Puszcza" Forest. This forest reaches until Chern-vietch on the Bialistock-Grodno railroad line and until the town of Supras'l.

Krynki is first mentioned in historical documents in the year 1434. In March of that year a summit took place between the Polish King Valdislav Yagella and the Lithuanian Nobleman Zigmunt Kestitovich. Yagella, while participating in a hunt in the Balavisher Forest, accepted an invitation by Kestitovich to meet with him in Krynki. It was in the town of Krynki that they renewed the alliance between the Polish Crown and Lithuania, (known as the "Unia") and worked on improving relations between the two countries.

The village of Krusheniani remains in the vicinity of Krynki as a memorial to an earlier epoch – to the time of the Tartar invasion into the area in the 13th Century. This was the largest Tartar settlement in the entire area of the Grodno region (of which Krynki was part).

Krynki first appears in the second third of the 16th Century as one of the estates of Queen Bona Sortza, wife of King Zigmunt the First in the "Ekonomiya" – the register of the Grodno region. On the 22nd of November, 1569, the King of Poland, Zigmunt August granted self-rule to Krynki, in the fashion of the Magdeburg Law. This law was imported to Poland and Lithuania by the Germans who were invited to settle in the Polish cities. The Magdeburg Law freed the area on which it fell from the rule of king and nobleman to whom it belonged previously.

For the "mitchzanim" (burghers) – the citizens of the towns, this law granted the right to elect a town council and city magistrate effectively enabling them to control their own affairs. According to the Magdeburg Law, all lands that had already been granted and surveyed remained in the citizen's hands. The exceptions to the rule were fish ponds and village meadows which were already designated as city plots and those lands which belonged to the Krynki estate.

In the Second Swedish-Polish War, King Karl the 12th encamped in Krynki on the cold winter day of January 12, 1706. This was in the middle of his retreat with his defeated forces northward from the Second Army which was hotly pursuing them.

"The Writ of Privilege"

The earliest archival document concerning the Jews of Krynki is the "Writ of Privilege" which King Kazmir granted to the Jews on January 12, 1662. This "privilege" was later renewed by King Zigmunt the Third, Vladimir the Fourth, Johan the Third and by August the Third.

The "Writ of Privilege" granted the Jews of Krynki the very same rights that were granted to other Jewish communities in the Lithuanian grand duchy. These rights consisted of the following: the right to acquire inheritable property in the market or in any street in the town; e.g. houses, garden plots, meadows, plowing areas, and to keep these properties and act toward them in a fashion of ownership. The right to build and establish synagogues, inns and new homes according to their own will. The right to repair old buildings, to produce whiskey and to brew mead and beer and to sell them in retail or wholesale trade in their own houses or rented houses.

[Page 32]

The right to engage in various types of businesses: to open stores in the market or in their homes. The right to engage in various trades: to establish and build butcher shops and to repair old ones, to buy animals in the market place and to trade them without having to pay taxes and levies. The Jews are permitted to rebuild a synagogue in the event that it burns down and to rebuild it in its original locale or in a new location. They are allowed to repair old synagogues. They are similarly allowed to have their own cemeteries and to even build the necessary buildings on the cemetery grounds. They are allowed to build bathhouses. The plots on which the synagogue and cemeteries are built are free from property taxes. All property taxes, levies on pubs and inns along with head taxes are to be paid solely to the treasury of the King in Krynki. It is permissible for the Jews and the "mitzchanim," non-Jewish citizens of the towns, to make use of the town meadows and to use the forest grove at the entrance to town. Additionally, the King formally transfers the official market day from Saturday to Thursday. He also gives permission to the town dwellers, the Jews and other groups—wagon drivers, small tradesmen, and butchers to come to the market from out-of-town with assorted merchandise for sale, purchase and exchange and to engage in trade in a free manner.

Concerning fees (especially for the needs of the army) placed on the city dwellers, the Jews must pay their portion according to existing rules and decisions of the government officials. The Jews are free (according to the statute of 1600) from paying postal fees.

The Burgher's Attack on Jewish Rights

The burghers, town citizens, in Krynki did not look favorably upon the rights granted to the Jews according to the "Writ of Privilege". They appealed to the government to repeal these rights. The commission established by the King to examine the burghers' claims originally ruled in favor of the burghers. However, the Jews of Krynki complained, explaining how this ruling would damage them. Nevertheless, a final ruling was never accorded and the matter remained undecided. Meanwhile the exorbitant expenses needed to fight the legal battle broke down both sides and in the end the King decreed to keep in force the rights granted to the Jews.

Yet, the burghers did not rest their case and on June 6, 1668 they issued a charge on the entire Jewish community and its leaders. The burghers claimed that according to the stories of the Bishop Godrytz, many items had disappeared and that rumor had it that the Jews were to blame. However, it was clarified that the claim had no basis in reality and only caused the burghers additional expenses unnecessarily. The burghers had to pay a fine and some of their rights granted to them under the Magdeburg Law were repealed.

Having no choice, the burghers came to an agreement with the Jews of the city on February 2, 1669, which was confirmed by King Yan Kazimir. According to this agreement, the burghers were obligated first and foremost to rescind all claims that they had made against the Jews since the year 1662, at which time the "Writ of Privilege" was granted. Similarly, they accepted upon themselves the responsibility in the future to give help to the Jews and to protect them in case of riots and attacks against them. Furthermore, the burghers also allowed the Jews to keep in perpetuity their synagogue "which stands between the houses of Yanova Kotlovayva on one side and Volf the son of Isaac on the other side and whose front faces the brewery and the house of the Jew Aharon…" The same law applied to the Jewish houses in the market and other real estate "which is in their hands and will be for them in the future."

[Page 33]

The agreement obligated all Christian city dwellers and similarly their descendants who might some time in the future try to break any detail of the agreement by acting against the Jews to pay a fine of 1,000 kop which is the equivalent of 60,000 Lithuanian groschens to the King's treasury and also compensation for any damages and expenses.

Whereas the King on his side added to the injunction and ordered an extra fine of 2,000 kop or 120,000 groschen on any burgher who tried to disturb the tranquility of the Jews through denying their rights granted them by the Polish Kings. Also such an attempt on the part of a burgher would result in the loss of his own rights.

All the above was again confirmed by King August the Third in Warsaw on January 19, 1745. It was registered for the records of the royal court of Justice in Grodno on the seventh of September 1745 by Kopol the son of Todros from Krynki in the name of Mendel the son of Leib, leader of the Jewish community of Krynki.

An Early Glimpse into the Community

The above cited document together with the "Writ of Privilege" itself not only shed light on the non-friendly and troubled relationship of the burghers to the Jews, (which was even worse in other Jewish communities) but they also show us that by the Sixties of the 17th Century the Jews of Krynki were already organized into a community structure. They had synagogues, a bathhouse, a cemetery and various property. We also see that they dealt in brewing alcoholic beverages and had taverns for their distribution. The Jews also dealt in trade, crafts and cultivated vegetable gardens in the framework of village agriculture. In addition we see that the Jews knew very well how to stand up for their rights – an attribute which describes the Jews of Krynki also in future generations.

Krynki Jewry was once again mentioned in an official archival document from the year 1680. This was concerning a Head-tax debt which the Jews in the Grodner district owed to the kingdom: of which one hundred and fifty gilden was assessed from Krynki Jewry.

Krynki – A Community Member of the Council of Lithuania

Krynki is mentioned in a Jewish source in the year 1679 in the "Pinkas" – record book of the Council of Lithuania, which will be discussed later. The chronicles of the Krynki community itself have not come down to us or were not preserved. The fate of "Chevra Kadisha" – burial society records, "Chevros Limud" – Torah learning societies records and registers of various other social and charity related societies were similar. None have been preserved. [1]

In the "Pinkas" of the Council of Lithuania, (the central organization for Jewish self-rule in the area of the grand duchy of Lithuania in the 16th and greater part of the 17th Centuries) Krynki is mentioned for the first time in a decree of 1679. This "takana" or decree concerned certain debts which the council owed to a number of creditors from whom it had borrowed money to pay for its operating expenses. Amongst these creditors is mentioned the "Captain, the Rav R' Leib from Krynki", who was owed 62.5 gilden. It is not clear whether R' Leib was the Rabbi in Krynki at that time. In any case, the use of the word "Aluf" – captain which is a general title of honor used for leaders of the Jewish community gives testimony to his elevated stature. It appears that he was also wealthy because he is mentioned two more times in the very same decree in connection with debts owed to him by the Council many more times the size of the above mentioned debt!

[Page 34]

The "Vaad HaMedina" (Council of Lithuania) and its Session in Krynki

In the year 1687, the Krynki Jewish community had the honor of hosting the "Vaad Hamedina" the Council of Lithuania. This was one of the Council's thirty-seven sessions during its century and a half of existence. In those times, a session of the "Vaad Hamedina" was considered a very honorable occasion in the internal affairs of the Jewish community. What exactly was the "Vaad Hamedina"?

As earlier mentioned, the Council was the highest representative organization of the Jews of that time in Lithuania. The "Vaad" was established right after the Polish Parliament had regulated a universal general head tax for the Jews of Poland, and for the Jews of Lithuania in particular. This was in place of the earlier system of tax assessment according to the number of Jews and taken directly from them. The Council of Lithuania was thus founded as the central Jewish representative body whose most important function was the composition and distribution of head-tax burdens and other special taxes upon the various local Jewish communities of the country. Another parallel function of the Council was the levying of internal taxes on the Jewish populace in order to support the organizational functioning of the Council itself and for the support of local Jewish communities.

The "Vaad" was composed of the representatives of three major communities (later from still more communities), amongst them, the community of Grodno, to whose region belonged the town of Krynki. Based on its above-mentioned official status, the "Vaad" also would liaison with the highest government officials concerning the lessening of the tax burden on the Jews and guaranteeing that Jewish rights and privileges were preserved. Thereby, it became the highest Jewish political organ in the land and often would consult with the Council of Poland - the "Council of the Four Lands" about matters which concerned Jewry as a whole; matters such as defense against libels and making efforts and bringing to bear various means in order to elude, repeal or mitigate anti-Semitic decrees.

Having the possibilities, due to its official capacity, to actually put its decisions into law, the Council became the most authoritative voice concerning general internal matters of the Jews in the economic, educational and religious spheres. For example, the Council, in order to protect certain traditionally Jewish businesses and trades, declared a prohibition of infringing and encroaching on the rights of businesses and established laws protecting rights of possession in businesses and trades. It enacted various rulings in the Jew's internal jurisdiction; problems of personal conduct, education, the strengthening of Torah study and also in the areas of "Tsedaka" – charity and social assistance. Besides all this, the Council organized regular support for its Jewish Brethren who had settled in the Holy Land – in "Eretz Yisroel".

In order to adhere to its large financial obligations, the Council, as shown earlier, was forced to take on loans from individuals and from other sources. This was needed especially in order to distribute bribes and hush money to notables in the Polish Parliament and in other offices. Large sums were also needed in order to save Jewish children from forced conversion by the unrestrained Jesuit Clergy and for ransom money. One of the creditors of the council was the above-mentioned "Rabbi from Krynki" R' Leib.

As mentioned, a session of the Council was held in the Town of Krynki in the month of Elul in the year 1687. It was a period in Lithuania when the Jewish communities had not yet fully recuperated from the destruction and ravages of the Cossack raids under Chmelnitzky, and from later Russian persecution during the Polish-Moscow war. Additionally, heavy tributes were demanded of the communities during the time of the Swedish Invasion. Due to these conditions, the Council chose a smaller and more out of the way location for its gathering, and it convened in the town of Zablodova, then a very inconspicuous town, and later the "mother" of the Jewish community of Bialistok.

[Page 35]

It turned out, because of a frame-up against the local leadership and Rabbis, the delegates to the Council were forced to leave Zablodova and convene in Krynki, which was one of the most important communities in the Grodno area and the most responsible concerning tax matters in its "neighborhood" –from among the smaller neighboring Jewish settlements and poor surrounding villages.

In the course of its twenty-second session held in Krynki, the Council completed the disrupted deliberations about the distribution of tax quotas and other rulings and finalized its decisions. Amongst its rulings, it was decided to strengthen the Talmud Torahs and to support Yeshivos in a number of communities. The Council additionally made decisions about rights of possessions and leases on properties and taverns. It also strictly enforced laws about falsifying weights and measures and even in dealings with non-Jews.

As a result of the structure of the Council, the smaller communities became dependent on the nearby larger community. This was true concerning tax assessment as well as religious matters such as appointments of Rabbis in their communities. The larger communities used their power in the "regional council" to cast onto the smaller communities a disproportionate and unjust percentage of the tax burden.

The Krynki Community Rebels

In the beginning of the 18th Century, together with a number of smaller communities in the Grodno District, Krynki rebelled against discrimination in the assessment of the head tax, which Grodno had so unfairly placed on the outlying towns. Krynki declared herself an independent region with the town of Amdur at its head. (The Amdur Jewish community was a more established one and is mentioned in the Pinkas of Lithuania as early as the year 1623.) However, the Lithuanian treasurer who was opposed to the revolt of these particular communities, intervened in the year 1720, and re-established the previous authority of Grodno on the communities who had desired liberation from her rule.

In the year 1761, the Polish parliament decided to change the head tax policy from a centralized, mass sum to a direct tax made on each family head. With this policy change, the Council of Lithuania lost its raison d'être in the eyes of the government and at the end of the year 1761 dissolved together with its district organs of self-government.

Coinciding with the initiation of the Jews' payment of taxes not on a mass sum basis, the Polish government ran a census of the Jews in every community from the end of the year 1764 until 1766. Children under the age of one were exempt from taxes and were not counted in the numbers of Jews for each local community. Besides this, the Jews made every attempt (because of monetary reasons) not to be counted in the census. In Krynki with its surrounding areas, 1,285 Jews were counted. And this was at a time when 13,815 Jews were tallied in the entire Grodno district. According to Dr. Yitschak Shiffer there were 2,555 Jews in Grodno itself. And according to other sources there were only 2,418 Jews in Grodno, including immediate surrounding areas. In Amdur there were 505 Jews. In Kosnitza (whose community was mentioned in the Pinkas of Lithuania already in the year 1623) 434 Jewish tax payers were counted. In the town of Sekelka, with its surrounding areas, there were 5,222 Jews.

The Jews of Krynki in the 19th Century

We have very meager historical sources concerning the Jews of Krynki in the first half of the 19th Century. A few contradictory sources exist concerning Krynki Jewry's involvement in the French-Russian War of 1812. Reuven Gamber, a Jew from Krynki received a citation for bravery when he endangered his own life in order to save the life of a Russian officer during the retreat before Napoleon's forces. On the other hand it is reported that Jews from Krynki were active in supplying provisions for the French forces, encamped behind the Bug River in the Polish area.

[Page 36]

The situation of Krynki Jewry together with the Jews of Amdur and of Volyn in the year 1823, is described in a government announcement issued by the governor of Grodno. According to this announcement, the Jews were in such dire straits that a number of them died of hunger. Accordingly, it was impossible for the authorities to reclaim their taxes via confiscations and fines. The governor, who had his doubts about the true picture in the towns, sent a delegate from the judiciary of Grodno to investigate. The delegate confirmed that quite a number of Jews in Amdur had died of hunger and sickness, while in Krynki the situation was better due to the presence of a local doctor who took care of the sick often at his own expense!

Nevertheless the governor quickly dispatched a group of tax enforcers into the communities (at their own expense) whose job it was to requisite by force all the taxes that had not been paid to the government coffers (the so-called "Kozna") for the last year and a half.

During the Polish Rebillion of 1863

During the Polish Rebellion in the year 1863, it is related that a number of neighboring Polish nobles ("Peritzim"), tried to influence the Jews of Krynki in direct and also in indirect contacts, to support the Polish revolt. But these attempts to influence the Jews and their accompanying promises of a golden future for them "after the victory" if only the Jews would support the Polish side, did not meet with success.

Krynki Produces Textiles

An important new development in the economic and social life of Krynki Jewry was the establishment in the late 1820's of the first industrial enterprise – a small textile producing plant. In the year 1827, the lessee, Yosel Geles established this small textile operation in his own house. By 1828, there were already five Jewish workers working on four weaving looms producing peasant clothing. This development coincided with textile industrialization taking place at the time in a number of Jewish towns of the Grodno district.

Although we do not have any additional information about the above mentioned loom industry in Krynki, it is known however, that in the sixties of the previous century there were already a number of busy textile businesses active in the town. In the 1820's, the Russian authorities made efforts to expel the Jewish population from the villages in the Grodno district. This edict was a definite factor in the growth of Krynki's Jewish population. The constant growth in population caused a need for more industry and jobs. These factors together with the excellent water quality of Krynki contributed to the development of Krynki as an industrial entity. Abraham Miller relates details about Krynki's contemporary textile industry in his memoirs, which will be quoted later in the Yizkor book. He notes amongst other facts, that practically the entire populace of the shtetel "from young to old, men and women" was plunged into cloth production, which developed very nicely. Wealthy Jews erected a number of factories powered by steam engines, "and the noise from the machinery created an impression of a rich industrial city."

[Page 37]

Krynki, however manufactured an inferior type of fabric and could not keep up with the economic competition and consumer demands for superior quality merchandise produced by the Bialistock and Lodz textile conglomerates. Krynki factories remained behind the times and their businesses quickly failed never to recover again. The looms and spinneries closed down and the various craftsmen left the shtetel and moved to the upcoming new industrial centers nearby. Other assorted workers who made their livings indirectly from the factories also left the town.

"The town" writes Miller, "was as empty as a cemetery. Because of the poor economic situation in town, the Jews began to buy up all saleable merchandise from the neighboring Gentiles with the hope to peddle it later in order to eke out at least a minimal living."

Fire Disasters

As if this was not enough, Krynki also became subjected to a plague of ruinous fires. Three such fires devastated the town. The first fire broke out in the year 1879. The second fire took place on May 19th 1882 and the third approximately in 1887. On a hot summer day the Synagogue, the Great Bais Medrash, The "Chayay Adam" Synagogue and the shtiebel of the Slonimer Chasidim were destroyed by fire. The damage was so extensive that nothing was left of the many deserted textile factories that had still been standing until the fire.

As usual, the Jews, of the neighboring towns, merciful by nature quickly came to help Krynki in its time of need. First of all, they sent bread for the hungry and clothing for those left only with the shirt on their backs. After a while, when the Jews of Krynki had recovered, they generously returned the aid and sent immediate relief to neighboring shtetels and cities, when they in turn were hit by fires.

Meanwhile, the town had previously adapted a new income-producing industry – that of the tannery business. Thenceforth this became the mainstay of the town economy. It also played a major role in the general and social life of the community, eventually enabling Krynki to recover and to replace her burned down wooden homes with modern brick structures.

Yaakov Zalman Levin from Horodok - supplied bread from Horodok to the victims of Krynki fire disasters

Footnote:

1.   According to the testimony of Krynki survivors, shortly before the liquidation of the Jewish community, the Krynki communal register (pinkas) was entrusted to one of the local priests. No one knows the fate of the register!

[Page 38]

Bibliography

Translated by Jerrold Landau

Sources:

1.   Krynki – In "S&322;ownik Geograficzny Królestwa Polskiego" (Geographical Dictionary of the Kingdom of Poland), Warsaw, Volume IV, 1883, and in Volume II, 15/2, 1902; Also in "Encyklopedia Powszechnie" (General Encycopedia) by Shmuel Orgelbrd, Warsaw;

2.   " Wileń;skiej Archiograficznej Komisji: Piscowaja Kniego Grodzień;ski Ekonomiej" (Deeds of the Vilna Archaeographic Commission: Registry Book of the Grodno Economy), Vilna, 1882, Volume II, page 235.

3.   "Ragesti I Nadpisi" (Lists and Writings), and anthology of documents regarding the history of the Jews in Russia, Petersburg, 1899, volume I, page 486, 1910, volume II, page 47.

4.   Ledgers of the State, or Ledgers of the Primary Communities of the State of Lithuania – published by S. Dubnow, Berlin, 5688 (1928), Enactments of the council during the year 5439 [1679], entry 772, page 192. And from 5444 [1684], from page 204 and onward; Additions and Completions to the "Ledgers of the State of Lithuania" added and edited by Yisrael Heilprin, Jerusalem, 5695 [1935], page 16 and onward; Ledgers of the State, introduction page XVI, and enactments 906 (and 966), page 265; Dr. Mark Vishnitzer, the "Council of Lithuania" "Lithuania" Anthology II, 1, New York 1951, page 181.

5.   Dr. Yitzchak Shiper, The Settlement of the Jews in Lithuania, in "Historia Yevreiskovo Naroda" (History of the Jews of Russia), Volume II, 11, Moscow, 1915, pp. 121, 123; Ch. Korobkow, Statistics of the Jewish Population in Poland and Lithuania in the Latter Half of the 18th century, In Yevreiskaya Starina, Petersburg, 1911, page 555; Krynki 'Indura" (Amdor), Koznica-Sokoloka – in the Jewish Russian Encyclopedia, Petersburg.

6.   July Hesen, the Socio-Economic Struggle in Russian Jewry from the 1830s to the 1850s, in Yevreiskaya Lietopis", Anthology, Leningrad-Moscow, 1926, page 46.

7.   Asher Margolis, History of the Jews in Russia (1861-1772), Centralfarlang, Moscow-Minsk, 1930, page 280.

About Jewish Life in Krynki during the second half of the 19th century until 1896

[Page 39]

About Jewish Life in Krynki during the second half of the 19th century until 1896

Translated by Jerrold Landau

D. R.

The first tannery in Krynki was set up already around 1864. Other smaller ones followed in its wake. As Avraham Miller relates, the "wet" tannery only worked with cattle hides – for shoes, straps, awnings, carriages, etc. These products were sold inside the city itself on the market day. That morning, the tanner would take all of his products, tie them with ropes to the "broken vessel" of the small wagon, and hitch himself to it. His wife and children accompanied him, following behind him, to help push it forward as it went up the hill. He arranged his meager "merchandise" next to the wooden pen of a merchant, and stood next to it to wait for a "trader," that is, a customer from the villages who would come to the market, and who might purchase some of the leather to make for himself a pair of plaited sandals (that were common among the farmers). During that time, the all the family members of the tanner guarded the wagon, so that no small thing would be stolen, for in those days, even minute, torn piece of leather would serve as a "purchase" for a poor farmer.

From these lowly, shaky tanneries, the Krynki leather manufacturing sector developed, which later became well-known for its volume and quality of its products.

This was during the 1860s. At the beginning of the 1860s, the serf farmers in Russia were liberated – a period of change for that empire at the beginning of industrialization. The Czarist regime even related in a positive fashion to the new economic situation. As we have noted, the tendency to ward manufacturing was already felt among the Jews in the Grodno-Białystok region during the 1820s. It found its expression in Krynki as well with the beginning of the textile manufacture.

The move toward tanning work in Krynki involved not only a willingness to engage in manual labor, even as a day laborer, but also involved overcoming of the revulsion regarding work that was unpleasant in the literal sense of the term, especially with the "wet" work with cattle hides ("carcasses") before they were dried – with the working of the "repulsive" [material] (that was also considered a "disgrace") and even damaging to health, especially given the sanitary conditions of those days in particular. Nevertheless, the difficulties with livelihood and the economic sense of the Jews of Krynki had their effect. Thus did the tanning sector grow in the town with the passage of time.

This happened even though Krynki was, from a geographical perspective, a remote place on the map of Jewish settlements in the area. It was far from both the water routes and the land highways, and it had no railroad at all. Despite this, it was blessed with an abundance of high-quality water flowing toward it from the wellsprings and from the artesian wells that were dug later on. Furthermore, it is told that one day, salty chemicals were found in those waters – minerals that are important for the tanning work and that improve the products.

A tanner, one of the pioneers of this work in Krynki, would work himself, and also employ some Tatars from the area. He would purchase raw hide "at a discount" from a flayer of carcasses or a butcher. He would process it into a coarse product and sell it to a shoemaker, or to a purchaser from the villages on the market day for fixing boots. The tanner would barely earn a meager livelihood from this.

The first workers in the factories in the "wet" work were, as we noted, Tatars and their wives. After some time, they also included Christian villagers.

[Page 40]

Germans worked in the "dry" work, for they were pioneers of tanning of horse hides ("Hamburger" hides) in Russia. Jews learned from the Germans until they became specialized in this field and themselves became expert tradespeople. Such tradespeople were even in demand outside of Krynki.

Hide processing quickly spread throughout the entire town, until the government changed its mind and stopped granting permits for setting up "wet" tanneries in the center of the settlement due to the inferior sanitary conditions. After a great deal of effort, the manufacturers later succeeded in receiving permits to open enterprises for the processing of hides on the other side of the river in the fields of "Janta" where the manufacturers obtained large areas and built giant tanneries. These had large windows and very comfortable equipment, such as concrete tubs and the like. There, they processed horse hides for various products, and employed hundreds of workers, tradespeople, and apprentices. Some of these factories became known not only by the Jews of Krynki, but also by many villages of the area.

Through the decades

Ab[raham] Miller

Translated by Judie Goldstein

Chapter on Textile Production

Before the leather industry arrived in Krynki, the shtetl had been busy for sixty years in the previous century [18th c.] with cloth production. In stables and in attics – stood (weaving) looms. Back and forth they ran without cease. Big and small, everyone worked. From morning until night the noise was heard and the clatter of the machines together with the singing of the bobbins. I still remember the old song that the young women would sing:

> "Mama, arrange a marriage and give me
> A man, a weaver;
> The day after the wedding I will travel
> In a carriage with rubber wheels".

A weaver was popular. He earned six to seven rubles a week while other artisans, for example a shoemaker or a tailor, earned more like eighteen gulden in the same time and not able to make ends meet.

The weavers had trouble with their hands. So before the spinning they used the strength of the waterfall from the big and small Nietupe and a little water helped with the task. There were also a lot of "roundabouts" (an arrangement using the strength of a horse, also used later in the leather factories to pound bark). Cloth production quickly developed and several fortunate manufacturers built steam factories with high chimneys. Krinik was noisy. The whistle of the steam factories and noise of the modern machines left its mark on the shtetl of an industrial center.

I would like to mention some of the manufacturers. It is thanks to them that Krynki reached its high status and they also bore the usual shtetl names: Yehusha Kugel's, Zundel Ite's, Mordchai Meyer Katsemakh, Meyer Yokhe's, Moshe Abraham the Wealthy, Munye the Tanner, Berl Pukh, Yidl Eli Chatskel's, Boruch David, Moshe Slava's, Yosel from Dobra-Valke, Chaim Jankel Hersh's, Hersl Sukenik, Yosel Tsalel Enya Kresh's, Jankel Moshe Abrham's, chaim Eli, Berl. Chaim Jankel's, Moshe Chaim Jankels, Feyvel the Ekideker, Moshe Yoshitser, Gdaliya Krupnik, etc.

[Page 41]

Besides the manufacturers, there arose in the shtetl a class of big merchants of raw material, commissioners and wagon drivers (there was no railroad in Krynki at the time).

Bialystok and Lodz, with their modern factories, that put out a better product, and due to demands at the time had begun to surpass the Krynki manufacturers who did not go with the flow of making cheap goods. They began to quarrel amongst themselves and in a short time became aloof and one fine morning they simply went bankrupt.

The work slowly went over to the neighboring towns – Horodok, Mikhalove and Vashilkove, etc. The factories were idle. The spinners, weavers and merchants left Krynki and the town became as idle as a cemetery. The windows and doors of the factories were broken, boarded over. The idleness and quiet cast fear into the population and passing by after the *kheder* [religious school], boys would avoid this area, as they believed that there were devils there. Jokers would blame the silent steam factories and composed a song about the troubles.

"Yidl approaches and says:

> The steam factory goes like a fiddle
> Eli approaches and says:
> The steam factory goes like an orchestra
> Gedalya approaches and says:
> The steam factory is out of order,
> Fayvel approaches and
> Rolls up his eyes."

Krynki in Confusion

Krynki's economic situation became very difficult. Looking at the community institutions in the shtetl, like the *Talmud Torah* [free religious grade school for poor boys], the *bote-medroshim* [synagogues, of study], the *hakhnoses-orkhim* [Sabbath shelter for poor wanderers], the hospital, etc. were poorly maintained. During the good years the bosses were too busy with their big businesses to notice any of this.

Krinik felt like after a wedding. The tumult was still humming in the head, but the pockets were empty. Everyone felt impoverished. People wandered around the market place like after a fire, not knowing what to do to earn a piece of bread.

Little by little people accepted the situation and carried on as best they could. They bought what the gentiles brought during a market day: a bundle of pig hair, seeds, flax, wax, wool and fought each other over an old, holy peasant shirt. They ran on the roads during a market day to stop a peasant with a little grain; then ran back to the shtetl, while the other whipped the horse in order that the Jew would not run after him. All this just to earn a kopeck profit from the trade. And from this business people had to live and pay tuition, pay for marriages and pay one's way out of military service. They wracked their brains trying to survive from one day to the next until times got better.

The Fires

The fires touched everybody!

One beautiful morning a fire broke out at the market place at Niome the tanner's and one quarter of the city went up in smoke. There was nothing anybody could do and so they asked for help from the surrounding cities. They received a little from here and there and they began to rebuild. First the Christian houses and later the Jewish ones. A lot of places stood empty and before the wound was healed another fire broke out - a larger one.

[Page 42]

It began on *Shivoser betamez* [17th of *Tamuz* June/July, a fast day to remember when Nebachanezar broke through the walls of Jerusalem in 586 and Titus in 70 b.c.e] and people had fasted the whole day. It was a very hot day. Everyone was tired. They were exhausted and went to sleep. Just before daybreak a large fire broke out. Screaming was heard. "Fire, it's burning!" People opened their eyes – there were lights in all the windows. Everyone woke up and grabbed the children. The father grabbed the axe – he ran to see where the fire was. I ran after him. I ran to the fire and saw Chemia Moshek's house was ablaze and nobody extinguished it. A second caught on fire, a third.

The Krynki rabbi, *Reb* Boruch crawled out a window in his nightclothes and begged the butchers to at least grab a hoe. He could not ask more of them. The fire was everywhere and destroyed the entire shtetl. Whatever things could be saved was carried into the synagogue, because it had not burned the time before and everyone was sure it would not burn this time. But it did not take long for the large synagogue, the "*Khayeh Odem*" ["Life of Man", title of a well-known compendium of Jewish religious laws] and the *Slonimer shtibl* [Hassidic prayer house], to go up in flames. All that was left were ruins. Three quarters of Krinik went up in smoke.

The Shtetl Is Rebuilt

The large fires erased all traces of the cloth factories that Krynki had. From all the tired, empty buildings nothing was left.

But it is said that after a fire people become rich. People in the shtetl began to stir, buying old bricks. They were ready to clear out a couple of blocks. It was lively. Some insurance money had arrived and some respected citizens were traveling the world with a document from the rabbi – to make money.

The large synagogue, whose walls were still standing, had not been forgotten. They were working on the building so that it would be ready for *Rosh Hashanah* [Jewish New Year]. Yudel Laskes helped a lot with the work.

Little by little the shtetl was rebuilt (with nice bricks in place of the rotten wooden houses) one with modern windows and doors (made with frames set into the openings.)

But the Kalter Synagogue was forgotten and was left standing without a roof. Who knows how long it would have stayed this way if not for Yankel Elke's (Mordchilevitsh) and Shaul Zelman from the courtyard. They did not rest until the synagogue was rebuilt. Yankel Elke's tried to make it as beautiful as possible according to the standards of the time. The vault was decorated with fine carvings of pears with an artistic knob in the middle. The carver was Shalom Pinkhas from Grodno and his name was cut into the carving. A lovely Holy Ark was also built (made by Efrim the cabinetmaker) and an artistic cantor's desk as well as a fine door (worked on by Eli Meyer Fishel's).

As known, the poor and guests of the community always prayed in this synagogue.

The Beginning of the Tannery

In Krynki, as in a lot of other towns, there were small wet tanneries that worked cowhides and also made simple soles (one of them was founded about 1864 and later restored by Jakob Kipel Zalkin). The entire morning during market day, the manufacturers would layout his entire "production" on a small, dilapidated wagon held together with string. He hitched himself to the wagon and dragged it to the market place. His wife and children helped pushed it downhill. He stood near the booth of Motl, Chaia Tille's, laying out the bits of leather, and waited for merchants and peasants who were the principal buyers of leather to make bast shoes. The wife and children stood around all day watching the wagon so that the peasants would not steal because back then a gentile buying a small piece of leather was a big purchase. The small piece was used for different parts of the shoe.

[Page 43]

The Holy Ark and Bima [Torah reading platform] on the Krynki synagogue

**Standing on the bima at the right is the shames [synagogue sexton];
on the left is the gabe [trustee of a public institution]**

[Page 44]

The large Krynki leather industry that began with these small leather pieces later became famous in Russia.

The tanners at that time were Yeshiya Shmuel Moshek's, Mates the Tanner, Moshe Velvl and Abrahaml Gimzshes, Jakob Shmuel the Tanner, Eliahu Abrahaml Holeveshke, Abrahaml Meyer Leyb's and Kopel *Safianik*. Kopel would make *safyan* [morocco leather] from sheepskins at Yoshe, Chaia Masha's.

This how they worked year in and year out. They bought horsehides from the "*kapitse*" [skinners[1]], a cowhide from the butcher and kept a couple of Tatars to help during the week (not on a market day). They sold cow hides to a shoemaker for gentile boots and with this they made a living, not having any idea that anything better existed.

People Become Tanners[2]

Hillel Katz-Bloom

In Krynki, a small shtetl of three to four hundred wooden houses in the 1890's, the population was poor and oppressed. They made their living from the village and the market place. When a peasant arrived by wagon he would be met by Jews in *kapotes* [long, black coats worn by Jewish men] and women with kerchiefs wound around their heads and there would be a tumult and yelling: "you, what do you have to sell?"

Down near the river there were several large wooden buildings where during the good years, in the past, when Jews had "*podvalen*" [cellars to store liquor] and taverns, there were liquor distilleries and breweries and Jews made a living from them. With the introduction of the monopoly in Russia, all the taverns and distilleries closed and Jews were left without the means to earn money. Men with entrepreneurial spirits began making tanneries in the old houses where leather was made to sell. Jews worked at dry leather and the Christians in the villages at wet hides.

A kilometer before arriving in the shtetl one could already smell the odor of the tanneries. Old, wooden, low, half-rotten buildings, the walls were damp and there was no ventilation. There was absolutely no sanitation. The workers had never heard of such thing and were not concerned about any of this. The only government official in the shtetl was the police officer. As long as he received his monthly stipend of fifty rubles from the manufacturers, everything was "kosher."

There was an exploitation of the workers and the working conditions. The majority were former impoverished small storekeepers and former idlers. In winter the wet workers would have frozen hands, as the owners did not heat the buildings. For the dry workers in the drying rooms the heat was unbearable.

[Page 45]

People worked in shirts and sweat poured from their bodies. They worked in these odious conditions without rubber gloves (the owners did not worry about these things). The wet workers hands were damaged from the lime and became infected from the hides of sick animals, with the terrible "*Sharbunke*" ("Siberian Plague", a type of ulcerated "carbuncle"). In just the winter of 1896-1897, fifteen workers died from it.

Nobody dared protest or complain about such conditions or the terrible treatment. Rebels like this would have been beaten black and blue and thrown out of the tannery.

From Tanners to Leather Manufacturers

Ab[raham] Miller

Jakob Kopel Zalkin was the first to begin working leather in large volume. He owned the factory that later belonged to Hershl Grossman. Although all the manufacturers tanned horsehides, some produced Warsaw soles. All of them worked according to the same system. The same wet tannery had the ceiling over head, broken windows, rotten vats, the same terrible odors from the skins, lime and extracts mixed together that would infect the air of the shtetl.

Never once on a Friday during the day, did we go without seeing a child or a wife bringing a piece of potato pudding to the tannery for a father or a husband. During the wet tanning he stood at the vat, with a scraping iron in hand, and pulled the hide from the carrion. He hurried to finish the work quickly, to be able to leave sooner for the bathhouse in honor of the Sabbath. He wiped a hand dirty from the leather and took the piece of pudding and "enjoyed the feasts" near the vat.

The first to begin production of leather in large volumes in Krynki, besides Jakob Kopel Zalkin ("*safyanik*") [morocco leather man] were: Nachum Anshel with his partner Ayzik Krushenyaner and Chaikel Alend who bought the small tannery from Moshe Gimzshes. There were also Jankel Mates' and Hershel Grossman, Leyb Mates', Jankel Moshele's, Yehusha Zatz, Hershel Yankel Elkes, Sevakh Elkes, Shmuel the American, Asher Shiya's, the Blochs, Moshe Szimshonovitz, Eli Kopel's, Israel Ertzki; Rechel's three sons – Archik, Velvel and Israel Leyb and others.

The leather industry quickly spread throughout Krynki until the government looked around and stopped giving out permits to set up wet tanneries in the middle of the shtetl because of the terrible sanitary conditions. After going to a lot of trouble the manufacturers were allowed to go to the other side of the river, at Yenta's fields. The industrialists bought large tracts of land and built immense factories with better facilities, such as large windows and cement tanks. In the new factories they worked horse skins and employed hundreds of workers, masters and apprentices.

The First Tanners

The first workers in the factories doing wet work were as previously mentioned, Tatars and their wives.

Not only the Jews in Krynki made a living from the factories. There were also gentiles who worked there.

When Nachum Anshel decided to take up leather manufacturing, he asked Kopel Zalkin for advice. Kopel told him: "If you have enough money to put into it – then do it." Nachum Anshel was not afraid and a few dozen years later he was the head of the shtetl, the leader of the Krynki manufacturers. He ruled like a strong government official and his word was law. His strong hand was also often felt on somebody's cheek.

[Page 46]

Germans did the dry work. The word "*garber*" [tanner] originated with the Germans. A lot of the words used in Krynki in the leather tanneries came from them. And when the Krynki young people went into the leather factories, they were taught not only the trade but also the German terminology.

The workday in the leather factories, during the early years, started at five o'clock in the morning and ended at dark during the summer. During the winter they worked from five o'clock in the morning until eight or nine o'clock at night. At five after five in the morning the doors to the factory entrance were already closed.

The weekly wage of a wet worker was three to six rubles.

The dry work was done by the masters who were paid by the piece or by two pieces of distressed leather (a horsehide of finely worked leather with minute projections). It took ten to eleven years of apprenticeship to become a master and it cost forty to fifty kopecks a week to learn the trade. The masters lived better than the manufacturers. They lived in nice dwellings, had servants, were well-dressed, splayed cards, drank beer and schnapps and slept until nine o'clock in the morning.

Like the children of Israel in Egypt, the Krynki workers also moaned and groaned under the yoke of the difficult, dirty work. The skin of the wet workers hands was cracked to the bone, from working the hide with lime. They were not able to change their boots, and on Friday afternoon would polish their work boots with cod liver oil and go to the synagogue. Even the dry workers would wear their greasy work trousers on the Sabbath and holidays.

Tanners in Krynki

Krynki Rabbinate

[Page 47]

Religious Leaders of Krynki

The First Rabbis and Preachers of Krynki

by D. Rabin

Translated by Jerrold Landau

Translator's note: The Content of this Hebrew section up until the final paragraph of page 47, is essentially equivalent with that of the Yiddish section starting on page 49. The translation here starts from the final paragraph of page 47:

During the tenure of Rabbi Avraham Charif as rabbi of Krynki, a renowned rabbinical judge and preacher lived in Krynki, known as "Der Alter Maggid" [The Elder Preacher], Rabbi Avraham Yaakov Lewitan. He had a fine manner of oratory. His style of sermons, his manner, and his struggles were in the fashion of the Maggid of Kelm. However, when Rabbi Baruch Lawski was appointed as the rabbi of Krynki, he did not tolerate any rabbinical judges in the town other than himself, and Rabbi A. Y. Lewitan was pushed aside from his post of rabbinical judge. He then left Krynki and moved to a different community, where he served as rabbi. He would go to preach in various places as "the Maggid of Krynki." However, he returned to Krynki in his old age. He was a teacher of older lads, and he gave classes in the Kowkoz Beis Midrash .

[Page 48]

Rabbi Yaakov Avraham Lewitan, "Der alter Magid"

About Two Heads of the Rabbinical Court

Translated by Jerrold Landau

Rabbi Yosef the son of Rabbi Asher HaKohen

Rabbi Yosef the son of Rabbi Asher HaKohen was a native of Krynki. He served as the head of the rabbinical court there during the 1830s. The approbations of the rabbis of his generations for his book *Kapot Zahav* (novellae, didactics, and sermons,

Vilna and Horodna, 5596 / 1836) testify to this, as they describe him as the rabbi of that time. They impart importance to the community of Krynki by noting that he was invited "presently to serve as the desired head of the rabbinical court of the holy community of Krynak." Rabbi Aryeh Leib Katzenelboign, the head of the rabbinical court of Brest-Litovsk, notes this especially, stating that Rabbi Yosef had earlier served as the head of the rabbinical court of Zabludow. Those who granted approbations for that book, which imparted fame in the rabbinical world to its author, mention Rabbi Yosef as "sharp, expert, and learned" and as "a splendid preacher in communities."

Rabbi Yosef HaKohen signed as the head of the rabbinical court of Krynki in two books: in the year 5593 / 1833 on *Avot DeRabbi Natan* (with the addition of two essays on the book of Rabbi Eliahu the son of Avraham of Delticz. That book also includes a long list of subscribers from among the notables of Krynki); as well as on the Vilna edition of the Talmud (Ramm edition).

Rabbi Baruch Lawski

Rabbi Baruch the son of Rabbi Shmuel-Meir Lawski was born in Lomza and was educated in Talmud and rabbinic decisors during his childhood by his father, the Torah scholar and wealthy leader who had studied in the famous Yeshiva of Volozhin for a period of time when it was headed by the two famous Yeshiva heads, the Netziv (Rabbi Naftali Tzvi Yehuda Berlin) and his son-in-law Rabbi Rafael Shapiro. During his early years, Rabbi Baruch also served as assistant to the rabbi of Brisk, Rabbi Yehoshua-Leib Diskin, who served as the head of the rabbinical court of Lomza for many years.

Already from his youth, Rabbi Baruch excelled with his straightforward, deep intellect, and in his ability to delve deeply into the words of the early sages. He filled himself with this knowledge, and became well-known. After Rabbi Baruch married a woman from Lomza, he was summoned to serve in the Krynki rabbinate in the year 5643 [1883]. He was recommended to the communal administrators in the town by his friend from the time he studied in the Volozhin Yeshiva – Rabbi Zalman Sender Kahana Shapira, the head of the rabbinical court of Kobryn at that time.

Rabbi Baruch Lawski

Rabbi Baruch settled in Krynki, and his influence was also great in communal and general affairs in the town. His knowledge of Polish and proficiency in Russian assisted greatly in this activism. He was considered to be a great expert in issues of Torah adjudication and general jurisprudence, and he was in demand by many as an arbitrator, to mediate in complicated disputes and general court cases.

[Page 49]

He was sought for arbitration by large-scale, well-known business owners, such as the Szereszewski family, who were famous tobacco manufacturers in Grodno; as well as estate owners and administrators.

Rabbi Baruch Lawski became well-known among the Torah personalities of the generation, due among other things to his work *Minchat Baruch* – responsa on the Code of Jewish Law, and the *Tur Orach Chaim*, as well as the laws of Passover and Torah lessons – published in Warsaw in the year 5656 [1896] (138 pages). The Torah personalities of that time would praise that book greatly for its bounty of extensive expertise, and deep sharpness. Large, Torah oriented communities of Lithuania wished to appoint him as the head of the rabbinical court, including the community of Ponevezh [Panevėžys], which sent him a rabbinical contract. However Rabbi Baruch remained faithful to the community of Krynki, preferring to remain there. He served in the rabbinical position there for 20 years, until his death in the winter of 5663 [1903] at the age of 60.

He was buried in the cemetery in Krynki. Masses of people came to his funeral, even from the nearby towns. He was eulogized by eight rabbis from the nearby settlements.

Rabbi Baruch's second book, *Nachalat Baruch*, was published in Warsaw in the year 5664 [1904]. This 48-page book consisted of 22 responsa and halachic novellae on the *Yoreh Deah* section of the Code of Jewish Law. It was a continuation of *Minchat Baruch*. In more recent times, a group of Yeshiva students in Bnei Brak published a second edition of *Mekor Baruch*, which eventually sold out. Its unavailability was felt by the students. That edition was entitled *Imrei Baruch*. Additional manuscripts of Rabbi Baruch Lawski on Torah topics and responsa that he left in his estate were not preserved.

The First Rabbis

We are in possession of details about the Krynki rabbis from 1883. Because of the lack of necessary community chronicles (such as the community record book, and the Burial Society records) we have only the names and details of the rabbis, as far as possible, as was found in the sources that were available to us.

As previously designated the first time a rabbi in Krinik is mentioned is in *"Pinkas Mdins Lita"* [Book of Records of the Country Lithuania], in institutions for the year 1679 where he is entitled "the Communal Leader, the rabbi Leyb of Krinik".

Later we have scant details about Krynki rabbi, first from the beginning of the 29th century, for instance:

Reb Osher son of *Reb* Avigdor ha Cohen was the rabbi in Krynki until 1810.

Reb Arye Leyb, the author of *Shaagas Arieh* [literally "the Lion's Roar"—a well-known work on Jewish Law] was at first the rabbi in Zabludova (after his father the rabbi *Reb* Boruch Bendet). He was the rabbi in Krynki until 1814 when he was invited to be the rabbi in Bialystok where he died in 1820. He was known as a sagacious scholar and versed in Talmud, Rashi's commentary, Tosfos and Codes. He was a master of style in Hebrew and was knowledgeable in religious poetry.

Reb Yosef son of Osher haCohen, author of "Kapos Zahav" [literally "The Golden Spoons, a book on Jewish Law and philosophy], the son of the previously mentioned Krynki rabbi, *Reb* Osher son of Avigdor – became the rabbi in Krynki in the 1830's until about 1838 when he was invited to become the rabbi in Kamenets-Litovsk.

After him, *Reb* Abraham haCohen became the rabbi in Krynki. He died in 1848. This is all that is known about him.

Reb Yosef of Krinik, *Reb* Yosele Lipnishker, was first the rabbi in Lipnishok and afterwards in Krynki where he died in 1867. He was a student of *Reb* Chaim Volozhyner in his yeshiva and in a letter in 1865, he described the situation of the study of Torah in Lithuania and Poland, before the above mentioned yeshiva was founded and stirred the Jewish community to open the locked yeshiva once again. In the shtetl *Reb* Yosele was considered a pious man and on his grave in Krynki there stands a monument where believers would come to lay request notes for him to defend them.

[Page 50]

Reb Abraham the sagacious scholar, "*Reb* Abrahamtchik", "*der alter rav*" [the old rabbi] from Krynki died there in 1872. He was known as a man satisfied with little.

It is likely that was after him until 1883 rabbi in Krynki, *Reb* Gad Moshe son of Zelman, a brother-in-law of the Novy Dvor rabbi *Reb* Abraham Tsvi Hirsh. At the same time the Rabbinical Judge in Krynki was *Reb*Shlama Chaim Mishelev, previously the rabbi in Novy Dvor who is buried in the Krynki cemetery.

Reb Boruch son of Shmuel Meyer Lavski who came from Lomza, studied in the Volozhyn yeshiva, and when he was young was described as a bright, upright man with an aptitude to penetrate deep into the ancient rabbinical authorities. He became the rabbi in Krynki in 1883 having been recommended by *Reb* Zelman Sender Shapiro, who was the rabbi in Kobrin and who was acquainted with *Reb* Boruch from their days on the yeshiva bench in Volozhyn.

Reb Boruch soon occupied an important place in community affairs and being well versed in Polish and Russian helped. He was a specialist in lawsuits brought to the religious court and in jurisprudence. People bringing lawsuits would turn to him, not only Krynki manufacturers and merchants, but also people from near and far in the area, for example the Grodno Tobacco manufacturer Shereshivski and noblemen, for him to decide or comment on their disputes.

Reb Boruch had also acquired a name among the Torah scholars with his work "Minchas Boruch" [literally "the Offering of Boruch"] – questions and responses on the "*Shulhan Aruk*", ["Prepared Table", title of a book containing all Jewish religious laws]. Because he was a great, well-versed, sagacious scholar of Torah, a lot of communities, like Ponovezh for example, offered him the rabbi's chair, but *Reb* Boruch was faithful to his Krynki community where he remained as rabbi for twenty years until his death in 1903.

Preachers

While *Reb* Abrahamtchik was the rabbi in Krynki, *Reb* Abraham Jakob Leviton was the judge and preacher – he was called "*der Alter Magid*" [the Old Preacher]. He was a good speaker and a follower of the Kelm *magid's* path and manner and his fight against petticoats.

But when *Reb* Abrahamtchik died, *Reb* Boruch Lavski took over as rabbi and he did not need somebody to help out as judge. So *Reb* Abraham Jakob was removed as judge and "*der alter magid*" left the shtetl and took up the rabbinate in another community and traveled around as the "*Krynker Magid*".preacher.

In his old age he returned to Krynki, was a teacher in the religious public school for older boys and spoke before the people in the "Kavkaz" synagogue.

Some time later *Reb* Tsvi-Hirsh Orlanski, "Hershele Dubrover" became the *magid* in Krynki. He was famous for preaching in favor of Zionist societies and the settlements in Israel. Among the common Jews he had managed to influence were the fervent Hasidim, but as told by Ab. Miller, Rabbi *Reb* Boruch and the bosses "were not convinced by him" and in 1887 he left for Szczuczyn (Lomza Province).

[Page 51]

The *Haskalah*
Rustling Winds of the *Haskalah* Movement

by Dov Rabin

Translated by Jerrold Landau

Translator's note: This Hebrew section is equivalent with the Yiddish section on page 52

Jakob Zalesk

[Page 52]

"Enlightenment" Winds

Signs of the winds of "enlightenment" began to blow also in Krynki about the last quarter of the 19th century. This is evidenced in the correspondence from there in the "*HazFira*" [newspaper] dated the 7th of *Nisan* [March] 1877, written by the enlightened man Jakob Leyb Zaleski in which he complains about the sad condition of Jewish education in the shtetl. He writes "education is being neglected and is run by the teachers who tire out the children with *gemore* [part of the Talmud commenting on the Mishnah], before they know how to read *Tanakh* [the Pentateuch or Five Books of Moses] as it should be. The *Talmud Torah* [free religious grade school for poor boys] students are ruined and hundreds of children from poor families wander around in the streets and nobody is concerned about them. They are not even able to write a couple of lines in correct Hebrew or sign in Russian.

"The previous summer there a teacher, an enlightened man from Grodno, M. Volgel, who had, on his own, and with a permission from the government, opened a school here in order to teach our children Hebrew and Russian. We hoped that his would be a modest beginning that would grow larger. Unfortunately, several people who felt that the school was a crooked business, began a smear campaign that the children would be led away from a Jewish life. The situation for the school has become very difficult and as a result it will not be able to hold out for long."

Later Zaleski opened a school in the shtetl. As mentioned in the Jewish Russian weekly periodicals "*Russki Yevrei*" [Russian Jews] and "*Voskhod*", since August 1881 he had gone regularly to endeavor to get a subsidy from the "Society for Trade and Agriculture among Jews in Russia." The subsidy was for a class to train young women as skilled workers in his school. He received the first subsidy in 1887 when the Krynki community agreed to pay an equal subsidy for this purpose. In 1901, 30 young women were enrolled at the school.

Zaleski also tried in 1881 to buy agricultural land, through the same society, for six Krynki Jewish families in the area, near Krusheniany. But in the mean time the Russian government had forbidden Jews to buy land outside the city limits.

About Jakob Leyb Zaleski, his son, Moshe Zaleski, today he is a manager of the Office for Hebrew Community Education in Cincinnati (United States) and Professor of Hebrew at the university. There he wrote that his father was a true Jewish enlightened man, devoted to the pursuit of "esthetics of beauty in G-d's tents." As for the broader picture and his proficiency in several languages he was self-taught. He was a reader of Hebrew and world literature and created a rich library, but mainly he was a trustee for various associations.

Footnotes:

1. "Kapitses" – Skinners who would handle animal carcasses, principally horses. They would skin the animals and deliver the hides to the tanneries. The "skinners" were also busy with other businesses.
2. Hillel Katz-Bloom, one of the founders of the "*Bund*" [Jewish Labor bund, socialist labor party influential in Poland and other East European counties until World War II.] had as a mission of the movement (active in Bialystok) visited Krynki in 1897. This was used in his book "*Zikhroynes fun a Bundist*' ["Memoirs of a Bundist"], New York 1940, page 148.

The flourishing period of Krynki (1897-1915)

[Page 53]

In the Flourishing Years of Krynki (1897-1915)

by D. Rabin

Translated by Jerrold Landau

The Size of the Jewish Population

In the census that took place at the threshold of the 20th century in 1897, 3,452 Jews were enumerated in Krynki, forming 71.45% of the general population – in contrast with the 3,336, or 84.62% (according to the "Geographic Lexicon of the Kingdom of Poland" 1883) in the year 1878, and in contrast with the 1,856 in the year 1847. It can be seen that the Jewish population almost doubled during the course of 40 years. From that point, however, it barely continued to grow during the 20th century, and the percentage with respect to the general population even declined slightly. This was despite the natural growth of the Jews, and the gains to the Jewish community from those who moved to Krynki and became permanent residents, especially during the flourishing years of the tanneries. The reason for the relative stagnation of the Jewish population in the city was – emigration.

Individual, daring Jewish youths from Krynki already immigrated to America during the final two decades of the 19th century. However, the waves of hundreds of emigres began to stream out of there from the time that the Czarist government began persecuting the tannery workers who were awakening toward a struggle for humane working and living conditions, and young Jewish revolutionaries were aspiring for freedom and equality. At that time, especially from the year 1902, many of them were forced to leave their homes en masse and escape from Russia due to the persecution. They especially went to the free United States. With time, this emigration increased, especially after the revolt in Krynki in the year 1905, and during the years of the depression that affected the tanning sector following that. When the first immigrants began to become acclimatized to their new land of refuge, they began to send ship tickets to their families and relatives, so they could join them. With time, the number of communities of Krynki natives in the diaspora increased to the point where that number came close to the number in the hometown itself.

The Situation and Struggle of Jewish Krynki

The Jews of Krynki had the same lot as the more than 6,000,000 Jews of Russia during the period under discussion, especially in the communal and political arenas. They suffered from the same decrees, oppression, and restrictions that the inimical regime decreed upon the general Jewish population of the empire, including Krynki. During that period, they continued to find means of restricting internal Jewish life – especially in the arenas of religion, culture, and general life – in which the [previous] oppressive, inimical, Czarist regime had not dared involve themselves with previously. Apparently, the writers of articles in Jewish newspapers, and even the researchers, did not report much about this regarding Krynki in particular.

A general Jewish event that especially shook up and frightened the entire nation in Russia was the slaughter in Kishinev in 1903. It found expression in the Jewish newspapers, even regarding Krynki (*Hatzefira*, Warsaw, from June of that year). These articles included the names of heads of families in the town who gave donations toward the assistance of the victims of the pogrom. The list included the amounts donated. These lists included tens of people who volunteered to collect the donations, and testify that all strata of the community participated – the manufacturing tycoons, as well as their employees, the tanners, and those of other sectors (see details on page 226).

The most important political event, as well as the most "sensational" that took place in Krynki, , the heroes of which were the Jewish tannery workers and the revolutionary youth – was the revolt against the Czarist regime in January 1905, when the local "sisters and brothers" (Yiddish nickname for the youth who fought for freedom and equality) expelled the leaders from the town and took the government into their hands for several days. We will relate more about this.

Jewish revolutionaries from Krynki, members of the general political streams (such as S.R. – Socialist Revolutionaries of Anarchists) also resorted to personal terrorist methods in their battle – became known even outside their native town for their deeds of bravery that they displayed with their self-sacrifice.

The local Jewish tannery worker, Sikorski, a member of the S.R. took part in the clashes that his faction organized against the murderous interior minister of Russia, Plehve[1], who was also responsible for the pogrom in Kishinev. Sikorski joined his two friends Sazanov and Kalyayev in ambushing the inimical minister next to the Warsaw paths in the capital Peterburg, with dynamite bombs in their hands. The first one, thrown by Kalyayev, killed Plehve.

[Page 54]

The 17-year-old Anarchist Niumke (Binyamin) Frydman, ended his young, adventurous life in a clash that he himself planned, based on his own conscience, against the cruel director of the Grodno prison, taking revenge on him for that which he perpetrated upon young Jewish girls. The girls were active in the tobacco factory in Grodno, where they went on strike, and were put in prison by the police when Niumke was imprisoned there. The head of that prison ordered that they be beaten, and their screams that reached the heavens frightened the heart of the young revolutionary. When he was freed, he ambushed the perpetrator, and shot him to death.

It is appropriate to note here that Yossi Galili, a commander of the Haganah in Israel and minister in the government of Israel, related in the name of the late Eliahu Golomb, one of the founders of the Haganah in Israel and its renowned leader (in the book *Eliahu Golomb – Chevion-Oz* volume II, Tel Aviv 5615). Minister Galili writes that at one point, Golomb incidentally discussed his youth in Krynki (he himself was a native of Wolkowysk, a city close by). Regarding this, he recalled the brave deed of the aforementioned Niumke, who died taking revenge for the disgrace of the striking Jewish girls.

No less important from a general perspective, especially in the annals of the Jewish workers' movement, were the daring, fierce strikes arranged by the Jewish tannery workers in Krynki in order to attain humane conditions in their work and lives. This is a long story, and we will later present it in full detail.

Tanneries – the Foundation of Life in Krynki

The tanning industry was established already in the middle of the 19th century as the vital cord of general life in Krynki. Even then, a portion of the Jews of the town continued to earn their livelihoods, or part thereof, from the weekly market day in the town, to which the villagers from the surrounding area would come to sell their produce and purchase their necessities from the peddlers or the products of the Jewish tradespeople. They would also taste "tasty food" and satiate themselves in one of the Jewish restaurants. However, the pulse of economic life in the town had now become the local hide factory, which not only employed and sustained its workers and owners, but in an indirect manner the entire network of local commerce, trades, and services.

By 1896, 20 tanneries were already operating in Krynki, tanning horse hides. These employed hundreds of workers, including a percentage of Christians. The revenue of the enterprises was large, and their owners became increasingly wealthy. Since there was no shortage of Jewish initiative in Krynki, the number of tanneries continued to increase, along with their employees. They grew in size, and their strength increased. Raw material started to be imported from afar, from Siberia and the Caucasus, and even from outside the country – from Germany, Austria, France, and even North and South America. The products were now marketed in southern Russia and other areas of Russia's vast expanse, as well as abroad. In 1897, the number of tannery employees reached between 500 and 700. In 1898, it reached 800, and in 1921 – 1,000. Later, it even reached 1,100 (of which 160 were gentiles), in 67 factories.

At the time of the Russo-Japan War in 1904, the value of the leather products increased significantly. The soldiers of the Czar, as well as others, required boots. The demand for leather increased, and the pride in the tanneries increased. This continued for several more years.

The Situation with the Tannery Workers

However, even when the hide tanning in Krynki was already taking place in full force, and the manufacturers, like their comrades in this branch in the northwest district of Russia, had attained the status of powerful tycoons, reaching the status of wealthy business owners within their people through their professionalism – the situation of the tannery workers was the worst of the worst. Their salary was negligible and their workday extended from 5:00 a.m. to sunset on the long summer days, and until 8:00 p.m. during the winter, and to an even later time on Thursdays and the eves of festivals. From time to time, they would even work on Saturday nights.

The salary of the "dry" workers was not set at all. The manufacturers would give over this work to "professionals [or experts] on a contract basis in order to ease their efforts and to earn more profit. These people would hire assistants and young apprentices for this purpose, and take advantage of them without bound. The wages were set by "time" and the accounting was calculated at the end of six-month terms. The professional would grant an "advance" solely according to his goodwill.

[Page 55]

The worker would require special mercy in order to be able to pay several rubles for a physician, in the event of a birth in their house, for a joyous celebration, or in the event of a tragedy, Heaven forbid. Throughout the entire "term," the worker was forced to purchase or order his provisions on credit, at a price and with the conditions that were appropriate to the issuer of credit. Furthermore, it happened more than once that the professional would announce a "moratorium"[2] or bankruptcy at the end of the term, or would simply disappear from town with the wages of the unfortunate workers stolen in his hands.

There was a set rate for a penalty for a worker for losing or breaking a tool, or for spilling a bit of tar. For complaining about such a travesty, and certainly for any refusal, the worker was liable to pay by being fired on the spot, possibly along with an appropriate beating. Furthermore, the "embarrassed" professional would inform the credit issuers to cut off the worker, for the fired worker could no longer be depended upon to pay his debts. Furthermore, in order to obtain work in a different enterprise, the worker would have to present a letter of recommendation from his former employer…

From the perspective of protecting the health and security of the worker, frightful conditions prevailed: crowding, filth, stench, a lack of air, and the absence of any ventilation. In the "wet" departments there was mildew and moisture. In the winter, there was a harsh cold, to the point where the fingers of the workers would freeze and even stick to the metallic areas of the tubs used for washing and soaking the hides. Burning heat pervaded in the dry rooms, with the constant sweat draining the body and energy of the worker.

Tuberculosis and rheumatism were therefore common illnesses amongst the tannery workers. The "wet" workers would often suffer from attacks of malignant abscesses – a condition caused by the hands touching the hides of affected animals. The skin on the fingers of the workers was usually fissured from constant immersion in the limewater used to soak the hides. The use of rubber gloves in this type of work was still unknown. The few directives regarding the Czarist factory laws indeed required such protection for the life of the worker, but the employers ignored them. The government inspector in charge of these laws was satisfied to receive hush money from the manufacturer, with the addition of a portion of liquor, as was customary.

The health and even the life of the worker, as well as his energy – was even more wanton in those days. No workers organization existed, and the Jewish day laborers were lacking any certificate confirming their most basic rights, let alone their social rights. The workers were dependent on the mercies of the employer, and they relied on his "propriety" in all workplaces.

It should also be no surprise that no small number of gentile workers were employed in the "wet" labor. These were "half" farmers, uneducated, whose tanning work was not their only source of livelihood; whereas the Jewish workers who came to the factory to work had the intention of training themselves in the work, and rising to the level of a professional who could supervise workers, and amass a sum of money so that they could open a small tannery or some other business of their own. Therefore, every worker attempted to attract the attention of the employer, so that he could get ahead and advance as quickly as possible. The Workers Union was still an unknown concept.

Tanning work was justly considered within the Jewish community, in accordance with the conditions of those times – as backbreaking, dirty, low-level work. The odor of carcasses and lime would "go before" the tanner and accompany him constantly, even on a day of rest – for he was unable to purchase a change of clothes or boots. The external form and the odors of the workers was unpleasant to the hide manufacturer when they came to worship together with him on Sabbaths and festivals in the common synagogue for all tanners – until the workers saw fit to separate and to set up a separate *Beis Midrash* for themselves. Furthermore, the tannery workers even made a Sabbath for themselves in the cultural-religious arena, and in 1894, they founded (according to *Hatzefira*, number 264 of that year) a union called Poalei Tzedek, whose "members were workers in factories, 400 in number." The purpose of the organization was "to hear lessons from a preacher in the house of worship that they set up for themselves for daily worship." Indeed, from that time on, their *Beis Midrash* served as a gathering place for meetings regarding secular matters, to consolidate the struggle that was to come to improve their conditions of work and level of life, and even more so, to raise their level of respect amongst the people.

[Page 56]

The Beginning of the Struggle of the Tannery Workers

The time of the struggle of the tannery workers in Krynki was approaching. Already in 1894, the first strike of the Jewish tanners in Vilna broke out, and the manufacturers were forced to raise the wages of the professional workers. The success of this strike struck far and wide throughout the tanneries of the entire district. Around that time, a local tanner who was a witness to the large-scale weavers strike that broke out in that year in nearby Białystok, arrived in Krynki. Similarly, a carpenter who worked in Grodno and knew about the awakening within the Jewish workers there to the struggle for their rights, also returned to his home. Individuals, youths, and workers, especially from Białystok, who had been taken by the "new" revolutionary political winds, also arrived in Krynki.

The memoirs of Av. Miller states that "In the summer of 1897, new faces began to appear in Krynki. *Melamdim* [traditional teachers] began to teach a new doctrine to the tannery workers in our town – beginning with the young and later to the older ones. They began by teaching the *aleph beit*, and those with sharper minds, with the study of Gemara. They began to secretly discuss the meetings that would take place in the evenings behind the Christian cemetery or in the Razbyonikow Forest. – – – Suddenly, the eyes of the workers were opened to see a path to improve their dreadful situation. The workers' songs, one more endearing than the next, had special influence. The youth joined the revolutionary movement with full enthusiasm. Krynki was frothing like a kettle. Everyone was confiding and whispering one to another. Pairs would go for a stroll, and turn through various alleyways, to a certain point in the forest, where they would listen to speeches and sing workers songs.

Things quickly became "practical" – with deeds. The activists were to gather in a large gathering (*Schodka* in Russian) in the aforementioned forest, 5-6 kilometers from the town to make a "covenant" of unity amongst the workers and to agree to keep the matter of preparing for action secret from the manufacturers and professionals. When those gathered arranged themselves into a semicircle, a mysterious voice was suddenly heard from a dark, hidden corner describing in an emotional fashion the difficulty, to the point of unbearable life of the tannery workers, and their slavery. The hearts of the audience were pulsating. The voice stopped when the emotions of the crowd reached their pinnacle.

Now, the crowd was asked to stand on their feet and arrange themselves in a circle. One of the participants said that rain began to fall, but the entire camp did not move from their places one iota. The voice was then heard once again, posing poignant questions to the crowd, such as: do they certify the description? Are they prepared to unite and keep everything that had been discussed from the employers? After the response, everyone shouted out in a loud, decisive voice, "We are prepared!" They were called upon to take an oath regarding this. Then, a certain comrade appeared with a pair of tefillin in his hand. He raised them up high (according to another version – also with a Bible), and the crowd repeated aloud the words that were uttered by the mysterious voice – to maintain the unity and to guard the secret about that which was said and heard at the gathering. At the end, the "people of conscience" amongst the crowd joined hands and sang a revolutionary song of oath.

The First Strike

One did not have to wait too long for the pretext to declare a strike. An opportunity arose when a professional in the tannery of Hershel Grosman slapped a worker on the cheek. This deed aroused the fury of the workers in all factories, and at a general meeting of the "dry" workers, it was decided to not come to work the next day.

At first, the manufacturers and professionals thought that this was only a prank by the workers, and that they would hasten back to their work when they had any suspicion that they would eventually starve. However, the employees quickly realized that this was not the case. One of them, Izik Krusznianer, even stated before his friends in public that "he was willing to swear that this was something that was organized and planed from the outset." Now, the manufacturers indeed got scared, and they sent messengers to the workers to find out what was going on. Then they found out that the strikers in the "dry" work were demanding that the secondary contracting with the professionals be cancelled, and that they be paid weekly directly by the manufacturer, as well as a 12-hour workday.

The employers had not imagined such brazenness. Now they searched for a way to influence 350 workers to return to their work – whether through pressure from family members, or through the involvement of the rabbi of the city. The rabbi, Rabbi Baruch Lawski summoned one of the "rebels" – Herschel Wajnberg (Pinks), whom he knew to be an intelligent person, who was also familiar with halachic jurisprudence. He agreed and went to the rabbi, but was greeted with words of reproof regarding the strike of the workers, which the rabbi interpreted as taking the law into their own hands, without first approaching the rabbi first as Jews do, and without going for a rabbinical adjudication [*din Torah*]. Wajnberg responded to the rabbi in his manner, also with words of halacha, and he proved to Rabbi Baruch that he was supporting the side of injustice, the side of the employers.

[Page 57]

When the manufacturers realized that the workers were standing strongly for their demands, they decided, with the agreement of the rabbi, to turn to the district governor in Grodno. A group of gendarmes were sent to Krynki. This was the first time that such a number came to that town. They immediately started to oppress the leaders of the strike by capturing them and beating them with murderous blows. The manufacturers also asked the police to lock the doors of the *Beis Midrash* of the tannery workers, so as to prevent the strikers from gathering there for deliberations. However, they too did not hide their hand on the plate[3]. On the Sabbath morning, they took over the large *Beis Midrash*, where the manufacturers worshipped. They also took over the seats on the eastern [wall] [4]. They set up guards to prevent the entry of the employers, and distributed the choicest Torah honors to themselves. After the services, they locked the doors of the *Beis Midrash* and took the keys with them. The manufacturers were forced to approach the police and request that they open their house of worship

However, the persecution increased the bitterness of the workers, and the battle grew sharper. In the meantime, tens of the strike leaders were arrested and sent to prison in Grodno, Hershel Wajnberg among them.

At the end, the manufacturers realized that they could not defeat the strikers, and they agreed that from that time, the workers would be paid a weekly salary, and that they would work from 7:00 a.m. to 7:00 p.m. – that is, only 12 hours a day. The "historic" strike in Krynki ended with a victory for the workers.

Av. Miller writes, "Thus began the period of strikes in Krynki. The workers realized that they had power. The arrogance of the professionals began to abate, and the workers no longer received slaps on the cheek from their employers. Workers in other sectors, including shoemakers, tailors, carpenters, and the like – learned from the tannery workers, and began to come with demands. They too were successful.

The Continuation of the Struggle of the Tannery Workers

The manufacturers were not happy with their downfall, and during the next work "term" after Sukkot of 5658 [1897], they convened a meeting with the rabbi, and decided to set contracts with the professionals for three years, and to only accept workers who were not among the "rebels" and who agreed to work for 14 hours a day. The workers, and this time also the professionals as well, did not agree to this, and began a strike. The employers requested that the district governor send the army to Krynki to impose order. They also gave over the names of the "rebels" to the authorities. There were arrests based on this, and the villagers were summoned to disrupt the strike. They were incited to beat the strikers. A father, who defended his striking son who had been attacked, paid with his life.

Army brigades that arrived in Krynki perpetrated attacks on the workers on the streets, and beat them. The soldiers even took over the house of worship of the tannery workers. They removed the Torah scrolls from the room and turned it into barracks. The workers then went to the *Beis Midrash* of the wealthy people and delayed the reading of the Torah[5]. The police were summoned, and they dispersed the workers. Their commander took out the Torah scrolls from the holy ark, making sure to cross himself first, in order to enable the Torah reading to take place.

The strike dragged on. The workers, hungry for bread, did not have the strength to stand up before the army and the strikebreakers who had been brought in from Białystok and other cities, even from far-off Berdichev. Finally, they were forced to give in and to return to a 14-hour workday.

In June 1900, another strike broke out, this time with the "dry" workers, who demanded a 12-hour workday. After the intervention of the government representative who arrived from Grodno, the manufacturers succeeded in convincing 50 workers (from among the 300 strikers) to return to their work. However, such a workforce alone did not make it possible to operate the tannery. Since the employers did not succeed this time to bring in strikebreakers from other cities – for the tanners there knew about the strike – strikebreakers were brought in from the surrounding villages, and the police were asked to treat the strikers with a heavy hand. They even conducted searches in their houses, and arrested them.

The strike dragged on. Under [financial] pressure, the workers went to the estates in the area and hired themselves out for seasonal agricultural work for a small wage, which they divided up among their striking comrades. Now the manufacturers approached the police chief to convince the estate owners to no longer employ "the rebels." After a strike of seven weeks, the hungry workers were again forced to work 14-hour days.

[Page 58]

However, in the following strikes, in the years 1903 and 1904, the tannery workers succeeded in improving their work conditions, and in 1905, the workday reached eight hours. With time, they also found effective ways to punish the employers for improper behavior toward the employee.

In the merit of their constant, tireless, strong struggle, the tannery workers not only succeeded in attaining humane conditions and much better physical circumstances in their work – but they also raised the status of their trade amongst the public. It was no longer considered "lower class" but was even regarded as honorable. Furthermore, through their struggle, the tannery workers themselves earned an honorable place in the front ranks of the Jewish workers movement in Russia.

The Political Activities of the Workers and Revolutionaries of Krynki

The root causes of the revolutionary movement among the workers of Krynki, with all the fame it attained, was similar to that of the Jews of Russia in general. There were three: human oppression and overlording at the hands of the harsh, barbaric (to our dismay, we must state: in accordance with the concepts of those days) Czarist regime; the harsh taking advantage of the workers, and the extreme oppression; and the persecution of the Jews and the rendering of their life valueless. Incidentally, most of the Jewish revolutionaries at that time thought and believed that the change of regime of the state would also bring redemption to their people in that land.

According to specific information, groups of Jewish revolutionaries already sprouted in Krynki during the 1890s. Some of their members even conducted publicity in Grodno, and attempted to organize the tailors, carpenters, shoemakers, and especially the employees of the Szerszewski tobacco factory there. We can surmise that these groups drew their revolutionary ideology from the manufacturing sector of Białystok. The Jews of Krynki maintained strong connections with that city, and continued to be influenced by it for many years thereafter, especially in the spiritual arena. These revolutionary groups were the ones who initiated, organized, and directed the strikes of the tannery workers in the town, about which we have already discussed extensively. Strong, daring youths who were only between the ages of 18-22 were the ones who were active in such groups. Many of them were imprisoned by the government, and were even put to trial in the years 1898-1899, some due to active participation in organizing strikes, and others for belonging to "workers groups." Some were sentenced to various harsh punishments.

Seventy tannery workers participated in the celebrations of May 1, 1901, in the forest near Krynki. They enjoyed themselves there until late at night. They listened to speeches and sang revolutionary songs. That year, the tannery workers raised a ruckus at the wedding celebration of one of their co-workers who had refused to take part in their strikes. Three of the perpetrators of the "disturbances" (in the language of the police) were arrested and put on trial.

At the beginning of 1902, a demonstration took place in Krynki during the funeral of a worker, where they sang revolutionary songs. That year, the immigration to America of the workers increased, and Krynki revolutionaries were persecuted by the police.

At the international Socialist congress of 1904 in Amsterdam, the Bund committee (the general union of Jewish workers of Russia, Poland, and Lithuania – the democratic Socialist movement) of Białystok was represented by 2,240 members, of whom 250 were from Krynki. This was a relatively large contingent in comparison with the clandestine movement in the town in those days, especially since other Jewish youths in Krynki were affiliated with other revolutionary movements, including the S.R. (Revolutionary Socialists), and especially with the local active organization of anarchists. In those days the Bund was the leading faction amongst the Jewish workers and revolutionaries in Krynki, as in the Jewish Pale of Settlement in general.

Anarchist Activities

The influence for the anarchist groups in Krynki came from Białystok, especially from the group headed by "Yankel Professor" – that is Yaakov Kropliak, a native of Zabłudów, close to that city. He later became a Yiddish writer, author of books, editor, and translator. Betzalel Pocbocki, a Krynki native, one of the first of Poalei Zion in the town, writes in his Yiddish article on that topic that there were followers from all streams and sub-streams among those groups. There were many spokespeople and counselors in this movement, different one from another, for the personal individual fundamentals were decisive. Most were among those who felt that acts of terror were a necessity, to be directed against the Czarist authorities and those who oppressed and took advantage of the workers. They also justified conducting confiscations and expropriations (*Achsim* in their language) – for they claimed that since the workers were prevented from receiving the full value of their toil from their employers, they should restitute what was stolen through different means.

[Page 59]

Indeed, various "operations" were carried out, called "actions" in the lingo of the perpetrators – not only confiscations. Thus, the manufacturer Shmuel Weiner, the "American" so to speak, was shot and killed on the last day of Passover by 17-19-year-olds, as he was coming home from synagogue services. Sometimes the anarchists would plant bombs, and not just for a specific reason. One was at a meeting of manufacturers, and it did not injure anyone. Anarchist demonstrations took place in the town several times, at which the revolutionaries dressed completely in black and sang anarchist songs. If the townsfolk would even "smell" the approach of such a "celebration" they would lock the shops (B. Pocbocki continues to relate), and passers-by would hide in the houses. The town strongmen would stand in organized fashion and wait for the Cossacks to come, to influence them to treat the stormy youths mildly.

There were cases when the anarchists were arrested, brought to trial, and accused for what they had done. Not only would they refrain from defending themselves, but they would also bring false defense witnesses, and would accept the guilt of their fellow upon themselves. This was all in order to take over the court lectern so that they could make declarations against the oppressive police and state oppression. They would do everything, including taking up arms, to free themselves from those who would carry out the verdicts against them. They would clash with the police even after they left Krynki, being unafraid of a death sentence, or deportation to Siberia for backbreaking work that would be decreed upon them. More than one paid with their lives when carrying out dangerous missions taken upon themselves.

Krynki anarchists were also active in various activities outside their town. One of them, Aharon Velvel (Yankel Bunim's) was the head of the attack brigade (*Hakravit—Boyuvka*) of Białystok. Among other things, he was the head of a group that attacks a police guard that was taking political prisoners, and freed them. Krynki youths would also be called upon to arrange "revolutions" in other towns. One of them was Yankel Caini, one of the most talented battlers. The Krynki anarchists attacked the post office in the town of Sidra in the Sokolka district. One of them was killed in this action. In 1905, a group of anarchists, including several Krynki youths, prepared to clash with the rule of the city of Odessa.

One of the strongest of the Krynki anarchists youths, very bold and who was involved with the most difficult actions – was Niumke (Binyamin) Frydman. Niumke merited being mentioned by the late Eliahu Golomb, the head of the Haganah in the Land of Israel in his time and a leader of its settlement and the Workers Unions (in the book *Eliahu Golomb – Chevion-Oz*, vol II, Tel Aviv 5715 [1955]) – for one of his actions in which he gave up his life. We will discuss this later.

Niumke, the son of a very poor family, had a father who suffered from a skin disease, based on which he was given a dishonorable nickname – joined a stormy group of anarchist followers (a group with no leadership or power of coercion) already at the age of 15. He already stood trial at the age of 16 for throwing a scare-bomb from the balcony of the women's section of the *Beis Midrash*, which exploded without injuring anyone. Those upon whom the bomb was thrown hired one of the best lawyers to defend the accused, and testified in court that not only did Niumke not throw the bomb, but also – they swore – that he was pious and worshiped daily in the *Beis Midrash*. It seems that the adjured judges found him not guilty, but Niumke found his own way. He declared that it was specifically he who threw the bomb, and that the witnesses testified in his favor out of fear of revenge from his brothers. He concluded aloud, "Long live the Socialist revolution!"

Due to his young age, they did not sentence him to death, but rather to deportation to Siberia for harsh labor. However, at one of the stops on the journey, Niumke participated in a prisoners revolt against the guard that accompanied him, and was thereby freed. His comrades provided him money to escape abroad, but he refused, claiming that he had yet another action to carry out.

He traveled to Grodno to take revenge against the director of the prison in which had had previously been imprisoned, and under whose watch some imprisoned Jewish girls were beaten. The girls were imprisoned for participating in the strike in Szerszewski's tobacco factory. Their screams and cries during the beatings moved Niumke, and he decided then to take revenge upon the cruel person at the first opportunity. Niumke's brother describes in his Yiddish article here that he ambushed the evil man next to the gate of the prison and shot and killed him with his revolver. When the police chased after him, he escaped into one of the houses, from where he succeeded in shooting to death one of the pursuers who tried to capture him. He continued to shoot at the rest of the police, and when he had only one bullet left, he put an end to his own life.

[Page 60]

This deed of Niumke, "who arose to take revenge for his people and shot the head of the institution that tormented Jewish young women" – was brought to the fore, as has been noted, by Eliahu Golomb. On one occasion, when he was dealing with the attacks of the Turks upon the Hebrew settlement in the Land of Israel during the First World War, he relates, according to Yisrael Galili, that when in those days Golomb was commanded, along with other Jewish workers, to work for the government on the Sabbath, "A burning fire overtook him, and he recalled the memories of tribulations and resistance from his childhood days in the city of Krynki in the year 1906, when his friend Frydman risked his life to the point of death for the honor of his sisters of his nation."

As has been noted, the Jewish tanner Sikosrski is numbered among the young revolutionaries of Krynki, who became known also far from their native town for their daring deeds, at which they they risked their lives. He was one of the members of the S.R. party, and he participated in the attack of the murderous Russian Interior Minister Plehve, who was responsible for the Kishinev pogrom. In accordance with orders from the party, he and his comrades Igor Sazanov and Sergey Kalyayev ambushed Plehve on July 5, 1904, next to the Warsaw crossroads in the capital Peterburg, with dynamite bombs in their hands. Kalyayev threw his bomb first toward the bloody man and killed him. Sikorski was later exiled to Siberia, from where he never returned.

Rebellion in Krynki

The general political event, as well as the most sensational in Krynki, the heroes of which were the Jewish tannery workers and revolutionary youth – took place in January 1905.

Already a month before this, the federative committee of the Bund and of the Polish Social Democratic party of Krynki decided to "confiscate" the mail in nearby Amdur. On December 6 (19)[6] 1905, the matter came before the Attack Brigades (*Boyuvka*) of the aforementioned committee. 1,368 rubles of cash were "confiscated" as well as stamps, postcards, a sword and a loaded gun – everything was "donation" to the battle against the oppressive regime.

However, the spirits in the town were stormy and shaken up after news of the bloody Sunday in Peterburg on 9 (22) January 1905, when a mass of workers, headed by the priest Gafun, while they were on their way to the palace of the Czar to deliver a letter of request for an improvement of their status – were attacked by bullets by the police, and many of them were killed. The storm increased further when they found out about the strike of railway workers that broke out in the town.

Without waiting, the aforementioned federative committee called upon the workers of the town to strike, to conduct demonstrations of solidarity with the railway workers, and to attack all the local government institutions. All the workers in Krynki, of various trades and factions, more than 1,500 individuals including gentiles, responded and gathered in the synagogue for a meeting. From there they went out to a demonstration, on a day of heavy snowfall. The city center was fully on strike, including all the shops. Bearers of red flags (according to the version of B. Pocbocki – also the black ones of the anarchists) were marching at the head. Calls against the police and in favor of revolution were heard from the crowd, accompanied by noisy pistol shots [bullet-less] and the singing of La Marseillaise, with the Attack Brigade [*Plugat Hamachatz*] advancing along with the group.

The police and government people disappeared completely. As the demonstrators advanced, they overturned telegraph poles and ripped the wires, entered the post office and damaged the telegraph machine and accessories and took them out of use – in order to cut off communications with the outside. They also destroyed the office apparatus and burned the stamps. They removed the picture of the Czar and shot it with bullets (as is stated in the report of the district governor of Grodno to his superior in Vilna). Then, they turned to police station and the Jewish registration office, where they destroyed everything that they found, especially the pictures of the kings of Russia and the "suspicious" citizens in the eyes of the authorities. The heads of the revolt removed hundreds of blank citizenship papers and passports, as well as the seal. This "loot" was later of great benefit for the revolutionary movement to provide "official" certificates for escaped political prisoners, and to enable them to reach a safe spot.

From there, they turned to the office of the director of the village subdistrict and destroyed it, as well as to the government liquor distribution office, where they took by force of arms the large supply of bottles of drinks. They completely destroyed the remnants of the government apparatus that still remained in the town, due to illness or other reasons. They removed their weapons. Now, the active militia prepared for actions to ensure local order.

[Page 61]

The demonstration also took place in the nearby Tatar village of Kruszyniany, where tannery workers of Krynki lived. There too, they destroyed the government liquor distribution depot. From there, they moved in a mass demonstration to the nearby village of Holynka and to the town of Greater Brestowica [Brzostowica], to wreak similar judgments.

In the interim, however, the Krynki police chief, who escaped to Sokolka, managed to call for help from the district governor in Grodno. When the army delegation reached the town two days later, they found the local youth in formation on Sokolka Road, armed with revolvers, metal rods, and axes. Even girls were standing at the gate, armed with stones.

The army captains entered into negotiations with the rebels, and promised not to harm anyone if they dispersed. These negotiations continues until the district governor himself arrived, with the regular army and infantry, who had been housed in the Yenta Beis Midrash. Now they decreed a state of emergency in town. Approximately 200 of the participants in the revolt were arrested by the police, who were assisted by spies and informers from the officials and residents, some of whom regarded this as an opportunity to extort "hush money." (After the workers recovered from these persecutions, they took revenge on the most murderous of these slanderers, and two of them were even taken out to be killed.) The prisoners were hauled to the prison in Grodno and placed in suffocating isolation cells. They were only freed in October of that year, with the government "manifesto" and amnesty that was declared in its wake. Some organizers of the revolt, including Niumke Frydman at that time, escaped from town. Some immigrated to America.

Disappointment and Setback

The revolt in Krynki concluded . The Bund organization was weakened, and its existence was no longer felt for a period of time. A mood of disappointment of helplessness pervaded amongst the workers. The intelligentsia was scattered, and reactionaryism reared its head. A "brotherly society" of manufacturers was formed in 1906 for the struggle with the workers. The organization of tannery workers was disbanded in 1907 due to the indifference of the workers. A recession hit the hide manufacturing, and the wages of the "wet" workers were reduced. The economy of Krynki was badly affected, and "Were it not for the support of the loan and credit organization, many small-scale businesses would have gone into crisis" – writes the teacher-activist Avraham Einstein in *Hed Hazman* on June 27, `1909, "However, the situation of the hide merchants improved lately, and the demand has grown."

He writes in a second article in the same newspaper, from August 8th of that year, about the spiritual-cultural situation among the workers in the town: "The boredom that took hold of many workers in Krynki after the days of the revolt brought them to disillusionment and forced them to seek something to spend their time. Some of them founded the Tiferet Bachurim organization. They study a section of *Ein Yaakov* and Talmud every day between *Mincha* and *Maariv* from the mouths of the Yeshiva lads. Some of them spend their time reading American literature in Yiddish, especially the thick novels that shake up the nerves. The intelligentsia busy themselves with reading Russian books."

Some sort of arousal was again felt in town with the improvement of the situation of hide manufacturing. A union of tannery workers was again set up in 1911, which succeeded in conducting a strike for 14 weeks in 1912, with the demand to return to an eight-hour workday. It even succeeded in improving the economic situation of its members. A legal library was also set up. The workers of Krynki again went on strike in 1914, even though depression and indifference again spread through the Jewish tanning sector.

Translator's Footnotes:

1. See https://en.wikipedia.org/wiki/Vyacheslav_von_Plehve .See also
   https://en.wikipedia.org/wiki/Igor_Sazonov where Sikorski, Sazanov, and Kalyayev are all noted as assassins of Plehve.
2. The term here is *shmita*, which is the same word as the Biblical Sabbatical year – when loans are canceled.
3. A Hebrew expression for sitting by idly.
4. i.e. the most honorable seats in the synagogue.
5. A common form of communal protest in those days.

6.   The dual date noted here, which is in the original, is indicative of the Julian-Gregorian discrepancy. Russia remained under the Julian calendar until 1917.

[Page 62]

The Golden Age of Krynki
(1897-1915)

Dov Rabin

Translated by Eszter Andor

General Overview

The Jewish population

On the eve of the 20th century, in the census of 1897, 3,542 Jewish souls were counted in Krynki. They made up 71.45% of the 4,957 inhabitants of the whole shtetl. According to the Polish Dictionary of Geography of 1883, 20 years earlier Krynki had had 3,336 inhabitants, and 2,823, that is, 84.62%, of them were Jewish. Since 1847 a total of 1,686 Jews came to the shtetl, and of them about 719 settled in the last two decades of the 19th century. This means that in 40 years the Krynki Jewish colony doubled. However, after 1897 the Jewish population almost stopped growing, apart from the natural increase and the influx of Jews who came to Krynki from the surrounding settlements in search of a better living in the shtetl which had been economically prospering for a number of years, and the percentage of Jews in the general population of the town even diminished a little.

The growth of the Jewish population in Krynki came to a standstill because many inhabitants left the shtetl and emigrated. Individuals, enterprising young Jews left the town for America already in the 19th century. The repression of the czarist police, however, which started to pour down on the awakened tannery workers and revolutionary youth of Krynki following their frequent strikes, forced the Jewish 'lads' (young, daring members of revolutionary circles)—especially after 1902—to leave their homes and escape--emigrate by the hundreds abroad, mainly to North America. As time passed this emigration intensified and later, when the first wave of immigrants settled down and became more or less 'Americanized' in their new haven, they started sending 'ship tickets' home to their families and friends, especially when the Krynki leather industry started experiencing a serious crisis which became even more acute after the First World War. In due course Krynki Jewish 'colonies' appeared in many countries and grew in size until the number of compatriots in these 'colonies' equaled those in Krynki itself.

The position of the Krynki Jews and their struggles

A regular part of the more than six million Russian Jews, the Krynki community also experienced the fate of the Jewish communities in the period under discussion especially in the social-political and spiritual-cultural domain. Krynki Jews endured the same vexations and restrictions introduced by the Russian government as the whole Jewish population of Russia. At the same time, however, they found enough opportunities to derive great satisfaction from various domains of internal Jewish life, and from the Jewish tradition especially, with which even the anti-Semitic despotism of the Romanovs did not dare to interfere. As can be expected, the Krynki chronicles—press reports and descriptions—and even the memoirs of the compatriots usually concentrate on the local events, especially on those that could be of general interest and even on things of global significance, that is on the incidents related to the Jewish labor movement, as for example, the 1905 revolt of the tannery workers in Krynki or their epic strike.

[Page 63]

Witnesses gave long lists of Krynki heads of the families who at the time of the Kishinev massacre in 1903, which shocked all Jews, especially the Jews of Russia, and of Krynki, hastened to give donations speedily for the victims of the pogrom. These lists, which appeared in the Warsaw paper *Hatsefira* in June 1903 (see p. 226), contain the names of rich middle-class manufacturers and their journeymen tanners, as well as of other strata of Krynki Jews.

The most important, and sensational, political event – with the tannery workers and revolutionary youth as its heroes – which affected the Krynki Jewish community was the rebellion against the czarist government in January 1905, during which the freedom fighter 'sisters and brothers' expelled the local lord and seized power in the shtetl for a few days. We shall describe this in detail later on.

The young Jewish revolutionaries of Krynki who belonged to political trends, which adopted terrorist methods in their struggle, became famous even far from their hometown for their daring acts and self-sacrifice. Sikorski, a Krynki Jewish tanner, member of the social revolutionary movement (SR) participated in the attempt on Viacheslav Pleve, the cruel czarist minister of interior, who was responsible for the Kishinev pogrom. With dynamite bombs in hand, Sikorksi and his two accomplices (Igor Sazonov and Sergei Kalaiev) waited for Pleve at the Warsaw station in Petersburg on June 15, 1904. Kalaiev threw his bomb first and killed the evil antisemite. Sikorski was sent to Siberia and he never came back.

The seventeen-year-old anarchist Niomke Friedman finished his very active life with an attempt on the cruel commander of the Grodno prison in revenge for his whipping and bullying the young Jewish female strikers of the tobacco factory who had been arrested.

Yisroel Galili, leader of the Haganah and minister in the Israeli government, recalls (in his book entitled *Eliyahu Golomb – Chevion 'Oz*, vol. 2, Tel Aviv, 5796) Niomke's name when describing the reminiscences he heard from the deceased Eliyahu Golomb, chief commander of the Haganah, as well as from the leaders of the Histadrut and from members of the Jewish colony in Palestine in general. In his recollections of his young years in Krynki (he himself was born in Volkovisk) Golomb portrays his 'comrade' Niomke as a "Jewish hero who risked his life to take revenge for the torture of Jewish women strikers".

No less important and also of general interest, especially for the history of the living conditions of the Jewish workers – a long affair about which there was much commotion in Russia – were the series of bold and heavy strikes organized by the Jewish tannery workers of Krynki for humane working conditions. Much has been written on these strikes and we shall also discuss them in detail in the present study.

The tanneries – the life and soul of Krynki

The tanneries – leather manufacturing – became the backbone of the economic life of Krynki already in the 1890s. Of course, even then many Krynki Jews made a living out of traditional petty commerce and crafts, and awaited the weekly market day when the peasants of the nearby villages came to town to sell their products, their poultry and cattle, and to buy and order what they needed, and to have a drink or fill themselves with beer or kvass and stuff themselves in the eating-houses on the market.

[Page 64]

Whether Thursday influenced the lives of the little shopkeeper on the market and of the plain traders, of the Jewish blacksmiths, cart-wrights, harness makers, cap makers, bakers, barbers, and the like is hard to say but it is certain that the leather factories and the masses of tannery workers were the main life force of the shtetl and of the artisans and merchants. The shopkeepers, tailors, shoemakers, quilters, bakers, butchers, coachmen, locksmiths, carpenters, masons, flour dealers, glaziers, and so on, all lived off the manufacturers and their workers. A strike in the tannery or a crisis in the leather industry steeped the whole town in crisis.

As early as 1896 there were already 20 factories which tanned horse skin and employed hundreds of workers, among them also a small number of Gentiles. The tanneries yielded large profits and the manufacturers were getting richer and richer. There was no lack of Jewish initiative in Krynki, the number of leather factories grew, the volume of production was on the increase and the number of employees multiplied. Skin was brought from as far as Siberia and the Caucasian mountains, as well as from abroad, from Germany, Austria, France, and even North and South America. The spacious realm of the vast Russian Empire and even foreign countries served as a market for the leather industry. In 1897 there were already 500 to 700 tannery workers in Krynki, their numbers grew to eight hundred in 1898, a thousand in 1901, and then to 1,100 (from which 160 were Gentiles) in the sixty-seven tanneries of the shtetl. The leather manufacturers were considered the richest people in the Northwestern region of Russia as early as the 1890s. Thanks to the Russian-Japanese war of 1904 the already booming leather industry began to flourish even more. Russian soldiers, and not only the military, needed boots. There rose a great demand for leather and the tanneries continued to grow for some years.

In the heyday of leather manufacturing when the manufacturers had already become rich and their master craftsmen well-to-do bourgeois, the tannery workers lay in the abyss. They worked 15 hours a day, and even more on Thursdays and before holidays, and sometimes they had to work even on Saturday night. The wages of the 'dry tannery' workers were negligible and they were paid irregularly and haphazardly. In the 'dry tanneries' the manufacturers would make their life easier and at the same time increase their profit by handing out the piecework (the work on a piece or part of skin) to master craftsmen as 'contractors' (subcontractors). These in turn would hire journeymen and underage apprentices for a 'term' (half a year from Pesach to Succoth) on a weekly pay and exploit them in the most extraordinary ways.

The master craftsman would pay only a wretched wage of few rubles and pay it when it was advantageous for him: usually after the 'term' was over. During the 'term' the workers were forced to appeal to the mercy of their boss, the master craftsman, to get a few rubles for the doctor, in case of the birth of a child, a wedding, or, God forbid!, some misfortune. The whole life of the workers was about trying to make ends meet by borrowing and buying from the shopkeeper and the baker on credit, and by asking the artisan to make or mend shoes or clothes on credit. They would send their order and pay the bill when they could. And to make matters worse, it would often happen that the master craftsmen did not pay even that wretched little wage earned by hard work, declaring themselves bankrupt or simply disappearing from the shtetl with the money.

[Page 65]

Punishment was a widespread custom if a tool was damaged or broken or a little cod liver oil spilt. If a worker talked back to the master craftsman or protested, the 'impudent man' was sent home and got a good beating too, and his creditors were informed that he had been sacked and he was no longer credit-worthy. Such a man would not be hired in any other tannery without a note from his previous boss.

The working conditions were dreadful in terms of hygiene and sanitation: stuffy air and foul smells, cold, and constant humidity characterized the 'wet tanneries', and great heat in the drying rooms the 'dry tanneries'. Consumption and rheumatism were frequent diseases among tannery workers and 'wet tannery' workers often suffered from the fatal Siberian plagues (a contagious type of ulcers which the workers caught when touching sick animals with wounded hands). At that time the health or life of the workers, let alone their toil, were forlorn. There existed no workers' organization in Krynki yet and the workers had no class consciousness and did not think of getting organized. People knew nothing of social legislation. No one complied with the few existing government decrees on ensuring hygiene in the factories and workshops and there was no one to enforce these decrees.

Part of the workers in the 'wet tanneries' were recruited from among 'half-peasants' and for them, working in the tanneries outside their villages was not their only source of income. The Jews, on the other hand, would come to the factories in order to specialize in the trade and become master craftsmen who stood above the average workers and to collect some capital to establish a little tannery or other little business of their own. It is not surprising then that for the sake of ascent they all tried to please their employer and had never heard of labor unity.

The average Jewish person considered work in the tanneries a lowly, hard and dirty trade. The workers smelled of the 'pleasant odor' of carrion and slack lime from afar. Krynki middle-class tanners did not tolerate this in the bes-medresh [*synagogue and study house*], so the workers built their own prayer house. The tannery workers separated themselves from their employers in the cultural-religious sphere as well and, as the Warsaw newspaper *Hatsefira* reported (see p. 264), they founded an association called Poalei Tzedek [*Righteous Laborers*] in 1894 whose approximately 400 members were all leather factory workers. The association intended to hire its own lecturer-teacher who would give the members daily Torah and Gemarah lessons in their bes-medresh.

The Bundist leader Sofia Dubnov-Erlich (daughter of the Jewish historian Shimon Dubnov and widow of the Polish Bundist leader and martyr Henrich Erlich) describes in her book *The Tannery Workers' Union and the Brush Makers' Union* (Warsaw, 1937) the typical young Jewish tannery worker of the Jewish Pale of Settlement. She writes that for the above-mentioned reasons "only those on the lowest steps of the social ladder would go to work in the tanneries. The tannery worker is the synonym of the ignoramus. A new type of factory worker started to gradually develop, at first in the Jewish quarter: the typical youth who was not diligent in Torah study but had mighty fists and a quarrelsome temperament. And this youth, with callus on his hands soaked in leather, gradually forces the others to treat him with respect."

[Page 66]

The first strike

The first significant strike of the Jewish tannery workers broke out in 1894 in Vilnius, the hometown of tanning in the Pale of Settlement. Years earlier a German master craftsman had established in Vilnius a little tannery to tan horse skin into 'Hamburg' leather, a type of leather produced in Hamburg, Germany. Gradually other tanners learnt the trade from this German master craftsman (as we have seen, the first tanners were German in Krynki, too). Thanks to the tannery workers' strike in Vilnius, the local manufacturers raised the wages of the qualified workers and the echo of the strike spread in the tanneries of other towns as well.

By 1897 a few Krynki workers had witnessed organized strikes in Bialystok and Grodno. This affected many tannery workers in Krynki and their first strike broke out. It was a heavy and prolonged strike, which ended with the first victory of the workers: a twelve-hour working day and "wages to be received directly from the manufacturer". This is how the brave and persistent fight of the Krynki tannery workers for humane working conditions started. "The Krynki workers", continues Sofia Dubnov-Erlich, "placed the tannery workers in the first rows of the Jewish labor movement." This was accompanied by a change in their way of life. "The tannery workers attained through their fight great improvements in their material circumstances and as a result their environment stopped treating them as pariahs. The parents among the artisan and petty trader started sending their children to work in the tanneries."

Krynki – A shtetl of Torah scholarship

The fight of the revolutionary workers although very significant was but one aspect of Krynki Jewish life in the period under discussion. Krynki was also a shtetl of Jewish tradition and Torah scholarship and even a prominent center in this regard.

In the period discussed, Rabbi Zalmen Sender Kahane Shapiro occupied the rabbinical chair of Krynki. A great Torah scholar of his generation and a prominent personality, he was respected and accepted by all strata of the town and his fame went well beyond the borders of Krynki. Rabbi Zalmen Sender had been rabbi in Maltsh and head of the well-known local yeshiva. When he came to Krynki, he brought a part of this yeshiva with him and continued to be its rosh yeshiva [*head*]. Even before his arrival, young yeshiva students from many Jewish settlements had come to Krynki to study Torah in groups. One of these students was Arye Leib Semiatzki who later became a distinguished Hebrew philologist and one of the most prominent editors of youth literature in Hebrew.

Under Russian cultural influence

From the beginning of the 20th century until the entry of the Germans in town in 1915, part of the Krynki youth, just as many young Jews in the whole Pale of Settlement, underwent a certain degree of Russification. This was brought about partly by the few schools in town with Russian as the language of instruction and partly the Krynki high school students who studied in the Russian high schools of the nearby towns and, most importantly, by the general spirit and mood in certain strata of the Jewish population. Speaking in Russian and singing Russian songs with reverence was 'in vogue', especially among the intelligentsia and the 'upper' circles, just as well as reading the witty and freedom-loving liberal Russian literature which had a strong influence on them.

[Page 67]

The beginning of Zionism in Krynki

The Zionist movement started budding in Krynki in 1898 and it soon set about to transplant its ideas into practice, in particular through a national Jewish education. The basis of a Hebrew education was soon laid down and in due course Krynki distinguished itself in this Hebrew education and it brought excellent results later in forming a nationally minded Jewish youth, which made devoted pioneers for building Palestine.

In 1908 Yisroel Korngold, a member of the Poalei Zion, became known in Palestine and he soon immigrated there. He worked in the Jewish colonies first in Judea and later in Galilee and he was secretary of the party at the same time. He became a guard, one of the first members of the Hashomer organization (the predecessor of the Haganah) but he was soon killed by Arab bandits on Pesach 1909. He was one of the first victims of the Hashomer organization and of the Jewish community who sacrificed their lives for protecting Jewish lives and property in the future State of Israel.

A proclamation of Poalei Zion in the Land of Israel, 5689 [1929], rearding the murder of Yisrael Korngold and his colleagues from Hashomer

Krynki, the tannery town, in creativity and struggle

[Page 68]

Krynki, the tannery town, in creativity and struggle

Translated by Eszter Andor

The tannery center in ferment

Krynki – a town with a name

Mordechai V. Bernstein

Among the annihilated settlements well known in the world, Krynki was famous for its leather industry, while among the Jewish public it was famous for its prominent rabbis, and it had a place of honor in the Jewish labor movement of czarist Russia. One of the first historic strikes of hundreds of Jewish proletarians, around which a sizeable literature grew up and which was considered a milestone in the history of the Jewish labor movement in Russia, took place in Krynki.

Krynki was one of the most important towns in the famous Tannery Workers' Union. In the 1905 revolution Krynki became well known all over the world. The telegraphic agency sent around the news that workers' councils were set up in Petersburg and Krynki.

It is an interesting story how such a wide tanning industry developed in Krynki, a remote shtetl far from any train station. Chemists are believed to have found that Krynki water was rich in certain important salts essential for the tanning process which helped the good tanning of the skin, and the leather that came out from the Krynki water was better and the production more precise.

The tannery

Shmuel Geler

Leather tanning requires much initiative, professionalism, knowledge and persistence – 'articles' with which Krynki was abundantly supplied – and, most importantly, unlimited water supply. Who would not remember the Krynki springs, especially the artesian wells, which flow with water all year long, summer and winter alike.

The process of tanning raw horse skin takes weeks. The skins 'go' from tanks (tubs) to tanks, from hand to hand, soak in various waters, swamps, slack lime and 'oak' (oak bark). They absorb all kinds of extracts and chemicals and are softened with fat. Many professionals worked hard and shared the work until the skin became the well-known Krynki leather.

The 'wet tannery' workers scraped the skin with sharp scythes to remove the hair and the meat from it. The so-called folders folded, smoothed, and compared the skins. The 'dry tannery' workers bleached, cut into strips, curled and rolled, colored and polished, spread out and stretched the skins on frames. The song "The hands be healthy with callus / The sweat running down the forehead!" was in the hearts of all the tannery workers. For them this was daily prose.

The 'wet tannery' workers were constantly soaked in slack lime during their work. The long leather aprons and boots could not protect them from the constant humidity around them. Their hands were always covered with wounds burnt by slack lime and their nails were yellow and green.

[Page 69]

They were enveloped in a strong smell that they absorbed through long years of working in the tannery. The 'wet tannery' workers liked taking a drink from time to time. The alcohol would warm their limbs and drive the bitterness of slack lime out of their mouth and the everyday bitterness out of their hearts.

The work of the 'dry tannery' workers who specialized in various trades was somewhat easier. The main advantage was that they worked mostly in a dry place and they often sneezed, especially in the winter, because of the heat and smoke coming from the nearby drying rooms.

'Fulling' was a trade in itself. The fullers used to make 'uppers' (tongues). The main art of fulling lay in making the 'uppers' strong and soft and making their little tongue protrude. The Krynki 'tongues' adorned thousands of peasant boots.

Folding was an 'aristocratic' trade. It took years to become a good folder, to acquire nimbleness in the fingers and a light professional mobility with the sharp folds. The folders received much higher wages. They taught the trade to their children and close family members in order to pass it on as a dowry to their future sons-in-law.

The strike epoch

The condition of the Jewish tannery workers

Mordechai V. Bernstein

Krynki had a high tanning production already in the 1890s, distributing tanned leather to all the corners of the Russian Empire. The Krynki Hamburg type 'cowhide' and boot legs were sent even to the most distant places as well. Before one entered the shtetl, from the direction of Sokolke or Brestovitz, one could already smell the odor of slack lime, the fleshy side of skin, and dry oak coming from the tanning tanks.

The exploitation of the tannery workers had no limits. They worked long hours in the stuffy tanneries and their wages were miserable. They toiled in stinking crowded workshops. They dragged first the wet skins into the tanks of slack lime and oak and then the dry skin in the 'dry section' to the folders and fullers. And still they could not make ends meet.

In the eyes of the Jewish public the tannery worker was inferior even compared to a simple worker – he was accompanied by the smell of skin, blood and slack lime in which the skin soaked. The manufacturers, these 'respectable Jews', did not even want to pray in the same shul [*synagogue*] as their workers, so the tannery workers built their own bes-medresh.

The beginning of the strike movement

H. Weinberg (Hershl Pinkes)

It was the winter of 1896-97. Some workers started to go around with strange secrets that they confided to only a few select people, as well as to me. Thanks to the agitation of Chaim Leyser Yonah the carpenter who had worked in Grodno and came to Krynki from there, a few workers looked around themselves and understood what a great injustice was committed against the toilers.

[Page 70]

They organized themselves into small groups, hoping that these groups will multiply in due course. However, the movement advanced very slowly and it almost died at the beginning of the following summer.

Tzolke Dretzhiner, a tanner from Krynki, then came from Bialystok where he had stayed for some time when the weavers went on strike there. He brought with him a complete plan on how to carry out similar strikes in Krynki. At first he chose only a few trustworthy workers and called them together to a secret meeting to which I was also invited although I was younger than they were. We swore an oath that we would be devoted to the work and would not betray each other. We discussed various plans on how to prepare a strike. Our demands were the following: working from seven in the morning to seven in the evening, and getting paid directly by the manufacturer. Our numbers grew from day to day. Soon some good speakers rose from among the masses. It soon became impossible to keep the larger meetings secret very often. In the course of a few weeks the majority of the workers of Krynki joined the movement.

Before and during of the strike [1]

Yosl Kohn

There were few 'enlightened' people in Krynki at that time. The Jews were firmly rooted in the Jewish ways and customs and what the agitators told them and wanted them to do meant rebellion and upset their lives and beliefs. The tannery workers who were being agitated through intimate chats during walks, and later through meetings in the forest, were no steady elements. The agitators had two objectives: to strengthen labor unity and to make sure that the manufacturers and the master craftsmen did not learn about their preparations too early. The younger ones who were already enlightened knew some of the 'brothers and sisters' songs but all these things were still foreign to the 'masses'.

When the first big meeting was organized in the Razboynikov woods, about 5 versts from the shtetl, the leaders, with the help of the 'steady elements', put on a real show. When the tannery workers sat down in a half circle, a voice started talking suddenly. It depicted the hard life and slavish conditions under which the manufacturers and the master craftsmen held the tannery workers. The fact that the face of the preacher could not be seen created a mood of mystery and great curiosity – an impression as if the scene when God revealed himself to Moses, our teacher, through a voice in the desert had been repeated - only the Burning Bush was missing. When the voice fell silent, everybody was asked to get up and form a circle. The voice started speaking once again: "Brothers, is all I have told you true?" "Yes", answered the crowd. "Will you unite yourselves?" "We will", responded the crowd. "Will you stand up all for one and one for all?" "We will", they cried out. "Will you keep all you have heard in secret and not let the manufacturers and the master craftsmen know?" "We will."

[Page 71]

"If so, swear an oath." A member appeared as soon as this was heard with a sacred book and phylacteries. He lifted the book high up in the air and the crowd, repeated after the voice, the oath of unity and secrecy. After the ceremony, people took each other by the hand and the 'enlightened' started to sing:

> "Brothers and sisters, comrades in work and need
> Come together all who are scattered and dispersed
> The flag is waiting for us
> It is burning with rage and from blood is it red
> We swear an oath of life and death."

As the 'unity' movement started to expand, the agitators who had been sent to Krynki returned to Bialystok. It was left to the local 'enlightened' to instruct the tannery workers. The main leaders were Hershl Pinkes, the shamash, Itshke Grodner, and my uncle Moishe Berl. My other uncle, Chaim Shloyme, was also active.

The oath that the workers swore on the sacred book and the phylacteries was held sacred. The strike broke out by accident. A master craftsman from Hershl Grosman's factory slapped a worker in the face and that was the signal to which workers in all factories rose in rage. A meeting was held with the participation of all the tannery workers and it was decided that no one would go to work the next day. At first the manufacturers and the master craftsmen thought it was a joke. They played jokes on the strikers and laughed at them: "Ah", they said, "they will soon be hungry and they will come back and take up their work." As this wish did not come true, one of the influential proprietors Eizik Krushenianer, my grandfather Chaim Asher's cousin, said: "As far as I can see, we will not get anywhere with them; it seems that this was prearranged by the association." The proprietors became restless and sent messengers to the workers to find out why they did not come to work. The workers gave them the following answer they had agreed on: "We demand the dismissal of the master craftsmen, weekly wages paid directly by the manufacturers, and a twelve-hour working day."

The manufacturers had not expected such a riot and they held a meeting where they decided to call the rebels to the local rabbi, Rabbi Baruch Lavski, may his memory be blessed. The workers and the poor did not like him very much but the wealthy considered him an influential person and respected him a lot. He was rich and his son Avigdor was one of the biggest manufacturers. The rabbi summoned Hershl Pinkes, the shamash, who was one of the leaders of the strike. When he arrived, Rabbi Baruch, surrounded by the manufacturers, started at once to reprimand him for letting Jewish workers participate in the rebellion.

My argument with the rabbi

H. Weinberg (Hershl Pinkes)

I came to the local rabbi at his invitation and found him sitting, surrounded by well-to-do manufacturers. He turned to me at once and said: "I am very much surprised at you. Tell me, is this a just and Jewish way to settle a dispute? When Jews have a complaint against each other, they go to the rabbi to seek the judgment of the rabbinical court and the rabbi rules who is right." "Rabbi", I answered, "You may be surprised at me but I am also surprised at you. One can turn to a rabbinical court only in a case when one party has the power and the other party is right.

[Page 72]

But in this case, as you can see, we have the power and we are also right. So, I am asking you, why would we need a rabbinical court?" "It may be true that you are right and you probably also have the power indeed", said the rabbi, "but it is the middle of the term; wait until the end of the term and your demands will be fulfilled." "At least this is what you say, rabbi", I answered him quickly. "It clearly means, 'the worker returns on the same day', and even in the middle of the hour?"

Terror and arrests

Yosl Kohn

Hershl Pinkes, the shamash, asked the rabbi why he was asking the community all the time to raise his salary. He also reminded the rabbi that his predecessor, the 'old' rabbi (the diligent student Rabbi Avromtshik) was satisfied with little. This 'impertinence' amazed Rabbi Baruch and the manufacturers and the rabbi told Hershl to leave his house.

Seeing the stubbornness and impertinence of the workers, the manufacturers, with the agreement of the rabbi, turned to the governor in Grodno. A large number of gendarmes led by a colonel (regiment commander) arrived in Krynki – this was the first time that the shtetl had so many 'guests'. The gendarmes started at once to terrorize the leaders of the strike. They caught them and struck them down with murderous blows. This only angered the craftsmen all the more and the strike became not only harsher but bloodier as well. The leaders started to hide. Their homes were attacked and people could not sleep in peace in dozens of Jewish homes. The fear that the gendarmes would attack them kept them agitated and vigilant. Hershl Pinkes, the shamash, and dozens of others were arrested and sent to the Grodno prison.

The first victory

Hillel Katzblum

The strike and the meeting before it in the woods were full of dramatic moments that vividly characterized the atmosphere of the strike and the means used in the fights in a Jewish shtetl in the 1890s. While the assembled stood for more than two hours in the rain swearing and singing the 'oath', some of them lay down on the ground and wept with joy or grief – who knows which. A strike meant hunger, suffering and misery.

In order to prevent the striking workers from gathering in the workers' bes-medresh and taking council about the continuation of the strike, the manufacturers persuaded the police to seal the bes-medresh. In return, the workers seized the big bes-medresh where the proprietors of the tanneries used to pray Sabbath morning. The workers sat down by the Mizrach [*picture on the Eastern wall*] set up a guard to make sure that no employer could enter and distributed 'slips' for leinen [*calling up to read from the Torah*]. After the prayer, they locked the bes-medresh and took the keys. The manufacturers were forced to turn to the police and ask them to open their bes-medresh. Later the manufacturers tried by all means to persuade the tannery workers to take up work under the old conditions but nothing helped and the workers won in the end. It was accepted that they would work from 7 AM to 7 PM and get paid weekly. They marched on the streets singing and clapping: "From 7 to 7 and money every week".

[Page 73]

The workers get a taste of their power

Avrom Miller

The manufacturers and the master craftsmen had to give in on all points. The sacred oath that the workers swore on two potatoes (bulbes??) in a bag for phylacteries united them until they returned to work victoriously.

This is how the tale of Krynki strikes started. The tannery workers got a taste of their power, the master craftsmen could no longer look braver than they felt and the manufacturers would strike the workers no more. Even Nachum Anshl's strong hand stopped 'working'.

Shoemakers, tailors, carpenters and other craftsmen followed in the footsteps of the tanners, and started to rebel and come forward with demands until they also won. Krynki was soon becoming a kind of Garden of Eden for workers.

The second strike of the tannery workers2

After Succoth 1897, on the eve of the new 'term' the fight of the tannery workers flared up again. The manufacturers summoned a meeting at the rabbi's house and following his advice they agreed to contract with the master craftsmen for three years and employ only those workers who did not participate in the rebellion and agreed to work from 6 AM to 8 PM. The manufacturers agreed to employ peasants if they could not find enough workers. The master craftsmen and the workers did not accept these conditions and went on strike. The manufacturers appealed to the governor to send soldiers into the shtetl. They gave him the names of the rebels. The strangers were sent away from the shtetl and the locals were arrested. The strike breaking peasants were incited to beat up the strikers. This is how a father, an older coachman, who stood up for his son who had been attacked was struck dead.

The red soldiers who came from Grodno attacked the workers on the street and struck them down with murderous blows. The soldiers went into the workers' bes-medresh, threw the sacred books out and used the building as their barracks. The workers then went to the bes-medresh of the rich and did not let them read the Torah. The chief of police arrived with a sergeant, dispersed the workers and, crossing himself, took out the Torah scroll from the Holy Ark. With the aid of the czarist army, the peasants and strikebreakers who went to Krynki from Bialystok, Berdichev and other towns, the workers were defeated. They starved for some time and in the end they were compelled to surrender and work 14 hours a day again.

The prolonged fight of the tannery workers for a more humane life

Sofia Dubnov-Erlich

On June 18, 1900 the 'dry tannery' workers (300 of them, among them 50 Christians) stopped working and came out with the demand for a twelve-hour working day. After the intervention of the representative of the government who arrived from Grodno the manufacturers persuaded 50 workers to return to the factory but they were too few to start the work again. The manufacturers set out into other towns to find workers but none of the tanners responded to their call because they all knew about the strike. The manufacturers brought in peasants from the surrounding villages and asked the police to take stricter measures against the strikers.

[Page 74]

The police together with the gendarmerie descended upon the tannery workers, carried out house searches at night and arrested some people on the street the following day. The manufacturers also handed over workers directly to the police. The strike was slowed down and many of the workers who found themselves in great need went to the countryside to do seasonal agricultural work for the landowners for 25 kopeks a day. They shared their earnings with the rest of the strikers. The manufacturers urged the police commissary to persuade the landowners not to engage the rebels. After seven weeks of strike the starving workers were forced to go back to work 14 hours a day as before.

When a general strike of the tannery workers broke out in Smorgon at the end of 1901 and the leather manufacturers of the North-Western region were mobilized to help their fellow industrialists, Nachum Anshl Knishinski, the 'leather king' of Krynki, went to Smorgon in person to urge the manufacturers not to surrender. In the strikes of 1903 and 1904 the Krynki tannery workers succeeded in achieving some improvements.

During the revolutionary storm in January 1905 the Krynki tannery workers who had become hardened through long years of violent fight represented the main force that seized power in the town for a few days. That summer the Krynki workers managed finally to achieve the eight-hour working day. But in 1906 when, after a hot spurt, a reactionary period set in and the manufacturers lifted their heads and some towns of the Bialystok district also declared lockouts, an Association of Brothers was founded to support the fight of the workers and a strike took place in Krynki. In the fall of 1907 the Tannery Workers' Union of Krynki disintegrated because of the indifference of the workers and systematic struggle became impossible. The practice of weekly wages was discontinued among the 'wet tannery' workers as well.

After a few years of crisis in the leather industry and a period of depression in the Jewish labor movement in Russia a certain revival was noticeable among the tannery workers. A professional union was set up in Krynki in 1911 and it developed serious activity. In the fall of 1912 the union succeeded in carrying out a fourteen-week strike demanding once again the introduction of an eight-hour working day. Several people were arrested after the strike but even this did not break the determination of the union and it grew into a mighty force.

The union carried out a series of economic improvements, introduced a system of punishing the manufacturers for bad conditions in the factories. The union set up a legal library and fought against the system of mediation which had been fairly widespread among the tannery workers before the reactionary period. The union had to put up with not only the manufacturers and the czarist administration but also with the local anarchists who led a bitter agitation against the union and the strike fund.

In 1914 while a revival could be felt in Krynki and the workers went on strike again, there was apathy and a stifling atmosphere in other towns of the tannery district. The earlier unity vanished. Workers arriving in a strange town were no longer given any work. Only in the more hospitable Krynki where there was a union could they find a bit of a haven. The example of the Krynki tannery workers was soon followed by thousands of workers in five factories of Vilnius who also went on strike.

[Page 75]

Revolutionary activity

The beginning of the revolutionary movement in Krynki

Dov Rabin

Krynki 'lads' in the first rows

Krynki, an important center of the tanning industry and a little toiling shtetl, was a natural ground for social fermentation. When the Jewish Pale of Settlement started to seethe with social and revolutionary fight in the 1890s, the Jewish youth and the workers of Krynki were among the first to start this fight. The hard and slavish conditions in the tanneries led the workers to declare a harsh and prolonged strike movement, while the general political and economic oppression of the people in Russia and the hopeless situation of the discriminated and persecuted Jewish masses triggered revolutionary activity. The Jewish 'lads' (youth) were in the front lines of the fighting parties which put the goal of general political and social liberation, that should also bring salvation to the Jews and free them from the troubles specific to them, on their banner.

According to certain sources, there existed revolutionary Jewish workers' circles in Krynki already at the end of the first half of the 1890s. Some agitators who were members of these circles led propaganda activity, even in Grodno, and tried to organize the carpenters, tailors, shoemakers and, most importantly, the workers of Shereshevski's tobacco factory. It is assumed that the above mentioned circles drew their spiritual nourishment from the industrial Bialystok, the town with which the Jews of Krynki had close ties and which later influenced them for many years, especially on the cultural and spiritual plane. These workers' circles took the initiative and organized, led and carried through the famous strikes of the Krynki tannery workers, among them the 1897 strike, one of the most momentous strikes in the history of the Jewish labor movement in Russia – we have already discussed this in detail above.

Who were the first activists?

The active members of these circles were mostly young 'lads' of 18-22 years of age. In a list 3 of 21 people accused by the czarist government of belonging to a "workers' circle" in Krynki only seven were older than 23 and three of these were 27-30 years old. The 'oldest' was Elijah Senders, a tinsmith, accused also of participating in strikes. The names of the others were as follows (according to A. Buchbinder): Avrom Zalmen Brevde, Michol Avrom Guz, Mordechai Moishe Glazer, Yosl-Eizik Moishe Heilperin ("also participated in a strike"), Yosl Avrom Harkavy (a tailor), Hirsh-Leib Lipman Virshubski, Menachem-Yudl Naftali Zogli, Avrom Mordechai Zalkind, Nachum Avrom Luria, Chaim Moishe Mareine, Leib Hirsh Nisht (a weaver from Horodok who "fled to Switzerland"), Leib Feinhersh, Yosef Avrom Friedman, Meir Hirsh Kviat, Simeon Nachum Kerber, Binyomin (Benye) Rom, Hirsh Yoshuah Reisen, Yisroel Yakov Riman, Isayah Yoshua Shimanski, and Ezekiel Leib Shmid.

[Page 76]

In the same police records (from 1898 and 1899) the following persons were accused of participating in the tannery workers' strikes in Krynki: Mendel Zalmen Chanutin (participated in the first strike of 1897), Yakov Moishe Mareine ("taken into police custody"), Elijah-Chaim Avrom Neshkes ("he was under special police supervision and immigrated to America"), Hersh Shmuel Polivnik, Avrom-Ichak Tuvie Sholem (under police supervision like the above and also "fled to America"). Two other organizers of the first strike, Menachem Motl and Moishe Berl, "went" abroad (see more about them on p. 202). Shmuel Geler recalls the name of some more revolutionary activists in Krynki: Chaim the tailor, Avrom Yakov Betzalel the baker, Pinkes Shevach Morduhovitz and Meir Epstein (the son of the "rabbi of Kazion").

In connection with the celebration of May 1, 1901 in Krynki the Bundist paper, the *Arbeter Shtime* (August 24, 1901) related that 70 tannery workers gathered in the woods, where they held speeches and they stayed there until late at night; they parted singing revolutionary songs. When the police commissary learnt about this, he mobilized the neighboring police forces and they were searching for the 'offenders' for 5 weeks until the seekers got bored.

Police records of the same year also mentioned another three people accused of taking part in 'riots' in Krynki which were initiated by a large number of workers on the wedding of a worker who had refused to participate in the strike of the tannery workers. They were the following: Hirsh-Yisroel Avrom Mazur, Avrom Shmuel-Hirsh Maletz ("who had already been accused in 1898 of participating in the strike of the tannery workers and sentenced to be placed under police supervision for two years") and Leib Avrom Meister.

At the beginning of 1902 the police started searching for a Krynki 'politician', Hirsh-Yisroel Mordechai Mazor who had been sentenced to six months in prison. At the same time a demonstration took place at the funeral of a worker in Krynki on which revolutionary songs were sung.

Fifty to a hundred workers participated in the May 1 gathering in Krynki in 1904. The same year the Bialystok committee of the Bund represented at the international socialist congress, held in Amsterdam, 2,240 members, of which 250 from Krynki (and 700 from Bialystok itself). At the same time Simeon Avrom Mordechai Mazor was accused of belonging to the Bund (he had been under police supervision earlier) and Simcha Mordechai Dimant, a 'political' who had 'vanished' from police supervision, was sought by the police.

The revolutionary propaganda

Betzalel Patchebutzki (senior)

The secret meetings used to take place outside the shtetl. The scenes of 'sealing the unity' were solemn and impressive, especially the ceremony of taking the oath on the Tanach and the phylacteries. The workers swore to be faithful to the ideals of the fight for the rights and freedom of the workers and against "tyranny and the enslavement of the workers", and to keep their unity and the meeting in secret and not let their employers know about them. It seems that even the Krynki 'lads' considered belief in God and the sanctity of the Tanach and the phylacteries as among the most sacred values.

The people who took part in these secret meetings used to gather and leave in small groups or one by one. From time to time the agitators went for a walk with a group of lads in the direction of Sokolke or on Shishlevitz Street, or to the Yentes, Shalkes or Razboynikov woods or to Virian's court where they would spell out the situation and the goals of the revolutionary movement. They often held speeches, distributed proclamations, books and pamphlets and sang labor and revolutionary songs.

A well-known song was Edelshtat's:

[Page 77]

In Storm and Fight

The melody outlined gloom and sadness; the dreary tune, the heart-breaking words call up to fight:

> "My youth faded in storm and fight
> I have not known love and luck
> Only bitter tears and aching wounds
> Weighed down my breast."

The two oaths were adopted from Bundist songs. One of them included a paragraph "Holy is nature with her dress of freedom", while the other anthem contained the blazing stanza starting with the words "Brothers and sisters, comrades in work and need" and ending with "We swear an oath of life and death".

The anarchists' activities

Anarchist credo

The anarchists occupied a special place among the fighters for a new and liberal regime in Krynki. As is well known, they did not accept any social and state rule based on coercion and law. In Krynki just as elsewhere there were various shades and trends within the anarchist movement. There were discussions in town about Proudhon's article *Property is Theft* and the notions of 'federalism' and 'mutualism' (mutual coexistence) became daily expressions among Krynki youth. There were, of course, adherents to Kropotkin's anarcho-communism and to Bakunin's preaching to destroy the state, the mother of all oppression, through 'spontaneous' terrorist acts. Among the Krynki anarchists one could even find admirers of the German Max Stirner who advocated extreme individualism and instinctive egoism, as well as of the Russian nihilist Nietzhaiev who believed that the use of even the most brutal terrorist methods against the ruling government was justified. There were also 'anarcho-syndicalists' and 'ethical' and 'philosophical' anarchists. The Krynki anarchist group was founded by 'professor' Yankl (the writer Yakov Krepliak). The carpenter Niomke Yonah, Moishe (Rives) and their leader Avrom Ichak of Vilnius were also active in this group.

Terrorist acts

In practice most anarchists justified terrorist acts carried out personally against the czarist executive power and the exploiters. They also justified and carried out appropriations or as they called it in abbreviated form 'approps'. If it was not possible to improve the workers' wages legally and give them back the surplus value of the work which had been taken from them, they argued, these must be wrung from the exploiters through other means.

In Krynki great 'acts' were in fact carried out. The manufacturer Shmuel Wiener, the 'American', was shot. He was called 'American' because he had once been to America. He had a permit to have a revolver on him and he used to boast about it. He even teased the youth pointing out his 'gear'. On the last day of Pesach when Shmuel 'the American' was coming from the prayer service with a group of influential community members he was attacked on Tannery Street. The attackers were 17-19-year-old lads.

The Jewish population of Krynki had not yet calmed down after the Shmuel 'the American' case when rumors about an attack planned to be carried out on a meeting of the manufacturers in the great bes-medresh spread. The attackers were supposed to throw a bomb prepared in Horodok. The Krynki group sent Moshke from Krynki to fetch it.

[Page 78]

On the way to Horodok Moshke was wounded and since he could not get medical help there, he was taken to Shishlevitz (Svislotz in Volkovisk county). The doctor who treated him informed the police about the accident. Moshke was arrested and imprisoned in Grodno.

Later it became known that his trial would be held in Warsaw. His mother Rive left no stone unturned to have the trial transferred to Vilnius. No efforts were spared to hand over the matter to lawyers. But Moshke, faithful to his ideals, decided to admit that he was to take the bomb to Krynki and at the same time made a political declaration against the regime of enslavement and tyranny. He intended to declare that he tried to kill the slaves of autocracy with the bomb. His mother threatened him with killing herself if he did that. In the end the Jewish kid, mummy's boy awakened in him and the revolutionary Moshke pleaded not guilty and was freed. Some time later he was arrested again and sentenced to prison.

Anarchist demonstrations

A few anarchist demonstrations took place in Krynki. The demonstrators went out on the street dressed in black shirts (overcoats), black tassels, black felt boots and black forage caps. They marched to the Polish church singing anarchist songs, the anarchist anthem included. When the quiet, provincial population felt that the demonstrators were becoming 'too merry', the shopkeepers closed their shops, the passers-by locked themselves in their houses and the notabilities of the shtetl, with Nachum Anshl at their head, treated the raging youth calmly.

Niomke (Binyomin) 'the anarchist'

I remember a meeting of the manufacturers in Krynki. It was heavily guarded by armed Cossacks led by a sergeant. Suddenly a shot and the breaking of glass could be heard. The sergeant started to chase the scabby Niomke Hershl and knocked him down. As it turned out, the bomb was thrown by Moishe Siderer. It exploded but no one was injured. Niomke was sentenced to eight years of hard labor by the Slonim court.

Niomke Fridman
('the anarchist')

On the way from the prison Niomke took out a revolver hidden in a loaf of bread and shot the guard and escaped to Krynki. A few days later he was arrested again and he was taken to the Grodno prison more heavily guarded. When he was taken to the first examination, he snatched the arms of the guards, attacked them and shot at them. Then he barricaded himself at a tailor's in the next house and continued to fire at the police from there. When he saw that he had one last bullet left, he shot himself.

[Page 79]

When the police went into the room, they saw a notice written in blood: "Long live anarchy, you will not get me alive!" (His brother has another version about Niomke's death. See Lipa Friedman, *Niomke, the Anarchist*, p. 201. [editor's note].)

There were attacks on several Krynki sergeants long after they had moved from the town. The Krynki 'minor' sergeant was shot when he was already living at a hat maker's in Sokolke. The attempt was carried out by Yosl Moishe Afroitshik the shoemaker and Moishe Siderer. Afroitshik was sentenced to the gallows. After some time his sentence was changed to 20 years of hard labor. In 1917 rumor spread in Krynki that he had been seen free in Moscow where he occupied a distinguished position.

The activities of the Krynki anarchists outside their shtetl

There were also cases when Krynki Jewish anarchists perished while carrying out secret and unexpected attacks. This is how Yisroel Isar the shochet and Meir Yankl Bunim died on their way to Bialystok in a horse cab; an explosion was heard and both of them died on the spot.

The activity of Ahron Velvel Yankl Bunim (of Krynki) among the anarchists in Bialystok made a strong impression in town. It was reported that when a group of prisoners had been taken from the prison in Bialystok to the bailiff (district police commander), the guards were attacked and the prisoners were set free. This act was carried out by Ahron Velvel who was at the time a member of the leadership of the Bialystok 'fighting squad' (fighting group). A little later, in 1897, the same Ahron Velvel carried out an attempt on a textile manufacturer named Nachum Kolner and he was sentenced to four years in prison in Irkutzk, Siberia. Ahron Velvel's love went with him in his long wanderings and they married in prison and had children in exile. Later the family came back to Krynki.

The Krynki youth were often called up to help 'make a revolution' in other shtetls. This is how Yankl Tshaine was sent by Yakov Krepliak to help 'make a revolution' in Shishlevitz. They both gave a speech to a large audience. Suddenly a warning was heard that the police was coming. Everybody ran off as fast as they could and Yankl Tshaine came back to Krynki. He was one of the most capable agitators.

In town people were saying that Yankl Tshaine joined the anarchist movement because he was not satisfied with the activities of the Bund, which was too moderate in his eyes. The following incident brought this about. The shochet Yisroel Iser took him to Bialystok and brought him in among the fighters. There was a meeting in Factory Street, and someone approached Yankl and handed him the ABCs of anarchism. Suddenly a commotion was heard. The police attacked the meeting place and shouted to Yankl, "you are one of the Krynki rebels!" and beat him up. Yankl Tshaine tried hard to avenge himself but the Bund was not appropriate for that. So he changed sides and joined the more extreme anarchist movement.

The Krynki anarchists were active in other towns as well. In Sidre (a shtetl in the Sokolke district) Krynki anarchists attacked the post office. One of them, the mason Dovid was killed by a postal clerk.

[Page 80]

In 1905 an anarchist group, in which there were some Krynki youth too, had to carry out an attempt on the mayor of Odessa. The following persons were involved in the preparations: Avrom Ichak from Vilnius, Moshke Rives and Niomke Yonah the carpenter.

The workers seize the power in Krynki in January 1905

Aba Lev/Betzalel Patchebutzki Senior4

In January 1905 there was some stirring in our town Krynki when the news got around of the bloody march that had been led by the provoker Priest Gapon to the czarist palace on Sunday January 9. However, the Krynki lads started to assault only when the news about the strike of the railway workers got around.

(B. Patchebutzki)

We received an appeal from the Bialystok committee of the Bund and also from the local branch of the Polish Social Democrats (PSD) to join the open fight of the comrades in Petersburg. We set up a federative committee consisting of the two organizations that decided to stop work in the town on January 17, go out and demonstrate and attack all government figures. In order to declare the political strike, the Bundist organization called together a mass meeting in the synagogue. All Krynki workers, more than 1,500 people, responded to the call and came to the meeting. The two red flags of the Bund and the PSD decorated the bimah.

After the meeting the enthusiastic crowd went out onto the street singing the Marseilles. The 'fighting squad' (fighting group) with revolvers in hand was marching at the head of the procession [a wet snow was falling and the flags were fluttering in the wind – B. Patchebutzki]. The crowd set off towards the center of town. The police vanished. The police commissary and a few village policemen ran away into the Yentes woods. Singing and shouting, the demonstrators went on to the post office in Shishlevitz Street. The gate was shut, so the demonstrators broke it in. We went into the office, broke the telegraph into pieces, tore and destroyed the books and burnt the stamps. No one touched the cash desk, which had 18,000 rubles in it, although the manager of the post office offered us the keys. We only took the sword and started out to the police station and the Jewish 'borough council'. There was no one at the police station, so we played havoc with all we found there: tore, destroyed and burnt the portraits of the emperors, books, papers, photographs of 'suspicious persons' and the like. We inspected the Jewish 'borough council' as thoroughly as the police station. We took several hundred passport blanks and passport booklets with stamps. This 'robbery' came in very useful for the revolutionary movement later, especially when the mass escapes from Siberia started. Dozens of arrested people who escaped were provided with passports from these Krynki blanks and thanks to them they arrived in peace wherever they had to get to. From the Jewish 'borough council' we enthusiastically went on to the district (village district) office and wreaked havoc there just like in the two other places.

[Page 81]

We found about 600 rubles in the cash desk of the district office. The anarchists took most of this (we allowed ourselves to take government money) and 80 rubles were taken by other workers who gave it at once to the organization.

In closed lines, singing and shouting, we went on to the 'Monopolka'. The vendor shut the door and when we broke it in, he started shooting from a revolver. We answered him in the same vein, taking his weapon from him and he fled at once. The store received the very same day a huge consignment of liquor. We put a group of young boys and girls around this government liquor store and they destroyed it to the last bit; they spent the whole day breaking bottle after bottle and pouring out the alcohol so that no one could use it.

We first went into the apartment of the local gendarme but we only found a medal and a sword there, so we took them. Only one inspector (a police superintendent who was in charge of certain 'offenders') remained in town. He was ill in bed and could not run off. We ordered him to hand us over his revolver and sword and he obeyed immediately. Krynki was 'clean' and we had complete control over it. The police commissary and some village policemen ran off to the Yentes woods. We also managed to organize a demonstration and destroy the 'Monopolka' in Krusheniani, a village where many workers had their family.

In the meantime the soldiers coming from the direction of Sokolke were getting nearer and nearer. It turned out that the police commissary had fled to Sokolke and alerted the governor from there and asked for help. The latter sent out the soldiers and we met them on Sokolke Street. The youth stood on one side, armed with revolvers and all kinds of iron bars and axes; the girls were also there armed with stones. The officers started to negotiate with us, and promised not to shoot and injure anybody if we were ready to disperse. We were gathering the whole day until the soldiers dispersed us without shooting at us. The governor himself arrived at once. Krynki was flooded with soldiers – infantrymen and cavalrymen, among them the Tsherkes who lodged in the Yentes bes-medresh.

(A. Lev)

The state of emergency was proclaimed and two hundred participants of the uprising were arrested. Put in chains, many of them were taken to the Grodno prison and many of them were locked up in one-person cells. They were liberated after the October Manifesto of 1905. A few people like Yankl Tshaine, Leibke Naskes, etc., who had organized the Bund in Krynki, escaped from the town (Niomke Friedman and the scabby Hershl were also among the leaders of the revolt). The state of emergency had its innocent victim – the baker Yankl Tzalel. He went out to fetch wood early in the morning and did not hear it when he was ordered to stop, and he was shot on the spot. The Krynki revolt ended and the town became calm and quiet again.

(B. Patchebutzki)

[Page 82]

A. Sh. Zutz renews the Bund

Nachum Bliacher/M. Fridman

During the uprising in Krynki in 1905 when the Cossack punitive expedition arrived in town and the state of emergency was proclaimed, up to 300 people were arrested and taken away and this led to the disintegration of the local organization of the Bund.

In 1906 the organization was already under reconstruction. This was led by Avrom-Shmuel Zutz, together with the comrades Baruch-Mordechai Bliacher, Yudl Kolter's son and Avrom Gordon (Yankl Tzales' son).

Born in 1887 in a poor family in Krynki (his father was a butcher), Avrom-Shmuel Zutz tasted work at a young age in the tannery, first as a leaflet maker and later as a laborer in the fullery. Although he received no elementary schooling he started to ponder over the illegal books of the Bundist literature in his early youth. In the stormy year of 1905 he became an active member of the local Bund and the small rooms in his house and stable served primarily as a meeting place for the leaders and a hiding place for illegal literature.

Avrom-Shmuel Zutz ('continual light')

In April 1907 Avrom-Shmuel was arrested for possessing illegal literature and he was sent to the Grodno prison. He was badly beaten up there several times and once a soldier hit him on the head with a rifle butt. He became ill in the eyes and a few years later he went completely blind. When he was freed he returned home. By 1909 the revolutionary movement was fast declining. The intelligentsia fled. A reactionary spirit reigned among the disappointed workers. They became frequent visitors in the inns and playing cards became their spiritual food. Avrom-Shmuel picked up his courage to activate the remnants of the movement and they accepted him as their teacher and guide, and things gradually started moving by 1911.

[Page 83]

Culture and Society
Krynki – A Center of Torah

by Moshe Tzniowicz

Translated by Jerrold Landau

Rabbi Zalman Sender Shapira and his Yeshiva [1]

Rabbi Zalman Sender Kahana Shapira was born in the year 5611 [1851] in Nieśwież, Minsk District, to his father Rabbi Yaakov, son of Rabbi Moshe HaKohen, son-in-law of the Gaon Rabbi Chaim, founder of the well-known Volozhin Yeshiva. Rabbi Zalman Sender was already known as a genius from his youth. He was sent to Volozhin to benefit from the Torah and learning style of his relative Rabbi Yosef-Dov Soloveitchik. There he became known as an expert Talmudist, with a sharp intellect and skill in innovative ideas.

In the year 5645 [1885], Rabbi Zalman Sender was appointed as head of the rabbinical court of the small town of Malech [Maltsh] in the district of Pruzhany near the Pulsia marshes. Rabbi Zalman Sender lived in that city, involved in his studies, acting in rabbinical matters, and discussing issues of the Torah with the rabbis and scholars of the area.

In the year 5657 [1897], with the founding of the Knesset Beit Yitzchak Yeshiva in Slobodka, Rabbi Zalman Sender was invited by the founders and supervisors to serve as Yeshiva head. However, it seems that the people of Malech urged him to not leave them, and that he acceded and remained with them on the condition that they agree that he start a Yeshiva in their city, to which he could dedicate some of his time. Indeed, the community of Malech willingly accepted this condition. Even though there were already splendid Yeshivas in Lithuania and Zamot at that time. The new Yeshiva of Malech, founded in 5658 [1898], took an important place in the tents of Torah. Within a few years, it grew from the ten students at its opening to 120. Even older Yeshiva students, who had previously spent time in large Yeshivas, preferred to now study in the Yeshiva of Malech with Rabbi Zalman Sender.

During his regular Talmud classes in the Yeshiva, his full spiritual stature and power of scholarship, without forgetting anything. was revealed. His classes developed the students' ability to innovate, to grasp any issue and Talmud subject, and to delve deeply into the roots. Rabbi Zalman Sender also concerned himself with the physical situation and spiritual support of the Yeshiva students. His home was open wide to them. He even attempted to raise their honor and value in the eyes of people, and he warned the householders of the town to not treat lightly their relations with the young scholars. He even asked that they be called "Yeshiva men" rather than "Yeshiva lads" as was customary – a nickname that had some sort of hint of disparagement. Rabbi Zalman Sender was also strict with his students that their clothing and manners be pleasant, so they would find favor with people.

Rabbi Zalman Sender did not take any salary from the Yeshiva coffers. He got enough money with the paltry salary that he received from the townsfolk. Aside from this, he supported a rabbinical judge to deal with questions and rabbinic adjudication, for he, like his relative the Gaon Rabbi Chaim of Brisk was loathe to make rabbinic decisions.

From among the students of the Yeshiva of Malech of that era, we must especially note the one who lives with us today in blessed fashion, the chief rabbi of Israel, Rabbi Isser Yehuda Unterman.

Rabbi Zalman Sender was accepted as the head of the rabbinical court of Krynki in Iyar 5663 [1903], after the death of Rabbi Baruch Lawski, and in accordance with his recommendation prior to his death. Rabbi Zalman Sender set a firm condition to his agreement of serving as the head of the rabbinical court of Krynki. And that a portion of his Yeshiva would move there from Malech, and he would continue to serve as the Yeshiva head. Indeed, the communal administrators agreed unanimously to this. Students from the areas, Horodno, Białystok, Łomża, and other places[1] – began to swarm to the Yeshiva of Krynki, which was now also called Anaf Eitz Chaim. Rabbi Zalman Sender's classes and Torah short stories found their paths to other famous Yeshivas, both orally as well as in various booklets and digests.

Numbered among his excellent students in the Yeshiva of Krynki were several Torah personalities who later became renowned. Among them we will note Rabbi Leib Goelman from the town of Jedwabne, who became known as a Hebrew linguist and Torah educator. Later Rabbi Leib arrived in Krynki as a war refugee in 5675 [1914]. On the recommendation of Rabbi Zalman Sender, he opened up a public *cheder* organized by age for the higher grades, which became known throughout the entire region.

[Page 84]

Rabbi Zalman Sender as a Person

In Krynki, as in Malech, Rabbi Zalman Sender conducted his rabbinate at a high level with respect to rabbinical matters. With this, he was revered in the town, even amongst the masses and the laborers. He also became known as a rabbi who could provide salvation and as a worker of portents, and people came to him for blessings. As a grandson of Rabbi Chaim of Volozhin, he himself was against portents, and he demonstrated to his students that everything he said or advised to those who turned to him with their bitterness, were things that were logical. Rabbi Zalman Sender would tell of things that people regarded portents, but through logic were not miraculous at all.

Rabbi Zalman Sender would apply his authority upon the sick and weak people, and decree that they must eat on Yom Kippur. He would even send a physician to examine them, and if the physician determined that a person would have difficulty fasting, Rabbi Zalman Sender would force him to eat. There were times where he would bring the person to his home so he could eat in his presence in accordance with the advice of the physician.

Rabbi Zalman Sender would conduct the Passover Seder in Krynki with great splendor, as he did in Malech, and just as was done in the Volozhin Yeshiva in its time. Rabbi Zalman Sender was an enthusiastic fan of music, and he even composed tunes. On festivals, when the joy was complete in the Yeshiva or the rabbi's house, he would sing songs and hymns that he or others had composed. Thus, Rabbi Zalman Sender's heartwarming composition of the hymn "Charming dove, why do you weep, your Messiah will come to you, come and go, for I will be your savior and redeemer for whom you are waiting" spread through all the Yeshivas of Lithuania. Similarly, on public holidays, he would sing the conclusion of the hymn attributed to Rabbi Shlomo Ibn Gabirol "Consumed and bereaved, why do you weep, has your heart given up regarding he for whom you are waiting?" These melodies attained renown throughout all the Yeshivas and would be repeated on holidays, especially at the Simchat Beit Shoeiva [Sukkot night festivities and on Simchat Torah. The writer of this article still recalls that they would use the special melody of Rabbi Zalman Sender for "May Your Name always overlook transgression"[2] in several of these Yeshivas.

In the year 5675 [1915] as the battlefront neared Krynki Rabbi Zalman Sender wandered through the depths of Russia with a group of his students, and remained in the city of Tula for a number of years. After the war, he did not return to Krynki, which was now part of Poland, but rather made *aliya* to the Land of Israel and settled in Jerusalem, where he spent his final years. He died there on 29 Shvat 5683 [1923].

A small number of the anthologized Torah works of Rabbi Zalman Sender were preserved in part in Yeshiva circles, as well as in the book of other authors of his generation. First and foremost, an anthology of his Torah novellae (short stories) are included in the large work of his son Rabbi Avraham Kahana Shapira, *Dvar Avraham*. Rabbi Avraham Dov Kahana was the head of the rabbinical court of Smilovich in the Minsk district, and later in Kovno. He was the final general rabbi of the Jews of Lithuania. The aforementioned novellae of Rabbi Zalman Sender demonstrate the character of his sharpness and intellect, and his brightness in the understanding of Torah. We also find his novellae, small in quantity but high in content, in the book *Zecher Yitzchak* by Rabbi Yitzchak Yaakov Rabinovitch of Ponovich.

Rabbi Zalman Sender's two young sons, Rabbi Yehuda and Rabbi Chaim, stood with their father in the founding of the Yeshiva of Malech, and were together with him for several years in Krynki, helping him establish his Yeshiva. Rabbi Chaim later served as the head of the rabbinical court in Kozienice, and from 5678 [1918], as rabbi as the Slobodka suburb of Horodno, where he died of an accident in the year 5685 [1925].

Two of the grandchildren of Rabbi Zalman Sender, sons of his son Rabbi Avraham Dov, will be noted here. One, Rabbi Chaim Nachman Shapira, readied himself for some time in the light of his grandfather in Krynki. He was an expert scholar, the author of books in the research of modern Hebrew literature, and a professor of Hebrew and eastern languages at the university of Kovno, where he perished in the Holocaust in 1943 along with the rest of the members of that community.

The second grandson, Dr. Noach Shapira, studied with his grandfather Rabbi Zalman Sender in Krynki during his youth. He was taken by the *Haskalah*. He studied chemistry and was a docent at the university of Kovno. He made *aliya* to the Land of Israel in 5695 [1935]. He was a professor of chemistry at Bar Ilan University, and the editor of the general encyclopedia in Hebrew published by Jezreel in Tel Aviv. He died there in 5724 [1964].

Translator's Footnotes:

1.   There is a footnote in the text here: It should be noted that lads and young men came to Krynki to study Torah in a group [kibbutz] already years before this. Among the others was Aryeh Leib Siemiatycki, a native of Sokol in the district of Łomża, who later became a well-known Hebrew linguist, a member of the "Committee for the Hebrew Language" in the Land of Israel, and one of the prominent editors of Hebrew literature for youth (he was the editor of the Amanot publication) – the editor.
2.   From the Yom Kippur service.

[Page 85]

Zionist Activity
The Beginning of the Zionist Movement in Krynki

by D. Rabin

Translated by Jerrold Landau

The Zionist movement, which maintained connection with the Zionist Center for Correspondence in Kishinev, was already established in Krynki in 1898. Shmuel Nisht (father of Baruch-Bendet Niv) was one of its founders. Chovevei Zion was active in the town before this. We should recall that already from 5646 (1886), Tzvi Hirsch Orlanski (Hershele of Dąbrowa) served in Krynki as the *Maggid* who preached the love of Zion and the settlement of the Land of Israel. He gained many enthusiastic followers from among the masses. The tradition of many generations of people, who were meticulous in keeping the mitzvot, and of making *aliya* to the Holy Land in their old age, of course did not pass over Krynki. Two such people, Yechiel-Tzvi and Freda-Rivka are known for receiving help in Jerusalem in 1890 from the "General Committee for Ashkenazi Kollels."

A correspondent from Krynki in *Hatzefira* (issue 236, 4 Cheshvan 5661 – 1900, written by Sh. H.) relates that "The Zionist idea awakened movement and great feeling among our townsfolk. The local Zionist organization founded a Tiferet Bachurim organization. The purpose of which was to disseminate knowledge of the Holy Language and the study of Bible among the masses of youth. It also founded an organization for reading of *Haskalah* books and other such books.

"However, in place of the original enthusiasm, now a sense of iciness and cold grew between the Zionists, certainly because of people of means did not support the issue, or more accurately – because of the persecution by the zealots who were hostile to the Zionist activists. Therefore, the groups disbanded, their activities ceased, and it was as if they never existed. Only a few people remained in the Zionist organizations, among them the pharmacist Yatom and Kniszinski, who tried with all their might to arouse the members to purchase the shekels [tokens of membership in the Zionist organization] and the like. However, these few special individuals were unable to do big things for the benefit of the public, or to improve the level of education, which was in the hands of the zealots who were among the haters and persecutors of Zionism."

With all this, the Zionist idea continued to strike roots among the people in Krynki. In 1903, we find that Agudat Zion in the town gave its donation to the Odessa Committee – the legal center of Chovevei Zion, which was active in the arena of settlement and education in the Land of Israel. Furthermore, at the beginning of that year, a Young Zion organization was founded in the town, the members of which were "primarily workers."

The Zionist Movement in Krynki
at the Beginning of the Century

by Baruch (Bendet) Niv

Translated by Jerrold Landau

Zionist activities already took place in Krynki from the outset of the movement. The adult Zionists gathered around one of the first ones, the pharmacy owner Yatom, an honorable man with higher education, and a warm, enthusiastic Jew. He educated his children toward Zionist actualization, and they even made *aliya* to the Land.

Young workers and students from the Russian school and the private Hebrew schools were numbered among the Zionist youth. The adults distributed shekels, turned their attention to the sale of Keren Kayemet [Jewish National Fund] stamps by the youths, subscribed to *Hatzefira* and *Hatzofeh*, gathered for prayer services in the Zionist minyan, exchanged ideas, and debated issues of the day at the Zionist Congress regarding the relationship to Herzl and the Uganda Plan, and other such ideas in the realm of Zionism in those days.

There were also youths who made *aliya* to the Land of Israel: The Hebrew teacher Malka Grosman and Hershel Fajnberg, who later went back because he could not withstand the malaria that afflicted him. On the other hand, there was the Poalei Zion member Yisrael Korngold, one of the first of the Hashomer organization in the Land, and who fell on the line of duty while standing guard in the year 5669 [1909].

Almost all of us, the students of the Russian school, were members of Pirchei Zion. We would distribute stamps of the Jewish National Fund, and gather to listen to speeches about Zionism and the land of Israel. They were arranged every Sabbath eve in the home of Fajnberg on the Street of the Tanners, after he returned from the Land of Israel. The Zionist movement in Russia was run in an illegal, clandestine fashion. We students of the government school, were forbidden for belonging to any movement, and most certainly not to a Zionist one.

One Sabbath eve, when I was going to one of the meetings in Fajnberg's home, I ran into the teacher Einsztein, who was leaving the courtyard. He called to me to also disappear very quickly. We both started to run, each in a different direction, to avoid the danger of being arrested. After approximately a half an hour, I saw that the police were arresting about 20 students from my school.

[Page 86]

By chance, the rest of the guests had not succeeded in reaching the gathering point at that time.

The entire town was in an uproar. The children were arrested, and the school authorities announced that all those who gathered at the aforementioned meeting would be expelled. The heads of the city became involved and exerted personal pressure. With the help of money, they were all freed after about two days, with a stringent warning that they must not continue to be involved in "forbidden" activities. However, despite all this, including the warning, we were of course not afraid from continuing our activities, albeit with taking precautions.

In Education and Culture
With the Changing Times

by D. R.

Translated by Jerrold Landau

At the beginning of the present [i.e. 20th] century until the German occupation during the First World War, Krynki also felt, as did the Jewish Pale of Settlement throughout Russia, an influence of the spirit of culture and essence of the Russian nation, especially among significant circles of the youth. Aside from the general national factors and gossip among the Jews in town, the Russian schools set up in the town worked toward that end, and not in a negligible fashion. The boys, and especially the girls, who studied in the *gymnasjas* of Grodna and Białystok would bring back Russian culture, and especially the language and social style of these schools. Speaking in Russian, and especially singing Russian songs with much enjoyment, were "typical" in Krynki as well, especially amongst the intelligentsia and the upper class. Bigger than these was the penetrating influence of the rich Russian literature, broad in scope and seeking liberty, causing the hearts of its readers to throb.

In 1897 the public government school, which opened in Krynki supported by the budget from the Jewish Korovka tax (on kosher meat and wine, candles, yeast, and the like), was already bustling with students from Jewish homes. On the other hand, an article in *Hatzefira* from 1900 states that "Approximately 70 youths are imprisoned in the Talmud Torah building from morning to night, but without any order in their education. The teachers are lacking in life experience and the ways of the world, and they lord over their unfortunate students as in years of yore." They do not teach them any language, and they also do not teach Bible appropriately. And "Aside from this, the school building is cramped, and stifling air pervades there."

However, within a few years, Hebrew education in Krynki changed for the better: two young Hebrew women from nearby Brzostowica opened the first Hebrew school for girls, and a modern Hebrew cheder also arose in 1905. The Hebrew teacher Einstein was already able to note in his article in *Hatzefira* from 14 Elul 5669 that the education of boys in Krynki is "in a good state. Students of the schools receive Hebrew and national education, and their influence has spread to the *cheders*. The *melamdim* [cheder teachers] have also begun to introduce various improvements in their teaching, and have set aside a special place for Hebrew, its grammar and literature, and Jewish history." However, "There are few lads of age 13 who are studying Talmud. Most of them move over to general studies when they reach that age."

He writes that regarding the situation of reading, the intelligentsia have their hearts fixed on Russian books; The liberal newspaper *Sobramnoya Slovo* and the inexpensive newspaper *Gazeta Kopayka* were the main Russian newspapers that were read. The Yiddish dailies included *Heint*, *Unzer Lebn*, and *Freund*. The Hebrew newspaper *Hed Hazman* [Echo of the Times], the *Hashiloach* monthly, and the weekly *Hapoel Hatzair* [The Young Worker] from the Land of Israel were also received in Krynki. Einstein adds that there were more people in Krynki who understood Hebrew than could read it, and there were only a few who purchased Hebrew books. However, the demand has increased of late, and the owners of the library were planning to expand the Hebrew division.

Jewish Students in the Civic School

In the "civic" Russian high school, the *Gorodskoya Ochilishcha*, which was founded in its time through the efforts of Yaakov Leib Zalski, a quota system was in place for the acceptance of Jewish students, as was the case in all Russian government schools. The number was restricted to approximately 10% of the students. It was my lot to study in that school together with one other of our fellow townsfolk in Israel, Shamai Kaplan.

[Page 87]

In our town, where the vast majority of the population was Jewish, and the school was established through their funds, it was impossible to have a Jewish student accepted unless there were nine Christians to make up the quota. These would be gathered from the villages of the area. With the transportation situation in those days, these villagers would arrive daily for their studies on foot, from a distance of 8-10 kilometers, and they would also return to their homes in that manner. Most of them were Pravoslavic Byelorussian children, and the minority were Catholics. The classes opened with Christian morning prayers in the presence of all the students, including the Jews. Classes took place also on the Sabbath, with the day of rest being Sunday.

A Jewish "Incident"

Jewish students were exempt from writing on the Sabbath, at the request of their parents. This included drawing. For them, this was a main principle in expressing their Jewishness, even though not all of them came from religiously observant homes.

Art classes took place twice a week on weekdays. The teacher was an elderly gentile, somewhat feebleminded, goodhearted, and boring. He depended on the students to somehow fill the curriculum. The students, without difference between religion and nationality, recognized the weakness of their teachers, and had fun during the classes, but not without limit.

It took place during one of the recesses between classes, when the students used to doodle on the blackboard, erase the "drawings" and "compositions" with a wet cloth, and repeat this over and over again. The mischief increased to the point of a rampage. The "knocking" of one another turned into a storm, and the entire classroom was filled with chalk dust, to the point when one could no longer tell what was happening there. It then happened that the dirty cloth hit the face of the teacher as he was entering the classroom. After he was hit, he reacted with a loud scream, and ran from the class as quickly as he could. The students were astonished, and the "transgressors" who were caught in the act quickly went to sit silently at their desks.

The door opened quickly, and the principal himself appeared along with the inspector (supervisor) and the victim teacher, who began to shout out loudly that he could no longer bear this and "an appropriate punishment must be administered." Due to the great confusion, they did not know who to punish. The principal then began a speech about manners and politeness, etc. He suddenly turned to the Jewish students, "I am primarily turning to you! On the Sabbath, you do not draw, but in the only class during the week in which you participate, you behave in in such a disgraceful manner!"

His baseless attack on us Jews, in anti-Semitic fashion, angered me, and I responded that there is no art class at all on the Sabbath. My reminder angered him, and he dismissed me in anger, "Go home, Jew, and do not come back here!" I hesitated for a moment, gathered my books, and turned toward the door as a protest. The entire class was astonished and astounded from the outburst of the director. He realized that he had overstepped the bounds, and added on, "Don't come – without your Father!"

I was informed later that after I left, the principal turned to the students in anger, "How was that one so brazen against me?!" The Jewish students burst out crying. Then, the heart of the principal softened, and he attempted to calm them, saying, "Oh, enough. I got upset with him a bit. You don't have to blame me. Tell him that I forgive him – he can return to class tomorrow as usual."

Our art teacher gained a bit from this incident, for from that time, the mischief in the classroom decreased during his classes.

The Modern Cheder

During a heatwave in the summer of 1904, a fire broke out in the Kavkaz alleyways, and spread until half of Krynki went up in flames. The *cheders* were closed, and many parents sent their children to relatives in nearby towns to study with *melamdim* there.

About a year later, a number of Zionist parents decided to open in the city a Hebrew school or *cheder metukan* [modern *cheder*], as it was called in those days. They would teach "Hebrew in Hebrew" according to the natural style, without translation into Yiddish.

At first, young children of ages 6-8 were accepted into the *cheder*, and one expert teacher was hired (Cirkl). The school developed, and a second teacher (Kulik) was hired for the third year. The number of students was small, however, because the *cheder* did not find favor with the masses of traditionalists who regarded it as a "heretical" school, in which they only teach the Hebrew languages, song and gymnastics…

[Page 88]

After several years, the curriculum was expanded, and another teacher (Farber) was brought in from Wolkowysk. Later, another teacher, who was a graduate of the pedagogic courses in Grodna was hired. Now, they taught all subjects, at high school level, only in Hebrew. They also taught Gemara, as required in those days.

The modern cheder lasted for about four years, until the teacher Farber left Krynki. At that time, the level of studies in the advanced class reached the level of six *gymnasja* grades.

In the interim, however, several Hebrew teachers came to Krynki and settled there, Avraham Einstein among them. They taught Hebrew to students privately or in groups, and most of the students of the cheder continued their studies with them.

The first girls' school, 1903: The teachers – the sisters Sima and Malka Grosman.
Between them, the student Hindka Nisht.

Di Hebrayishe Lehrehrkes - The Hebrew Teachers

Translated by Hadassah Goldberg

"Di Hebrayishe Lehrehrkes" - "Hamorot HaIvriot" - This was how the sisters Malka and Sima Grossman were known, two young women who came to Krynki from the next town, Brestovitse, and founded the first Hebrew school for girls at the beginning of the current (20th) century.

[Page 89]

Prior to their arrival, there was the girls' teacher, Novik, and the modern cheder of the teachers Cirkl, Kulik, and Farber. However, it was at the hands of the two sisters that almost all of the girls in town between the ages of five and eight were enrolled into their institute.

Sima, the elder of the two sisters, taught the older girls, and Malka, the younger ones. My teacher was Malka, and we loved her very much. In our eyes she was the epitome of beauty, a thread of gentleness and nobility was drawn through her. And both women together were graced with the highest virtues.

They taught us Hebrew in Hebrew, using pictures in a big book, I believe "Learning the Language of Ever" was the name of the book. Each of the many pictures in the book was like an entire story. If, in the first one a table was pictured, all of us learned and repeated in unison: "This is a table, this is a table." "What is this?", they asked us and all of us responded "This is a table". And again, "The table is on the floor, the chair is near the table, the girl is near the chair, the girl is under the table", and this time, as a concrete example, one of us was placed under the table. And so, after three months, we were already able to say the words and even speak in Hebrew.

Even the system of learning to read was modern: no more "alef, beit, gimel", "kamatz, aleph, oh", "patach, veit, va" and so on, but with the consonants beit, gimel, daled, and the vowels, kamatz alef, patach alef, patach beit, and so on. To write, we were taught that every letter in the alphabet shall be simply, pleasingly and precisely written.

But, what can be like the first stories told from the bible - on the creation of the world and on the sin of the first man, actually of Chava, our ancestor with whom we were so angry for she craved a taste of the apple from the tree of knowledge and thus deprived humankind of eternal life!

In three whole years - with holidays during the days of Pesach and Sukkot - we progressed beautifully. We wrote without errors, we knew grammar, we learned Tanach up to the book of Isaiah. Even when we finished the phase of Hebrew studies and moved to the Russian state school, we continued evening studies with the teachers Avrash and Rozpinsky We read the books of the latter Prophets and Hebrew literature - and all this before the First World War.

In those years, our teacher, Malka Grossman made Aliyah to the Land of Israel. And we, her students, who meantime had grown up a little, accompanied her to her departure. We wrote her many letters and received many from her. She didn't succeed in setting roots in the land (of Israel) and she returned from there. She brought us news of the Herzliya Hebrew High School. The dream then was to leave the Russian high school and to continue in the Land of Israel. The longing for Israel was awakened in us with the study of Hebrew. But the outbreak of the world war stopped us from this path.

Credit goes to the two teachers "Di Hebreyishe Lehrehrkes", Sima and Malka Grossman, whose path in teaching Hebrew was continued by their students in the Hebrew School in Krynki established during the (first) world war for the children of refugees and also for local people. Girls aged 13 - 14 were teachers to the younger children during that time, and they were known for their good reputation in the "Tarbut" - an educational movement - that was established after the war. They were: Leah Vine hy"d, Ester Terkl z"l, her sister Brynatbl'a, now a citizen of the state of Israel (she is a member of Kibbutz Yagur), Hindke Nisht (Aida Avidov) Leah'che (Za"k in Kibbutz Geva) and others.

From the Cultural and Social Life

Krynki – A Center of Torah

Translator's note: This Yiddish article is equivalent with the Hebrew article on pages 83-84.

[Page 91]

Education and Culture

Translator's note: This Yiddish article is equivalent with the Hebrew article on pages 86-87.

Founders of the first library in Krynki,
1907/1908 – Libka and Ahrchik Lew

[Page 92]

The Modern Cheder

by Bendet Nisht (B. Niv)

Translator's note: This Yiddish article is equivalent with the Hebrew article on <u>pages 87-88.</u>

[page 93]

The First World War

Mutual Aid to the Refugees

Translated by Jerrold Landau

The outbreak of the First World War in August 1914 led to a draft of the youths and reserves. This created a chance for a boom in leather manufacturing in Krynki, as the demand for footwear for the vast army increased greatly. However, when the Czarist army began to suffer defeats in East Prussia in 1915, leading to retreats to their own areas, the Russians liquidated and transferred the majority of the factories of Krynki eastward to the interior of the country. At this point, the anti-Semites in the Kingdom of Russia required a scapegoat upon which to blame the retreat. As usual, they easily found it: the Jewish people! Rumors spread and grew that this treasonous nation was helping the enemy in various ways including espionage, for they hoped to benefit in the event of a victory.

An edict was quickly issued by the commander in chief of the Czarist army, a member of the family of the wicked Archduke Nikolai Nikolaev, to deport the Jews from the area of the battles, and the adjacent area. The roads and paths were filled with caravans of wagons laden with homeless Jewish refugees. They were fleeing to wherever they could, with the aim of finding a new shelter for themselves and their family. Some of them stopped in Krynki and established their lives there.

An "Aid Committee" was quickly set up to deal with housing, food, and clothing for the refugees. A special committee called "The Vaad" was created to deal with their children, especially with their education. It was headed by Sonia Pel, Yaakov Kirszner, Bender Nisht, and Pinchas and Menashe Garber. They were assisted by several teachers, enthusiastic and idealistic young girls: Leah Nisht, Esther and Breina Terkel, and others. The committee succeeded in opening a public school with three grades for the children of the refugees and the poor local children. It was not long before the echoes of their tender voices began to burst forth from the walls of the school, to the great satisfaction of the teachers and educational activists, who spared no effort for these unfortunate children.

Days of fear and danger approached and overtook the Jews of Krynki after the German army conquered the Osowiec fortress on the Biebrza River, opening up for them to the Białystok-Sokółka district west and southwest of Krynki. The news and the arriving refugees from the towns near the front told of atrocities and deeds of revenge perpetrated by the retreating Czarist troops, who executed judgments against the Jews and their property.

The local wicked people were diligent. They began to go around the market near the Jewish shops, and the yards of the wealthy Jews, "sniffing around", plotting and discussing openly who of them will inherit this bounty in the upcoming days.

However, providence was good to the Jews of Krynki, for the evil people, in their great haste, did not have the chance to carry out their plans before the armies of "Reb Velvel" (as Kaiser Wilhelm was nicknamed by the Jews) entered the town, and a new chapter of life began in the entire district.

According to Baruch Niv (B. Nisht) and other sources.

The First World War

[Page 94]

The beginning of the Russian defeats

Translated by Eszter Andor

Aid to the homeless refugees

Bendet Nisht (Barukh Niv)

When the Russian troops started to retreat from Eastern Prussia under the pressure of Emperor Wilhelm's army in 1915, the Russians needed a scapegoat that could be blamed for their defeat. They found it soon: "the Jews!" An order was issued at once to expel them from all settlements near the border and the front lines. Long lines of wagons appeared on the roads, packed with homeless Jewish refugees yearning to find a place where they could shelter with their families. Many of them stopped in our town Krynki and settled here.

A Committee for the Homeless was soon set up to provide them with a roof over their heads, as well as with food and clothes. The committee had several sections and one of them was responsible for cultural matters. Its activists – led by Sonya Fel, Yakov Kirzhner, Bendet Nisht, Pinkhas and Menase Garber, and others – devoted themselves to teach and educate the innocent homeless children so that they would not, God forbid, remain backward in their spiritual development.

With the help of some teachers, such as Leah Nisht, Breyne and Esther Terkl and others who, although still almost children themselves, were unselfish idealists, the cultural committee succeeded in establishing a three-grade Hebrew elementary school for both homeless and poor children of the town. The little voices of the pupils soon rose from the classes and delighted the teachers and the founders of the school amidst their hard work.

At the end of the summer of 1915

D. Selkof

Around Tisha be-Av of 1915 during the First World War, the entire Jewish population lived in deadly fear of each new day. One morning the rumor spread that the Jews of Krynki would soon have to leave the town because of the great Russian defeats on the whole battle front and the advance of the German army. The entire region between Grodno and Bialystok was classified as a strategic zone since the Germans concentrated immense forces in the region of the two big fortresses in Grodno and Osowietz. The Germans besieged the Osowietz fortress for six months and the shelling could be heard in our town. It was reported that the Jews of Grodno, just as those of the nearby shtetls, were expelled into the heart of Russia. We feared and expected that it would soon be our turn and we would have to abandon our homes and trades. It was especially frightful to think that the Gentiles would appropriate all our properties after we left the town.

And we would talk among ourselves about the imminent distribution of our property like this: "Look, there is Tzapan, the limping shoemaker from Sokolker street, standing on the marketplace with a band of Gentile lads around him. He is showing his friends with his thick stick which shop and its stock he will inherit when the Jews flee the town. Or take Yurhilo, the wet tannery worker, who walks around barefoot with his feet black and bruised and begs some kopecks from the Jews every Friday. He wants nothing less then Itshe Mostovlionske's brick house!"

[Page 95]

The entire local police force ran away from Krynki one night and abandoned the shtetl. An officer with a group of barefooted soldiers took over the power, declared a state of war and proclaimed himself interim commander. We all feared that he might order us to leave the town.

One evening a whole crowd of Gentiles descended upon us with spades and axes on their shoulders. At first we thought that they were rioters ready for action but it soon turned out that they were sent to Krynki to dig trenches against the attacks of the enemy. We learned from the Gentiles that they came from Sopotzkin where they had also dug such trenches, but German planes flew over them and started dropping bombs and in the end they were forced to retreat. Thus we learned again that the Germans were close to Grodno. Meanwhile Virion's grove was cut down to make room for the trenches. The Jewish youth was not hired for this work even though many of them would have been eager to earn two rubles a day. The Jews were excluded from the war operations because of dreadful false accusations against our brethren, the sons of Israel, which said that we were on the side of the Germans and even supported them in many ways. Naturally, after such rumors the Jews could not expect anything good either from the Gentile population or the Russian soldiers.

The pits were finished, ready to be used in battle but a miracle happened and the Russians had no time to use them. The Germans arrived and the Russian army was forced to retreat. As they were retreating they burned down everything on their way. Flames were blazing in all the villages around Krynki. The Russian soldiers spent a whole night trying hard to burn the great water mill which was not far from the town. But as if to spite them, the wooden wheel, which was thoroughly wet, did not catch fire and the mill remained intact. Later when the Germans came into Krynki the mill became very useful: all the poor Jews could go and grind a pood *(a Russian weight of about 36 pounds)* of rye there to bake bread for their families.

Under the German Occupation (Fall 1915 - Spring 1919)

Under the Pressure of the Occupier

Dov Rabin

Translated by Jerrold Landau

Transaltor's note: This Yiddish article by Dov Rabin is largely equivalent with the Yiddish article with the same title on page 98

Distribution of potatoes in the synagogue

[Page 97]

In Starvation and Distress

by Shamai (Shima) Lider

Translated by Jerrold Landau

As is known, the economic situation in Krynki during the time of the German occupation of World War I was very bad, as it was in the entire occupied area. The tanneries stopped their work. The situation of the shopkeepers and the merchants was not bright. Most of the shops were pillaged during the time of regime change, other than those of iron implements and agricultural machines, for the soldiers were not very interested in such merchandise at that time.

The hunger began to show its signs upon the masses. Entire families, with adults and children, would go to the fields to collect the left-over produce after the potato harvest. Even if the farmer had combed over his field a second time to retrieve potatoes that were hiding here and there, the people who came from the town would dig the ground once again, and, after great effort, find a few small, inferior potatoes. They would also spread out to the forests far from the city to collect wild berries or mushrooms in the summer, and to cut trees for cooking and heat. On occasion, we would even sneak into the nearby forest of Wyrion to cut dry trees, even though it was forbidden.

Once, a full convoy from our street was found as we were returning home with our cut-down bounty on our shoulders. We succeeded in escaping in all directions. However, one was caught and interrogated (Nyunia Stambler), and was unable to withstand the beatings. He gave over our names. We were summoned to a trial and fined. Some of us were also sentenced to jail. I remember how they came to arrest Mother. The Jewish translator Shabtai Chajes gestured to us children to burst out in great crying. We obeyed, and wailed and screamed, "Mother, Mother!" until they released her. At the end, we were freed from this tribulation.

Changes in Society

by Shamai Kaplan

Translated by Jerrold Landau

Rabbi Weintraub

As the Russians retreated in the autumn of 1914, Rabbi Zalman Sender left the city. Only one rabbi remained. The conquering Germans imposed their regime, and the Jewish community began to live its life in a restricted fashion during the period of occupation.

The majority of the community, who were observers of tradition, were faced with the problem of appointing a spiritual leader. In 1916, the synagogue people gathered together and invited Rabbi Weintraub, a refugee from Kovno, to serve as the rabbi of Krynki. He was an educated man, filled to brim with Judaism and its Torah, as well as with general education. He was also proficient in languages, including German. Rabbi Weintraub gathered together a group of lads and taught them a page of Gemara each day. I was one of them. We would go around from home to home in the city every Friday to collect money for the rabbi's weekly salary.

The German occupation regime, with its stringencies and decrees, led to a situation where many heads of families became impoverished to the point of struggling for a loaf of bread. At that time, there were some Jewish youths who collaborated with the Germans and profited from this. Rabbi Weintraub was a man of the humanist school. On Sabbaths after the third Sabbath meal he would deliver a sermon in the home of Yehuda Worlinsky, mainly on topics of morality, and he would speak out against this. There were those in the audience who understood his innuendoes about those serving the needs of the Germans, but they would not disclose who they were.

One day, he was summoned to appear before the district captain, and he found favor in his eyes. The captain recognized that he was a rabbi, and even agreed to free his Gemara lads from the forced labor that was taking place at that time, for he interceded on their behalf. As Passover approached, he also received from the Germans potatoes, which were in short supply, to distribute to the poor of the town. We carried this out on a volunteer basis. Thus did the prestige of the rabbi increase greatly.

However, this was not acceptable to some of those who were close to the regime, who were afraid of bankruptcy. They began to search after him. One Friday, as I was walking with Moshe Marain through the Kowkoz quarter to collect money for the rabbi's salary, several youths followed after us, and started up with us, leading to a dispute. From that time, they began to persecute us in various ways. We were even taken to forced labor. They damaged the rabbi's reputation, claiming that he was spying, so to speak, against the German regime.

Finally, they succeeded in bringing about a situation where one Friday, Rabbi Weintraub was ordered to leave Krynki within 24 hours.

[Page 98]

The German occupation (From Fall 1915 to Spring 1919)

Under the pressure of the occupier

Dov Rabin

Translated by Eszter Andor

When the Germans entered Krynki, the Jews in the surrounding communities sighed with relief. At first the Jews felt liberated from the Russian regime which had discriminated against them and persecuted them, and threatened their physical survival for many generations.

But a harsh occupational regime established itself very soon. There began a series of forced labor on the highways. Food and various merchandise such as leather, metals and chemical products were requisitioned. Unemployment started after the requisitioning of the small piles of supplies and the prohibiting of leather production, which led to the closing of even those few tanneries that still remained in Krynki. Free movement was restricted and a special permit had to be acquired if someone wanted to leave the town for example. It was prohibited to take in and out of town, food an other products of primary necessity, etc.

Commerce came to a standstill. Many shops and businesses had been plundered during the retreat of the Russians and most of the remaining goods were soon requisitioned or bought up and what was left vanished due to all the smuggling and speculations that went on.

Serious food shortage, turmoil and immense scarcity sprang up. The Jews, young and old alike, set out to the nearby villages to get whatever products they could from the peasants, whose cattle and grain had also been confiscated by the Germans. People were lucky enough if they returned home with a little piece of hard village bread, a little barley or rye and the like for themselves and the rest of their household.

Even those who still had some savings soon lost it when the order was issued that all Russian rubles had to be exchanged into the worthless banknotes of the occupying power. An evil decree was also issued which ordered the "selling" of all copper products, (including household articles such as door-handles, frying pans and other tableware), to the German lord for almost nothing. The wind of poverty started to blow soon in the Jewish homes. The time of hunger and need arrived when, as Krynki Jews describe it in their memoirs, "mothers and sisters, wrapped in tatters and with clogs on their feet, poured out of all corners of the town at daybreak and tread the fields for 20 versts *(about 13 miles)* to find a forgotten stalk of rye or a frozen rotten potato." Others also went to the nearby woods to gather a little waste wood to cook and warm themselves.

Jewish and Christian forced laborers loading and pulling trolleys
on the highway leading to Little Brestovitz

[Page 99]

Living under distress

Meanwhile the Jews of Krynki did not sit idly. They sought ways to make both ends meet and endure the bad times. They leased orchards and gardens from landowners in the neighborhood of the town and dozens of families made a living out of growing potatoes for years. Others took up impromptu trades of the times: the more adventurous engaged in smuggling forbidden goods from one zone to the other, while the less daring became coachmen who transported these goods and made a living from this. It is true that some of them "would have made a better melamed [*teacher of children in cheder*] than have anything to do with a horse and a coach", writes a Krynki Jew, but they did not have an alternative. People also tried to make a living out of other things as far as they could.

[Page 100]

In the abandoned tannery yards

Shmuel Geler

When the front line approached Krynki during the First World War most of the leather factories evacuated into the heart of Russia. After the entry of the German troops into town, the remaining tanneries were closed, the factory yards were overgrown with wild grass. The "raw materials" were left lying around, the "tanks" were dry, the "rolls" and the benches were covered with cobweb.

The huge abandoned factory yards were a paradise for the cheder youth. There, they jauntily and happily played hide and seek, and Cossacks and robbers. The hundreds of "poles" left there served often as guns, swords and for playing devils.

The revival of Jewish culture

D. R. N

Soon after the entry of the Germans in town, a radical change could be felt in Jewish cultural and social life in the nearby occupied territories. As the front line was approaching Krynki the Jewish members of the Russified circles were the first to leave the shtetl and go to the heart of Russia and those who remained were deprived of their spiritual nourishment. Russian language was withdrawn from circulation. The Germans banned it from the educational institutions and from social life in general and they even prefered Yiddish, which was close to their own language and which they thought could serve as a tool in Germanizing the population.

Yiddish, which the nationalist Jews had always regarded as a shield which protected the Jews from assimilation and as a natural tool for the development of Jewish culture, was maintained for some time, despite the general conditions.

The Jewish public, especially the youth, experienced not only bitter economic deprivation but also spiritual distress. People yearned for opportunities to enjoy themselves and drive away the oppressive mood, hear a little Yiddish and gain some spiritual.

When the Germans started to allow the organization of various performances the income of which was to be donated to help the needy, the Jews of the nearby towns and shtetls soon set up associations to cultivate Yiddish arts and drama, at first with the above-mentioned aim.

In Krynki, too, a Literary Society was quickly founded by leaders of various social groups, and literary evenings and other events were organized. The association set up a drama circle which ventured to produce plays in Yiddish – a delight that the Russian regime had forbidden and that the Jewish public had not tasted for years. A fresh spirit entered the shtetl and reached even those who had until then been far from Yiddish culture in all its manifestations.

German compulsory school for Jewish children, with their teacher Potshebutzki

[Page 101]

Beside their activities in the general Literary Society and in the drama circle, the Zionists, especially the youthful Tzairei Zion, which had organized itself undercover in the meantime, also opened a special gathering place, the "Center". This label served as a disguise under which illegal Zionist activities were carried out as far as it was possible in those times.

Young teachers and activists undertook, with a lot of energy and devotion, the education of Jewish children The Hebrew elementary school was opened again and later a Yiddish elementary school was also established by labor leaders. Meanwhile, however, the occupying forces looked around and opened their own schools where teaching was in German with the intention to abolish Jewish education. The Germans demanded the introduction of German as the language of instruction in the Jewish schools and when the Jews resisted this they closed the Jewish elementary schools, although this did not make the German schools more successful. The Jewish schools opened again later.

The Literary Society also suffered from the occupying power. The situation changed only after the revolution in Germany at the end of 1918.

The Literary Society and its fight[1]

Yisroel Veyner

It is 1916. We are in the middle of the First World War. Krynki, like all Lithuania, is occupied by the German army. An intensive cultural revival can be felt in almost all the towns and shtetls and Krynki, of course, cannot lag behind. A Literary Society was founded in our town at once under the leadership of the brightest forces, such as the teacher Eynshteyn, Dovid Gotlib, the Potshebutzki brothers, and others.

The society started to develop a wide variety of activities, organizing frequent literary evenings, at which lectures on literary topics and social questions, as well as recitals and recitations, and readings were held. The cultural elite of Krynki Jewish society participated in these events. The evenings always attracted a large audience, which greeted each performance with great applause. This audience, however, started to demand serious programs, such as lectures, recitals and recitations, because it badly needed culture and literature in order to drive away the hunger and poverty, which reigned in the town. An amateur drama circle was formed and it produced plays in Yiddish under the guidance of the Literary Society at the local bank.

[Page 102]

I remember to this day the first play of Yakov Gordin that we staged, *Kashe the Orphan*, in which Trakhtenberg was played by Eynshteyn the teacher, Matie Shtreykhl by Shmuli Tenor, as we used to call him, and Kashe the orphan by Rokhl Stambler.

The performance was a great financial and moral success.

The theatrical evenings were also attended by the German military personnel stationed in Krynki and in the nearby villages, as well as in the Lishk manor and in Alekshitz where they were quartered. The Germans stationed in Krynki were even interested in the performances and they often intervened in the direction of the play. Once at the performance of *Hertzele the Aristocrat*, they even forced Rokhl Stambler to sing Schubert's serenade at the end of the play.

The Germans are "victorious"

The Germans soon became jealous of the pleasure the Jews took in the performances and the overlord issued a strict decree that the management of the Literary Society should add a dance after each performances to make it possible for the Germans to dance with the Jewish girls. Unable to refuse, the management had to accept the decree against their will and for a few months each play finished with a dance for the benefit of the Germans who were very much attracted to the Jewish girls of Krynki.

The performance of "Hertzele the Aristocrat"

However, murmuring started among the Jewish people of the town against such entertainment, at first quiet but getting ever louder. Scandalmongers took the opportunity to "intrigue" and "exaggerate" what really happened. The management of the Literary Society was powerless. They could not put an end to these dances because repealing the decree of the German military power in wartime would have entailed the death penalty or at the very least being sent to forced labor in Heynovke or Bialoviezh. There seemed to be no way out.

Then comrade Dovid Gotlib, chairman of the Literary Society announced in a meeting of the management that he would not allow the dance after the next performance and would assume responsibility for it. All members of the management tried to dissuade him, warning him of the great danger that such an act might bring, but nothing helped. He stubbornly stuck to his own opinion. And so it was: when a new play was put on and at the end of the performance people started making room for the dance, Gotlib got on the stage and gave out strict orders that nobody was to dance and have boisterous festivities at a place where Mendele, Peretz and Sholem Aleichem was recited.

[Page 103]

The Germans were stupefied as if struck by lightening. "How dare that filthy 'Ostjude' [*East European Jew*] oppose the omnipotent Germans!", they said to themselves. Comrade Gotlib took advantage of the confusion to disappear from the hall with some of his comrades.

When the Germans recovered from their astonishment, they started to look for Gotlib in order to take revenge on him. Late at night they invaded the house of Dovid's father, Reb Yudl Gotlib, peace to his memory, and other Jewish houses, too. As they did not find him, the German police announced to the Literary Society the following day that if Dovid Gotlib did not surrender himself in six hours, all the members of the society's management would be arrested and the society would be abolished. Precisely six hours later Dovid Gotlib showed up at the police station and he was arrested.

When the authorities tried to decide later what punishment he should get, the police sergeant Grabak, demanded the highest punishment. A series of mediation started then trying to influence the head of the office and other circles, and they finally agreed to just sending Gotlib to Heynovke. But Gotlib was unexpectedly saved by his cousin Batsheba Mordekhailevitz who was on friendly terms with the secretary of the head of the office, Shturmak, a deeply religious German Jew, graduate of a rabbinical seminary. (They got married later.) No effort was spared and Dovid Gotlib was finally rescued from the clutches of the German military.

However, he was freed on condition that the Literary Society would call together an exceptional general meeting at once and not only relieve him of the chairmanship but exclude him from the society altogether. The meeting took place two days later and all members of the society, as well as several representatives of the German occupying forces participated in it. The meeting was presided over by the vice-chairman, Anshl Potshebutzki, who explained to the assembled why the meeting had been convened. For the sake of the continued existence of the Literary Society he asked those present to vote for the dismissal of Dovid Gotlib from the chairmanship and his exclusion from the society by raising their hands. But nobody raised their hands.

Seeing this, the chief representative of the Germans warned the assembled that they must find a way out; otherwise sanctions would be applied against them. Gotlib himself intervened, however, to save the situation and implored the assembly to vote for his exclusion for the sake of the Literary Society. But the second voting could not take place because the firemen sounded the alarm – this had been prepared by the Germans and their servants on purpose – and the assembled scattered.

The Germans were "victorious" . . . Officially Gotlib was considered excluded from the society but in reality no meeting of the management, no discussion, no cultural event took place without Gotlib being actively involved in it. And he received dozens of letters from the nearby Jewish shtetls, which appreciated his courage, daring and fearlessness. This is how the Jewish youth of Krynki fought against the evil German power in 1916.

[Page 104]

Zionist activities and Hebrew education

The "Zionist Center"; "Tzeirei Zion"

by Baruch Niv

Translated by Jerrold Landau

During the First World War, when everyone was tied to their own location for several years, with no possibility of even going out to the broader area, the youth were thirsty for activity and for salvation from idleness. Thus did the "Literary Society" (an organization for Jewish literature and culture) and the Zionist Center sprout up. We conducted Zionist activity under the auspices of the "Merkaz" [The Center]. The German authorities were angered by this. We conducted activities for the Jewish National Fund, we organized a memorial for Dr. Herzl on 20 Tammuz, etc.

Members of the Tzeirei Tzion [Young Zion], founded at that time, organization met in the Merkaz. It was headed by young people who displayed great action and diligence throughout all the years of German occupation. Through their various activities, they earned a respectable level of influence and communal status in town. Tzeirei Tzion reopened the Hebrew school and participated in leading and sustaining it. Since most of the Jewish children of Krynki studied there at that time, they also made connections with the parents and those who were involved with the school. Tzeirei Tzion established the large local library. They also maintained connections with the movement outside of Krynki. A delegate from the organization (the writer of these lines) participated in the convention of that organization in Białystok in 1916. A delegate from the Krynki chapter (Avraham Einstein) participated in the Zionist convention of the south Lithuanian district in Białystok in 1918, and was elected as a member of the central headquarters.

Tzeirei Tzion was also active in the aforementioned Literary Organization and in the drama troupe and its performances.

The Hebrew Kindergarten

The Merkaz Hatzioni [Zionist Center] locale (in Alter the painter's house)

The Hebrew School

Th activities of the committee for refugees in the town ceased its operations with the entry of the Germans to Krynki, and the Hebrew school, founded for their children, was closed. A few of the members of the culture committee of the aforementioned organization who remained in town – Menashe and Pinchas Garber, Yaakov Kirzner, and the writer of these lines – decided to reopen the school, and did so. However, after that, the relationship of the authorities to it took a turn for the worse, and they closed it and forced its students to attend the German school that they founded. Despite this, the Hebrew school was reopened after a period of time through the efforts of its activists, albeit at a more modest level.

At the end of 1971, after the Balfour Declaration, members of the Tzeirei Tzion committee – Alter Pocboski (died in Israel in 1964 after surviving the Holocaust of the Second World War), Berl Zakon (today in New York), Melech Zalkin (perished in the Holocaust), Pinchas and Menashe Garber, and the writer of these lines – gathered together and decided to enlarge the school in light of the hoped-for possibilities of *aliya* to the Land of Israel and the need to prepare the younger generation for such. The matter became feasible, but only after the revolution in Germany, when the fist of the occupying government weakened, and the students who had been forced by the Germans to transfer to their school began to return to their own school.

[Page 105]

Those active in supporting the school at that time included Avraham Einstein, Heshil Sapirsztajn, Melech Zalkin, Yosef Gabai, Feigel Epsztajn, Menashe Garber, and the writer of these lines. Later, they were joined by Efraim Efrimson, Shamai (Shima) Kaplan, and others.

The Hebrew elementary school

Bendet Nisht (Barukh Niv)

Translated by Eszter Andor

After the German occupation of Krynki, the Committee for the Homeless ceased its activities, and instruction was interrupted for a few months in the Hebrew elementary school, which had been founded for the children of the refugees and the poor at the beginning of the war.

The population was suffering from hunger, poverty and the cold. But soon four members of the cultural commission of the Committee for the Homeless, who had remained in Krynki –Menase and Pinkhas Garber, B. Nisht and Yakov Kirzhner – assembled and decided to open the school again saying that "even when there is no flour, there is the Torah" (one must study even when there is nothing to eat).

In one year the school, the only Hebrew school in town grew bigger, and the rulers who had at first tolerated it, took a dislike to it and closed it, and compelled the children to attend the German school. But thanks to the efforts of its leaders our school opened again, albeit on a smaller scale.

At the end of 1917, after the Balfour declaration, the committee of the Tzairei Zion convened in Krynki. (It consisted of the following people: Bendet Nisht – now in Israel; Alter Potshebutzki – died in 1964 in Israel, having survived the cruelties of the Second World War; Berl Zakon – now in New York; Melekh Zalkin – perished; and Pinkhas and Menase Garber.) It was decided that the school had to be enlarged, especially because of the prospect of an aliya to Palestine and, connected to this, the need to teach the pupils Hebrew, the local language.

It only became possible to carry out the resolution in 1918 when new winds started to blow – the winds of revolution first in Russia and then in Germany. When the inhabitants of Krynki started feeling, too, that the iron grip of the occupying forces became weaker, the Tzairei Zion organization enlarged the school and the pupils who had been forced to transfer to the German educational institution were also allowed to come back.

Among the active leaders who fully devoted themselves to maintaining the school were the following people: Avrom Eynshteyn, Heshl Sapirshteyn, Melekh Zalkin, Yosef Gabay, Menase Garber, the author of this article, and later Efraym

Afrimzon, Sheyme Kaplan, etc. They spared no efforts and they managed to overcome all the difficulties that arose: political persecutions of the school authorities and especially lack of money.

Forty to fifty percent of the budget was always missing. Great self-sacrifice was required from the school committee and the Tzairei Zion organization in order to cover the deficit. They received piecemeal support from our American brethren and later from the town authorities.

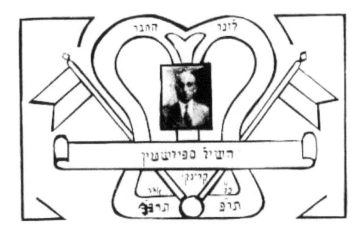

In Memory of the member Heshil Sapirsztajn, Krynki, 22 Adar, 5684 [1924]

[Page 106]

Despite the hard material situation of the school, the teaching staff always maintained a high pedagogical level. The moving spirits of the school were such educators as Eynshteyn, Gotesfeld, Dr Reys, Dr Tzveygl, Moshe Zaleski (now doctor and director of Hebrew education in Cincinnati, USA), etc.

A class in the Hebrew school

Hundreds and hundreds of pupils graduated from this educational institution in its eighteen graduating classes. And those graduates who left Krynki and emigrated to North and South America, and the numerous graduates who made aliya to Palestine, occupy most distinguished places in the cultural and social life of their country.

The original idea was to educate Jewish children in Hebrew and in the spirit of our national values and survival in Palestine – and indeed the school made this reality. This is shown by both the spiritual foundation with which the pupils were provided, and the enviable rich hakhsharah [*training for would-be immigrants*], which was to help them take root in the country, build it and fight for it.

Fighting with the Germans for Yiddish education

Sure Fel-Yelin

It is the First World War. Homeless, starving, and shabby people wander about in town. Something must be done. I call together the intelligentsia of the town – the high school students, the pharmacist and the teacher couple – and we decide to create a school for the children and to pay attention to them.

The fight against the German occupying power is a splendid chapter in the history of Krynki. The Germans demand that German be the language of instruction in the schools. We teachers agree that Yiddish should remain the language of instruction and German should be taught only as the vernacular. Among the teachers were the Rotbort sisters (the daughters of Rubke, the Governor of the Province), Potshebutzki, Falk and I, and there were a few German teachers and a high school teacher. The Rotborts had already been linguistically assimilated. I, the socialist-Bundist, was a rather militant Yiddishist. Once I made a sharp attack in public against the representatives of the occupying power and because I was young I did not realize how dangerous it was to oppose a military power. "We have not invited you . . . You came to us uninvited . . . Yiddish is our mother tongue . . . We love Yiddish and we will not give in!" This is how I was thinking at the time.

The same night my friend, the German high school teacher, knocked on my window and advised me to leave the shtetl at once. . . . I woke up my father and left in the cold grey dawn. I got on a cart to Bialystok. Later I often came to the shtetl to work – in the school, in the self-defense group, or to give a lecture. My father used to call me the "gabe's wife" and he had hardly any time to see me.

[Page 107]

During the Times of the Revolution

by Shamai (Shima) Lider

Translated by Jerrold Landau

When the Germans Left

On one autumn evening, we suddenly found out that the Germans left Krynki, as they lost the war. Masses of men, women, and children began to stream to the area of the Wyrion farm to collect booty from the large amount of property that was left there, especially sheep and cattle. The gate was broken open and the pillaging began. It is difficult to describe the mania that overtook everyone to snatch and pillage.

Even the civilian committee that was founded on a provisional basis sent delegates to inform and influence the masses to stop the pillage, for the committee was intending to organize local affairs, including the distribution of necessities, in a fair fashion. They did not find an attentive ear.

The battle regarding the nature of the committee, which was aroused in the houses of worship, had not yet stopped – when stories began to circulate in the city that a draft for the Polish legions was taking place in the region, with the purpose of taking over the local government. It was further said that the Lithuanians were also beginning to draft people around Grodno. The

Lithuanian announcement also reached Krynki, and one lad, Shmuel (Mulia) Stambler, was even drafted to their army. (He was later killed in one of the battles that took place in those days.) A Russian youth, apparently a Communist, arrived in Krynki, and started to organize a workers council. They also started gathering weapons and organizing a militia. Its members included among others: Shlomo Stambler, Tevel Koncwycki, Chaim Gedalia Kopel, Shmuel Lewski (Taner).

The Rule of the Workers Council

Within a brief period, the Germans left Krynki, and a different national government had not yet been established. For a period, the Workers Council ruled in collaboration with the town council. The Workers Council set up its headquarters in the building of the national bank on Poctowa Street. Its prominent members included Yehoshua Gotlib (the brother of David Gotlib), Yeshayahu Zuc, Yoska Terkel (Chatzkel's), Moshe Puria (Mosheke Sacur), Binyamin Puria, his brother Yaakov, Kahanowic, Neiporuznicer, Gershon Tarlowski, Velvele Ekstein, and others.

The local workers authority conducted an orderly distribution of food to protect the prices of staples against inflation, and to protect the storehouses of food in the town that they not be smuggled outside. For that purposes, guards were also posted on the roads leading from Krynki to the wider area. They also did so to preserve local order and to prevent theft and hooliganism.

In the interim, supporters of liberated Poland began to organize themselves in the area. They drafted soldiers and set up committees in their effort to establish Polish rule. Rumors spread that there was a great deal of ammunition in Krynki, and that the town intended to declare an actual independent government. Nearby neighbors, including the landowner Rozenblum from Makarowce, where brigades of legionnaires were training, as well as others, requested that the people of Krynki refrain from bloodshed, for there would be no hope that this settlement could maintain its stand in the hostile area, and it would be best to avoid provoking a war.

After days and nights of serious debate within the workers council, it was decided to remove the cannon from the roof, to hide the weapons, and to refrain from mounting resistance – but also to not invite a different government. After a few days, however, the Polish legionnaires entered Krynki, and began searches for the heads of the workers council. If they did not find them, they arrested their family members to force them to reveal the hiding places of the members of the council. Those interrogated were even tortured with the points of the skewers used to clean the guns.

[Page 108]

In the time of the revolutions

The workers' rule in Krynki

Yisroel Stolarsk

It is the end of 1918. The First World War has ended. The Germans are about to leave Krynki. The secretary of the county convenes a meeting in the big bes medresh [*synagogue and study house*] and informs us that the Germans are leaving and the Poles intend to take over the power. He selects some respected Jewish and Christian inhabitants and gives them the keys of the granaries and some twenty thousand German marks and creates a civil committee, which will take over the lead. Dovid Gotlib convenes a meeting of the Bund, the Poalei Zion, and the anarchists, and we decide that with the outbreak of the revolution in Russia and Germany the time has come for the workers of Krynki to take over the power. Following the good old tradition of the Krynki lads we broke into the meeting of the civil committee, scattered it, and established a labor council. We took over the keys of the granaries and the money and the power in the town.

We promptly distributed flour and potatoes among the poor and sent some men to buy weapons in Bialystok. We already had 200 guns and two machine-guns and a lot of crates with weapons. We set up the machine-guns on the roof of the "little bank" – the loan and savings bank. We organized a workers' militia, which was lead by Heykl Barkan (Heykl Mutz). We provided them with guns and red armbands and we started governing the town.

When all the cereals were gone from the granaries, we levied a tax on the rich and organized public work to give work to the poor and the unemployed. They were sent to cut ice on the Krynki lake for the "poorhouse".

Our militia had a very difficult task trying to fight theft and hooliganism, which started to spread towards the end of the German occupation. Rich Jewish boys and Christian hooligans terrorized the population and people were forced to suffer and keep silent. When the "gang" disregarded our warnings to hand over their weapons, we shot two bandits in the market place and that helped. The population was very grateful to us, and later when the Poles took over the power and arrested us, the priest interceded for us and helped us to get free.

This is how we ruled the town for a while. Bialystok was already governed by the Poles. Messengers from Pilsudski himself came to Krynki a few times and called us up to give over the power. We refused. We surrendered only when we were already surrounded and the Poles were coming at us from two directions, from Sokolke and Amdur.

The activities of the workers' council and its demise

Volf Ekshteyn

I arrived back in Krynki after the First World War as a demobilized soldier who had gone through the storm of the Russian revolution in the Russian army. When I came home, I joined the Krynki committee of the Bund with the intention to cut off the left wing of the local movement in order to found a separate communist party, following the example of the "Kombund" in Russia.

The following people were members of the local committee of the Bund in Krynki: Dovid Gotlib, Issakhar Fink, Avrom Shmuel Zutz, Hakhum Blakher, A. Sh. Liberman, who was a crockery shopkeeper, his sister-in-law, Khame (Nekhame), who was a midwife, and I. Among us we held the continual debates that were going on at that time between the Mensheviks and the Bolsheviks along the lines set by the two geniuses of that generation, Plekhanov and Lenin.

[Page 109]

Meanwhile the revolution broke out in Germany and the German power around us ceased to exist. A workers' council made up of several parties was set up in Krynki. The chairman was Yerushe Gotlib, Dovid Gotlib's brother, the secretary Velvel Furie, and Yoske Hatzkls, Moshke Furie, Sorke the midwife, Velvel Ekshteyn, Heykl and Shloyme Mutz and Issakhar Fink, as the representatives of the Bund, were its members. There were also a few Christian members, such as Mikhniuk and Anisimovitz, young demobilized officers of the Russian army and tsar Nicholas.

The first action of the workers' council was to levy a tax on the richer inhabitants of the town in order to help the demobilized soldiers who came back from Russia and from German captivity and went around tattered and hungry. There were heads of families among them who had to be given first aid to help them get back on their feet. A soldiers' committee was set up and it successfully carried out the necessary actions. There were very few people who refused to pay the tax. The workers' council organized a big demonstration to protest against the pogrom in Lemberg and almost all the Jews of Krynki participated in it. The demonstrators, together with the tanners, marched through Kostzial and New Street to the town hall and the little bank and back. The red banners were carried by the eldest worker of the town.

Within the workers' council an arms committee was set up, which went to Bialystok every week to buy weapons. We collected money for this from a special tax, which we imposed on the mills of Krynki and its environs around which we deployed our militia.

A problem arose with the "illegal" youth that went around armed and tried to take advantage of the situation. The workers' council approached them and tried to influence them rather than threaten them. And when we caught a well-known Sokolke thief in Krynki, the "illegal" youth even helped us hand him over to the Germans in Sokolke, who shot him. (A few Germans were still left in the towns at that time.)

The Bund committee, 1928

The Krynki workers' council was closely linked to such nearby shtetls as Horodok and Brestovitz, in which there was no stable power either.

We ruled the town thus until the Polish army started to mobilize and the news came to us from Amdur that the legionaries were coming to Krynki. They stopped in the middle of the way and sent ahead a delegation to us with the proposal that we should surrender and give over the power. Dovid Gotlib told them that we would not give over the power to anybody, but they should come and take it if they could. The leaders of the workers' council left Krynki and went to Vilna on a minor road, the Odelsk-Grodno road, to avoid an unnecessary bloodshed.

[Page 110]

By the way: when we arrived in Odelsk, we encountered a pogrom mood but when people learned that the Krynki workers' council was in town, the tensions died down.

The activities of the Bund during the war

Hershl Giteles Oygustovski

When Krynki was under German occupation during the First World War the Bund, together with other trends popular among the Jewish population, was active in the cultural life of the shtetl. The literary Saturdays that took place in the "little bank" are memorable. A wide Jewish public gathered there to hear a little Yiddish – lectures on Yiddish literature and Jewish history and the like. And if the representatives of the German occupants were not present, which happened from time to time, the lecturer would sneak into his speech his opinion about daily happenings.

After the disintegration of the German occupying regime, when the inhabitants of Krynki organized their own town administration, the Bund came out in the open and participated in the elections to the town council. When the workers' council took over the power, the Bund joined it. The party was also active in the cultural life of the town. Under the leadership of Shmuel Tenor, a Jewish workers' choir was organized and natural science and cultural studies evenings were also held for the young.

I remember the happy evenings when we gathered, thirsting for culture on the premises of the Bund in Itshe Afroytzik's house. There was a lending library, which had a wide selection of books: world literature, as well as the works of the Yiddish classics, of course, and a rich collection of scientific and general social-economic works.

The Bund played an important role in Yiddish education and theater. The plays of the best Yiddish dramatists (Hirhbeyn, Yakov Gordin, Sholem Ash), as well as of world dramatists (Strinberg, Ibsen, Molière, etc.), were put on stage with amateurs. We would have to search hard to find another town or shtetl where Anski's Dybuk was put on stage without any help, but in Krynki we did it. It required a lot of courage and perseverance, as well as inexhaustible faith and love to realize such a performance. School children dragged all kinds of sacks and blankets to the lake, washed them and sewed them together clumsily, and then Note Kozlovski painted sceneries on them. Great was the excitement when the curtain rose.

War Years

Ab Mille

We struggled with hunger,
We ran over the fields to feed ourselves.
Our will to live grew stronger,
We appeased our hunger as best we could.
We were seeking on the fields,
We burrowed ourselves in garden beds,
We wanted to provide food for the winter.

We carried potatoes and rye on our shoulders,
We knew that the languishing would last for years.
The war starts with destruction and fires,
Then come the orphans and widows, cripples and plagues.

Footnote:

1.   From page 101: From the *Grodno Echo*, Buenos Aires, No. 10.

Jewish Krynki between the Two World Wars

May 1919 – September 1939

Under Renewed Polish Rule

[Page 111]

In Krynki After the First World War

by Zeev Tzur

Translated by Jerrold Landau

I arrived in Krynki from my native town of Werejki [Vyareyki] near Brzostowica [Berestavitsa] at the age of three, with my mother and sister Elka, after the outbreak of the First World War, when father was drafted to the army. I lived continuously in Krynki with my family from 1914 until 1926, when I went to study in the Technion in Vilna. Until I concluded my studies in 1929, I would visit there only on Passover and the summer vacation. After the disturbances of 5689 [1929] in the Land of Israel, I went out to a *hachshara* kibbutz in Congress Poland, and only came to Krynki prior to my *aliya* to the Land in May 1939 in order to bid farewell. Even during those years, however, I maintained correspondence in writing with friends in the town.

Therefore, my memories of Krynki related primarily to my period of childhood and youth. As the years pass and the memories become cloudy, several typical themes stand out, through which the communal image of Krynki is etched upon me. Without doubt, these memories also had a great influence on my future way of life.

These impressions are of a town bustling like a beehive with labor and toil, a center of tanneries, with many workers working in that industry; a city of commerce and labor, with connections to the gardens and agriculture of the surrounding area.

Communal life in Krynki was reasonably developed, especially in this period after the First World War. The weakening of the rule of the Czar in Russia and the Kaiser in Germany, the Socialist revolutions, the destruction and ruin left behind in the wake of the war; the rise of Poland as an independent country – all of these had a shocking and harrowing influence on the arena of Jewish life, first and foremost upon the youth.

In the wake of the destruction, want, and poverty left behind in the wake of the war, with the loss of the former markets in the expanse of Russia for manufactured products – the generation coming of age faced the question: to where?

Even though the influence of the circles zealous for tradition was large in the city, both from a religious perspective, and from the perspective of guarding the accepted way of life – the youth, with their difficulties, with the unemployment, and lack of opportunities for local productivity, started searching for new ways and a change of situation.

The Russian Revolution and the Balfour Declaration aroused a strong longing for redemption. Their influence upon the youth was strong not only from the social and communal perspective, but also with regard to choosing a path for their lives and their future, leading toward emigration.

Many hundreds of Krynki natives immigrated to the United States, following the paths of relatives and acquaintances who preceded them. With the quotas on immigration there, the immigrants began to stream to South America. Another group, smaller in scope but more directed in their aspirations and pioneering in their actions – sprung forth and made *aliya* to the Land of Israel.

[Note, the photo is missing in the original, but the caption is: **A group of youths just before their immigration to various countries, including *aliya* to the Land of Israel.**]

[Page 112]

We are also witness to the formation of centers of cultural activity and strong rise in factions and youth movements during that period in Krynki, following the First World War until the 1930s. These factions and movements had a strong influence in the community and within the youth as they directed their steps toward the future.

In Krynki, there were important centers of Communist youth, the Bund, and pioneering youth – first centered around Tzeirei Zion and then around the socialist Zionist party (left-leaning Poalei Tzion) and the Freiheit movement, organized into Hechalutz and Young Hechalutz.

The ideological, organizational, and political struggle among the factions was not only felt at the time of elections and important communal challenges. Rather it formed the essence of many of the youth as they concerned themselves with their personal lot in life, and sought solutions to the purpose of their lives. Belonging to Hechalutz and Young Hechalutz implied a practical realization of the idea of the movement – *aliya* to the Land of Israel. This was while the Bund and Communists sharply opposed this path in an extreme and "reactionary" manner, so to speak, distracting the interest of the community from the local revolutionary tasks. Furthermore, while the people of those factions permitted immigration to America, they opposed *aliya* to "the Land of Zionist dreams, of bogs, fever, and Arab Bedouins."

The pedagogic council and members of the committee of the Hebrew School, 1923

From right, seated: Beila Klotnicki, Bendet Nisht, Avraham Einstein (principal), Diamant (teacher of Polish), Rozka Cukert
Standing: Bobcha Freidman, Falk, Shama (Sheima) Kaplan, Ethel Terkel, Efraim Afrimzon, Moshe Zolski, Yosel Gabai, Pszpyurka

The centers that served as the sources of educational and ideological influence for the aforementioned factions were primarily the schools: the Yiddish school under the supervision and leadership of the Bund on one side; and the Tarbut School, led by the left-leaning Poalei Zion and forming the base of Hechalutz on the other side.

The first group of Krynki pioneers, who made *aliya* in 1920, belonged to the generation of the founders of the Hebrew school. The following generations of pioneers were primarily graduates of the school who were members of Hechalutz, and later on, those who had been through the *hachshara* kibbutzim.

The story of the development of Hechalutz in Krynki is decisively connected to the Hebrew school. Through the years, it underwent changes in its educational aims, in the direction of emphasizing general knowledge and ideological neutrality.

However, in the period that I remember, this school was a focal point of pioneering education. It is no wonder that incidents took place in Krynki where children escaped from their houses with the dream of reaching the Land of Israel, similar to Velvele the Fool in Shaul Tchernikhovsky's "In the Heat of the Day." I recall how the teacher Ethel burst forth in front of the students who had come to class on May 1, 1922, apparently a normal day by directive of the school leadership, and preached to them: "Is this how you sanctify the name of Y. Ch. Brenner?!" (he was killed on May 1, 1921)[1].

Hechalutz

At celebrations and festive evenings organized by the school, the stress was on the educational content and connection to the ideas of labor, physical toil, agriculture, simplicity – in short: toward pioneering, *aliya*, and practical actualization.

The teachers in that school formed groups [to discuss] issues of the movement in the area of culture and ideology.

[Page 113]

With time, the school also served as a headquarters for the pioneering youth. However, the Hechalutz movement reached its pinnacle in terms of its scope and organization power during the 1930s, with the worsening of the general depression, and the increase in anti-Semitism. The influence from the Land of Israel also increased, via emissaries from the Kibbutz and the Histadrut, and with the rapid development of *hachshara* kibbutzim.

I had already made *aliya* to the Land of Israel by that time, after having spent approximately two years in *hachshara* kibbutzim, especially the Borochov one in Kielce.

Translator's Footnote:

1.   See https://en.wikipedia.org/wiki/Yosef_Haim_Brenner

The Jewish Community in Krynki Between the Two Wars

by Dov Rabin

Translated by Jerrold Landau

Note: The Hebrew sections by Dov Rabin, from pages 113-123, is largely equivalent with the Yiddish sections by Dov Rabin and Shmuel Geler from pages 151-163. Some detail may differ, and the headings and topics are organized differently.

[Page 116]

The committee and leadership of the Cooperative People's Bank of Krynki, 1927

From left, seated: Yaakov Leib Zaleski, Yaakov Lewi, Yaakov Chaim Gosztynski, Baruch Zdytowski (chairman of the bank), Yisrael Kolianewicz (chairman of the committee), Anshel Potseboski, Wolf Wiener

[Page 118]

The leadership of the parade in honor of May 1

The active members of the Yiddish Folks School

The Yiddish Folks School

Committee of the Heshel Papersztejn Library

[Page 120]

Esperanto course, 1928

The council and committee of Linat Tzedek of Krynki, 1937

Seated from right: Moshe Afrikaner, Beilka Korngold, Sh. P. Nisht, Baruch Stolarski,
Shmuel (Sam) Lewin (guest from Chicago), Dr. Hochman, Garber the dentist, Moshe Garber, Shimon
Kotler

[Page 121]

Women's sewing school

Women's Committee, Krynki, 1930

Seated from right: Zlata Grosman, Michla Stolarski, Slova Jaglam, Yache Lopate
Standing: Lifsha Garber, Rachel Kaplan, Sonia Lubelinski, Fani Dzokowicki

[Page 122]

Torah and Traditional Devotion in Krynki

In Krynki After the First World War

by Hanoch Sorski

Translated by Jerrold Landau

A Community Rooted in Torah and Commandments

The Krynki etched in our memory is not like that of previous generations. Our town was an offshoot of an ancient root, with a splendid tradition of rabbis and righteous individuals, great in Torah. With them was a community of Jews rooted and imbued with truth and faith, with life and ideology in Torah and knowledge, commandments and good deeds.

From time to time, when one would be in the old cemetery of the town, one would stand next to the graves of the greats of Krynki, such as: Rabbi Yosef, a rabbi and head of the rabbinical court in our town, and one of the greatest students of the Gaon Rabbi Chaim of Volozhin; Rabbi Baruch, the head of the rabbinical court of Krynki, author of the books *Minchat Baruch* and *Nachalat Baruch*; Rabbi Chaim Tzvi of blessed memory, a Hassid of the Admor of Slonim, author of the book *Yesod HaAvoda*, and a worker of wonders. Next to them was their flock, spread out around them. The feeling and thoughts one would have was that the inscriptions on these monuments testify to the continuous chain, merging worlds and generations, the world of the living and the dead, the past and the present.

The Cemetery

Rabbi Chizkiyahu Yosef Mishkowski

by David Mishkovski

Translated by Jerrold Landau

Note: This Hebrew section is equivalent to the Yiddish section on page 163 by the same author (albeit the final paragraph is absent in the Yiddish).

Rabbi Chizkiya Yosef Mishkowski, may the memory of the holy be blessed

The Committee and Workers of the Orphanage of Krynki, 1931

From right, seated: B. Stolarski, Izik Leib Lystokin (vice chairman), V. Weiner (chairman), Baruch Ajon, Zalman Ostrinski
Standing: Sara Lowler, Rishka Mendelowicz, Shmuel Lewski, Zalman Kotler, Reizel Tewel, Itka Sziszlican, Golda Terkel, Fani Cukert, Roza Gel, Lea Logsinski

The leader of the General Cheder, and its teaching staff.
Rabbi Chizkiya Mishkowski is seated in the middle.

Note: Final paragraph of this section is missing in the Yiddish. It is at the bottom of page 124 in the Hebrew:

A Yeshiva named after his memory, Knesses Chizkyahu, was established in Kfar Hasidim in Emek Zevulun. It is headed by the local rabbi, Rabbi Eliahu Eliezer Mishkovski, son of the deceased.[1]

Translator's Footnote:

  1.   See https://en.wikipedia.org/wiki/Knesses_Chizkiyahu

[Page 125]

Rabbi Shmuel Leb, may G-d avenge his blood,
a rabbinical judge and rabbi

by Hanoch Soraski

Translated by Jerrold Landau

The noble image of the rabbinical judge Rabbi Shmuel Leb was full of honor, splendor, purity, and holy majesty. He was head and shoulders above all others, in human height as well as supernal height. He was the central figure and living spirit of the Hassidim of Slonim in Krynki. His entire personality evoked honor and holy awe. Rabbi Shmuel was one of the veteran Hassidim of the Rebbe of Slonim. As per their holy custom, he would worship with wondrous devotion and stormy enthusiasm. He loved all Jews with his soul, and suffered all their pains.

He was quiet and modest, never engaging in conflict or debate. He lived a quiet life, content with his lot. He was involved in communal life, for he founded the Beis Yaakov girl's school that existed in our town at various times. In the ghetto, during the time of the occupation of the Nazis, may their names be blotted out, he discreetly collected charitable donations for Passover [*Maos Chittin*], and clandestinely baked matzos for the townsfolk. On the eve of Passover 5702 [1942], when he went to kasher utensils from chometz, he was murdered by a murderous brigade of Nazis, may their names be blotted out. Although this was in the midst of the war, he still merited to be brought to a Jewish burial. May G-d avenge his blood.

Hosts of Torah and Religion

by Hanoch Soraski

Translated by Jerrold Landau

As is remembered, a large Yeshiva called Anaf Eitz Chaim existed in Krynki until prior to the First World War. It was founded by Rabbi Zalman Sender Shapira, may the memory of the holy be blessed, the rabbi of our town. Students from the entire surrounding area came to it. That world war shook up the existence of the Yeshiva and destroyed it.

However, after that war, a Yeshiva for youths existed in Krynki as well, as a branch of the Beis Yosef Yeshiva of Novhorodok, founded by Rabbi Yosef Yozel Horowitz, may the memory of the holy be blessed. It was set up in the Chayei Adam *Beis Midrash* on Garbarska Street.

On some days, as you passed through the streets of Krynki, you would hear the voice of Torah echoing in your ears – the voice of the words of the Living G-d, bursting forth from the mouths of the excited Jews, whose entire life was connected to Torah and Divine service.

Houses of Prayer and Study

With trembling and holy awe, I recall the *Beis Midrash*es of the town of Krynki. Three buildings stood close to each other in the center area of Garbarska Street. First and foremost was the synagogue, "Di Shul" as it was called. According to Jewish law, a synagogue dedicated for worship does not have to have a mezuza on its door, provided it is designated for worship and not for study. The synagogue was founded and built hundreds of years ago with the help of residents of the nearby settlements, who would gather to worship there on festivals. For the most part, ordinary folk worshiped there. It was a gigantic, wide building, built in ancient style. There were two rings [i.e. stocks] at its entrance to punish transgressors and display their shame to the public. There was a large yard in the front, called Shulhoif (the synagogue yard).

The large *Beis Midrash* stood next to it. The prominent members of the community worshiped there – including the rabbi (who would also give a Talmud class there), the leaders, wealthy people, studying householders, and great scholars.

Next to it stood the Chayei Adam *Beis Midrash*, in which members of the middle class worshiped. Regular classes took place there morning and evening in all Torah subjects: Talmud, Mishna, *Ein Yaakov*, *Chok LeYisrael*, etc. The Novhorodok Yeshiva was also housed there in the latter period.

Further on, on nearby Czysta Street [Street of the Bath] stood Yente's *Beis Midrash*. It was located next to the building that this Yente built, and housed the communal council, the *Hachnasat Orchim* [organization for tending to guests], and *Linat Tzedek* [for providing lodging to poor wayfarers].

Then before us, on Grochowa Street (Paltiel's alleyway) was the *Beis Midrash* of the Slonim Hassidim, built on the lot that Wolk had dedicated for this purpose. Those who were faithful to Slonim Hassidism in Krynki did not spread out far and wide, but rather laid down deep roots in this location. There, we would find people of spirit, immersed in the service of G-d, regarding the matters of the world as a passing shadow in their eyes. Their connection and love for the customs of the Rebbe of Slonim were without bounds. Hassidism was a candle at their feet and a light for their path. They also made donations to the Slonim Kolel in the Holy Land by selling small packets of its earth.

Skipping over several streets and wooden houses, we would come to the *Beis Midrash* which was called Kavkaz for some reason. It was on Białystoker Street. The wealthy people of the city worshiped there. The *Beis Midrash* of the Stolin Hassidim on Plantajska (Tepershe) was set up in the latter years.

[Page 126]

Houses of worship and regular minyanim in Krynki

The Synagogue
The Kavkaz *Beis Midrash*
The Large *Beis Midrash*
The Yenta *Beis Midrash*
The House of Worship of the Hassidim of Slonim
The House of Worship of the Hassidim of Stolin
The Zionist Minyan
The Minyan of the Tanners / Garbarsker

[Page 127]

The vast majority of the Jews of Krynki were Jews of the *Beis Midrash*.

Cheders, Teachers, Personalities, Organizations

The General *Cheder* [*Cheder Klali*]

The religious school (General *Cheder*) was founded in the year 5680 (1920). Until its founding, there was a great lack in the area of religious education for the children of the Orthodox residents of the town. A minority studied with private teachers [*melamdim*], and dedicated their time solely to religious studies. The teaching was without appropriate order and regimen.

When Rabbi Mishkowski arrived, he immediately became involved with founding the General *Cheder*, the aim of which was to unite all the private *melamdim* together with certified teachers under one framework, and to impart religious education on healthy foundations to the young generation. A curriculum of religious and secular studies was established, which would equip every *cheder* graduate with sufficient knowledge to continue their studies in either a yeshiva or a *gymnasja*, according to their preference.

First of all, the rabbi concerned himself with finding a spacious premise for the cheder, appropriate to its role. To this end, he sold the house of the old Talmud Torah on Gmina Street, which was too small to house all the required grades. With the help of the townsfolk and donors from the United States, he purchased two large buildings, and renovated them with rooms and halls that would be fitting for their purpose. He also hired and brought in experienced, certified teachers to teach secular studies.

Many of the townsfolk received the foundations of their education in the General *Cheder*. People even came from surrounding towns to study in this *cheder*, which gave Krynki positive renown.

Melamdim [Religious Teachers]

Several of the *melamdim* of the cheder, who nurtured the foundation of the towns folk, were especially accepted and revered by the people of Krynki. They were wise scholars, great in both Torah and awe of G-d, connected to their young students with the strands of their soul, with love and great fatherly dedication.

The lion of the cadre of *melamdim* was Rabbi Yisrael "der Tzigene Berdl" (with the goatee), a teacher of children in our town. Most of the townsfolk of the previous generation studied with him, and revered him. He was a great scholar, dedicated to his young students with his whole heart, and loving them greatly. (In his old age, when his strength waned, his wife, Tsharna the Rebbetzin, assisted him.) When it was time for his students to stop their games and they did not heed his calls, she would warn them and urge them. He was a private melamed, and when the religious school (the General Cheder) was founded, he worked within his rubric.

The other *melamdim* were the late: Reb Shmuel (The Rebbetzin's), a wise Jew, who could explain things clearly; Reb Shmuel Tencer; Reb Meir (The Sholker); Reb Heshel of Grodno (Grodner); Reb Yisrael Jeruszabski (the father of our fellow townsperson, Chava Jeruszavski, a resident of Israel); Reb Mendel Listukin (the *Melamed*); Reb Eliuta Szapir; Reb Chaim Yuches; and others whom I did not know and some whom I have forgotten, to my dismay.

One of the Hassidim of Slonim

Reb Shmuel Chona Zakheim, may G-d avenge his blood, the baker, was the essence of a beautiful character. He was one of the prominent Sloniimer Hassidim of Krynki. He had a good eye and abundant spirit. He was modest and humble, restricting himself to his four ells, and acting in a straight forward fashion with the supernal worlds.

He never had an argument with anyone, for he loved his fellow, and drew people close to Torah. He toiled hard at his trade, despite his age, and his baked goods (Shmuel Chone's Kuchens) became famous for their excellence, because he added positive flavor to them. He was wise and intelligent, levelheaded, and infused with the joy of life. His melodies added a unique charm of pleasantness. (He was asked to sing: "Bake the buns, chase the flies…") It was the same with the melodies of his prayers, in their expert, holy manner, as instructed by the *Admorim* of Slonim to their Hassidim.

Reb Shmuel Glembocki (The Rebbetzin's)

by Chaya Glembutski-Rabinowitch

Translated by Jerrold Landau

My revered father of blessed memory, who was called Reb Shmuel Der Rebbetzin's, was the youngest child of Rabbi Yossele, may the memory of the holy be blessed. He was beloved, honored, and revered by all the townsfolk. He had a splendid countenance, exuding goodness of heart and uprightness. He taught Torah to the People of Israel, and gave a class to the worshippers of the Kavkaz *Beis Midrash*. He was accompanied with great dedication and reverence to his home on snowy, frozen, winter evenings.

[Page 128]

His sweet voice when studying Gemara alone still rings in my ears to this day. His set place was near the holy ark in the aforementioned *Beis Midrash*. On Rosh Hashanah, he would blow the shofar blasts in a ringing fashion, with holy reverence..

Mothers would turn to him with requests for a complete recovery for their sick children through incantations (removing the evil eye). He would utter a silent prayer and conclude: "For Recovery!" The mother would believe with full faith that her child would recover.

With our curiosity, we children were anxious to interpret the silent incantation, but Father of blessed memory refused to disclose it on account of the holiness of the tradition from his ancestors. For us, this remained in the realm of a deep secret.

Agudas Yisrael and its Youth in Krynki

by Hanoch Soraski

Translated by Jerrold Landau

Religious Jews in Krynki, headed by Rabbi Mishkowski of blessed memory, were involved in the ideology of the Agudas Yisrael organization of Poland. The chapter of the Aguda in our town was founded in the year 5693 (1933) by the writer of these lines, who forged contact with the Aguda headquarters in Warsaw. Reb Yisrael Dubinski of blessed memory served as chairman of the chapter.

Members of the chapter would send their donations to the *Keren Hayishuv* [fund for settlement] of Agudas Yisroel, which was dedicated to the fortification of the settlement and the institutions of Agudas Yisroel in the Land. Through the initiative of the chapter, a Beis Yaakov school for girls was founded in our town. It existed for a set period.

The following was etched on the seal of the chapter: "The Agudas Yisrael Organization of Poland, Krynki Chapter." In the center of the seal was a drawing of the globe of the earth, held up by three pillars, upon which, according to the Talmud, the world exists: Torah, Divine service, and benevolent deeds[1].

The movement that incorporated the religious youth of Krynki was Young Agudas Israel of Poland. Its chapter in our town was also founded by the writer of these lines in 1934. Shlomo the son of Rabbi Mishkowski of blessed memory served as president of the chapter, and Baruch Soraski of blessed memory served as the treasurer.

The youth conducted a class on the *Daf Yomi* [daily page] of the Talmud in the building of the General Cheder. Some of the members joined Hechalutz Haagudati [the Aguda Pioneers] and underwent *hachshara* in various kibbutzim to prepare for *aliya* to the Land.

Notable Krynki Natives Who Lived Outside the Town

Krynki had so many notable natives that the page is too short to include them. Some of them represented it in a fine manner outside its boundaries already during the past generation: Reb Chaim Aryeh the son of Reb Asher Handler, the author of the book *Kitzur Alshich Hashalem* on the Torah, printed in Piotrków in the year *Be'et Haketz*[2] – 5667 (1907), who lived in Białystok; Rabbi Chaim Tzvi Lider of blessed memory, one of the heads of the Ohel Torah Yeshiva of Baranovichi, the Admor of Slonim. Rabbi Mordechai Chaim Slonim, may the memory of the holy be blessed, the author of the book *Maamar Mordechai*, who made aliya to the Land of Israel around the year 5635 (1875) with his father Rabbi Yehuda Leib Kastelianicz, and died in Jerusalem in the year 5614 [1954]; and many other such people.

Translator's Footnotes:

1. *Pirkei Avot* 1:2.
2. In religious writings, Jewish years are often referred to by a fragment of verse, the numerology of which is equivalent with the year.

[Page 128]

Krynki's Zionism and its Activities

The Aims and Status of the Movement

by by D. Rabin

Translated by Jerrold Landau

Between the two world wars, The Zionist Movement had a pioneering platform – to prepare the youth for *aliya* to Israel as *chalutzim* [Zionist pioneers], to educate the Jewish child in the Hebrew-national spirit, to win over the souls of the people to the idea of our redemption in our historic homeland, and to bring it to fruition. Within this movement, its leaders and activists acted with concern for the needs of the local Jewish community.

Even though there were members of the various factions of the Zionist movement in Krynki, the most prominent bloc in the town, with its constant activities, was the Working Land of Israel, and especially Tzeirei Tzion [Young Zion]. From 1926, it united with the right-leaning Poalei Tzion, with the name Poa'Tz'Tz'S. [Poalei Tzion, Tzion Socialist].

[Page 129]

It also took into its rubric, the Socialist-Zionist and pioneering youth, dedicated itself to the enterprise of Hebrew education in the town. Of course, this was over and above its activities in the general Zionist movement for Keren Hayesod (1,737 zloty collected in the town in 5689 [1929], in comparison with the 3,462 zloty of the district capital of Sokolka), for the Keren Kayemet [Jewish National Fund], for the distribution of the shekel [token of membership in the Zionist organization] (193 in 5686 [1926] and close to 500 in 5699 [1939]), in the Tarbut organization (5 delegates to the first national convention: A. Einszejn, Y. Gabai, M. Zaleski, B. Nisht, Sh Cukert, and others).

As I remember, Tzeirei Tzion (as the word Tzeirei means – they were youths) was already bustling and active in Krynki during the German conquest during the First World War. However, after the revolution in Germany at the end of 1918, it conducted a battle for precedence in the general communal forum – with the elections for the communal council and the town council, conducted for the first time on a democratic basis.

B. Nisth (Niv) relates: "We were then a youth movement without a significant past in general communal activities within a town of workers – and we had to measure up to the much older and stronger local Bund. Furthermore, many members of Tzeirei Tzion were not yet of voting age for the town council. However, they stood with us with their energy and appreciation that they earned for themselves through their activities in various communal affairs, especially in the field of Hebrew education, and we earned a victory."

Similarly, I have in my hands an article from Krynki, from the central publication of Tzeirei Tzion in Poland, *Bafreiung* in Warsaw, from February 11, 1921, which notes: "The influence of Tzeirei Tzion in the communal arena was great. Our faction in the town council was the only one that participated in all important activities, and all work of the communal council was directed by our members."

The Tzeirei Tzion Committee, 1929

From right: Moshe Szmulewicz, Chaim Bunim, Moshe Morajn, Izik Ostrinski, Bendet Nisht, Beila Klotnicki, Efraim Afrimzon

The first chapter of Hashomer Hatzair

That article also tells about evening classes for adults, sponsored by Tzeirei Tzion. Courses included Jewish history, geography, natural sciences, political economics, Hebrew, and Yiddish. There were also special classes for Hebrew, and the history of Jewish settlement in the Land that Tzeirei Tzion arranged for the groups of laborers who were preparing to make *aliya* in the near future.

In another article in the aforementioned publication, from April 3, 1926, Ben-Amram writes among other things that there were 80 members in the united organization of Poalei Tzion Zionist Socialists, and it was the only organization with influence in political and cultural life in our town. Furthermore, "Tzeirei Tzion consisted of about 100 members from the circles of workers, and from the first three cohorts of our school, who are moving into creative labor and are active in the activities of our organization. Our members are active in the communal institutions – in the People's Bank, in the committee for care of orphans, etc., and their influence is great."

That year, our party also participated in the elections for the chapter of the government sick fund in our town. On May 1, 1934, the daily newspaper of our party in Warsaw states that 500 workers, members of the commonfolk and the youth, participated in a parade in honor of the laborers' holiday, which was arranged in Krynki by the League of the Working Land of Israel. "They were under the red flags of Poalei Tzion, Socialist Zionists, Hechalutz, Haoved, Freiheit, Hechalutz Hatzair, and Hapoel. The members Borowski and Wiener delivered speeches in the yard."

[Page 130]

Freiheit chapter

The status and influence of the Working Land of Israel movement of Krynki grew greatly in the final months before the Second World War. "The number of members in our youth movement here in Freiheit-Hechalutz-Hatzair reached approximately 200, and approximately 50 in Hapoel" writes Melech Zalkin in his article of June 30, 1939 about Bendet Nisht in the Land of Israel.

That month, elections to the 21st Zionist Congress took place. From the 449 registered voters in Krynki, the Working Land of Israel bloc received 406 votes. (The Histadrut Hatzionit of Poland list received 35, and Mizrachi – 7.)

Poalei Tzion, Socialist Zionists, 1934, flag celebration

For the elections to the town council during those days of great danger in the world and in the Land of Israel, M. Zalkin writes further in the aforementioned article: "We marched with the motto 'For or against the Land of Israel at this time.' "This was the era of the publication of the British White Paper against *aliya* and Hebrew settlement in the Land. We hit the mark in the depths of the people who were faithful to the nation in their hearts. Our motto bore its fruits: from among the eight Jewish delegates elected to the town council, the Bund only received two, whereas we (the bearers of the flag of Working Land of Israel) received six.

However, the central and primary activity of the movement in Krynki, especially among the youth – that is, those of Tzeirei Tzion and later with its union with the right-leaning Poalei Tzion (Poalei Tzion – Socialist Zionists) – was the preparation of Hebrew education.

The Jewish Education Enterprise

by Efraim the son of Efraim [Afrimzon]

Translated by Jerrold Landau

The Hebrew School

Our school was founded by the Tzeirei Tzion organization in the year 5678 (1918). These were days of the revival of the world. The shofar sound of the revival of the nation passed through the camp of our youths, and we were all armed with energy and dedication as we set out to build the Hebrew school.

We began our efforts without outside help. We arranged several celebrations. Our members donated their last coins, and we set up an abandoned dwelling to serve as the school. We toiled and obtained desks. With great dedication, we obtained supplies. We did not yet have experience in the field of education, but we did not turn backward, and we were happy with our lot and our activity.

To our good fortune, A. Einsztejn stood at the head of our institution, and our good friends taught on a voluntary basis – and the school opened.

This was immediately after the German conquest. Our city declined and was destroyed. Its residents became impoverished. Of course, their hearts were not open to improving the education of their children. However, bit by bit, the community began to recognize the value of our school, and masses of children began to come to us. The teachers related to their work as a holy task, and prepared themselves to be fit to serve in the sanctuary. They did not spare themselves any toil. They weighed all their actions, and toiled to acquire pedagogic expertise. The internal situation of the institution improved day by day, and the number of students grew continuously. All the *cheders* in the city closed, for the students left them. We acquired more than 300 students, which was unexpected at the outset.

[Page 131]

Seeing that the student size was too large for its creators, and feeling the full responsibility involved in this, we increased our efforts, as did the teachers. The hearts of the founders of the school rejoiced when they saw that they had succeeded in establishing an institution that would save an entire generation from boorishness. In truth, the Orthodox complained about us. They could not accept the idea that the education of the younger generation was given over to the hands of apikorsim (heretics}. However, we did not pay attention to them or their complaints, just as we did not pay attention to the complaints of the Yiddishists who tried to undermine our school. We then began to determine a tuition fee for all the students, first of all in order to ensure some sort of maintenance for the institution, and second, we intended to uproot the "begging" that came with the occupation. Of course, the poor paid in accordance with their abilities. The income was small, only about 30-40% of what was required. Nevertheless, our school was maintained, and continued to develop and improve. We thus endured a year and a half of birth pangs. During that time, we realized that it had struck deep roots in the ground, and that even an unusual wind would not uproot it from its place. However, the Bolshevik occupation overtook us suddenly in the summer of 1920, and threatened to forcefully undermine the entire structure of Hebrew education that we had set up with such great effort.

In an emergency meeting of the leadership of the school, we decided: "We ill not give them anything." We divided up all the school supplies among the members, who brought them to their homes clandestinely. Only the desks remained, for we could not hide them.

Page 132]

When the Bolsheviks conquered the city, they set up a commissaÂ¬ry for education, as was their custom, headed by one of our "Reds" into whose hand we had to give over the fate of all the education in our city. We reopened the school as if nothing had changed. All of our students returned. Not one enrolled in the government school. The entire teaching staff set out to their tasks, and not one accepted the offer of the commissary to transfer to their institution. The rulers issued an edict that the Hebrew school must close, and all of its supplies must be given over to the commissary of education. Our teachers were instructed to gather all the students to the classes to say good bye to them. The final class was then dedicated to the issues of the day. A silent lamentation united the teachers and students at that time. These were schoolchildren who wept, and knew why they were weeping.

Fearful days overtook our members. They were libeled for hiding the school funds and inventory. After an inquiry, the verdict was that the members of the school leadership would be deported from the city. However, the Bolsheviks left the city due to the victory of the Poles on the banks of the Wisła.

It was destroyed by them from a financial perspective, but we nevertheless renewed the work with the school. We gathered the equipment, and we succeeded in salvaging the portion that was stolen by the Bolsheviks. We even came out with a profit, for we found that the hall of the institution had been renovated by the commissary of education.

The students returned to their classrooms like captive birds that had gone free and returned to their nests. Anyone who did not witness the joy of the children at that time has not seen true joy in his life[1]. The work began and was conducted with double energy and dedication.

The People's School of Tzeirei Tzion, first cohort Krynki, 5682 / 1922

From top right, first row: 1) Freda Margolis, 2) Devora Chasid, 3) Esther Kirpic, 4) Tzipora Shapir, 5) Diamant, 6) Moshka Kirpic, 7) Shoshana Zaleski, 8) Chana Kaminski
Second row: 1) Chaya Slapak, 2) Moshe Zaleski, 3) Przpyurka, 4) Shoshana Cukert, 5) Beila Klotnicki, 6) Shoshana Lewin, 7) Liba Poria
Third row: 1) Chana Farber, 2) Bobcha Frajdman, 3) Yosef Gabai, 4) Avraham Einsztejn, 5) Bendet Nisht, 6) Ethel Terkel, 7) Batya Szolchowic
Fourth row: 1) Cymbler, 2) Chanoch Furman, 3) Shraga Ostrinski, 4) Avraham Cukert, 5) Efraim Afrimzon, 6) Shmuel Zaleski, 7) Zeidel Lasz, 8) Yisrael Sapir, 9) Simcha Furman

However, there was no extended period of calm. The Polish authorities began to afflict us, and always found issues with the school. We overcame all obstacles, fought with all our might, and obtained a complaint regarding the lower authorities from the ministry – and our school was not closed. Many parents assisted us. In their meetings, which had the appearance of a mass meeting based on the number of participants, they decided to struggle for the existence of our educational enterprise, and to support it to the extent possible. Even our opponents from among the Yiddishists were unable to overcome it, and we educated about 90% of the children of the workers in it. The meetings that they called and the bans that they placed on workers who gave over their children to our school were to no avail. After these meetings, we received encouraging letters of thanks from those workers.

To the announcement of the government that all children of the city, without any difference based on nationality, must transfer to the Polish school, our parents responded with a notice signed by hundreds of parents protesting this type of relationship to Hebrew education in our city, and demanded that it be funded by the state.

We utilized our representatives in the city council and struggled for the rights of the Hebrew school. We indeed succeeded, and the city council allocated appropriate sums to our benefit.

The first era of the school concluded in 1922 – the era of founding and building. We also earned the right to see the fruit of our labors: the first graduating class with several tens of youths faithful to their nation, culture and land, armed with knowledge and education.

Translator's Footnote:

1.   This expression is based on Mishna Sukka 5:1.

More About our School During the Changing of Ruling Authorities

by Shamai (Shima) Kaplan

Translated by Jerrold Landau

After the First World War, three types of Jewish schools existed in Krynki: The Hebrew School of Tzeirei Tzion, attended by the majority of the children of the city, about 500 students of the Yiddishists, directed by the members of Left Leaning Poalei Tzion, Bund, and the Communists; and the General *Cheder* of the Orthodox, attended by about 200 children.

The local communal council did not yet have legal status. However, it was active and was recognized by the JOINT, which was a very important force in Poland in those days due to the extensive help that it gave to its Jews after the ruin of their status during the world war. In the communal council, Tzeirei Tzion was represented by close to half of the delegates, including people of the synagogue and non-factional. At one point, the communal council received 100,000 marks from the JOINT to provide food for summer camps for the students, for the nutrition in their schools was wanting. According to the agreement between the communal council and the JOINT, 70,000 marks were allocated to the Hebrew School, and 30,000 to the Yiddish School. Since the people of the General *Cheder* were unable to organize summer camps on their own, the Hebrew School had to provide food for the children of the cheder as well, to the extent that requests were made for that purpose.

[Page 133]

It was the summer of 1920, and war broke out between Poland and Soviet Russia. The front began to approach the city of Krynki. The local Communists were awaiting the arrival of the Red Army. When it became clear to us that the die was cast, and the Bolshevik army was already standing behind our walls, and we knew their attitude toward Hebrew and Zionism – we summoned the leadership of the school and the Poalei Tzion council to an emergency meeting. We decided to hide the money that we had received from the JOINT distribution and that had not yet been used for its purposes, and to prepare for what was to come.

During those days of battles on the front near Krynki, many incidents of pillage were perpetrated in Krynki by Polish soldiers. Some of the Jewish residents put pressure on the treasurer of the school, Shima Kaplan, to use the aforementioned sum of money for a bribe to the military commanders to rein in their men and prevent them from pillaging. Having no choice, 10,000 marks were used for that purpose, and 60,000 remained in the treasury of the institution.

I recall that after the Bolsheviks entered Krynki, we held a secret meeting in the women's section of the *Beis Midrash*, and decided to open the school. In our naivete, we surmised that the Russian occupation of a region full of Jews would permit the development of local Jewish culture, perhaps taking into account the realities, and behaving in a liberal manner. If we could get through the emergency period, perhaps changes would take place, and the Soviet persecution of Jewish culture would cease. We knew that we could not now find the means to uphold the school from the income of celebration and flower days[1], for the vast majority of the community remained without livelihood. We therefore assumed that the money remaining from the JOINT allocation would hold us up in the interim to pay the teachers, and we would thereby be able to maintain the school now, and see what would come next.

Thus, we opened the school with a full staff of teachers. The children all came. The negative propaganda from the Bolshevik police began immediately but was not successful. The Communists themselves, whose children had attended previously, did not remove their children, for the desire of the children overcame that of the parents. Our opponents convened a public meeting on the topic of "two populations." The publicity at the meeting was conducted in the spirit of the Bund. The Hebrew School was described as a "nothing other than a cultivator of nationalism, without fundamental general culture that would be worthwhile for workers and their children during their lifetimes." There were calls from the audience refuting these false words. The head of the local division of culture of the Soviet regime threatened one of those who issued the calls, Izik Ostrinski, from the podium that anyone who interrupts the meeting will be put in jail.

Since the propaganda against our school did not succeed, and the children continued to attend, an edict came from the commissariat of education one fine day to close the institution. The final class that day in all the classes was based on the story of the final class given in Alsace-Lorraine on the eve of its transfer from France to Germany after Germany conquered the area in 1871. The content of the story echoed the spirit in our school at that time, and the children burst out crying. With tears in their eyes, the students even welcomed the delegation from that "cultural division" who appeared that day in the school. They even began to stone its people with stones. Of course, the cultural division later claimed that the children were "incited by the Zionist reactionaries."

After the Bolsheviks closed our educational institution and confiscated all of its property, they issued a demand to give over the treasury. Investigations and even arrests began. However, they did not last for a long time there, for their army was forced to retreat from the area after its defeat.

When the Poles returned, we again opened the school and continued the classes as previously, without paying attention to the plans of the authorities, for indeed our district was considered to be an occupied area until its fate would be determined by a referendum. We continued to teach Russian as the local language, in addition to Hebrew. However, when the Polish government was formed, and it established its ministry of education, it became necessary to ensure that the institution would be recognized by the government. Then we changed the language of instruction from Russian to Polish. A special teacher, Diamant, was hired for that purpose. He had academic credentials, and would be legally recognized to serve as an official principal for the population.

Even so, this was insufficient to satisfy the government supervisor of schools, who came to us from Grodno and visited all the classes. We found out that he had decided to close our school, for he regarded it as a "den of Russification." He got this impression during his visit, since not one of our teachers, aside from the aforementioned official principal, was fluent in Polish. This was the same as the rest of the intelligentsia in the area, who were educated in their time in Russian schools. Indeed, this was an issue to which the Poles, who had suffered from Russian oppression for generations, were very sensitive. Great efforts were demanded of us to annul the decree, and to ensure that our mission would exist into the future.

[Page 134]

With this, we knew how to preserve the Jewish-national style of our education. This was also the case when the Poles commanded our school to participate in the annual festival parade of May 3, the constitution day of the State of Poland. Including the youth, we formed 70% of the participants of this parade. However, rather than sing Polish songs, we began to sing in Yiddish, and even more so in Hebrew, with songs of the Land of Israel. Thus, the parade turned into a huge Jewish-national demonstration. After that time, the Poles no longer invited us to participate in parades of this nature.

Translator's Footnote:

1.   This expression is based on Mishna Sukka 5:1.

The Hebrew High School

by Efraim the son of Efraim [Afrimzon]

Translated by Jerrold Landau

The first group of the Hebrew school completed its primary course of studies in 1922. The question now stood before us and before the parents: What now? The children were young, and it would be too bad if we had to send them to work. Most of them were talented. We decided to make efforts to continue our efforts with secondary education.

The teachers of the school were self-taught. They learned and grew as they taught the classes. They did not have any teaching certificates for high school, and none of them had the resources to obtain such certification. The only place in Poland which certified academic teachers in Hebrew culture was Galicia, which was formerly part of the Austro-Hungarian Empire, where freedom prevailed and there were people with higher education to train Hebrew teachers.

We knew one such person, Dr. Cwygel, who had been the principal of the Tarbut Gymnasja in Białystok. We sent our member A. Einsztejn to Lwów. With his good imagination, he presented to the academics a rosy picture of the rich, firmly-based group in Krynki, promising a bright future to those who would teach in the high school that was being established in our city. Thus, he brought three teachers to Krynki: Dr. Rajs, who was killed in Rovno during the Holocaust; Dr. Gelernter for Hebrew; and Dr. Cwygel, who died in Israel, where he served as the principal of the teachers seminary in Givat Hashelosha.

This was the period of inflation, and their contract with us stated that their salary would be tied to the cost of living. From the outset, we were not experienced in such details, and we signed the contract. The high school covered its expenses primarily from the income from tuition fees, which placed a heavy burden upon the parents of the students, whose situation was difficult.

During those days, Krynki was cut off from the markets to which it had formerly exported its leather products, and had not yet accustomed itself to the new economic situation. This was the period of a chronic depression, and the people of the city earned their livelihoods with difficulty, as the cost of living jumped by 200-300% from time to time. We had to pay the teachers double or triple, whereas the tuition had been collected from the outset, one month previously, and we could not ask the parents to add on to the past accounts. We went from crisis to crisis We borrowed money at a cut rate so that we could pay the teachers whom we had brought in from the outside – so that they would not leave us – while the local teachers who taught in the elementary school received a much lower salary than their aforementioned colleagues, and always late by a month or two.

We realized that we could not continue like this. Shima Kaplan and I approached the teachers of the high school classes and said: "My sirs, do what you must do – we cannot fulfil that which we have taken upon ourselves: finish the year somehow." Dr. Cwygel did not agree to any compromise. Dr. Gelernter was a Jew who did not regard money as the main thing. Dr. Rajs, a man of culture and a gentleman, "understood the issue." Through his influence, the three of them announced that they were prepared for significant compromises in order to finish the year. Thus, we finished it somehow. The high school continued for another year, but we could not add anything to ensure its existence.

Indeed, we were even forced to struggle with some of the parents of the students, including the wealthy ones. The tuition, which increased each time, was divided into three categories: average, to cover the needed costs to maintain a student; low, for the workers, and for social situations. Some did not even pay at all; and a third category – for the wealthy, who also had to pay to maintain the students who did not have the means. The progressive tuition fees were a thorn in the eyes for some of the wealthy people.

[Page 135]

Their complaint was: where is the democracy and equality? They would also grumble, from mouth to ear, that we were Bolsheviks and were doing things that ought not to be done. There were even those who went so far as to attempt to take over the leadership of the school at a meeting of parents. There was a concern that they might succeed, but we knew that the group at the head of the institution knew how to stand up to this crisis. We continued to collect progressive tuition fees until the final day of the existence of the school. We also ensured the continuation of the high school as we had previously.

With the Hebrew Teachers in Krynki

by Arnold Rozenfeld

Translated by Jerrold Landau

It was in the year 1923, after I had served as the principal of the Tarbut School in Ostrów Mazowiecka for a year. I had been one of its founders. During the large vacation, I approached the office of the Tarbut educational network in Warsaw and requested a workplace outside of Ostrów. In the office, I met a person who aroused my appreciation and my heart, and I discussed work issues with him. This was Avraham Einsztejn, a permanent resident of the town of Krynki, who was serving in those days in Warsaw as the inspector of Tarbut schools of Poland.

He recommended that I go to Krynki to teach the Polish language, history and geography in the Tarbut School. I was very concerned at first when I heard of the distance of that town from the headquarters, for I was too young to distance myself from cultural life and the society of the big city. However after investigating through my acquaintances, I found out that we were speaking of a Jewish town that earned its livelihood from the manufacture of hides {for the maunfacture of clothing}, and it had many merchants and interested youth, where one could spend time in a nice fashion, without having to travel even to nearby Białystok or to Warsaw.

When I accepted Einsztejn's recommendation and I returned to my native city of Radom, I discovered to my joy that one of my dear friends, an exemplary teacher, Josef Korman, was also about to begin teaching in the Tarbut School of Krynki.

Even before the beginning of the school year, we decided to live in a joint room in Krynki. It is worthwhile to note that there was not yet any transportation between Krynki and Białystok in those days, and one could only get there by diligence[1], after a very wearing journey.

When we arrived in Krynki, we met at the school two young men who were its living spirit: Bendet Nisht (Baruch Niv) the administrator, and Efraim Afrimzon, the secretary. They received us as good friends, and helped us to the best of their ability. They also found us a place to live. We roomed with the Brustyn family, who were quiet, modest, good people. The room that we rented was spacious. After some time other new teachers arrived including Guta Frankberg, Bracha Rappaport, Za'k, and others.

After the renowned educator Yissachar Rajs, the principal of that good school, left, it was hard to find an appropriate principal to take his place, and it was only after several months that Gottesfeld was appointed to that position and arrived.

We began our educational work and were very satisfied. The institution was large, as was the number of students. Most of the children were educated, and had a great desire to learn. Teaching there was not difficult with such students. The school was housed on the second floor of a hut, and the stairs leading up to it were narrow. However, it felt that it was organized well. It had a rich library, a lovely nature room, and all the necessary work implements. The economic situation was not the best in most of the Tarbut schools , and the teachers would wait with great patience to receive their meager monthly salary. However, I did not complain, for we knew that it was not easy for the parents to obtain the tuition fees for their children. After some time, my friend Korman and I found another source of livelihood aside from our school, where the income was higher than our salary. I was the only teacher in that city who was knowledgeable in the Polish language and literature, and was willing to prepare students for the examinations for the gymnaszja in the big city. It was not difficult to find opportunities to give private lessons for payments in dollars, because the Polish zloty was not accepted at that time, especially beyond the borders of Congress Poland. Thus we did not suffer greatly if we did not receive our school salary very late.

The level of studies in our institution was very high. The children studied willingly. After they finished their course of studies, they had no problem in being accepted to high school. With time, we also made friends with members of the communities, and we would spend evenings in a more interesting fashion than in the big city. With time, we also earned well without having to make extra expenditures, and we were able to put significant sums into savings.

[Page 136]

We used the dollars that we saved for charitable purposes. If one of the merchants was traveling to Białystok or Warsaw to purchase merchandise, they knew that they could receive a sum from the teachers Rozenfeld and Korman. The merchants also knew how to return us the favor. If we wanted to purchase merchandise or a good suit on occasion, they would sell it to us for a token sum.

As spring approached, we also knew how to enjoy ourselves. Bendet Nisht, a pleasant youth, loved and appreciated by all, was the living spirit for everyone. He was good at singing Russian and sentimental songs. Anyone who heard him would never forget his singing. Even today, in my old age, I immediately remember our Bendet if the sound of a Russian song reaches my ears. I remember his Russian song, "Clown Around, You Clown!." Not only did he excel in this, but also in his pleasant manners, his joy, his ability to tell pleasant jokes, and to bring joy to those around him.

In the spring and the beginning of the summer, we teachers as well as several male and female youths from the finest group in Krynki would gather almost every night in the grove close to the town. We would sing, tell jolly stories, joke around, and play nice games. Some of us could play the guitar very well. On occasion, we would return from our excursion to the grove at dawn, always joyous and happy.

During the winter, I would travel to Warsaw for the weekend. At that time, I was an enthusiastic music fan. I would board the diligence[2] for a difficult journey of several hours to Sokolka already on Friday afternoon. From there, I would take a train to Białystok, and then a fast train to Warsaw. At night, I would already be hearing a fine philharmonic.

I would spend the Sabbath on the sports fields, and Saturday night at an interesting performance. Early the next morning, I would return to "my shtetel Krynki." These were perhaps the happiest days of my life.

I also had romantic occasions in Krynki. I did not have to complain that I had no luck with women. At first, I would often visit Tzila "the skinny" (Tzila Garber), a fine beautiful girl. My friend visited "the plump", she was also beautiful,… but heavy.

If you search for the teachers, you would know that one of them was with "Tzila the thin" and the other was with "the plump one." However after some time, I began to see a girl whose parents were very Orthodox. She was a very beautiful girl, intelligent and also very refined. She captured my heart, and things were even coming close to "actualization," but her parents did not want to hear about me, for I was like a complete gentile in their eyes. They did not even want me to visit them. However, we continued to take strolls until late in the evening. When she had to return home, I had to bend down, and she would stand on my back and go over the fence of her house. Once, they invited me to their home, and when her father saw me without a cap, he left the guest room and began to scold and curse his daughter. I never visited that house again. The girl left Krynki and moved abroad after a brief time.

The end of the school year was drawing near. The salary owed to the teachers of the school was large, and Bendet and Efraim did not have the ability to pay the debt to the teachers, despite their good will. How did those who worked hard all year and did not receive their salary react? For the good of the school, they did without everything that was owed to them! Thus were Hebrew teachers in those days willing to sacrifice for Hebrew education. After I left the school in Krynki after one year, I did not think that I would ever return there, even as a teacher.

Translator's Footnotes:

1.　　Days when flowers were distributed to raise funds for an organization.
2.　　A diligence is a solid type of stagecoach. See https://en.wikipedia.org/wiki/Stagecoach (especially the part of Contenental Europe).

An Energetic Pioneer for the Hebrew School

by Daniel Perski[1]

Translated by Jerrold Landau

(A. Y. Einsztejn, may G-d avenge his blood)

Avraham Yehuda Einsztejn (one of the first Hebrew teachers in Krynki) was born in Å½elva, Grodno District, in 1885. He had a religious education. From the cheder, he went to the Yeshiva in Volkovisk. At the same time, he diligently read the new Hebrew literature, and earned his meager livelihood from giving private Hebrew lessons. When he returned to his hometown, he opened a modern cheder there, which served as a spiritual center and driving force for the Hebrew movement in the entire area. After his marriage, he settled in Krynki and was a Hebrew teacher for individuals and groups. When the Hebrew school was founded during the First World War, and was expanded afterward, Einsztejn was its principal and living force.

When the Tarbut educational network was founded later, Einsztejn was appointed by the organization as the chief superintendent of its schools. He then set up his residence in Białystok.

[Page 137]

Throughout all those years, he would frequently visit hundreds of Jewish communities in Poland in order to set up and organize Hebrew schools at various levels. His dedication to the idea of the renaissance revival of our language, and his organizational and pedagogic talent contributed greatly to the flourishing of the movement and Hebrew culture in all its manifestations in that country.

Einsztejn educated a generation of people faithful to the spirit of Israel. Many of his students serve today as teachers and guides for our youth in Israel and America.

Sturdy as an oak, tall and broad shouldered, action poured forth from his bright, lively eyes and this facial expression, as "one who revised the dead and wakes up the slumbering." There was nobody like him: faith and trust were like the candle at his feet. He did not know the term impossible when it came to "our culture." He was a populist by nature, a conversationalist and a friendly man. He was an overflowing wellspring of popular jokes and populist understanding. Joy of life brimmed forth from him. He was an activist and orator. He lectures thousands of times at gatherings, all on a single topic: How to organize Hebrew schools, and how to develop and maintain them.

Einsztejn was brought to the gas chambers together with the Jewish community at the time of the liquidation of the Białystok Ghetto. May G-d avenge his blood.

In Conclusion by the publisher

Already in 1931, the 15th year of the people's school and a decade of its first graduating class – the number of graduates of the Hebrew school reached 300. Many of them continued their studies and became teachers, doctors, engineers, researchers, etc. The number of graduates continued to increase as time went on.

Avraham Yaakov Einsztejn

A group of students of the Hebrew School with their teachers

Alongside the school, there was a restaurant for the students, and a Hebrew library for children and studying youth, that was named for Mendele Mocher Sefarim. Already in 1926, the number of volumes in the library reached 500. There was also a drama club that put on performances successfully.

"The Hebrew School in our town was a spiritual achievement of great people" -- states Moshe the son of Yaakov-Leib Zaleski, today a pillar of Hebrew education in the United States. "This was a daring act by a group of stubborn youths, to found an exemplary Hebrew school in a small town under restricted conditions, and to raise it to a high educational level."

Tenth graduating class of the Tarbut School

"I, the youngest of the group, had the difficult task of organizing and directing the general studies. I approached my work without a curriculum, without Hebrew textbooks for geography, general history, mathematics, and nature:

[Page 138]

My students, many of whom were only two or three years younger than me, would copy the study manuals by hand.

"This school taught many students. Its graduates who escaped the inferno and who scattered to all corners of the earth, continue their holy tradition of national Hebrew culture wherever they are."

Translator's Footnote:

1.   There is a footnote in the text here: From HaDoar, New York, 27 Tammuz 5706 [1946].

A class of the high school

At the Margins of the Hebrew School

by Efraim the son of Efraim [Afrimzon]

Translated by Jerrold Landau

A Libel Against the Teacher Etel

This took place in the year 1922, when Etel Terkel of blessed memory taught grade two in the Hebrew School, which was housed in the building of Alter Farber. The stifling atmosphere in the classroom was unbearable, as usual, and the teacher went out on an excursion outside the city with the students in the afternoon. When they returned from the excursion, Etel permitted, as was her custom, the older children to return home alone, while she herself led the younger ones. When she was still on the way, she heard a shrill, warning voice directed to the children who had reached the city first. This was the wife of the church organist who was chastising them for apparently spitting on the holy icon on the porch of her house. Etel attempted to calm the woman. She called the children and accompanied them home.

However, this was not the end of the story. The organist lodged a complaint to the police against Etel, claiming that she purposely targeted his house with the students, took some of them out of line, placed them before the icon, and ordered them to spit at it, thereby desecrating the holy object.

In truth, it was the daughter of an Orthodox family, whose custom it was to spit three times when they passed by a holy icon or a cross, and conclude with "you shall utterly detest it"[1]. Thus did a libel form around her. We made sure that the girl would disappear from the town, thinking that the matter might hopefully be forgotten.

However, the next morning, as Etel was teaching in the class, a policeman came to summon her to the police station. I requested that he wait and not disturb her until she finished her class. We waited for an hour or two after she went to the police, and she did not return. I went there, and found out that she was arrested by command of the judge, who was known as a firm anti-Semite, and that they were preparing to take her the next day to the infamous prison in Grodno.

Etel was sickly, and we were very concerned that she would not be able to withstand the conditions of the prison. We therefore called an emergency meeting of the school leadership and teachers, and decided that Dr. Rajs, the official general principal of the school, and I would approach the judge and request that Etel be released on bail. The judge acted politely to us, but pointed out to us a section of the law that specifies a ten-year prison term for the crime which the teacher was accused of. Therefore, he had no permission to release her on bail, and she would be transferred to the prison in Grodno that night.

We decided that Etel's uncle Moshe Kuris and I would travel to Grodno to advocate on her behalf to the extent possible. This was Friday evening, and the trip would involve a violation of the Sabbath, especially for our house. When father returned from the synagogue, we explained to him the situation of risk of life[2] and the necessity for the trip. Thus we set out on a wagon and we arrived in Grodno.

The children of the Tarbut School strolling to the outskirts of Krynki via the market on a Lag B'Omer excursion

As we were searching for a lawyer, we found out that they were on vacation in camps.

[Page 139]

Nevertheless, toward evening, we got some type of attorney, but he told us that he could not do anything until Monday. Since we were very concerned that if Etel remained overnight in prison, who knows when she would be freed – we decided to take the iron while it was hot.

We went ourselves to the prosecutor. We did not find him, but rather his deputy Milner, and we poured out the bitterness of our heart to him regarding the teacher, Terkel, who was innocent of any wrongdoing. He responded that he was sorry, but he would review the case on Monday. After a brief rest, we went to visit the lawyer again. Etel was called before us, and she said that she was suddenly summoned to the director of the prison and informed that she was freed.

When we investigated the matter, it became clear that even though Milner told us that he would review the case on Monday, as a Jew by birth (he was an apostate), his heart did not rest, and he investigated the matter immediately. When he was convinced that the claims against Etel [were false], he commanded that she be freed.

Translator's Footnotes:

1. Deuteronomy 7:26.
2. Sabbath violation is permitted when life is at stake.

An Incident in the Literary Society Theater

by Shamai (Shima) Kaplan

Translated by Jerrold Landau

The upper floor of the only hall in Krynki for cultural performances served as the office of the "loan and credit" ("Benkel") organization during the time of the German occupation during the First World War. The hall was owned by the Literary Society ("Literishe Farein") a non-factional organization in which all the streams[1] in the city, especially the youth, participated.

This society disbanded later, even though the hall continued to bear its name. There was a form of unwritten mutual agreement that performances – which served as one of the important sources of income for the schools – would alternate between the Yiddish School and the Hebrew School. We were rehearsing then for a performance that was to take place on Friday night. When we came to get the keys to the hall, the people of the Yiddish school stated that the hall was designated for them on that evening. During the debate between us, we became suspicious that they were intending to take over the hall for themselves. To avoid such a precedent, we decided that, if that was the case, the hall would not be for either of us. Several of our youths went to steal the screen and thereby prevent performances from taking place in the hall.

From the performance "A Wedding in the Town" by the Drama Club of the Hebrew School

However, one of the neighbors, from the people of the Yiddish School, discovered the matter, informed the police, and even told them who had stolen the screen. Gandler and two others of our group were arrested for this. Informing the police, who the Jews, regarded as hostile, aroused a great deal of bitterness in the community.

In the market square, the gathering place of the city where debates between the factions took place, we informed our opponents that if they intend to solve their disputes with us through the police – they have more to fear than we do. The levelheaded people among them understood that they had taken an improper step. Then it was agreed that the joint leadership of the society would resolve the matter. The leaders, Bendet Nisht and David Gotlib, turned to the investigating judge, an anti-Semite who awaited opportunities to find complaints against the Jews, and informed him that there was no theft, but rather that they themselves, the directors of the society, sent someone to remove the screen.

The investigating judge was therefore forced to annul the investigation. However, in order, to take revenge against the Jews, the screen was not returned.

Translator's Footnote:

1.   Streams refers here to the various factions in the city. Many of the organizations (youth groups, etc.) would be based on political factions. e.g. bund was decidedly secular and non-Zionist. The Zionist groups had several 'streams' -- socialist Zionist, middle of the road, religious, right wing. Poalei Zion, a common Zionist organization in these translations, had a left leaning stream and a right leaning stream. This literary society did not belong to any of those factions (or streams).

Labor Zionism and Aliya

by D. R. (Hechalutz)

Translated by Jerrold Landau

Hechalutz

The Hechalutz [Pioneer} organization was set up in Krynki in 1919. Without waiting too long, its founders sought to train its members for manual labor and communal life. A large garden was leased next to the bath house, where a number of male and female youths began to study and train in agriculture, as much as possible, until the time would come that the gates for *aliya* to the Land of Israel would be opened.

[Page 140]

When the first convention of Hechalutz of Lithuania convened in Grodno in the autumn of 1919 – and this included all the areas around Grodno and Vilna – a delegate from the organization in Krynki, Bendet Nisht, participated. He also represented it about a year later in the general Polish convention of the movement that convened in Warsaw, and was even elected to the central council of Hechalutz in the country.

Indeed, during the summer of that year, 1920, the first group of pioneers from Krynki made *aliya*: the late Shima Za'k and Tzvi Carmeli (Rothbort), Izik Ostrinski, may G-d avenge his blood, and may they live: Avraham Najman, Yafa Furman (Chaklai), her brother Motka, and Tzvi Rothbort.

After making *aliya*, they worked together with the pioneers of Grodno in the forests of Mount Carmel and Itlit, in the orchards of Petach Tikva, and later in building in Rishon Letzion, Ramla, Jerusalem, and Motza. Finally, most of them joined agricultural settlements, some of them in Kibbutz Geva in the Jezreel Valley, where they joined Leah Nisht (Za'k) and Liza Rothbort (today the wife of David Tuviyahu[1], the first mayor of Beersheba and one of its architects and builders) – who also made *aliya* with the Third Aliya.

During the years 1919-1920, Krynki also served as a transit point for pioneers from other places – for *hachshara* and *aliya* to the Land. Shima Kaplan relates the following about this:

A group of chalutzim [Zionist pioneers] from Ukraine during their stop in Krynki on their route to the Land of Israel, 1920

"At that time Krynki and the district, were considered as an occupied area and various Polish laws did not apply there yet. Therefore "*arnavot*"[2] came to us – youths from areas annexed de jure[3] to the country, with letters of recommendation from Zionist organizations stating that they were pioneers ready for *aliya*, and requesting that we help them. The intention was that we furnish them with identity papers stating that they were residents of Krynki, so that they could obtain an exit permit from Poland for the purpose of *aliya* to the Land of Israel.

"First, we trained them to know the names of the streets and specific residents of the town, to prove that they were indeed local residents – in the event that they were captured and interrogated. Furthermore, we used to invite the head of the town council, Adolf Kozman, to a "feast of kings" at Chaikel Olian's house, and we would give the "sire" drinks as he requested. When the king was tipsy, we would ask him to certify appropriate documents through which the lads could receive testimony that they were from Krynki, and were therefore permitted to travel to the Land of Israel."

Chalutzim [Zionist pioneer] at work at the Hachshara kibbutz in Krynki, 1933

[Page 141]

In Nisan 5681 (1921), the members of Tzeirei Tzion of Krynki started an effort to collect work tools for the workers of the Land of Israel, as declared by the headquarters of that faction in Warsaw. Many agricultural tools, work tools, household utensils, and a significant sum of money for the designated purpose were collected in the town. The people of Krynki even conducted this campaign in the nearby towns.

That year, Tzeirei Tzion also sponsored trade lessons for preparing those who were to make *aliya*.

Further on, we will discuss more about the continuing activities of Hechalutz in Krynki. However, here is the place to note that in 1933, at the time that six pioneers from the *hachshara* kibbutz in Krynki began to work in Pruzhanski's factory to prepare themselves for *aliya*, the opponents of Zionism from among the tannery workers displayed an unfriendly attitude toward them. They even intended to force the pioneers to leave the factory.

This opposition in Krynki, as in other places in Poland at that time, was unable to disrupt the activities of Hechalutz, which at that time were not only to actualize the Zionist ideal, but also to save the Jewish youth from despair and hopelessness in their lives. We should note the merits of the founders of Hechalutz, and those who continued on in their path, and of the Zionist movement in Krynki, for in their merit, there are approximately 250 families of Krynki natives in Israel, among its builders and defenders. May the number grow.

Translator's Footnotes:

1.   See https://en.wikipedia.org/wiki/David_Tuviyahu
2.   Literally "rabbits" probably because they "hopped" in.
3.   De jure is a political term for a legally binding situation. During an annexation, it could be informal, or it could have been entrenched by law. 'de jure' means it was entrenched by law. The area they were living in did not have a de jure annexation, so people wanted to come in.

From the Labor Zionist Movement

by Shmuel Harbarm-Krupnik

Translated by Jerrold Landau

The Hechalutz Chapter

In 1942, the Hechalutz chapter in Krynki reached its pinnacle in essence as well as numbers. There were more than 100 members, male and female. Vibrant life was felt in all areas of activity of the chapter.

With its founding, it was located in the people's school in Farber's home (Alter "Der Farber" [the painter]). Later, it moved to the Bath House Street ("Da Besl"), in a house which had once served as the senior's residence next to Linat Tzedek. In that building, a branch of the Tarbut School was opened, and we would attend there each evening. Aside from organizational, political and publicity efforts, there were evening classes in Hebrew and knowledge of the Land. Our teachers were the comrade Alter (a teacher in Tarbut, not a native of Krynki), and Berl Stolarski, a graduate of that school.

Some of the students began to go on *hachshara* with the aim of making *aliya* to the Land, and a significant number started to study a trade locally in preparation for their *aliya*. This was not an easy matter at all, and the parents disturbed us throughout that time, because it was difficult for them to come to terms with the idea that their sons and daughters would leave them and make *aliya* to the Land to work there as hired laborers, whether as employees or tradespeople. However, we overcame all the obstacles and disturbances. There were those among us who suffered beatings from the parents, and there were those who were kicked out of their homes more than once. There were also those who left their homes and went out *hachshara* without the agreement of their parents. The desire to actualize the Zionist-pioneering idea was strong. We would carry out with dedication all the actions declared from the headquarters of the movement in Warsaw, as well as all the decisions of the chapter. Our will was strong that our chapter would be among front ranks in our movement in Poland.

For the Hechalutz Fund

Many of us toiled and wracked our brains thinking how and through what means we could increase the income of the national Keren Hechalutz [Hechalutz Fund] – over and above the donations of our members and the public ribbon days that we arranged in the town. We decided to go out to cut trees for the local residents. Later we accepted that work as contractors for the Krynki electricity station in the yard of Yisrael Hertzka on Kancelarska Street. This was a revolutionary move for us toward manual labor, which only gentiles from the villages would perform for the Jews. One can imagine what the relationship of the parents to this, and what type of reception they gave us when returned home after this work.

A flower day for the benefit of the Hechalutz Fund

[Page 142]

On the days before Passover, we would send our male and female friends to work in the baking of matzos (in the matzo *Podryan*). This work would also bring in significant sums for Keren Hechalutz.

The Purging of Vessels on the Eve of Passover

At the beginning of the spring of 1925, we decided to set up a new activity for the benefit of Keren Hechalutz – to purge (*kasher*) vessels[1] for its benefit. It was a new thing in the city for *chalutzim* to perform this work. However, some of the members of the committee of the Hechalutz chapter were concerned that the householders of the town and the rabbi might object to placing this holy task into the hands of *chalutzim*. In my opinion, it was appropriate to approach Rabbi Miszkowski and receive official permission for this activity from him. However, it was difficult for me to influence several members to join me in a delegation to the rabbi. Finally, we girded our strength, and three members of the committee went to the residence of the rabbi, who lived in the yard of Kniszinski (Berl Nachum-Anshel's) factory at the edge of Garbarska Street.

Along the way, we had a debate as to who would be the chief spokesman. Each of us proposed the other. Finally, we decided at the last minute to not rely on an individual, but to help each other in the negotiation, and to not leave the rabbi's house until he agreed with us.

To our surprise, Rabbi Miszkowski received us in a friendly fashion, and asked us to be seated. When we revealed our plan to him and explained to him its purpose, he peered at each of us with his wise eyes, examined us with his splendid countenance, and asked who our parents were. Then he told us about the strictness, caution, and level of detail that this task would require, so that we would not fail those who placed their faith in us, heaven forbid, and not violate their joy of the festival.

At the conclusion of his words, I girded myself with strength and announced that we accept upon ourselves to be stringent in all the directives that we would receive, and that I myself am the son of an Orthodox family and a grandchild of Hassidim. Then he stood up, clasped our hands, blessed us with peace, and wished us success.

As is known, Rabbi Miszkowski in his time was affiliated with a political stream that did not support Socialist Zionism in the least. Nevertheless, he treated us properly. It was his custom always, in the Diaspora and in the Land, to avoid creating divisions among people with his religious and communal activities – and especially among the Jews of Krynki, whatever their political outlook was. He understood the spirit of each and every person, and offered his assistance to the best of his ability, especially in his latter years in the Land.

After we received the approval, we publicized the matter with handwritten signs in all the houses of worship and barber shops in the town, noting that we had received the approval of the rabbi for this.

One evening, three days before the festival, many members went out to gather wood to heat the cauldron that we had set up in the empty yard of Chaim Juches, behind Szajnberg's house, which was a sort of public domain. We piled up heaps of wood that we had brought from our parents' homes and that we had hauled from the yards of the bakeries, especially from the nearby bakery of David Leib the baker.

We met early the next morning in the designated place. Our comrade Dines brought a large, clean cauldron. We placed it atop a foundation that we made of stones and bricks, and set up the first pyre. When the water came to a boil, we placed very hot rocks into it, and began to call aloud to the people to bring their vessels for purging. To our great joy, women and children quickly responded, and began to bring various vessels. We diligently performed the work with reverence and awe.

The income of Keren Hechalutz from the purging of vessels reached 45 zloty. The participants included: Sh. Dines, G. Dubinsztejn, B. Wajnsztejn, B. Falk, Y. Guz, the writer of these lines, and others.

The Hechalutz Carpentry Workshop

In 1925, we opened a carpentry workshop under the auspices of the Hechalutz chapter of Krynki. A guide who knew the trade well, Comrade Kantorowicz from Oszmiana [Ashmyany] near Vilna, was sent to us from the district secretariat of the movement. We rented a large hall in the yard of the tannery owner Alter Shegam (Kunes), and purchased tools and a work bench – all through our own finances. We spared no effort or energy for the success of our enterprise, despite the opposition of the parents and interference from the local carpenters.

The carpentry workshop developed well in a brief time. We had many customers in the town, and carried out various projects. After a year, we moved to the yard of Moshe Leibowic, who also had a tannery. Many local members of Hechalutz and Hechalutz Hatzair received their professional training there.

[Page 143]

I recall that already in the first days of the existence of the carpentry workshop we received an invitation from Rabbi Miszkowski, who requested that our carpenters come to fix the floor in one of the rooms of his house. As the central force in the carpentry workshop and one of its organizers, I went to him along with the advisor and one of the working staff. The rabbi was very happy to greet us. Throughout the entire time that we worked at fixing the floor, he chatted with us and took interest in our new enterprise. He did not quibble with us over the price, and paid us generously. He praised us and our work as diligent workers.

The Left Leaning Poalei Tzion Party

Following the convention in Warsaw in 1925, at which the right leaning Poalei Tzion merged with the Socialist Tzeirei Tzion, and in which Bendet Nisht participated on behalf of the Krynki chapter – many of the members of Hechalutz joined the united party, and its activities began to take place with double energy. In a united celebration that took place in lofty spirits at that time in the hall of the Tarbut School in the Farber building, the chief spokesmen were the members Menashe Garber and Beila Kotnicki of blessed memory, and may he live, Bendet Nisht.

A drama club existed alongside the party. It performed various performances on frequent occasions, the income of which was dedicated to local communal or national causes. A technical committee operated alongside the club, headed by the member Tzvi Gandler, who excelled with his talents and attention to detail.

A mandolin group also existed alongside the party, most of the members of which were graduates of the school or students in the upper grades. Its directors and teachers were the members - M. Borowski and the brothers Asher and Tzvi Gandler.

The dramatic club affiliated with the Hebrew School

The Heshel Sapirsztejn Zionist library

A large library named for Heshel Sapirsztejn ("Heshel Bibliotek" – The Heshel Library) existed in one of the rooms of the Tarbut School, affiliated with the united party. The room was filled to the brim with books, most of which were in Hebrew, very new and from the latest and best editions. The local youth and most of the residents of the town were members of this library.

Asher Gandler and Binyamin Ostrinki were the regular, dedicated librarians, working gratis. Every evening, they would respond to the request of anyone who approached them, as they circulated the books to the community. Those two were the pillars of the institution. The younger members of the movement were represented in the library committee, and bore the yoke together with the older ones.

For the Benefit of the National Funds

Many people worked on behalf of the national funds, especially for the Jewish National Fund. They organized ribbon days, in which pairs would pass through all the streets of the town, even visiting every house. Every pair would make efforts to collect the largest sum of money. We would also send members to private celebrations to canvass the attendees for the Jewish National Fund. The member Bendet Nisht stood at the helm of all these activities.

The Cherut-Hatechia Organization

At the beginning of the 1920s, a Cherut-Hatechia youth organization also existed in Krynki. It developed and flourished nicely, and formed the cradle of the Working Land of Israel movement that developed later. Its activists include Ostrinki, Moshe Borowski, and Asher Gandler.

Translator's Footnote:

1.   Vessels (dishes and utensils) used throughout the year must be immersed in boiling water or scalded at high heat (depending on the use of the vessel – the *halachot* are very complex) prior to being fit for Passover use.

Jewish Sport Groups

Translated by Hadas Eyal

'Maccabi'

Shmuel Harbarm–Krupnik

The Maccabi gymnastics team was founded by the local 'Zion Youth' Party and active in 1921–1922. My older brother Gdalyahu was among its devoted and excellent members who regularly performed in the 'People's Bank' public hall. They would usually form human pyramids and entertain the audience with amusing gymnastic routines.

The 'Bar Kochva' Soccer Team

A soccer league for the benefit of Eretz–Israel workers was held in Krynki during the mid–1920s. Although the team used the Christian grazing meadow for local and regional home matches, the religious Jews were angered nonetheless because some games were held on Shabbat. They were also furious when the team travelled on Shabbat to away games.

"Bar Kochva" soccer team

[Page 144]

'The Young Chalutz'

Dvora Levin–Shpatz

Local Training for Aliya to Israel

I joined 'The Young Chalutz' youth movement in 1928. The Krynki branch had around 100 boys and girls, most of them Hebrew speakers, all with national spirit and yearning to see their future in Eretz Israel. The cultural activities in the branch were organized by alumni such as myself. I was the branch secretary for a long time. Among other things, we would collect the donations from the Jewish National Fund (JNF 'Keren Kayemet') donation boxes and coordinated fund raising for the Chalutz Fund. There were many obstacles to overcome to get government legalization.

Despite the 1929 violence in Eretz Israel and the difficulties to make Aliya at that time, many friends joined the training program, myself included. When Aliya was renewed in 1932, dozens of youth honored the Krynki name by demonstrating the high quality cultural education and excellent Hebrew language skills they received in our branch.

Seated in the middle: Zeev Tsur (Velvel Shein)

The Momentous Activity of 'The Young Chalutz'

Haim Sheinberg

During the 1930s, the Krynki 'Young Chalutz' branch was one of the largest and most active in Poland. Its membership included the majority of the educated contemporary youth who were immersed in Hebrew language, literature and culture. They competed against the conservative–religious youth, the Yiddish 'Bund' and 'Zukunft', the socialists 'SKIF', and the Communist youth (who were commendably organized and active in the underground). The rivalry added interest and energy to our activities.

[Page 145]

As members of a movement that advocated personal fulfilment, we held conventions, summer camps, weekly educational seminars, weekend parties, and debates with other youth groups on local Jewish issues as well as global affairs of the time. Additional invigorating enrichment activities included literary clubs and Q&A gatherings with candidates before elections to the city municipality, to community committees and to Jewish conventions.

Our adolescent exuberance was devoted to practical Zionist work collecting donations to the Jewish National Fund (JNF 'Keren Kayemet') and United Israel Appeal (UIA 'Keren HaYesod'); we even enlisted our families and neighbors to action. Our success earned us praise and esteem from the movement's central institutions: prizes and flags, invitations to large conventions, and requests to send our youth counselors to fill various official roles. There were indeed many Krynki pioneers in the training Kibbutzim throughout Poland.

Krynki Chalutz Committee

Flower Day to benefit the JNF

Under Renewed Polish Reign

(May 1919 to September 1939)

[Page 146]

General Overview

By Dov Rabin

Translated by Eszter Andor and finished by Judie Goldstein

The Beginning Of Polish Rule

In the first few years after the Poles occupied Krynki and the surrounding area, in the spring of 1919 it was considered as an occupied territory, within the so-called Curzon line, the fate of which was to be decided later by a plebiscite. As a number of Polish laws, for example compulsory military service, did not apply to this territory for the time being, the Poles were interested in winning public support for their state in the region. In Krynki where the majority of the inhabitants were Jews and most members of the town administration were also Jewish, the *starosta* (the governor of the district) convened a special meeting of the town council. He hoped that the population would express their wish to belong to Poland on this meeting.

"Following the provisional decree of the Polish county administration the seat of which was in Vilnius," relates Sheyme Kaplan, "each ethnic group of the area had the right to express themselves in their own language in official places. Therefore, we declared in Yiddish that we had received a mandate from the population to administer the municipal economy of the shtetl [although] we had no legal power to represent it in political matters. The 'solemn meeting' ended with this, and the *starosta* and his whole retinue, which had come to the meeting with pomp and circumstance, had to leave like mourners, with empty hands…."

The "Eastern counties" were, by law, incorporated into Poland after the Polish-Soviet war in the summer of 1920. From that time until the destruction of the community the fate of the Jews of Krynki was tied to the fate of our brethren the sons of Israel in Poland.

Jews and Christians in Krynki

According to the Polish census of 1921, the Jewish population of Krynki numbered 3,495 souls, 67.1 percent of the 5,206 inhabitants of the shtetl. Of the rest 904 were Eastern Orthodox and 922 Catholic, many of them Catholicized Belorussians who had settled in the town when the territory was under Polish papal rule. The ethnographic structure of the Christian population of Krynki corresponded in fact to the ethnic-geographic position of the shtetl on the frontier of Polish and Belorussian territory.

The Gentiles usually lived in the outskirts of Krynki close to their agricultural or semi-agricultural property, while the Jews were concentrated in the center. The Jews lived in topographic compactness and made up the majority of the town council, so they considered themselves – and to a certain extent rightly so – the owners of the shtetl, and indeed it was a thoroughly Jewish settlement in its character and way of life.

[Page 147]

In Krynki the relationship of the Jews and Christians, among them the Poles who were now the ruling and privileged state-forming ethnic group, was usually fair until the Nazi period, and it was not affected by the open and even official anti-Semitic agitation, which intensified especially during the 1930s.

Locally the Jews were a visible political force. In the elections to the Sejm in November 1930 the Jewish parties and blocks received 1,193 votes in Krynki, while the Christians collected only 940 votes. The Jews constituted a majority both in the town council and the town administration, although they elected a Christian as town president -- for an understandable reason. In the interwar period the vice-president, however, was always a Jew– sometimes Bendet Nisht from the Tsairei Tsion, [Zionist

Socialist] (the first from among our brethren, the sons of Israel, to fill such a post in Poland), sometimes Dovid Gotlib from the Bund or Meylekh Zalkin (in 1939) from the Poalei Tsion [Youths of Zion].

The Jewish councilors and "aldermen" were fairly active in the municipality and thanks to this they also managed to protect Jewish rights and interests, in particular the town subsidies to the Jewish school system and the institutions for social help.

1920 – the Krynki Relief Committee

The active Jewish community leaders (with the delegate from America, Lewis Sheyn-Leybke Noskes) Sitting row from right to left: Yisroel Stolarski, Yankl Levi, Lewis Sheyn, A. Eynshteyn, Barukh Stolarski, Avrom Rubinshteyn. Standing row from right to left: Dovid Gotlib, Danevitser, Nakhum Bliakher, Barkan, V. Veyner, Ephraim Afrimzon, B. Nisht, Yitzkhak Yosem, Moyshe Shmuelevits, unknown, Sh. Feyvl Nisht.

Economic Discrimination

In terms of its economy, Krynki was cut off forever from its wide unlimited Russian market where it had sold its leather products, and this ruined the economic basis of the shtetl for many years.

In the first years of Polish rule a high inflation raged in the country and the masses of people who had already become impoverished in the world war became even poorer and this resulted in the shrinking of the internal market as well. The sources of the supply of raw skin became also very meager. "The leather production which gave half the shtetl their living came to an almost complete halt", reported Giterman the representative of the Joint when he visited Krynki in 1926. He left 200 dollars, which were to be distributed to those who were left without a job.

Craft and trade and other branches of industry that lived off the factories and off the people who made their living in the factories were also affected. Moreover, the traditional Jewish occupations fell victim to serious state discrimination and destruction, which were continuously showered on the Jews.

Under the pretext of progress for example, compulsory rest was introduced on Sunday and on non-Jewish holidays, as well as on Polish national and public holidays. This meant that Jewish shopkeepers, craftsmen and even manufacturers had to be content with an average of four and a half working days per week. At the same time the government distributed various concessions on cigar stores (where cigarettes, soft drinks, chocolate, etc. could be sold on rest days as well) among all kinds of "proper" Christians (the widows of policemen for example).

[Page 148]

A public kitchen (set up by the Joint) right after the First World War

At first a "patent" was imposed on the various trades and occupations in order to extract heavy fees from the pockets of the impoverished Jews. Then an evil decree was introduced according to which Jewish craftsmen had to get a special permit to own a workshop and employ apprentices and they could only get it if they passed an "official exam" in Polish for which they had to pay a high sum. Volf Eksteyn, who was a member of the management of the Union of Jewish Craftsmen in Krynki until 1925, describes the situation as follows:

"Our task was to fight as far as possible against all evil decrees that the anti-Semitic Polish government of the time showered on the Jews. We were in contact with the central committee of the Union of Jewish Craftsmen that was in Warsaw. But one day we received a letter that said that the Polish government would issue its new guild laws that aimed at completely stifling Jewish craftsmen. My father Khayim the carpenter, an elderly man, who had been working in his trade from the age of 15 had to defer to a Polish Gentile lad who was an apprentice in our workshop, to be recognized as a craftsman. My father was a good artisan and he could not endure this and he chose to leave Poland."

But the worst affliction were the heavy taxes and fees, like the poll tax, apartment tax, town tax, marriage tax, property tax, house tax, and all kinds of other taxes that the Polish anti-Semites could invent in order to shatter the last miserable opportunity of Jewish existence. And there was something worse than this system of pressure; it was the merciless method of admonition in practice – which went as far as confiscating and selling out the last bag and baggage and bedding of the impoverished and hungry households.

[Page 149]

Krynki – An "Economic Ruin"

"Krynki had once been a town where people could easily make a living", wrote Reb Khezkie Mishkovski, the last rabbi of the shtetl, in 5689 [1929] to his compatriots from Krynki living in Chicago, USA. "Now it is completely ruined, unemployment is high, the masses have become disheartened and the town is devoid of all signs of life: the factories became abandoned ruins, memorials to bygone years. Clouds of deep worry furrowed everybody's countenance, as it is said in the Book of Lamentation [Hebrew citation].

"The tanneries are closed in our town. The families of the workers have long been suffering from hunger because of the unemployment", describes a report on Krynki in the Bundist weekly *Grodno Echo*, on March 7, 1930. "Last week several hundred unemployed people demonstrated on the street, and they went to the city hall to demand aid."

Dynamism And Mutual Aid Initiatives

The energetic Jews of Krynki who were usually full of initiative and were veterans of social fighting were not watching idly their painful distress and the harsh persecutions.

The tanners studied and examined the tastes and the demands of the internal market in Poland and started to produce a new, more elegant, thicker and whiter type of leather from calfskin to increase production and sale. The Craftsmen's Union started to prepare its members for the "master exam", which was required of those who wanted to remain in their trade.

The coachmen demonstrated particular dynamism when they were in arrears and had nothing to drive their coaches with. They started to work as chauffeurs, founded two bus "spools" (companies) and established a modern travel connection with Sokolke, the nearest railway station to Krynki. Instead of bouncing in a cart or a stagecoach for long hours, often in rain or snow, one could "jump" those 22 kilometers from Krynki to the railway station quite comfortably. And later when the Poles were "smart" enough to "monopolize" the bus service (that is, they drove the Jews out of it), the former coachmen coped well with this, too: they took up trucks and developed a new trade in Krynki.

The "shopkeepers" established a mutual aid society to help each other in times of trouble, especially with a little credit to make sure that those who were hard up could breathe a little easier again. The tannery workers, who were the veterans of the professional militant movement in Krynki, maintained their association to ensure that it would support them in hard times – help them to avoid or delay dismissal from work, to find a new workplace, to protect the better working conditions that had been won in hard struggles, and to further improve the working conditions when the opportunity presented itself.

In the most bitter times the Jews of Krynki, just like our brethren the sons of Israel in Poland in general, took the initiative in creating societies and institutions of mutual aid the most important function of which was to provide credit and charity. The Jewish cooperative, the "People's Bank", or the so-called little bank, which had been founded in Krynki back in 1912 by the social activist of the time, Yakov Leyb Zaleski, carried out an especially important activity. With its modest loans granted on accessible conditions, it saved from downfall many Jews from the common strata, shopkeepers, artisans, and other oppressed toilers.

[Page 150]

The charity offices developed a prime rescue activity – literally the rescue of souls – in the shtetl by giving small loans without interest, without the fee for an official stamp, which people could get anew any time after they paid up their previous debt.

In the 1920s two workers' production cooperatives were founded with the help of the Yiko society, one for tannery workers and the other for fullers. In 1919 there was also a workers' and artisans' consumer cooperative.

The Charity Committee, its activists and personnel:

Herb Mishkovski, Matus Tarlovski, Sh. Feyvl Nisht, Lipa Kviat, Hanukh Yaglom, Eyzik Neyman,
Epfraim Eli Rodi, Meylekh Likhtshteyn, Meylekh Zalkin, Orke Shimer, Moyshe Ekshteyn

The Jewish Public Life

Social Competition

[Page 151]

Vigilance and Activity

The daily social life of the Jews of Krynki reached its full bloom during the interwar period. The representatives of the basic trends and parties of the Jewish public in Krynki were active in local politics, in the town council, and in Jewish communal matters, namely in the community council, which had a say first of all in the affairs and needs of the religious institutions and had a significant influence in financial matters, and in education and social help as well.

As to religious life – and we will talk about it more in detail on the coming pages – the rabbinical seat of Krynki was occupied by a rabbi who was a great Torah scholar and a prominent personality. Reb Khezkie Yosef Mishkovski, may the memory of the tsadik be blessed, was a passionate Palestinophile (i.e. supporter of Jewish emigration to Eretz Israel) and a tried and tested activist in public, whose reputation went far beyond his rabbinical seat.

Krynki also had a well-respected yeshiva, the "Beyt Yosef," for the youth, and there were a number of study groups for grownups and young people. Later the younger strata organized a Tiferet Bakhurim society for studying the Tanakh, "Eyn-Yakov" and the like. Religious education was completed and modernized by the creation of the so-called cheder haklali (regular cheder) and there was also a "Beys-Yakov" school for girls.

Ideologies and Political Currents

All major movements of contemporary Jewry were active and competed with each other on the social scene of the town. On one end of the ideological spectrum were those who considered the "keeping of the mitsvot" (commandments) the main constituent and essence of Jewish life. They believed and hoped that the worship of God would protect the Jewish people from trouble and from the evil decrees and bring about the coming of the redeemer, even if he tarries. On the other end of the spectrum there were those, among them some workers and youth, who believed in a radical upheaval, in the style of the Bolsheviks and the Yevsektsiye (the Jewish section of the Soviet Communist Party), which would bring complete salvation to all the working people, including the Jews.

Those who believed in "eternal galuth"(exile), at least in those areas of the Eastern European Slavic countries where there was a large concentration of Jews, stood on the basis of the "here and now"dogma. This was close to the beliefs of the communists but it was the social-democratic version of the communist's ideals of the salvation of the working classes and it also incorporated certain elements of the Jewish national cultural autonomy movement.

The activity of the young and enthusiastic Zionist pioneers who stood on the opposite end of the spectrum from the above-mentioned ideologies and their adherents became more and more perceptible and efficient in the interwar period. They were ready to realize in body and spirit the ideal of redeeming the Jewish people and the Jewish individual in his homeland, Eretz Israel.

The Competition Of Social Forces

Even the incomplete data at our disposal concerning the results of the elections to the town council, and to the council of the Jewish community in 1928, allow us to get an insight into the power relations of the Jewish society of Krynki in the 1920s and 1930s.

[Page 152]

Of the eight members of the community council four came from the Orthodox list, one from the Hassidic list, one from the Zionists, and two from the Bund. The Poale Tsion [Youths of Zion].would have needed one more vote to get a mandate. The results of the elections to the Krynki town council were as follows:

In 1919, there were 4 Polish, 4 Belorussian and 16 Jewish members; of the latter 4 Orthodox, 4 Zionists, 4 Tsairei Tsion [Zionist Socialist] members, 2 Bundists, and 2 artisans. The town council chose Bendet Nisht (from the Tsairei Tsion) as the vice mayor and vice president of the magistrate (town administration).

In 1927, there were 8 Polish and Belorussian and 16 Jewish members; of the latter 5 Bundists, 4 artisans, one Zionist, one Orthodox and one merchant, 3 Poale Tsion members and one from a personal list. Dovid Gotlib from the Bund was chosen as vice mayor.

In 1934, there were 10 Christian and 6 Jewish members. Of the latter there were 3 Bundists, 2 unaffiliated and one Poale Tsion member. Sixty votes were cast for the communists and, as it was rumored in town, several communists had been elected to the Bundist list.

In 1939, there were 8 Christian and 8 Jewish members. Of the Jewish members, the Poale Tsion received 6 and the Bund 2. Meylekh Zalkin from the Poale Tsion was chosen as vice mayor.

The Bund

We had already dwelt in a number of essays on the resolute fight that the Jewish industrial proletariat of Krynki pursued since the 1890s for the rights of the workers and for the safeguarding of their significant achievements. The Bund had a dominant role in these fights. In those days, when the Jewish factory workers were truly firmly established in the tanneries of Krynki, the town became a fortress of the Bund.

May 1 manifestation (Bund, Tsukunft, Skif [the scout group of the Bund])

The late Mordekhai V. Bernshteyn, a Bundist man of letters and historian, says the following about the Bund: "The Bundists of Krynki renewed the old Jewish revolutionary traditions of the shtetl. They maintained various cultural institutions, a Jewish elementary school and professional unions. A Bundist youth came into existence through the Tsukunft and the Skif organizations. The head of the Krynki Bundist organization was Dovid Gotlib, a renowned person in interwar Poland. And the "stars" of the Bundist public representatives included among others Yankl Levi ('the sane'), alderman in the town council; Tevl Kuntsevitski, member of the town council; Yankl Temkin, warden of the synagogue; Nakhum Bliakher, secretary of the Tannery Workers' Union; Rakhel Shuster, the 'mother' of the Bund; and Ephraim Petritser, the leader of the Tsukunft."

"And the shining star that excelled all was the Bundist pioneer, the former tanner and fuller, Avrom Shmuel Zuts, 'the blind eternal light' who was the light of the tannery town despite his blindness. He got the nickname 'the blind eternal light' and he entered Bundist literature under this name. He was the librarian of the big library which he had founded in Krynki" [until the Bolsheviks destroyed Avrom Shmuel's oeuvre, the library, when they occupied the town in 1939]."

[Page 153]

The Communists

The once vehement, rebellious anarchists were no longer heard of in Krynki and in the surrounding area. The government started to seriously persecute instead the illegal communist party. The party was especially active in the 1920s, when the economic crisis reached its peak in Poland in general, and in Krynki in particular, and better times did not seem to be in sight, and the morning star of the Soviet Union shone still with its full radiance as the savior of humanity and the liberator of enslaved nations, among them the Jewish people. Jewish workers and youth were often arrested in Krynki and in the surrounding area and condemned as standard-bearers of the Bolsheviks. The Reds cooperated with the Bundists in internal Jewish affairs, such as secular education in Yiddish. In certain cases, as was shown above, they also voted for the Bundist list in elections in which the communist party could not put out its own candidates due to police persecutions.

On the other hand -- as we have already alluded to -- the Zionist movement, especially its labor and socialist trends, were becoming an increasingly significant force in the Jewish public of Krynki. – We will return to this later. In 1933, the religious Jews of Krynki, headed by Rabbi Mishkovski, organized a local branch of the Agudat Israel of Poland and in 1934 a local branch of the Tsairei Agudat Israel of Poland came into being.

Education And Culture

Translated by Eszter Andor and finished by Judie Goldstein

The Secular School In Yiddish

It was in the field of children's education that the Jews of Krynki carried out the most exemplary work in the period under study, devoting a lot of efforts and hard work to it. We have already discussed their achievements in the field of religious education with the creation of the cheder haklaki in Krynki. In the field of a more or explicitly secular Jewish education there was a rivalry between the Hebrew educational system and the secular Yiddish elementary school, which was established in 1919.

*The administration of the secular Yiddish school with the guest from
America, Lewis Sheyn ("Leybke Naskes")*

[Page 154]

"In the dark and bitter times when people were swollen with hunger, the Jewish workers of Krynki thought of founding an elementary school", wrote Issakhar Fink. "The school constantly struggled for its survival because it had very little money and it had to work in an atmosphere characterized by a lack of understanding on the part of the Jewish public of the town. But many children from Jewish worker and artisan families finished the school year after year with a significant amount of knowledge and erudition, which helped them to push their way through in life."

By the beginning of 1920, the school had 138 pupils and another 93 students followed evening classes. The school was regularly harassed by the government, which closed it for some time at the beginning of the 1923/24 school year. The school, which was named after the Warsaw center of the Tsisho, had an exceptionally devoted teaching staff. The school was influenced by the Bund, and the Bundist scout group (the Skif) recruited many of its members from among the pupils of the Yiddish school. Krynki compatriots recall the school with pleasure especially because of the nice performances and celebrations, which were organized a few times a year.

The leadership, the teachers and the activists of the Yiddish elementary school in 1928

The Hebrew School

As we have already described, the Hebrew co-educational elementary school was founded during the German occupation at the end of the First World War with the assets of the Tsairei Tsion without almost any outside help.

[Page 155]

"A few 'evenings' were organized for the benefit of the planned school. Comrades contributed their last penny to the cause and all this was used to repair an abandoned apartment where the school could be set up", relates Ephraim Ben Ephraim (Efrimzon). "This is how we acquired desks and tools. We had no teaching experience but we were determined to carry out the work. The shtetl was impoverished because of the war but our young teachers approached this task as divine service and spared no efforts to perfect themselves."

"Liliput" dance at a children's performance
in the Yiddish elementary school

"Orthodox circles incited against us saying that we 'heretics' led the children off the Jewish way and that parents should not send their children to our school. But many cheders were closed so the children transferred to our school and we soon had 300 pupils. The Yiddishist circles also plotted against us. But we were not scared and we soon introduced a tuition fee to ensure at least the survival of the institution, and to avoid begging. Thus already in the first one and a half years, we had an income amounting to 30 to 40 percent of our budget."

The drama circle, 1930

"We lived through a horrible time when the town was occupied by the Red Army in the summer of 1920 and the Bolsheviks started to uproot the national Hebrew education completely. But we resisted by all means at our disposal. When the Poles returned to the town, they set upon our school and tried to discover some shortcomings, which would allow them to get rid of it and have the Jewish children transfer into the Polish state school. We had to start fighting again but in the end we won and managed to legalize our school as well."

"The senior class graduated in 1922 and we also opened a Hebrew high school. Our enthusiastic supporter and Hebrew educational activist, Avrom Yehuda Eynshteyn, harnessed himself and tracked down and brought us graduate teachers all the way from Galicia.

The administration and pedagogical council of the Hebrew elementary school, 1928

[Page 156]

Unfortunately a huge inflation raged in Poland in those days and despite the devotion of the teachers and the goodwill of the parents of the pupils, we could not maintain the high school for more than two years."

A class in the Hebrew elementary school

The elementary school, however, continued to develop. A canteen was set up for the pupils and as well as a Hebrew children's library, named after Mendele Moykher Sforim. Already in 1926 it possessed 500 volumes. There was a drama circle, which regularly organized successful performances. By the 10th jubilee of the first graduating class in 1931, already 300 pupils had finished the school and the number of graduates continued to grow.

Historical studies circle in the Hebrew elementary school

For the post-WWI generation of Jews in Krynki, the Hebrew elementary school was a primary source of educational and ideological inspiration in the spirit of the pioneers. It was like a stock farm that turned out Zionist-socialist youth. The history of the Hekhalutz in Krynki was closely linked with Hebrew education, thinks Zeev Tsur (Velvel Shteyn), a former graduate of the school, who was a leading figure in the Israeli Labor Party, member of the Knesset (the Israeli parliament), and deputy minister in one of the former Israeli governments. "The whole atmosphere in and around the school in the various social events and 'circles,'" adds Z. Tsur, "aimed at ingraining in the pupils the love of manual work, agriculture, simplicity, in short, pioneerism, aliya to Eretz Israel and self-realization."

Libraries

The above-mentioned rivalry of the two educational institutions in Krynki came to light in the field of culture, namely in the libraries, as well. The Bundists had their so-called "big library", and the Tsaire Tsion also established a library in 1920 named after Heshl Sapirshteyn, one of the pioneers of the Hebrew school. By the end of the decade it had 2,000 books in Hebrew, Yiddish and Polish, 200 subscribers, and it was the largest library of the town.

The "big library", directed by "Eternal Light" collected primarily Yiddish books and the most recent Yiddish newspapers. The collection included mostly literature, poetry, social sciences, political economy and socialism. It was supported by party members who were originally from Krynki but were by then living in America. The library had two main supporters: Leybke Sheyn (Noskes), who often sent newspapers and journals, and Khatskl Miller.

[Page 157]

The Zionist Movement

Translated by Eszter Andor **and finished by** Judie Goldstein

Trends Within the Movement and What They Supported

In the interwar period the most important activities of the Zionists in Krynki were to prepare the youth for aliya to Eretz Israel, educate children in a national-Hebrew spirit, and win people over to the Zionist idea and its realization. At the same time the Zionists were also ready to tackle the various needs of the Jews in Krynki.

The most important elements of the Zionist movement in Krynki were the groupings called "For the Labouring Eretz Israel," especially the Tsairei Tsion, which later united with the rightist Poalei Tsion. They pursued a wide variety of activities. They attracted the Zionist-socialist and pioneer youth and devoted themselves to Hebrew education in the shtetl. Beside this, they carried out a vigorous general Zionist activity in the Keren Hayesod, the Jewish national fund, the so-called Shekel campaigns, the Hebrew Tarbut societies, and so on.

The leadership of the Hashomer Hatzair organization

The elected representatives of the Tsairei Tsion were active in the town council as well as in the council of the Jewish community since the first democratic council elections, which had been carried out at the end of the First World War. "Despite the fact that many of our comrades in the Tsairei Tsion had no franchise because they were too young, and not only could they not be elected but they could not even vote in the elections to the town council, we had a great success thanks to the popularity of our leaders in the various domains of social life of the shtetl, especially in education", writes Bendet Nisht about the leaders of the above-mentioned trend.

The Tsairei Tsion founded the Hekhalutz movement by 1919 in Krynki. They provided Hebrew evening classes for the workers who were preparing to make aliya to Eretz Israel and in 1921 they arranged locksmith courses for the olim (the new immigrants). In the same year -- similarly to other areas in Poland -- they carried out a successful collection of tools and money to buy tools for the workers in Eretz Israel in Krynki and the neighboring shtetls.

*The council of the the Poalei Tsion with the drama circle
and the leadership of the Hebrew elementary school*

[Page 158]

Committee of Poalei Tsion [Youths of Zion] – Krynki 1929

In the same year they also opened general evening courses on Jewish history, geography, natural sciences, political economy, Yiddish and Hebrew.

By the beginning of 1926, the Poalei Tsion Union had already set up a youth organization with 100 members and 80 adults. "Our comrades", describes a report from Krynki, "participate actively in various social institutions, like the People's Bank, the orphans' committee, and so on, and they have a great influence on the life of the local society."

In 1934, 500 workers, common Jews and young people from the Poalei Party, the Hekhalutz, the Ha-Oved (The Worker), the Freedom Party and the Ha-Poel sports club and the Hekhalutz Hatsair kibbutz, participated in the solemn First of May demonstration organized by the League for the Laboring Eretz Israel.

But the movement flourished and reached its greatest influence in the last year before the outbreak of the Second World War. That year the Freedom-Hekhalutz Hatsair movement had 200 members and the Ha-Poel 50 in Krynki. And in the elections to the 21st Zionist Congress, the League for the Laboring Eretz Israel received 406 out of the 449 votes in Krynki.

The Poalei Tsion Party entered the elections to the Krynki town council with the slogan "for or against Israel now" at a time when the English government had just published its White Book against Jewish immigration to Eretz Israel and its colonization by the Jews. [The party] won 6 seats out of the 8 seats accorded to Jewish deputies (the other two seats were won by the Bund). The Jewish public of Krynki identified with the "for Israel" slogan.

The Hekhalutz Aliya To Eretz Israel

As mentioned before, a Hekhalutz union was founded in Krynki in 1919. And it started immediately to prepare its members for manual work and communal life. They leased a huge garden near the bath-house and a group of young boys and girls started to "learn agriculture" there and to get as much practice in it as possible until the gates of Eretz Israel would be open to aliya again. In 1919-20, Krynki was a transit point for pioneers who arrived in the shtetl from the surrounding area in order to go on a hakhsharah and then make aliya to Eretz Israel. This is how Sheyme Kaplan describes this phenomenon:

Pioneers at work in the hakhsharah-kibbutz in Krynki, 1935

[Page 159]

"At that time Krynki was within the so-called Curzon line, which was considered a territory occupied by Poland where a number of Polish laws, such as compulsory military service, did not apply. 'Hares,' that is, young boys from the territories that were already annexed by Poland by law, used to come to our town. The young people arrived with a recommendation letter from their local Zionist organization in which we were kindly asked to help the bearer of the letter, pioneer candidates for aliya to Eretz Israel. The idea was that we would provide these boys with documents proving that they were residents in Krynki (that is, that they were not liable to military service) so that they could get a passport and an English visa to Eretz Israel."

"First of all we memorized with each of them street names in Krynki and the names of some local residents so that the boys would be able to argue and "prove" to the authorities if necessary that they were really locals. At the same time, we invited the chairman of the town council to a feast at Heykl Olian's and made the "gentleman" rather drunk with liquor. And [Hebrew quotation] we would have him sign the appropriate certificates on the basis of which the pioneers who arrived in our town could get the necessary documents and make aliya to Eretz Israel."

In 1919 Bendet Nisht participated in the first conference of the Hekhalutz of Lithuania (strictly speaking, of the Grodno-Vilnius district), which assembled in Grodno, as the delegate from Krynki. He also represented Krynki on the national Hekhalutz conference organized in Warsaw a year later and he was elected to be a member of the central committee of the movement.

The first group of pioneers from Krynki made aliya to Eretz Israel in the summer of 1920. Among them Sheyme Zak and Zvi Rotbart (Carmeli), may he rest in peace, Eyzik Ostrinski, and Avrom Neyman, Yofe Furman (a farmer today) and her brother Motke.

They spent the first few years in Eretz Israel working in a group with the pioneers from Grodno on the forestation of Mount Carmel and in Atlit and in the citrus plantations in Petakh Tikva, and later in construction in Rishon LeTsion, Ramlah, Jerusalem and Motza. Then a part of them went into agriculture with the Geva Group in Jezereel valley where they were joined by Lea Nisht (Zak) and Lize Rotbart (who is now the wife of Dovid Tubiu, the first mayor of the reconstructed Beer Sheva and its builders).

The first pioneers, including the young Krynki pioneers, laid the foundations for the subsequent wider aliya to Eretz Israel, which built a country for the Jewish people that would be independent until the end of time.

The Life Pulse Of Krynki

By Shmuel Geler

Translated by Eszter Andor and finished by Judie Goldstein

The Economic Life of the Jews

When the First World War ended, new frontiers and new countries appeared on the map of Europe. Independent Poland came into being. Life started gradually to return to normal. Although there was still great poverty, the first buds of renewed, creative and constructive work appeared here and there. The aftereffects of the war could long be felt in Krynki. The financial assistance of the Joint [international Jewish relief organization] and former Krynki compatriots now living in America helped Krynki Jews a lot to make it through the difficulties of the transition period.

[Page 160]

In the first years of Polish independence, most of the manufacturers that had evacuated their enterprise to Russia during the war returned to the town. The shtetl slowly started to come to life again. The closed tanneries opened their gates that had been locked for so long. The leather workers rolled up their sleeves; and after a long interruption the tanners gave out a sharp smell of wet skin, slaked lime and oak once again.

Disregarding the differentiation between the various tannery trades, all leather workers were united by their common fate and fight. The tannery owners experienced good periods of prosperity as well as bad periods of crisis. The leather workers never had any good times. They could hardly make ends meet even in the better periods when there was plenty of work. And their situation was much worse in the frequently recurring years of crisis. The Krynki leather workers knew well what it was like to be unemployed for long months on end, when poverty reigned in their homes and the shopkeepers and bakers gave no more food on credit. The children of the workers looked yearningly on a piece of rosy bread. The unemployment benefit distributed by the state was hardly enough to buy water to make porridge.

But the leather workers did not crack. The suffering and the constant fight made them harder and tougher. They were all organized in their professional unions and it was impossible for someone who was not a member of the Union of Leather Workers to get seasonal work even for a day. Krynki was always famous for being a stronghold of the Bund, which had many members and sympathizers among the tannery workers. The Bundists were in a majority in the leadership of the Union of Leather Workers. Their leader Nakhum Bliakher was the secretary of the Union for many years. The communists also had a visible influence among the tannery workers. They were represented by Zeydl Zaleski in the leadership of the Union for a long time. Although there were a lot of Zionists among the tannery workers, they had no influence in the Union of Leather Workers. The Zionist tannery workers preferred to indulge themselves in the "Merkaz" (the Center) rather than in their professional union.

The cramped union hall was always crowded. The workers came here to talk about all that was weighing on their minds, to ask for protection and work. Many of them had no stable work place. The Union made great efforts to secure work for all its members but it was not always successful. Sometimes the manufacturers did not want to employ a newly sent worker, and sometimes the permanent workers of the factory would also object to a new worker.

Although the leather workers and the manufacturer prayed in the same beys medresh [synagogue] and went around with the same Torah scrolls on Simchat Torah, they did not have an idyllic relationship. The shtetl was small but the class conflicts were great. The town saw frequent work conflicts and strikes, which lasted for days and sometimes for long weeks. And there was no strikebreaker among the Krynki workers. The leather workers displayed a lot of persistence and class-consciousness in the strikes. True to their revolutionary tradition, they fought hard for their rights.

If we disregard their daily worries, the leather workers lived an intensive political and spiritual life. One of their main concerns was the education of the younger generations. The majority of the leather workers' children studied in the Yiddish elementary school where they received a secular education. The parents displayed a lot of love and devotion in maintaining the Yiddish Tsisho school.

[Page 161]

A group of elementary school children and their teachers

They often gave their last zloty to help cover the ever-growing costs and debts of the school. The leather workers could not afford to give more than an elementary education to their children. None of their children studied in gymnasium and only a few chosen ones continued their studies in a teacher training college or in a trade school.

The Krynki leather workers were interested in reading Yiddish books, daily newspapers and followed with great interest what was going on in the wider world. The trial of Sacco-Venzetti, the civil war in Spain and the notorious trials in Moscow were all echoed among the workers in Krynki. They felt sympathy for the freedom fighter and condemned the show trials staged in Moscow.

The tannery industry in Krynki experienced a certain degree of prosperity in the last few years before the Second World War. The tanneries increased their production; beside the "traditional" leather products such as sole, "distressed leather," bootleg and tongue, a new product came out: a soft, thick "piece sewed under" which functioned as uppers, especially for leather fancy goods.

A considerable number of local Christians and peasants from the surrounding area made a living from the leather industry. The Christians worked mostly as wet tannery workers and in other simpler trades. The number of leather workers continued to grow on the eve of the Second World War.

[Page 162]

Technology reached Krynki as well. Machines appeared in the Krynki factories. The majority of the manufacturers had their own steam engine and electric power and finally high wind turbines also appeared. The workers no longer had to turn the drums by hand for long hours. As one was driving along the highway from Krynki to Grodno or Sokolke, one could see the tall smoking chimneys of the factories and the wind turbines – it was like a "little Manchester." The shtetl was working; an intensive economic life was pulsing in the city. Jewish initiative and capital, the efforts and hard work of Jewish professionals created an economic value, which was beneficial for the whole shtetl. Shopkeepers, commissioners, packers, artisans and coachmen all made a livelihood from the ramifying leather industry.

The Second World War, which broke out unexpectedly, and the bloody German occupation destroyed everything that the Jews had built up over many decades. Jewish manufacturers and workers, the poor and the rich, all had the same fate: Treblinka, Auschwitz and death.

Religious Life

Translated by Eszter Andor and finished by Judie Goldstein

Torah and Traditional Devotion in Krynki

"In previous generations," wrote Henoch Suraski. "Krynki was known as an aristocratic shtetl with a proud tradition of rabbis and righteous torah scholars and of a community of Jews occupied with religion and Torah knowledge – that lived to the end in religious law and good deeds.

"In the old city cemetery there were gravestones on the graves of the Krynki great men, among them Rabbi *Reb* Yosef – *Reb* Yosele the Righteous and *Reb* Chaim Tsvi, a Slonimer Hasid who decided on rabbinical law and who was also a miracle worker. The writing on the gravestone says a lot about the changes in the community and the world.

"As known, there existed in Krynki before the First World War a great yeshiva "Anaf Eitz Chaim" [The Branch of the Tree of Life] where there were many students from the entire region.

"But later a new yeshiva existed in Krynki for young men, 'Beit Yosef' – a branch of the Navaredok [Novogrudek] *muser* [morals and ethics] yeshiva that was founded by *Reb* Yosef Yusel Hurvits. The yeshiva was in 'Chai-Odem' on Garbarska Street."

"There, in the synagogue, writes Abraham Soifer, "sat fifty youngsters who studied diligently the beautiful pages of *gemore* [part of the Talmud]. The songs, coming from deep in their hearts, never frightened Christians passing by.

"Young men with ear locks wound around their ears would eat with dozens of Krynki families. It was considered a great and good yeshiva. The head trustee, *Reb* Naftali was mainly busy with recruiting yeshiva students from the entire area. But dialects from a lot of Galitzianer and Polish youngsters were also heard. They came to study in the Krynki yeshiva because it was considered one of the best and also graduated several rabbis."

"In the Krynki streets," finishes Henoch Suraski, "the voice of Torah was heard, G-d's living words – by Jews whose lives were intertwined and thoroughly imbued with divine service, prayer and good deeds. 'It used to be…'"

[Page 163]

Rabbi Reb Khizkiyahu Yosef Mishkovski

David Mishkovski

After the First World War and until the outbreak of the second, the prominent Reb Khizkihau Yosef Mishkovski sat in the rabbi's chair in Krynki. He was the last rabbi in the shtetl. He was a great Torah scholar, a dedicated social worker and a lover of Israel, heart and soul. He was born in 1885 in Stavisk, Lomza District, to a religious rabbinical family.

He studied in a number of yeshivas such as Maltch, Radun and Navaredok and was already described as a genius while he was studying. In 1904 at the age of twenty, he immigrated with his father-in-law to Israel and settled in Jerusalem where he studied at the "Ets Chaim" yeshiva. He published his father-in-law's book *"Pri Yitzhak"* [Fruit of Yitzhak] as well as his own work.

Reb Khizkiyahu also took part in community work in Jerusalem and was a member of the first "Vaad-ha'ir leYehudi Yerushalayim" (community council).

In 1914 he returned to Poland where he was invited to be the rabbi in Zsheludok. In 1922 he became the rabbi in Krinik (after *Reb* Zelman Sender who left during the First World War and later went to Israel, and after Rabbi Weintraub who was the rabbi in Krinik a short time during the German occupation. Because of a betrayal he had to leave the shtetl).

After the First World War Krinik experienced a difficult economic situation. Rabbi Mishkovski was committed to helping the many needy and expended a lot of effort on the Jewish community institutions especially in the field of religious education. He founded the *"Heder HaKlali"* [the Public grade school for boys] from what used to be the *Talmud Torah* [free grade school for poor boys] and it became a model of a well-organized school for Jews and also secular education.

Rabbi Mishkovski was also busy caring for *"Linat HaZedek"* [a society whose volunteers stayed overnight with patients so their families could get some rest, provided doctors and medicine for the poor] and *gemiles khesed* [loans without interest]. (He initiated the founding of such funds with the help of the *"Joint"* [Joint Distribution Committee of the USA, charity to help poor European Jews] in all the large cities of Poland). He was also active in the orphanage, in the "Women's Committee" and wherever help was needed.

The activities of Rabbi Mishkovski surpassed by far the limits of Krynki. When the prohibition against Jewish ritual slaughter started in Poland, Rabbi Mishkovski – then vice-president of the *"Agudas HaRabonim"* [Federation of Rabbis] in the country – he stood at the head of the struggle against the evil decree.

With the outbreak of the World War in 1939, he traveled to Vilna where he was invited to be the chairman of the Union of Refugee Rabbis from Poland and with the initiative of the "Joint" developed a broad relief and rescue operation that also crossed over the border. In the spring of 1941 he went to Israel where he was invited to become the director of the *"Vaad HaYeshivas"* [the Council of the yeshivas] in the country.

A class in "Heder HaKlali" 1934

[Page 164]

Society for the Sake of Orphans, with the support of School for Tailors/Seamsters and its teachers and its students

But basically he gave himself body and soul to saving Jewish refugees and especially those wandering far from home deep in Russia.

He searched for addresses, especially of Krinkers, and moved heaven and earth to contact them so that they would send packages to save the unfortunate refugees from hunger and cold and to give them courage during this perilous time.

Selected as a member of the Israeli Relief Committee by the Jewish Agency, Rabbi Mishkovski left for Europe (in poor health) to help save the surviving Jewish souls, especially Jewish children who had been hidden in monasteries and to bring them to Israel. He was a fervent leader of the Relief Committee in Europe and in the United States.

He returned to Israel on the eve of the Jewish New Year in 1947, a man broken by the great sorrow for our murdered people. But his weak heart could go on no longer. The day following Rosh Hashanah he died. Over ten thousand people attended his funeral and he was laid to rest in Jerusalem on the Mount of Olives.

Krynki Melamdim [religious teachers]

By Betzalel (Alter) Patshebutski

Translated by Eszter Andor and finished by Judie Goldstein

Two Reb Shmuels

Reb **Shmuel Tentser** the *melamed* had a *heder* [religious grade school for boys] where once hundreds of young boys studied. He had several assistants.

The *Heder* – a huge room with a clay floor, three large wooden tables set up in a "U" shape. On both sides there were long benches so that the students sat face to face. The rebbe [teacher] sat across the table..

The assistants would stand around the table or go around among the children and make sure that they stayed quiet and listened to the rebbe.

In the second room – where the *rebbe* lived – it was dark and squalid. The walls were soaked with dampness. The damp and steam from the cooking pots poured down them. There were no windows.

The teacher's wife, Paya, was, the poor thing, blind in one eye and it ran all the time. She would yell and curse and would invade the *heder*. She was dirty and the seams of her blouse were split. With a loud voice she would let out her bitterness to her husband. Shmuel Tentser would not even move. He did not even turn his head to her and would continue with "kometz alef oh, kometz bes, bo."

There was a special punishment corner – a "prison" that was closed with a door as high as a child's head. The sinner would have to hold in one hand a poker and in the other a broom. The child would stand and yell: "beh, beh, a busha!" [beh, beh, a shame!]. After a couple of minutes he would go back to studying. The duration of the punishment was decided by the *melamed*.

[Page 165]

Reb Shmuel " der rebetsin's"

Reb Shmuel "*der rebetsin's*" was a "secular" *rebbe*. He was famous not only for his knowledge, intelligence and for his ability to teacher grammar, but first of all for this; several weeks before Passover he would produce wine. The *heder* boys were glad to help, at the expense of studying less.

The wine "production" was an interesting trade. It was necessary to pay very careful attention to the small boys so as not to arouse the wrath of the *rebbe's* wife who was worse than the rabbi's ethics lessons.

In the dark evenings the students would go back to the *heder* with lanterns in hand and snow creaking under the feet. One frozen hand holds the holy books and the other the lantern, rocking in the wind. Behind it sways the figure of the student – the Jewish zealot.

Shmuel "*der rebetsin's*" did not beat the students – as he had physically weak children. He had a blackjack, but did not use it. The parents of his students were more or less sure that their children were in no great danger that Shmuel "*der rebetsin's*" *heder* would beat them.

Reb Shmuel Glembutski

Yishie Drayzi

We, all the Krynkers, who have since spread through out the world, while still in our hometown went through and studied in *heder*. It was in Rabbi *Reb* Shmuel son of Yosef haTzadik [the righteous man] Glembutski, or as he was called, *Reb* Shmuel "*der rebetsin's*" *heder* where we studied.

With him we wandered the paths of this great and dear asset. There were Jewish teachings and ethics, based on the most beautiful and glorious principles of the Torah, the rich baggage of light and knowledge, of virtue, the deep spirit of Jewish traditions, morals and honesty.

My great uncle, *Reb* Shmuel "*der rebetsin's*" did not use the torah as a "spade with which to dig" – he kept the rule of "love work, hate domination." Therefore he dedicated his entire virtuous life, body and soul, to educate generations of Jews, taught them the way of knowledge and anonymity, to plant religion in the hearts of his young students.

Reb Shmuel "der Rebetsin's"

Reb Shmuel's *heder* was in its category the highest in Krinik and grown up boys from the best families studied there. They had already gone though other *heders* of *"khumesh"* [Pentateuch] and the books of the prophets – the degrees. *Reb* Shmuel taught the students traditional scholarship, such as *gemore*[the part of the Talmud that comments on the Mishnah] with *toysefes* [critical glosses on the Talmud], the way of *ha-p'shat* [a literal translation of the Torah] and cabala. It was an honor for parents and pride for the children to study with him. And we who sat for many years on the benches around his table soaked up Torah and wisdom from him as well as his love of Judaism and belief in the triumph of Israel.

[Page 166]

The model, clean, virtuous life of the rabbi served as an example for all his students. *Reb* Shmuel *"der rebetsin's"* (*Reb* Yosele's son and spiritual heir) was a good-natured man, of stately appearance and great scholar and at home in secular knowledge. People came to him from all walks of life to ask his advice, to charm away an evil eye and to pour out their heavy hearts. And everyone, when they left, had more faith. *Reb* Shmuel was respected and loved in the city.

Reb Shmuel prayed in the *"Kavkaz"*synagogue. His place was at the Holy Ark. The cantor always waited to start the "main" *Shmona Esrah* [the eighteen benedictions, a daily prayer] until Rabbi Shmuel had finished the silent prayer. The respect for him was immense.

How dear and since *Reb* Shmuel was to people – so strict with his pupils. Every minute was precious and holy. One had to exert all his sense in order to follow what he said. The students truly thought of him as the pillar of fire. He not only instilled in his pupils a love of learning and the love of Judaism, but also a sense of Hebraisism that has stayed with each of them.

Thursday might *Reb* Shmuel prepared for the Sabbath. He paid careful attention to everything so that it would be done according to religious law, in honor of the Sabbath Queen and prepared the snuff himself.

When he was finished his work, he would pay the first tithe to the Odelsker rabbi who then lived in Krinik and to other scholars. And I had the privilege of carrying out the "holy" mission of carrying the little boxes of tobacco to them.

[Page 167]

Once there was our Krynki

Our Krynki

by Frida Zalkin-Kushnir

Translated by Hadas Eyal

The name Krynki sprouts from the water springs that shaped its industrial character and tanning trade. It was a typical medieval town built around a characteristic market center from which streets branched in all directions.

The Jewish residents - manufacturers and merchants - lived in the city center while most of the Poles were farmers on the outskirts of town and built their homes on the edge of their fields. Among the Polish scholars were a doctor, a judge, a priest and policemen.

Church Lane

It was an industrial town with more than 20 tanneries. During the Russian Czar regime, leather and hide merchants arrived from as far and wide as Crimea and Siberia. The majority of the Jewish population, including the youth, worked in the factories, giving it a proletariat atmosphere. Alongside the manual workers were several shops and craftsmen such as tailors who also worked for the farmers in nearby towns.

The area farmers were mostly illiterate and primitive and it was only after the Polish authorities opened free public elementary schools that the town people began sending their children to study.

For the Jews of Krynki it was always important to develop cultural life. They kept close relations with the large regional cities like Grodno and Bialystok for continuous supply of newspapers and magazines, and Polish and Russian performance artists. The Jews also played significant roles in the local municipality as party representatives and deputies to the mayor.

Especially noteworthy is the political awareness and revolutionary activity of Jewish Krynki youth. Up until the establishment of the general schools, the boys studied mostly in "cheders" [traditional Jewish primary school] and the girls in the Russian elementary school. One of the teachers was Liza Rotbort, the wife of David Tubiyahu, the future first mayor of Beer Sheva in Israel. The Krynki youth was thirsty for knowledge but unfortunately there were no complementary education options in the town itself for many years.

Some of the youth had a deep Zionist spirit. "Tsirei-Tzion" [Zionist Youth] movement laid the foundation for the first Hebrew "Tarbut" [culture] school. At the same time, youth from wealthy families broke away to make Aliya to the land of Israel as Chalutsim [pioneers], some joining Kibbutz Geva in the Jezreel Valley.

A group of Yiddish Elementary School pupils with their teachers

[Page 168]

The teachers – Reiss, Gelernter & Tsvigel

Two schools were established simultaneously: The Hebrew School and the Bund Yiddish School. The competition between them for academic achievements and attracting the new generation elevated each school to high standards. The teachers were recruited from Galicia and Congress Poland – cultural people with high degree education such as Dr. Reiss, Gelernter, Tsvigel, and Sarig (later the renowned principal of the teachers' seminary in Kibbutz Givat HaShlosha).

There was a hope to open a Gymnasia [high-school] in Krynki but it was not feasible for lack of students. Children of proletariat parents could not afford to continue their education beyond elementary school. Some were able to travel to larger places such as Grodno or Vilna to study, train, or acquire a practical profession while somehow sustaining themselves in those places. The Krynki youth earned a good reputation for their cultural background and it was paraphrased that: "The law will go forward from Krink" [מקרינק תצא תורה].

Seven days in our town

by Shmuel Geler

Translated by Hadas Eyal

(This section is in Hebrew written by native Yiddish speakers)

Weekday

Dark grey smoke rising towards the pillar of early twilight from the chimneys of the hunched huts – announces the beginning of a new work day in Krynki: above tripods and cooktops, Jewish mothers prepare breakfast for their husbands, sons and daughters who are early to rise for their day's labor.

The rising day is not rid yet of the night and already the streets of Krynki are busy with tanners marching heavily down the streets and alleyways to the tanneries, fulling mills, and other work places. Quickly they will don their aprons, roll up their sleeves and quietly and gravely approach their hard work. The steam engines will come to life, the gears will hum, the cylinders will roll, the craftsman's instruments will shine. Diligent trained hands create the praised Krynki leather.

It is 7 am and the streets and alleys of Krynki are bustling with life. Loud calls and youthful laughter erupts from all directions – the children are marching to school. Satchels on their shoulders, bags in their hands, this one in new trousers, that one in patched trousers – all eyes shining, all faces happy. The class rooms quickly fill up - in elementary schools, in the general cheder: a new learning day begins for torah and haskalah. The joyful voices of youngsters can be heard.

Once the women send their wage earners and children from the house – they turn to their daily tasks: shining the floors, washing the clothes, mending underwear and clothes, going to the grocery store, the baker and the butcher. When lucky they pay cash, other times defer payment. Laden with baskets they return home to prepare afternoon fare. Flames are lit in ovens and cooktops. In cauldrons and cast iron pots they will cook either meat feasts, dairy meals or meager broth stews.

The streets fill again: Factory workers leave for their daily meal; youngsters return home from school with much ruckus and commotion. When it rains they will slosh through the puddles. In the winter they will proudly ice skate on self-constructed blades tossing snow balls at each other. Not lacking of appetite, it is unsure whether the scant food at home will satisfy it.

The hour ends, the adults go back to work, the students do their homework and impatiently look forward to moments of joy when they will be free for play and mischief outdoors. Housewives, like hard working bees, each persevere with what needs to be done. Does the stream of our mothers' work ever dry?

In the market center, summer and winter, women vendors sprawl next to their fruit and vegetable baskets and crates. Heat, cold, rain or snow – they will never desert their post. Rambunctious bickering over shoppers and mutual juicy profanity frequently rise to the heavens. The struggle for every morsel of income is not easy.

At the height of the day, groups of unemployed and plain bums of which there also were in Krynki hang around the market arguing about world affairs and town gossip. Some set this as a meeting point with the postman, in case he has a letter from America in his satchel with a dollar in it. Others seek any kind of work, any bit of livelihood. Everyone waits impatiently for the fifth day of the week, market day.

[Page 169]

Market Day

The morning of the longed for market day. By the crack of dawn, the square is already set and ready to greet its guests. Dozens of tents are pitched here, stalls, counters, tables, truly full of all good. What can you not find here? Women hat-makers with colorful heads and shiny black foreheads; leather shoe parts such as "tongues", lining and soles cut to size; cattle accessories; horse harnesses, reins and straps that stink the air with tar; artisanal spindles; heaped shelves of dark chiffon and white flour bread loaves, bagels, buns, cakes and plenty of other mouth-watering appetite-provoking baked goods; a splendid display of sweets and candies; and various cooking and household utensils arranged everywhere you look.

And the taverns, they are full of sausages, herrings, alcohol, soda water, kvass and beer.

Krynki Market

On farm carts and by foot, farmers flow into town from towns near and far. Neshot Chayil Bnot Yaakov [diligent Jewish women] in charge of budget savings are already waiting for them on the outskirts looking for findings at half price at least. In broken Goyish-language seasoned with Yiddish they haggle with the town folk, grope the chicken buttocks and blow into their feathers to check how plump they are. Experienced negotiators will eventually succeed in the difficult task of exhausting the farmer and striking a deal on a good chicken for Shabbat, eggs, a butter portion wrapped in coarse farmers' cloth or a wide leaf. Satisfied with their "winnings" they now trudge back to prepare meals.

Meanwhile, market day reaches its peak and is busy, crowded and noisy. Jews squeeze between the carts, rummage in sacks, check bundles and use all their talents to bargain until they settle their squabble with a hand shake and a friendly pat on the shoulder. The farmers' purses fill up and their carts empty out. Kosher butchers buy cows, calves, sheep. Horse merchants check the animals' teeth, assess their age, and test their fitness and tolerance amid the combined commotion of neighing animals and haggling people.

[Page 170]

The stores, chicken pens, and stalls brim with people buying utensils and supplies for their farms and homes. The women farmers buy cotton dresses, the younger among them also get colorful polka-dotted scarves and pearl-glass necklaces. The piles of bread loaves and other foods dwindle.

These are happy days in the eateries of Poliak & Snarski, Haykel & Lieder and pubs like them. With pockets full of cash, groups sit together, chatting loudly and taking rounds buying drinks, herring, sausages, bacon and sauerkraut. The more glasses they empty, the higher their spirits, the rosier their cheeks, the waterier their eyes. Some of them hug and kiss their buddy friends. One will begin singing, the others will drunkenly join in. When someone drops a coin into an automatic music box the audience will enjoy an energetic mighty march tune. Suddenly one of the celebrators remembers a past injustice…a bottle is thrown towards the offender, chaos erupts, tables shake, bottles and bowls shatter, and liquid splashes on the assembled…

Market day is over, it slowly empties. The grocers count their proceeds: G-d willing, there will be enough to make a tuition payment, return a debt, buy raisin-wine for Kiddush and Havdalah [orthodox Jewish rituals before and after the Shabbat].

Krynki welcomes the Shabbat

Translated by Hadas Eyal

Krynki began bustling in preparation for Shabbat from the early hours of Fridays. Cooking fragrances rose from the homes of Israel of baked challah, cooked fish and other Shabbat fare. The women of Israel, busy bees, clean, scrub, launder and iron. Storekeepers, laborers and craftsmen ready themselves for the day of Shabbat-Kodesh [Holy-Shabbat].

Most joyous was the children's anticipation for the end of the school week. With grand commotion and glee, they hurry out. Each preparing in their own way for Shabbat.

One of the greatest mitzvahs [a commandment] from youth to old age was to bathe in honor the happy day [Yom haSimha]. The children fulfilled the mitzvah in the stream on the slope of the Tanners' Garbarska Street near the grazing meadow where the water was shallow and did not rise above the ankles. The youngsters would crawl on all fours splashing marsh water on each other with sheer delight.

The pond down Mill Street near the flour mill was deep enough for youth to swim in the water, or mud, hard to tell. Those who ventured further from the town washed behind the "new" flour mill where it was possible to bath in fresh water and emerge perfectly clean.

The true taste of bathing however could be found in the river. Carters would hitch their horses and transport those who had enough money for the return journey. The Krynki teenagers would march the 6 kilometers in groups or alone to the serene river that flowed among fields and grass. The river was full of people. Here you had to know how to swim. The brave flaunted their abilities – diving, stroking to the deep waters, frog leaping. The water was clear and cold. The swimmers felt all their senses and after the soak would roll naked in the cool fragrant grass (in my youth, Krynki has not yet heard of bathing suits).

The women conducted themselves separately, at a distance from the men. Among the men who swam well were some who quietly made their way to "sneak" a peak at the half naked daughters of Eve.

Refreshed, light and relaxed everyone returned cheerfully back to the town; becoming tired and covered again in dust but returning home in good spirits.

The local bathhouse was also full on Shabbat evening. The reigning king here is Aharonchik the attendant. He generously provides large jars for water and twigs with which to scrub. In the first washroom people lathered soap and rinsed. But the proper Shabbat pleasure [Oneg Shabbat] was felt in the steam room. On wood benches laborers, craftsmen, landlords sat and reclined – everyone is equal here.

The group is enjoying the heat. Every once in a while they cheer: Steam! More steam! A few jars of cool water onto the scalding stones in the furnace send new waves of hot steam into the sweat room. It is not easy to see each other and breathing is difficult but soon they resume: Steam! Give us more Steam! The twigs are used to rub the skin clean and the men treat each other to a back scrub. This is the only place where a common person can beat the back of a rich landlord and it will even be considered a mitzvah…With glowing and flushed faces, everyone returns home.

[Page 171]

Meanwhile, the mothers already sent the cholent pots [traditional Jewish stew] to the bakers' ovens. Now they wash the children's hair with pails and water basins. Howling and crying, the toddlers attempt to flee their mother's hands, the soap suds bitter in their mouths and burning their eyes. Thick combs will go through the infants' hair – something might be found there…

Quietly and in moderation, the daughters of Israel will wash and arrange their own hair (rain water is known to bolster growth). Mothers lovingly braid it. The homes are shining clean. Old and young – everyone is ready to welcome the Shabbat.

One house after the other, Shabbat candles are lit. For some in silver candlesticks, for others brass, and yet others in a couple of potatoes… Head-covered mothers in kerchiefs and scarves whisper their prayers. With quivering hearts and teary eyes, they will accompany their husbands and children to the prayer houses.

Shabbat evening

Translated by Hadas Eyal

As Shabbat dinner is drawing to an end, the Krynki youth begin to flow from all corners of the town to the market. In couples and groups, they will roam around between the houses of Vacht and Hykel. Blaring conversations, loud calls, laughter, the market buzzes with adolescent joy. Groups congregate on sidewalks in passionate debate, defending opinions and supporting rabbis.

Bit by bit the audience dwindles and couples or circles of friends will turn down the street towards Viryon Estate and to side alleys. The main strolling wave will descend Shishlevitz Street, through the chestnut trees near the "Bolnitze" (the Goyim/Christian hospital) adjacent to the government elementary school. They shortly arrive at "Yente" woods which is actually the size of a little finger but is loved and precious, engraved deep in the heart of every Krynkian.

Throughout the woods singing can be heard. Who can sing better than Krynki youth? We sang with elegance and emotion. One will break into song and right away his friend will assist with a "seconda", the third and fourth will join in harmony:

> "Facing the dawn of the day we stand,
> The new young guard of the proletariat…"

[translated from the Hebrew translation of the Yiddish]

Sings a group of "Tsukunft" [Future in Yiddish] of the "Bund" youth:

> "From Warsaw to Paris
> From London to Canton
> Moskow launched a red flag!

[translated from the Hebrew translation of the Yiddish]

The crooning revolutionary youth demonstrate their belief in a new liberated world.

And from the edge of the woods the pleasant delicate voice of a young girl is heard:

> "You promised me you would come,
> You promised and you did not,
> I looked for you all night in the alleys,
> And yesterday so it was, so beautiful and delightful,
> So desiring-passionate the hearts!..."

[translated from the Hebrew translation of the Yiddish]

Singing about "Nights of Canaan", "Sea of Galilee", and the "Jezreel Valley" ends with energetic hora dancing. Bunds, communists, Zionists sing different versions but all share the throbbing spirit of the wonderful Krynki youth tribe.

Under the cover of the dark night couples embrace tightly and share their dreams. The trees of "Yente" woods soak many sweet secrets. Tired and exhilarated, the youth return to their homes at late hours, sneaking in quietly.

Shabbat calmness rests upon the town.

[Page 172]

In the atmosphere of Judaism and Zionism

by Yehudah Eckstein

Translated by Hadas Eyal

Hebrew Public School Class of 1928

Krynki my town – some things of the time I sat an entire day on the study bench in the "cheder" [traditional Jewish primary school] and "talmud torah" [traditional Jewish elementary school] I will never forget.

Late in the evening, in the winter; we jovial students return from our studies holding candle-torches. Who of us will not remember our melamed, "Rabbi" Bezalel z"l, whose cheder was on Cherkovna Street?

And here the school of "Tarbut" [Culture] on Garbarska Street and the big library next to it. The course of study – to Zion, to pioneering, fulfillment and implementation. Its dedicated principal Asher Gendel, the trips and excursions with fire torches to Yente woods or farther to Schalker forest on Lag ba'Omer, on Kaf beTamuz and other holidays.

And our "Young Halutz" [Young Pioneer] youth movement, the cultural-educational activities it provided and the summer-winter seminars all towards Erez-Israel, towards Aliyah [immigrating to Israel].

And the Shabbat in Krynki. Following six work days, the Shabbat-ness ["shabbatdikyt"] that prevailed everywhere; and after the mincha-meal on Shishlevitch Street the entire town from infant to elderly strolled around.

From the way of life

by Ashe Golob

Translated by Hadas Eyal

Like the other field towns in Poland, Krynki lived the typical Jewish way of life. The parents attempted to pass their religious traditions to their children.

But our town was blessed with various other types who provided much entertainment material and pranks. The Krynki clowns knew how to play practical jokes. And above and beyond, Krynki was blessed with an abundance of rumors about ghosts and spirits.

[Page 173]

Countless tales and jokes spun over generations around the "groisse schul" and the "schulhoff" (the grand synagogue and its grounds). These tales of demons and the dead that spread among the people would cast fear on the majority. I will recount one of the episodes here.

There was a Jew in Krynki named Herschel the "snob" or the "distinguished" who one fine day passed away – a natural ordinary incident, but the rumor was that Herschel returned home, spoke, turned and disappeared. Others said he appeared to them in a dream and asked to be re-buried because he rolled over onto his stomach and needs help rolling back. The emotional flurry among the town people grew and grew.

At the same time – so I heard directly from the storyteller – two pigeons were stolen from the Goy on New Street. The thieves' trail led to the path near the cemetery. When the Goy passed the cemetery in search of the pigeons and he saw a white figure walking around who turned out to be Herschel the distinguished snob. To the Goy's question what he was doing there, Herschel responded that he lost something. Frightened, the Uncircumcised almost fainted and quickly left.

That evening, as always, I was at the "Center" (the common name of the Zionist Movement Center in the town) on Garbarska Street meeting my friends who arrived from Heschel Library or the drama club at Alter's the painter z"l and I told them the entire story as I heard it from the Goy. An argument ensued. Some accepted the story as something that happened, others laughed at the expense of the Uncircumcised.

Finally, Shimon Rudi our famous hero rose and said he was willing to place a bet that he isn't afraid of anything. He will go alone, now, in the evening, to the cemetery, and stand there on the fence. We are to come later and see if it's so. We agreed. It was a dark night. Shimon left.

At the scheduled time we rose, a group of friends, to check whether the guy passed the test. As we approached we saw a figure standing on the fence. According to Rudi he yelled out loud that we were cowards and that he ran full of confidence and on purpose into the cemetery.

But coincidentally, in the burial plot of one of the saints, a group of communists were preparing flags and illegal printed material for their activities. They heard the commotion, thought law enforcement caught up with them, opened the gate and ran as fast as they could.

We too did not catch at that moment what was going on and we too ran for our lives. The next day, when the story spread, the clowns had an abundance of material to work with.

A story about an informer

by Efraim Ben-Efraim

Translated by Hadas Eyal

As I was walking one day in 1922 on Swislocz Street with Nyumka Terkel who was one of the radical leftists in Krynki at the time, he abruptly stepped away, went over to the young Yankel Kopel the "Oziranchik" (meaning from nearby Oziranie) and slapped his face. When Nyumka returned and I asked him why, he responded that the young man is a "moser" (a snitch) involved with the hostile Secret Police and a harmful Informer.

At first it seemed that the young man simply got caught up in hoodlum mischief but it soon became apparent that he was a regular guest of the Secret Police and associated himself with the detectives.

Because Duvke Lev - a young attractive maiden whom this Kopel tried to woo with love letters - did not accept him, he snitched on her that she is an active communist until the young woman was jailed in Grodno Prison as the Polish regime routinely did to anyone suspected of contact with that movement.

The people of Krynki from all factions attempted to prove there was no basis for the accusation imposed upon the young woman and even used the love letters from the "Oziranchik" as proof, but the Grodno Secret Police that took him under their patronage crushed the attempts in her favor.

The Informer continued to spin false accusations. He would secretly infiltrate assemblies of the Left, throw provocative notes, then invite the police to "find" them and make arrests. Things got to the point that the promenade in Krynki, that in normal times was full of adolescent cheerfulness, was almost silent that summer. Many of the youth even left the town for fear of the snitching and provocations.

[Page 174]

Those of us who were members of political parties and had mutual friendships between us, heard one day that the Communist Youth Underground "is organizing something" against the "Oziranchik". And indeed on the evening after Shavuot [a Jewish holiday] as we left a municipality management meeting, we suddenly heard alarm cries: Fire! It was indeed a fire… in the apartment where the Informer lived with his father on the outskirts at the end of Pochtova Street. We assumed it was an act of arson and we didn't go there.

The next morning, we learned of the details directly from the Communist Youth: they scattered two bundles of hay on both sides of the "Oziranchik's" apartment, poured kerosene on it and lit it that night. Armed with hand guns, two young inexperienced youth were situated to ambush the Informer when he tried to escape. The Informer, who knew he was sentenced to death by the underground Resistance Movement, came out with guns drawn in both hands. The terrified youngsters fled. The Informer summoned the police who searched homes and arrested four young men: Herschel Oberstein the son of the female roofer, Pinya Tavel the son of the female mikveh attendant, David Lev, and Itche Ahun the son of Heshil the servant.

The police opened an investigation. It was found that Itche's clothes smelled of kerosene. When asked about it he said he bought a bottle of kerosene and on his way home he tripped and fell, the kerosene spilling on his clothes. As a witness he named the grocer Beyla-Rachel the daughter of Alter-Meir Abbes. But she denied selling him kerosene, contradicting his claim. Still, the four suspects were able to secure an alibi and the people of the town who invested efforts towards acquittal saw the matter as trivial, assuming the police was harassing them as they frequently did in those days.

Actually, that was not the chain of events as the matter was moved to military court. The prosecutor, having found no grounds for the accusations, was interested in postponing the verdict by holding the prisoners and transferring deliberations to a civil court. He asked the defense to support his suggestion reminding them what was known to all – that a verdict by a military court could not be appealed. The defense, confident the defendants will be acquitted, asked that the court release them immediately for lack of grounds for the accusation. The verdict however was guilty as charged.

The lawyers, all well-known, were barely able to save them from being executed and they were sentenced to life in prison with forced labor. The people of Krynki were shocked. The families, especially the mothers cried out and with David Lev's mother leading them, they marched to the municipality building screaming to the heavens: Libel! Alilah [Hebrew/Yiddish word for libel]!

The Holy Arks in prayer houses were swung open. Weeping and rage were heard throughout the town, boiling, storming. A defense committee was formed. Letters were sent to the Bnei-Krynki Organization in the United States and money arrived from there. Lawyers were hired without any expected result because only the Polish Parliament (the Sejm) itself was authorized to decide on conducting a new trial. For that to happen it was necessary to prove that the verdict was based on false testimony while the witnesses in this case were the "Oziranchik" and his father who threatened terror if anyone dare go against them.

Eventually - a miracle happened. The Informer fell out of favor with the Secret Police who looked for an excuse to get rid of him. He used the time meanwhile to snitch in Grodno causing many arrests, trials and harsh sentences. Once dispensable, the Secret Police provided the "Oziranchik" a travel-passport and money, and ordered him to disappear from Poland. Awakened, anyone who had damaging proof against him brought it before Parliament and after a thorough investigation it ordered annulling the verdict of the four. Great credit to Valvel Weiner, Alter Ayan, David Gotlieb and several other Krynki activists.

Yankel Kopel the "Oziranchik" fled to Argentina. It is told that some time before, the young Krynkian Menashke Bieber, who served in the Polish Army in Grodno, happened to see the "Oziranchik" crossing the Neman River bridge in Grodno and assaulted him in an attempt to throw the Informer from the height of the bridge into the water. But Bieber failed and was forced to desert the Army and escape from Poland, settling in Argentina. When he heard the "Oziranchik" also arrived in Argentina he set out to find him. It is told that it was there and then that the death verdict of the Communist Youth Underground was fulfilled.

<u>Our Shtetl Krinek</u>

[Page 175]

Our Shtetl Krinek

Translated by Judie Goldstein

From My Childhood

Before the Destruction

Beilke Shuster-Greenstein

In a valley of Poland, east of the middle road between Bialystok and Grodno, lies my hometown Krinek, where I spent my youth; a beautiful childhood – full of memories - where I can never return…

The round market place was the center of the shtetl. During the day it was the place where storekeepers made a living and at night it was the promenade square for couples who filled the evening hours and amused themselves on these dates. So they would endlessly walk around the market place, until it became tiresome and then go to Shishlevitzer Street, as far as Yente's woods and often to the Sholker forest. That's where all the young people met. They would lay a fire and dance and sing around it - each with his group, each group singing its own tune.

I would like to mention episodes that I still remember from childhood. – how a group headed by Geler and Chaike Kirpisht went for walks in the forest. The Christian Anisimovitch played the guitar. Comrades sang. How happy and beautiful those evenings were…and we youngsters so envied them…

Winter evenings were entirely different. How happy the children were when a sled and driver was hired for a ride around and around the market place, while singing songs and the our laughter went up to the heavens. Oh, those beautiful winter evenings that can never be repeated…

Everyday living was something else. Everybody worked and everybody had their own anxieties – from making a living for the children, to a young woman who had no possibility of marrying as she did not have a dowry and her parents were old and gray.

On a sled in the Krinki marketplace

The shtetl was divided into three parts: rich, poor and middle class. The poor labored long and hard for the little money they earned. The rich lived in luxury. But the shtetl was made up largely of proletarian elements, for the most part tannery workers, also shoemakers, tailors, and so forth. The large factories with the tall chimneys left their mark on the municipality. Five times a day busses came from Bialystok and Grodno and each time the whole shtetl would go to see who was arriving - perhaps a bridegroom? And later they would go find a bench in order to get a good look at the strangers.

[Page 176]

The Sabbath was felt by everyone, even those who were not religious. In every house this day ruled as a holiday. Jews felt free in the shtetl. The vice-mayor was Jewish and Jewish city councilors were: Yankel Levi the "Klorer" [Clearer] and Nachum Klorer, who was a great achiever, were Jewish City Councilors. Because his language was never clear, every strike was led by him: Blind Abraham Shmuel Zutz and many other people as well, went down in the pages of history for their heroic struggle in 1905.

Also in the cultural domain, Krinek was no different from other towns. Besides the "Heder HaKlali" [public grade school for boys], there was also "Tarbut" [Zionist Hebrew school] a school run by Bendet Nisht and others, for whom we all had great respect. The Jewish secular school distinguished itself with its good educators and beautiful performances for each holiday that brought so much delight to the parents and the population in general.

Now – a little about organizations of all persuasions, like "Poali Zion" [Zionist Socialists], "Bund" [Jewish Socialist party, which set up Jewish trade unions, ideology based on the negation of Zionism, the struggle for Jewish working masses and secular culture], "HeHalutz" [Zionist youth organization to train pioneers for Israel], "Frayhayt" [Freedom], "Tzukunft" [Bund youth movement], "Skif" [Socialist Children Fareyn, a Bund children's organization]. Everyone in the youth organizations felt a strong bond for the other members of the group. Who does not remember the First of May demonstration when all the youth marched in special uniforms and with what self-sacrifice they all prepared and impressively carried it through with pride.

The Dramatic "Circle" 1926

String Orchestra and the Hebrew Public School

"Skif" marches in the First of May Demonstration 1937

Krinik

Avrom Soyfer

In a valley, between flat little mountains lies my hometown Krinik. The round market place was the center of the shtetl. Two rows of stores – the source of Jewish retail income – were divided by so called "gates" that united both sides of the market place. People bought and sold there during the day and walked around during the evening until late at night. Endless circuits were made until the couples became tired and marched away to Shishlevitzer Street. Then past the "bolnitzes" [hospitals] further down the road, often going as far as "Shemianitze".

[Page 177]

The main employer in the shtetl was the tanning industry. The workers fed the storekeepers, bakers, shoemakers and tailors. Every young boy dreamed of becoming a tanner – a man, a wage earner.

It would remain engraved in the memory of every visitor to Krinki, that a shtetl such as this had laid down sidewalks, arranged a municipal electric works – with a Jewish engineer, Golinski, and a Jewish technician, David Zack.

Jewish automobile owners in Krinik would drive passengers through the streets of Krinki to Bialystok and Grodno five times a day. This was called the "Spulke Ekspres" [spool express]. The "entire town" would go to an automobile every several hours to get a look at who was arriving and to get newspapers.

Electric works in Krinki

Later all this was nationalized and the Jewish automobiles were no longer allowed to be used to drive passengers, so Jews waited for the trucks that helped Jewish commerce in the shtetl.

The "Pazharnikes" (firemen) were the reflection of the town administration. Twenty "pazharnikes" – all Jews; the elder was Vladko Anisimovitch and Vice-Commandant – Chemia Meyerovitch. And it was the same at the city council. The majority of councilmen were Jews. There was a Christian Mayor, Pavel Tzarevitch and a Jewish Vice-Mayor. The "Christian" mayor, Pavel "Tzar", as people called him, was a very friendly man, spoke Yiddish well and had a good relationship with the Jews.

[Page 178]

1930 "Linat Hazedek" Managing and Oversight Committees In the center – Ziskind Mordhilevitch, chairman
Standing from (on) the left – Moshe Grodski, secretary

The "Sabbath Guardians" (an Orthodox group) had a little bit of work, but only Friday afternoons. It is before lighting and blessing the candles – a disturbance, running: it is already late, it's the Sabbath! The doors and shutters of the stores are closed, Ben-Tzion Donde calls out over the entire market place: "Jews, go to shul [synagogue]!" Young boys yelled after him: "Go to shul!"

Friday night the "Society of Sinners" (a secular group) shaved themselves. The "Sabbath Guardians" carried out a violent war against them.

Several people from Krinki community life – honor their memory:

Velvel Weiner (the carpenter), who gave up a large part of his life to activities in the municipal government, "Heder HaKlali" [Public Boys' Grade School], and Orphans' Committee.

Meilech Zalkin was an important social worker in the "Tarbut" [Zionist Hebrew School] School, the Jewish Community Council, the Folks-Bank and in the "Poali Zion" [Zionist party] political party. The Nazis burned him in Treblinka.

Yankel Levi, "der Klorer" [the clearer], a man who gave his great energy to community activities in the bank, the Jewish secular school organization, in the "Bund," a councilman in the municipal government and alderman to the city council. Murdered in Auschwitz, January 1943.

Abraham Shmuel Zutz, Zishe the "eternal light", became blind while in one of the Tzar's prisons and held a position in the brand new Jewish library, always active in the secular school organization, in the "Bund" and with youngsters. Perished together with his sisters Itke and Mulinke.

Nachum Bliaher – Secretary of the Tanners' Union, a strike could not be taken care of without him. During the ghetto period, at his house there was a working, illegal radio and people could listen to foreign news broadcasts. This news would later be spread throughout the entire ghetto. He gave up his soul in Treblinka.

And so that is the line-up of the very public figures in Krinki Jewish life.

[Page 179]

Krinki Institutions and their accomplishments

The mainstay of the Jewish economy in the shtetl was the local "Folksbank". Its money would be loaned to small storekeepers and artisans – those always hard-pressed to make a living. The major figures in the bank were Jacob Chaim Grinshchinski, Yankele Shafir and Kaganovitch (the "Ardent").

"Linat Hazedek" [medical assistance society] provided the entire Jewish population with a doctor and a pharmacist. The poor would receive free medical help, according to a receipt, stamped by the secretary Mordchai-Shimon Grodski. Also a "lodovna" [ice cellar] was built – a real public treasure, because to get a piece of ice for a patient during the summer was not a small thing. Every Purim there was a special "campaign" for the good of providing ice.

A beautiful activity was the development of the "Jewish Home for Orphans" with half-board [day home] for several dozen small children. During the time it was active, a tailor school under the direction of Blumke Zakheim was established and from then on dozens of orphans ended up with a trade.

At the "Gmiles–Khosdim " [loans without interest] fund, a Jew could get a loan, with a promissory note, without government taxes (free of the "stamp tax") and without interest.

A group of orphans with their supervisors

[Page 180]

Half-boarding school (day home) for orphans
In the picture (from the committee)
Rachke Caplan, Beylke Korngold, Shmuel Levski, Itshke Shishlitzian, Rishke Mendelevitch, Wolf Weiner, Shprintze
Shnayder, Boruch Garber, Falia Lev, Hashke Shuster.

Dear, kind Moshe Ekshtein ("Pintl") was the technical secretary there.

From my first years in heder [boys' grade school] I remember how in school, at the right side of the ante-chamber (foyer), we would fight against "knowledge" from "Israel the melamed" (a teacher called "the tin beard"). Others related that they would often receive their small share of "wet towels" and even a day standing in "prison." Later a "public Heder" was created – a modern heder where boys from the surrounding towns - Amdur, Brestovitch, Yalovke and Horodok - would come to study.

About fifty young men sat in the "Chai Adom" besmedresh [meeting place of study] and studied with determination the eternally beautiful gemore [a section of the Talmud] pages, and their tunes, that came from deep in their hearts, would never frighten the Christians passing by.

Young men with ear-locks wound around their ears would spend their "eating days" at dozens of Krinki families. Step by step, a large and good yeshiva became active in the shtetl. The head gabe [manager] Reb Naftali was in charge of recruiting yeshiva students from the entire area. But dialects from a lot of Galicianers and Polish young men, who came to study in the Krinki yeshiva, could also be heard. The yeshiva was considered one of the best and graduated several rabbis.

Krinik During The Week

Shmuel Geler

Dark gray smoke, in the early morning, rising from the houses into the still half-dark sky, announces that in Krinik a new workday has begun.

Jewish mothers put out three legged stools and plates then prepared breakfast for their husbands and children who are about to leave for work.

The night had still not managed to depart with the coming of day and Krinik streets were already lively. Alone and in groups the leather workers walk with heavy steps up Garbarska Street, Gmina Street and other streets – to the leather works, mills and other work places.

They quickly put on their work aprons and roll up their sleeves. They quietly get down to work. The steam is already puffing, the transmitter buzzes, the drums are turning, the utensils are shiny. Diligently the tradesmen's hands work to create the famous Krinik leather.

Seven o'clock in the morning and already the Krinik street and alleys are even more lively. Loud shouts, the sound of youngsters' laughing rings from everywhere. Krinik's Mosheles and Shlomoles, Chanales and Racheles are on their way to school. With knapsacks on their shoulders, binders in their hands, some with patched pants, others with newer pants, all of them with sparkling eyes and mischievous looks – they hurry into the public school and heder. There are a lot of schoolrooms: in the "Tarbut" [Zionist Hebrew school] School, Jewish secular school and "Public Heder". A new school day begins. With curiosity and thirst the children soak up general and Jewish knowledge. The sound of their voices singing Jewish and Hebrew children's songs rises up from the small schoolrooms and spreads throughout the nearby area. In secular and religious schools, in Yiddish and Hebrew, Krinik children study the Torah and wisdom.

[Page 181]

Now that the husbands and children have been dispatched from the house, the wives attend to their daily work. They clean house, do the laundry, mend shirts and clothes. They go to the food store, the baker and butcher. The fortunate ones use money, the others buy on credit. Loaded with baskets and bags, the wives return home to cook lunch. The fire is started in the oven. In cast iron pots they cook meat or dairy lunches. Some of the wives are ashamed of their daily fare. They cook "with nothing" – no meat and no dairy, only with water.

The Krinik streets become livelier still. The factory workers are eating lunch, children return home from school filling the streets with mischievous shouts, trying to outdo each other with their childish pranks. It is raining and everyone is wearing rubber galoshes. During the winter people slide on runners, a local product (a cut piece of wood with a wire underneath), allowing people to slide on the ice and use "sniezhkes"

Men, women and children went about their work, children doing their lessons, waiting impatiently for the time when they could run off into the streets to play and have fun. Wives, like busy bees, were working at home. How were our mothers able to get all that work done.

On a market day

Its only morning and the Krinik market is already lively. Food and flour stores, dry goods and iron stores – all waiting for customers. A whole week to realize a sale. Rich merchants are financially secure with their business. The small, poor ones – run around fainting trying to find a loan, a loan without interest: the need to pay a promissory note, in order to settle the revenue duties.. If not, the bailiff will seize what little he has.

In the middle of the market place, opposite the "gate" sits, during summer and winter, the market women surrounded by loaded baskets and wooden boxes of vegetables and fruit. In the heat, cold and rain, they never leave their "work places". During the summer people bake in the sun; during the winter, they warm up at the chafing pan. Loud quarrels between merchants break out over perspective clients, but they speak softly to their customers. It is a hard struggle to make a living.

At the end of the day there are constantly groups of unemployed, ordinary idlers - and such - wandering around the market place discussing world politics and town news. Some are waiting for the "distributor", perhaps a letter with a couple of dollars will arrive for them from America; others search for a little work, looking to earn a living. They all wait impatiently at the market place on Thursday. And here it is, and already before daylight there are dozens of booths, market stalls and tables, large and small put up on the market place with a variety of hats with shiny peaks in a variety of colors. Leather merchants laid out their goods: tongues, uppers, soles. Harness makers hung out horse collars, reins, and breeching, which had a strong odor of lime and tar. Turners put out foot wheels, on the ground, to make flax threads. Bakers prepared loaves of soft white bread and rye bread, stacks of bagels, round breads, cakes, "stritzlelkh" and all kinds of baked goods.

[Page 182]

Small tables with all kinds of candy, caramels and sweet things, with various articles for the house - were put out everywhere. The beer halls and restaurants were loaded with sausage, all kinds of herring, liquor, lemonade and small bottles of beer. Everything was ready and geared up for the market.

On loaded peasant wagons and on foot, in groups and alone, streamed the peasants to the market, from Poretch, Lapitch, Nietupe, Makaritze, Spodvil and a lot of other villages near and far. Clever housewives wait for the peasants beyond the shtetl in order to purchase something at a bargain. They felt the fowl and blew under the feathers to see if a hen was fat. The women worked hard at haggling. They talked to the peasants using half Yiddish and a kind of "gentile language" until they managed to buy a fowl for the Sabbath, a few dozen eggs, a piece of fresh butter wrapped in a piece of white peasant linen or in a green sheet of paper. Loaded down with good things, the Jewish housewives returned home.

Meanwhile at the market place there is already a tumult, a commotion, Jews walk around among the densely placed wagons. They rummage in the sacks, look at the peasants' packs and they haggle. They slap the gentiles' hands, a sign that they have come to an agreement. The peasants' wallets and pockets will be full, the wagons empty. Jewish butchers buy a cow, calves and sheep. Horse dealers try out the horses. They look at the horses' teeth. Their neighing and the mooing of the cows mix with the shouts of the buyers and sellers.

Surrounded on all sides by a mass of villagers, a young gentile stands up on a wagon and calls out at the top of his voice about his merchandise and bargains. For only one zloty he offers a spoon, fork, small comb and a mirror. But this is still not enough, so he also adds for the same zloty a needle with a spool of thread. And he yells more – he also throws in a pair of buttons and a ribbon. The peasant women move toward the gentile and grab the bargains.

All the stores, booths and stalls are besieged. The peasants buy various utensils and articles that are needed for the home and housekeeping. Peasant women buy calico clothes and the girls – colored pieces of cloth and strings of beads. The piles of breads, rolls and various baked goods become smaller and smaller. Wealthy villagers are able to eat, even during the week, white bread and wheat rolls.

In the restaurant owned by the Pole Snarski, at Chaikl's, at Lieder's and in many other eating houses, treats and beer are consumed with joy.

Peasants sit with companions, treating themselves to vodka. They snack on herring and sausage. They talk loudly. With each glass emptied, their voices rise. Their faces are already red, their eyes half closed from drunkenness. Some embrace and kiss. One of them starts humming a melody, and half-drunk voices join in. From Chaikl's restaurant a loud noise is heard from the automatic street organ. A peasant puts ten groschen in and out comes a march in all its detail.

Suddenly – a cry for help, a tumult, a peasant treated his drinking buddy to a bottle over the head, having remembered an old "loss".

Little by little people are leaving the market place. Long lines of wagons stretch from the shtetl to the roads to the dozens of surrounding villages.

Jewish storekeepers add up the cash: thank God, there will be enough to repay the loans, money for tuition and enough to make the Sabbath.

The market place looks like the aftermath of a battle, the entire, large area, that not two minutes ago shone with various colorful articles, lively and noisy – is wrapped in silence, the market place quickly caught its breath and rests.

[Page 183]

The dear Sabbath comes

Friday all morning, the Sabbath can already be felt in Krinki. From Jewish houses the smells of fresh baked challah [bread made with eggs and braided, served on the Sabbath], cooked fish and other Sabbath foods drift in the air. Jewish housewives, like busy bees, cleaned the house, polished the floors, cleaned and ironed the Sabbath garments. Artisans, storekeepers, workers and manufacturers – everyone prepared for the Holy Sabbath.

The greatest joy belonged to the children. They would wait impatiently for school to end. With a great rush and happiness, like free birds, the children would leave the schools. Each in his own way prepared for the Sabbath.

One of the great commandments for young and old was to bathe in honor of the Sabbath. Children fulfilled the commandment in the river off Garbarska Street at the "nashielnitza", at "Vigon". The water there reaches a little higher than the heel of a foot. They would crawl on all fours and get sprayed. There is great joy here.

Off of Mill Street, in the pond at the mill, the water is somewhat deeper. There they can swim a little – in water as well as mud. It was difficult to stand here because of the mud. Some of the youngsters would go to bathe outside the shtetl at the new mill, in Slusker-mill. There was real water, where one could come out of the water clean!

The real bathing was in the Lishker River. The wagon drivers loaded their wagons and drove there. Only some could afford to pay an entire zloty to drive there and back. Friday afternoon, alone and in groups, the Krinki youth went the six kilometers to the winding, calm flowing river, among fields and grass.

The deep river is full of people. There one must know how to swim. The swimmers do all kinds of tricks: they "dive," some can only swim a "single stroke," others swim like "frogs". The water there is clear and cool and everyone feels in seventh heaven. After bathing everyone rolled naked in the cool, fragrant grass (when I was young, nobody in Krinki knew about bathing suits!).

The women go elsewhere, further than the men. Some youngsters, good swimmers, would quietly steal away and go near the women, to catch a glimpse of a half-naked daughter of Eve.

Fresh and rested, everyone would go sprightly back to the shtetl. On the way they would become covered with dust, tired out - yet they came home happy. The feel of swimming, the cool, clean water stayed in their bones.

The night before the Sabbath the shtetl bathhouse was also full. Aronchik, the attendant, ruled there. He treated them to a good bucket and a small broom to hit themselves with. In the first room they would wash with soap and rinse off. But the true pleasure of the Sabbath was felt in the steam bath. Workmen, artisans and manufacturers sat or lay on long wooden steps. There everybody was equal. Once in a while a shout was heard "steam, steam!" and several pails of cold water would be thrown onto the stones in the oven and steam billowed up, filling the steam bath, refreshing them with the heat, even though they could hardly catch their breath. And they shout again: "steam, steam!". Sitting on the stairs, they rub themselves and beat themselves with the little brooms. One treats the other with an invigorating rub down.

That is the only place where a "common person" can beat a bossor a rich man and still earn merit. With beaming, red faces, everyone returns home.

[Page 184]

The mothers have already sent the cholent [a slow cooking stew made for Sabbath lunch, kept warm overnight at the bakery] to the baker's oven. Now they are washing the children's hair – in the wash tub. The child wriggles out from the mother's hands. They scream and cry, their eyes burning from the lather. Thick combs are used on the children's hair – always one can find there…

Calmly and leisurely Jewish daughters wash their hair. (A remedy for the hair is rainwater.) The mothers braid their daughters' hair with love. In the houses it is sparkling clean. Old and young – everyone is ready to welcome the Sabbath.

One after another the Sabbath candles are lit in the houses, in some there are silver candlesticks, in others brass and some are only a pair of potatoes!…

Mothers with scarves and shawls on their heads bless the Sabbath candles and whisper a quiet prayer. With a tremor in the heart, with a tear in the eye, they accompany the men and children to the botei medroshim [houses of study].

Friday night

Barely waiting for the end of the Sabbath dinner, the Krinki youth stream in from all corners of the shtetl to the market place. In couples and in groups they walk around - make a half turn at the watchman's house and from Chaikl's brick house return to the watchman's house. There is loud talking, yelling and laughter. The market place bubbled with happiness. At the edge of the sidewalk stand "speakers". They direct discussions. All of them defend their positions with fervor…

A house (Yosel Fonte's) in the Krinik market place

Little by little the people at the market place scatter. Couples and groups go off to Mill Street in Viryian's courtyard, some go off on the side streets and on balconies. Most of them walk down Shishlevitzer Street, through Chestnut Tree Alley at the "hospital", past the "povshekhneh". They are already at "Yente's woods" that is as large as a yawn, but dear and is embedded in the hearts of every Krinker.

Songs resound from everywhere in the woods. Who is able to sing as beautifully as the Krinker youth? Krinkers sang with zest and feeling. Somebody started a melody a second joined in and took the second part. And here comes a third, a fourth to sing and the harmony echoes around:

> "The red tomorrow in front of
> us, the young guard of the proletariat…" –
> sings a group from "Tzukunft" the youth from the "Bund"
> "From Warsaw to Paris
> From London to Canton –
> Moscow has sent out a red flag…" –

Sings Krinker revolutionary youth about their belief in a new, free world…

From a corner of the woods is heard a beautiful, tender girl's voice singing a Hebrew song that was interrupted by a stormy "hora" [Zionist folk dance, danced in a circle], danced by the young Krinki pioneer youth.

[Page 185]

Bundists, Communists, Zionists were singing. Different songs and lyrics, but they were all united as a wonderful tribe of Krinki youth who fought for and believed in a better tomorrow in a more beautiful world…

Protected by the dark night, couples cuddle together weaving dreams. The trees in "Yente's woods" imbibed a lot of sweet secrets.

Late at night, tired and with happy faces, they return home. They steal quietly in the house, not to wake up their sleeping parents.

A Sabbath quietness spreads over the shtetl.

Baruch Vladek Visits The "Eternal Light"

Daniel Charney

(The prominent journalist and noted leader of the Jewish Workers Movement, first in Russia (in the Zionist Socialists, then in the "Bund") and later in America – B. Vladek (Baruch Nachman Charney) – once sat in prison together with the Krinker "Eternal Light" (Abraham Shmuel Zutz). They became very good comrades there. Visiting Poland in August 1936, Vladek traveled to Krynki, with his brother the poet Daniel Charney, especially to visit his one time prison mate.)

In the morning the entire Krynki "Bund" gathered at the library with the "Eternal Light" and waited and waited until they decided to go to the highway to meet us. In front were two young women from the public school with two large bouquets of flowers from the Krinki "Bund" and from the library. Between the young women was blind Abraham Shmuel. Behind them marched the entire "Bund" from the shtetl, large and small.

That Sunday was a fair day in Krynki with all the Jewish population outside. When the people saw the curious procession, lead by the blind "Eternal Light" with two young women carrying bouquets, all the idlers in the shtetl began joining the procession and the highway was soon black with people…

When the peasants at the market place saw that among the "Zhids" a large "movement" was taking place, they immediately began to harness their horses to the wagons and quickly left the shtetl. The market place emptied in a matter of minutes. Then the storekeepers and traders also closed their businesses and went to meet the famous "American" (Vladek).

When our machine was a couple of kilometers from Krynki, the highway was already besieged with people. We were surrounded on all sides by the Krynki welcoming committee, but not one of them knew Vladek personally besides the totally blind Abraham Shmuel Zutz.

"Bund" committee, "Tzukunft" and "Skif" 1937

[Page 186]

But Vladek recognized him and after the representative of the Krynki "Bund" had managed to start his welcoming speech, Vladek threw himself on Abraham Shmuel and both embraced and kissed for a long time until they began to cry.

This meeting in the middle of the highway touched us deeply and nobody's eyes were dry.

I was deeply moved by the moment when Abraham Shmuel used his finger "to see" by moving it all around Vladek's face, as if he wanted to "see" how much Vladek had aged during the several dozen years they had not seen each other.

Later, after the official welcome in the only hotel in Krynki, we went to take a look at the library where Abraham Shmuel blindly filled the position of librarian.

That Sunday the library was full of young people who came to borrow books. In truth they only wanted to have a look at the guest from America…

It was really marvelous how blind Abraham Shmuel quickly got hold of the right book that he had been asked for, by using his finger. He ran it over the spine of the books, like a proficient musician over a piano keyboard.

Here is Peretz's "Popular History", here Sholem Ash's "Shtetl", here Sholom Aleichem's "Tevye the Dairyman", here is Maxim Gorki's "Mother" and here is Dostoeyevsky's "Crime and Punishment".

During the time we spent in the children's library, Abraham Shmuel did not make any mistakes getting a book. He "read" the depressed letters and numbers with his finger from the spines of the books, like a sighted person.

The "Skif"

Hershel Zakheim

With Hitler coming to power in 1933, throughout all of Poland there was a heavy Fascist cloud. The Jewish population was very disturbed and every day brought new extremes. The circumstances made it necessary to stand up and oppose the hooligans. All the youth were mobilized in due course and the time came when even the young children were organized. Krynki also created a "Skif" [Socialist Children's Union]. The first members were older students in the secular Jewish school and "Bundist" children. The first speakers in the circles of "Skif" were Tanya Gotlieb, Sorala Gabeh and the teacher Rosenberg. They lectured on the history of the "Bund", the 1905 Revolution and the romantic heroic story of Hirsch Lekert, the favorite theme in all the circles. The "Skif" idea also intruded among the students in the "Public Heder" and the Yeshiva.

The members of the Skif committee were quickly taught so they could lead the circles on their own and take on the job of enlightening poor children. The young activists first searched in the library for the necessary material and then the themes were properly presented at the circles. Very often "living" newspapers were arranged, written and read by the participants, as well as "academicians" and lecturers. "Discussion evenings" were held with opponents from the youth organizations "Freiheit" [Poalei Youth Organization] and when "Merikz" [center] youth held discussion evenings, our speakers took part.

More youth and children joined the ranks of "Skif" after the pogrom in Pshitik, especially after the protest strike against the Polish anti-Semitic pro-fascist government, a strike that was proclaimed throughout Poland on Tuesday the 17th of May 1936 by the central committee of the Bund and the trade unions. I remember that Monday the 16th, in the evening, the order arrived from the central committee in Warsaw to call the general strike and to mobilize everyone, Jews as well as sympathizing Christians, in a mass demonstration. An urgent meeting was called by the Krynki "Bund" committee at Abraham Shmuel Zitz's room, together with the delegates from "Tzukunft" and "Skif" and very quickly, in the space of several hours, everything was organized.

[Page 187]

The next day, early in the morning the Skifists were the first ones at the market place stores and booths to tell everyone they must stay closed. There was a complete strike and it encouraged the Jews to fight for their rights as citizens and to stand up against the anti-Semitic hooligans.

The Krynki Skifists all took part in the Bundist "press days" by distributing the party's central organ, the "New People's Newspaper". The Skifist strikers even received a mention in Dubnov-Erlichs book "Der Garber un Bershter Bund" [The Tanner and Brush Bund"].

Bund "Press Committee"

An outing of the Krynki Skif

The Sholker forest during the summer became the property of the "Skif." With singing in nature's lap, we would spend from morning until night there – eating, singing and laughing among comrades. Later we would stand in rows, well disciplined, and after shouting "Khavershaft!" [comradeship!] - we would march back home.

The bloody Nazis did away with them and their dreams along with all our brothers.

From The Krinki "Hakhalutz"

Shmuel Herbarem-Krupnik

In 1924 the Krinki "Hakhalutz" [Zionist pioneer movement, part of Poalei Zion, supporters of socialist education] already numbered over one hundred comrades. Some of them went to "Hakhshore" [preparatory training for prospective agricultural emigrants to Israel] and some learned an appropriate trade for Israel. At that time this was not an easy thing: parents were strict – on no account would they consent to this. They would not allow their sons and daughters to make aliyah [immigrate to Israel] to Israel to be day laborers or artisans. But the comrades overcame all the obstacles, not paying any attention to their parents. Some received slaps from their fathers and were literally from the house for wanting to leave their parents and for going to Hakhshore without their consent.

[Page 188]

At that time "we were scratching our heads", trying to find other ways to increase the revenue of the "Hakhalutz fund" in Poland, besides through our own helpers and carrying out endless "Bliml-Teg" [fund-raising days], which we ordered in the shtetl, for the good of the fund. Therefore we began sawing wood for local households and then also took it on as an "enterprise" for the town electric works. For us this was quite a transformation – to do such physical work that previously only village gentiles would do for Jewish orders. You should have seen the welcome our parents gave us when we returned home from doing such work!

Hakhalutz 25 April 1925

Just before Passover we sent our comrades to work in the "warehouses" (matzah "contracts") and dedicated the entire income to the "Hakhalutz fund". And the same in 1925 when we undertook to arrange a new enterprise; to kosher utensils for Passover. We even received a special "permit" from the town rabbi, Rabbi Khezekiah Mishkovski who even honored us with a blessing for prosperity.

That year "Hakhalutz" opened a carpentry shop, overcoming the disturbances and hindrances on the part of the parents and local carpenters. The carpentry shop developed very quickly and well. We established a large clientele, among them Rabbi Mishkovski who was interested in our achievement and believed in our work and our courage.

A Summary

That was how the Krinki "Hakhalutz" literally carried out its activities in the coming years, especially in the 1930's. One after the other comrades went to the Hakhshore kibbutzim [large collective farms] to be trained in agriculture and immigrated to Israel – to build and restore it – by themselves – and to defend and to bring into existence the land of Israel as an independent country for generations. And today the number of Krinki families in our country is two hundred and fifty, so may they increase!

[Page 189]

Memorable Characters of Old Krynki

From the second half of the 19ᵗʰ century

Translated by Hadas Eyal

My memories

Rabbi David Moreni – A Landlord from Those Days

Yechiel Kotik

Rabbi David Moreni was the son–in–law of Rabbi Israel Salanter, the founder of the "Musar (Ethical) Movement". Rabbi David was a powerful landlord and schnapps dealer, a smart diligent Jewish scholar but hot–tempered. Hashem protect us from his anger! If he felt someone offended his honor he would attack the person with mighty insults. That said, he was also easy to appease and when he forgave, he hugged and kissed.

His office was always bustling with people and you would find all the Krynki bartenders there, as well as Jews from distant villages. Not far from Krynki was a large schnapps brewery that also belonged to a Jew. The mover and shaker there was his wife Yente – a typical 'Eshet Chail' (i.e., capable woman, woman of valor), beautiful and very smart, whose husband served as a fifth wheel to her wagon. Nobody knew him and the factory ran under her name. Some didn't even know she was married. The husband was not at all a simple person, he was educated and knowledgeable but she was the one who "wore the pants." Even when he sat in the office, no one spoke to him about business.

Yente held many leased properties which she managed, including two schnapps breweries. She was forced to sell her merchandise wholesale because the bartenders preferred to trade with Moreni, who had integrity and was loyal to his word. He never changed the price even if the market value increased or decreased. Although people were often burned by his hasty scorching tongue followed soon after by a plead to be forgiven, his integrity was a magnetic gravitational force. Even bartenders who were thrown out of his office for unpaid debt and went to buy directly from Yente, eventually returned to him.

I also bought from him. One day an incident between us sent him on an attack, publicly shaming and scorning me, with G–d help us from such insults. I left before Rabbi David had time to catch and placate me as he usually did. I was saddened by the event, especially because I needed to buy from Yente whose schnapps was lower quality and more expensive.

Many in town told me Rabbi David's heart is heavy for insulting me the way he did and that he yearns to make amends to the extent of announcing a fair money reward to whomever succeeds in bringing me there so he could apologize. After some consideration I decided to write him a letter in Hebrew (my weapon those days) which I carried with me ready for the right moment. When I happened to drive my carriage past Rabbi David's office and saw him talking with someone at the gate, I waved the letter at him from afar. He ran to me, took the letter, opened it, began reading, became emotional to the point of tearfully hugging and kissing me begging my forgiveness. I forgave him. By and by he pulled my horse through the gate leading me himself to his office for all to see how he is reconciling with me.

And so it was. He ordered a bottle of old schnapps, pastry and cookies, and with a "L'Chaim!" – we kissed. Since then we "fell in love" and connected in a true friendship.

The Lifesaving Act of Rabbi Yossaleh

Yishai Dryzik

My teacher and grandfather Rabbi Yossef known as Rabbi Yossaleh HaTsadik, may he rest in peace, was a rabbi in Krynki. On his grave site was a tent into which people came to insert wish–notes. Many tales and stories about him were told in our family and in town.

[Page 190]

So it was also told that in his wartime youth, it happened that a Cossack attacked several Jewish Krynki women who ran for refuge in the ezrat–nashim (women's section) on the second floor of the beit–midrash. There appeared, heaven sent, the young prodigy Yossef who saved them from the impure criminal hands: with the full power of his momentum he threw the Cossack through the top floor window onto the sidewalk below. The thug dropped, crashed and died.

Although he clearly saved the women's life and honor ('pikuach–nefesh'), Rabbi Yossef declared a self–imposed punishment of daily cleansing 'tvilah' ritual in the town stream, winter and summer. And so he persisted in the heat and cold until suffering a paralysis from which he did not recover the rest of his holy life.

Kopel Zalkin – Pioneer Krynki Tanner

Y. G. Steinsapir

Kopel Zalkin, the first tanning industrialist in Krynki as well as in Bialystok and its surroundings, was born in the early 1840s in Yanova near Sokolka where his father Shaymeh (Shamai) tanned sheep skin in the primitive method that was customary in those days – a pit dug in a small shed. Shaymeh manufactured leather called "sapian," earning him the nickname Shaymeh "sapianik" which was passed on to the young Kopel.

Kopel settled in Krynki and married a local girl. He began using the same primitive tanning methods on cattle skin (instead of the sheep skin) to make villagers' shoe soles. When he heard that German craftsmen developed excellent new methods to manufacture top quality products, he set out yonder, returning with the German expert Gustav Moerman.

Blessed with energy and initiative, Kopel set out to improve his tannery and expand the variety of products. His father and extended family moved to Krynki to unite forces. Kopel learned the secrets of processing "Hamburgian" skin (also known as "Spiegel" skin) and began, for the first time in this region, to manufacture this merchandise which was immeasurably more profitable.

Every week Zalkin's horse–led carriages would leave Krynki loaded with his goods on route to Bialystok and from there – worldwide. This is how Kopel Zalkin began in Krynki, continued later on a much bigger scale in Bialystok, and became very rich.

In Bialystok he became absorbed with the idea of Zionism (Chibat–Zion) and joined a group of wealthy Jews who dreamt of Aliya to Eretz Israel and settling there. Zalkin decided to move his factory and craftsmen to Israel. At the end of the 1880s he and his wife travelled there, combed the country far and wide for nine months but eventually returned, disappointed. 'There is no customer in Eretz–Israel at this time for whom to manufacture leather, because the Arabs walk barefoot and do not need shoes' is what Zalkin explained to those who wondered about his return to the diaspora.

Yankel – My Teacher and Grandfather

Moshe Weinberg (Pinkas)

I knew two blind people during my childhood in Krynki: Itche and my grandfather Yankel whom I would like to write about. A carpenter–builder, he fell from a scaffold, sustained a head injury and became blind. He sold his house which was close to the beit–midrash to Michl the tailor under the condition that he be given a room in which to live for the rest of his life so he could walk independently to the beit–midrash.

Every morning before leaving for prayer he would leave a bowl of milk for the cat who regularly visited him. In the same way my grandfather never forgot to bless "hamotsi" on his bread, never did he forget to whisper "and his mercy over all his works" as he poured the milk into the cat's bowl. He could recite the entire Mishna – correctly engraved in his brain – and I was to follow him with the script for his fear of omitting or changing any detail.

[Page 191]

I also fondly remember Yodel Bratchkobs who regularly read the Hebrew–language weekly newspaper Hatzefira. He told my grandfather that surgeons in Petersburg perform operations to restore the eyesight of blind people. Yodel suggested that my grandfather write his two daughters in America to send him money for such surgery. To this my grandfather replied, "No, Yodel, I have no wish to re–open my eyes and sin again!"

And so he continued his God–fearing life. He made Aliya in 1903, as a blind person, to the holy–land, where he passed away and was buried in Jerusalem.

A few words about Rabbi Michl Belarcher, who was killed by the preying Nazi teeth with all Krynki kdoshim (holy ones). He was a kindhearted Jew, remorseful each time he was forced to slightly slap the cheek of an unruly student. He would beg his wife who couldn't hold her tongue: "In faith Rachel–Leah, why do you curse others? You'd be better off blessing yourself!". Indeed, he was often successful in calming his wife.

Two characters:
Pinchas the Builder & Rabbi Shmuel Tentser

Abraham Miller

Pinchas the Builder

Pinchas the builder was an exceptional expert. His craft in laying building foundations of unhewn rough stone was excellent quality and amazingly beautiful. The vaulted basements he installed had a good reputation throughout the entire Krynki region and no fire blaze could destroy them.

Once when Pinchas was plastering the front of the great synagogue, he fell off the scaffolding and remained standing on his feet. On winter days he visited Jewish communities as a messenger from Israel dressed as a Chassidic leader with a "Streimel" (a festive fur hat). He was a truly handsome Jew – without blemish.

Rabbi Shmuel Tentser

Rabbi Shmuel Tentser was my first teacher ('melamed'). While people sipped drinks and sang zmirot (Jewish hymns) around Shabbat and holiday meal tables, Rabbi Shmuel ran between the town homes in the worst weather and deepest mud to insure that every poor person had a Shabbat and holiday meal. Only after he took care of all those in need would he turn to set his own home table. He was also an excellent melamed of young children who loved him and carry his memory deep in their hearts.

Rabbi Menachem Mendel
Devoted his life to the poor and the distressed

Study Group Teachers

Berl Zakon

Rabbi Moshe Yehoshua, the potter, studied day and night. He also taught Torah in study groups. Despite being a poor Jew in a town of rich industrialists, he held all of Krynki's money for safekeeping because everyone trusted him.

His wife was the breadwinner, selling pots in the market. The only time Rabbi Moshe Yehoshua would leave the beit–midrash was to help his wife sell pots on market day. When a farmer would haggle excessively, offering a price too low, he would answer: "You mean you don't want the pot? That's fine!"

When he passed away, Velvel the "Cavasnik" (who fermented the Cavas beverage) and Bezalel the tailor took over teaching the study groups. Bezalel studied very little in his youth and didn't know much but, like Rabbi Akiva, he devoted himself to years of torah study.

[Page 192]

Yehuda Vilensky
Distinguished landlord

The Polish Doctor

D. Selkoff

Pan Rajchkovski was the doctor in Krynki of the days I remember. He was a tall Christian with a thick Polish mustache under a thick pink nose. No one knew his age. The elderly Jews considered him an expert but hoped they would never need him. The "Pan–Doctor" did not know the meaning of haste and was always slow.

On Shabbat, he would stroll the Jews' alleys to visit patients. The boys would welcome him with a proper "Shabbat tova" removing their hats in respect. He would wish them "Shabbat shalom" and amicably ruffle their hair. For a house call he was paid 30 cents but he would not ask it of them if he saw a patient who could not pay even that amount. Moreover, there were cheerful tales of chicken and wine that he gifted the poor women who just delivered babies. The husbands would salivate at these stories convinced the "Pan–Doctor" is a righteous Gentile that is destined for an honorable place in heaven.

Actually, the Krynki community paid him 100 Rubles a year for his 'free' visits to the poor. If at the end of the year the public committee claimed they had no money for the doctor, trouble began. The poor banged for hours on the doctor's locked door; the women would yell and cry that their daughters are in labor and must be saved. Unmoved, the doctor sent them to the public committee for payment of the debt. Some ran to the Rabbi, others to public officials. When all else failed everyone reverted to the most efficient Jewish ammunition over generations: delaying the Shabbat prayer and Torah reading by standing–put on the Bimah until the Rabbi and landlords promised to settle the balance with the "Pan–Doctor."

This type of mayhem would usually erupt on wintery days when the dampness and mildew already spread in the tiny dismal shacks of the poor and some of their ailments could no longer be cured. The evening after delaying the prayer, the "Pan–Doctor" resumed his visits to the poor, serenely humming a polish song, his galoshes slushing in the mud.

Doctor Pan Rajchkovski was not seen in town after he was drafted in World War I. It is told that he died in Russia, lonely and derelict. Whether he indeed found a place in heaven, remains unknown.

Krinik In The Past - From The Distant Past

[Page 193]

Krinik In The Past · From The Distant Past

Translated by Judie Goldstein

From my Contact with Krynik and Krynkers[1]

Yehazkel Katyk

Krynker Thieves

From Grodno I would bring to my *kretchma* [inn] sweet liquor, and from Krynik – mead and wine that Yochbed the widow would make and was famous for throughout the province.

When I arrived for the first time in Krynik, I drove up to Yochbed the wine tavern keeper's. It was a nice day. I tied up the horse to the rail in front of the window of the large house opposite the stores, in the middle of the market place – I went into the house. When I looked out the window a while later, I saw the horse standing and the wagon separated from him: the "coupling bolt" had been pulled out.

I ran around asking who had taken out the "coupler" from the wagon, such a strange thing to do – I discussed this with Yochebed's sons and decided that it is really unimportant.

The story is: There were in Krynik two brothers who were the leaders of all the thieves in the area: They were called the "Akhim" and all the merchants, villagers, land holders, dairy farmers and tenant farmers had to absolutely deal with the "Akhim" and reward them. They also gave them respect and when the "Akhim" drove around the district they were received with great respect everywhere. One must deal with them and then one is safe from thefts.

So as soon as the thieves see that there is an understanding with the "Akhim" – they will return it; and so as I am a newcomer, they hinted that I must deal with the leaders and make it seem like a "treat."

I was frightened and astonished: That means, I must deal with thieves and look them in the face and then shake hands? I knew that Yochbed's sons were smart and honest people and would not lead me down the garden path.

Still, it was for me to accomplish, to make the acquaintance of the master thieves and buying a new coupling bolt, I rode back home in peace.

But my friend advised me that I must not rebel against the "Akhim": The District Police Commandant and the Assessor, a government official, cannot protect me from the gang of thieves. Since I live in a *kretchma*, alone on a highway, I must get along with them and when they come I should receive them well, give them and their horses food, drink and so forth.

David Moreynu

In Krynik I would buy liquor from *Reb* David Moreynu, one of the *gaon* [sage] *Reb* Israel Salanter's sons-in-law. He owned the Krynki courtyard with the distillery. He was a rich man with eighty thousand rubles, a Jew, scholarly, smart, but an angry man – God should observe! He offended everybody but it seemed to him that he was the one attacked with the greatest abuse.

[Page 194]

But he was capable of behaving decently: his anger would soon pass and he would immediately ask this person's forgiveness, even a frivolous person. This must have cost him dearly. Each one had to say that he was forgiven and then he would kiss the person.

In Moreynu's office there were always a lot of people, all Krynki tavern keepers and inhabitants of the furthest villages. Near Krynik a *verst* [Russian measure of distance, about 2/3 of a mile] or two, was an even larger distillery that also belonged to a Jew. The wife Yenta ran the entire business – a clever, active woman, very pretty and smart. Her husband was a fifth wheel on the wagon. Nobody knew anything about him and the distillery was in her name. There were some people who did not even know that she had a husband. He was a tolerable man, a teacher, somewhat of a scholar; but she was such a strong woman "a woman in pants". When he was sitting in the office nobody spoke to him about the business.

She owned a lot of courtyards and two distilleries and ran it all alone. But her liquor she had to sell wholesale, not retail, to the tavern keepers from the surrounding villages – because everyone preferred to deal with *Reb* David Mareynu because of his honesty and his word was iron. He bought, then sold, and it was expensive, but he never went back on his word.

Truth be told, he often made people suffer because of his angry tongue, his inclination to hate. And then he would beg forgiveness. He could never entirely remove the insult from the hearts of his victims; only his honesty, his honesty! It attracted everyone even the tavern keepers who owed him money and wanted to pay. They would buy liquor at Yenta's, but in the end they would return to him, pay what they owed and do business with him again. They were drawn to him like a magnet.

I bought liquor from Moreynu regularly. But once he attacked me suddenly with such abuse that God should have pity (I had delivered too much in a message). The room was full of people and I was too embarrassed to raise my eyes. I quickly left and *Reb* David was not able to grab me and beg my forgiveness, as was his habit. I was deeply vexed by this story with Moreynu, especially because now I had to go to Yenta's and her liquor was inferior and more expensive.

In the city people told me that *Reb* David was eating his heart out because of the story with me, that he had insulted me and wants to give twenty-five rubles. They should bring me to him so that he can beg my pardon and make peace. I had to think about it and wrote him a letter in Hebrew (my weapon at that time). I drive by once and see *Reb* David with a Jew near the gate, at the road. I get down to give him the letter. I show it to him from a distance. He runs, takes it in his hand, opens it and begins to read. Soon after beginning the letter he was so moved that he grabbed and kissed me and begged me, with tears in his eyes, to forgive him; he did not know me, was confused, disturbed, and so on. I forgave him and then he pulls the horse's bridle and through the gate. He must drive me to the office so that everyone can see he asked my forgiveness.

And so that is what he did. Then he took out a bottle of old liquor, fifteen years old, with cake and cookies and said "*l'chaim*". We kissed each other. In the past, this is how a very rich man conducted himself.

From then on *Reb* David Moreynu "was enamored" of me and between us there was a kind of love.

[Page 195]

Yosel Lieder

Yosel Lieder owned the Krynki *korobke*[2] [meat tax], and when people said this word, it made their blood run cold. Yosel was the worst of the murderous meat tax holders.

When he came to take the meat inventory, to be sure that nothing was stolen from the meat tax, he was worse than the auditors. When he found meat at somebody's, he would take from the house various articles as a pledge so that they would remunerate him well. He was not afraid of the Assessor or the Police Commandant because they trembled before him, mainly because of the information he had. He was even able to denounce a Governor, about whom he knew something. He was a ruler and no functionary was going to stop him. He would take things like liquor. What could you do?

Yosel also owned a distillery and stole the excise tax, as much as he wanted, and nobody could do anything about it.

The city of Krynik held a large trial. It seemed that somebody was buried without a permit and the corpse should have been inspected. Twelve men, the best of the sextons, and from the Burial Society with Yosel in the lead, should have been banished to Siberia.

The district judge arrived in Krynik for the trial and the entire city was upset. They were afraid of one witness, a gravedigger. According to him he had taken part in the guilty act. To make off with him was difficult because the police had already detained him and were watching him carefully.

When it came time for the gravedigger to testify, everybody shook. Would he bring misfortune to everyone? Yosel Lieder was frightfully red and excited. Suddenly he began to scream with a terrible voice and grabbing his teeth:

"Rubin escape, Rubin excape, escape, escape…!"

The Chairman asked what he was screaming about. Yosel started to stutter and pressed his hands to his mouth and screamed like a wild animal" "Oy my teeth! Rubin escape! My teeth, not for you to think…Rubin escape… my teeth I cannot endure this…Rubin escape…escape, escape, escape."

Seeing a man in pain with a toothache, people ran to get a remedy, and Rubin the gravedigger, who had understood the meaning of the screams, had quickly extricated himself. When Yosel, who was smart and tricky, noticed Rubin he began his terrible screaming. When he saw that the danger was over, that Rubin had escaped – he took his hands from his mouth and calmly said:
"It is better now".

And in this way everybody was freed. The important witness, the one who had done the guilty deed, was missing

Reb Yosele Hatzadik
(what people said)

Issy Drayzik

My great-grandfather, *Reb* Yosele *HaTzadik* [the pious man], peace to his memory, was the Rabbi in Krynki and on his grave stood a structure, where believers would put notes with petitions.

In the family and in the shtetl several stories and legends were told about him, for example, that in his younger years, during wartime, it happened that a Cossack attacked Jewish women in the synagogue, in the women's section, where they were hiding. There arrived, as if sent from heaven, the young genius Yosef and saved them from the dirty murderer's hands. He threw the Cossack through the window and he died from the fall. Not taking into consideration that lives had been at stake as well as the honor of the Jewish women, *Reb* Yosef *HaTzadik* voluntarily took on the punishment of immersing himself every day, summer and winter, in the city river. For years the *Tzadik* behaved in this manner, immersing himself during the heat and the cold until he became paralyzed and remained lame until the end of his life.

[Page 196]

Before his marriage to the woman who was to be his *rebetzin* [the rabbi's wife], after she had agreed to the marriage, he sent her questions pertaining to her health in regards to her ability to have children. *Reb* Yosef gave her to understand that she would give birth to ten sons and a daughter; and so it was.

It was further said that before the *Tzadik* died he blessed the *rebetzin* with a living and he confided in her that in the dresser there was money for her to take to live on. For years the *rebetzin* did this and the gold coins that were lying there never ran out. One day a Jew asked the *rebetzin* the question of how she made her living, and she told him about the blessing from the *Tzadik* and about the pair of gold coins that never ran out. However, soon after they did run out.

With the last gold coins the *rebetzin* bought flour and wood and baked bread. In this way she renewed the miracle and the wood and the flour never ran out. The *rebetzin* had once again a living. But another time the *rebetzin* spoke about how she made a living – to a good friend who wanted to know. This time she said her source of income absolutely never ran out.

From the Period of Krynker Revolutionaries

Yosel Cohen

I See Everything Again

A.

Nights past come towards me,
Memories bring me forgotten days.
I remember as if today, as kids we would –
Start fights with children from Mill Street.

I remember as if today the "*Kavkazer*[3]" revolutionaries:
Noisy and chaotic, with hot blood flowing,
Drilling like soldiers we were lead by
The hero of my childhood – Yankl Kotyut.

His face burned by the sun,
With bare feet, already without a color,
He would stop to remind us
"*Kavkazer*" heroism is without limit.

During the day he would lead us comrades in battles
Against youngsters from Mill Street with Feyvel Shnantz;
In the evening he showed us, how at night
The demons dance in the synagogue.

We see corpses, they are studying Torah there –
Our blood turns cold with the rustle of a page;
Yankel Kotyut laughs and drives away our fear:
He dares, as befits a "*Kavkazer*" revolutionary.

B.

Krynik – difficult, men did not catch its name,
But for me, cozy and close:
There is the market place, the row of stores,
There Jews carry on *Shabes* [the Sabbath] the *cholent* [slow cooking stew].

[Page 197]

From very far away I see the images,
My own past life is in them,
I sense the odor of bear paws and horse hides
As sure as the smell of hay wet with dew.

There is my grandfather *Reb* Yankl-Bunim,
He whirls through the streets and shtetl;
Writing the *pinkus* [book in which shtetl events of importance were recorded]
And who would win the great prize, an entry by him.

His smart blue eyes look at me,
His deep voice is heard far away:
It is not true that everything has flown away
I see a renewal of what used to be.

C.

Standing in front of me are the Krynker tanners
Who dreamed of revolution, a workers' government
Played in Crime and Punishment on the Sabbath,
Cracked kernels Friday night.

I see the fighters, the revolutionaries,
Wanting to turn the whole world upside down,
Krynik flooded with a multitude of soldiers,
My mother, on the balcony, concealing money.

From the churches the bells ring
In haste young girls run with stones in pinafores
To be revolutionaries with fiery songs:
"Come, sisters and brothers, shorten Nikolai's years!"

I see them together, I see every one of them:
Shlomo'ke Dubrover, Azriel the Fibber,
They whisper, I hear: "In Virian's forest -
Brothers and sisters now we have a date".

I even remember everyone's face,
The passing years did not make them fade,
Nights they come to me always in a dream,
Memories like a fire glowing in the distance.

My First Master

A. M. Weinberg (Meshal Pinkus)

I remember it, as it happened that afternoon: the moment that was to be the luckiest for me and by the same token, the saddest for my dear mother. I came home from the Volkovisker yeshiva with the idea of stopping my studies and taking up a trade.

On hearing my decision, my dear mother's eyes ran with tears and she did not say one word. She moved off to a corner and had a good cry. For her this meant that her hopes were ruined. She had three sons and she had taken good care of all of them, so that they should become great men. She believed that she would live to see one of them with a *shtreymel* [fur hat worn by Orthodox Jews] on his head and taking up a rabbi's chair, if not in a large city, then in a small shtetl in our area. Only it turned out entirely differently: one after the other they went off on dangerous roads – on roads that lead, according to her, to the nether world.

Now she has only her last son and here again is the same trouble: the devil had again mixed in and torn her last child from the righteous path.

For me it was the luckiest moment of my life: I would no longer be an idler, a "parasite" or a hypocrite because my desire to study and, for the most part, my belief had been lost some time ago. For me this meant that I could now go and be a member of the large working family and also help overturn the present evil order because I was already by then, as it is said, a little caught up in the story.

[Page 198]

There only remained for me to find a place where I could start to learn a trade. I had not thought of any work other than tanning because this was the main occupation in our shtetl. It was as if – I wanted very much to get a job where the master would be, as it is said, "one of ours" and a little bit friendly, and advise me the right road to take and the secrets of the trade.

As luck would have it, a young man who frequented our house was a master and also "one of us," as I wanted. He would come around it seems, to see my sister. So, we spoke to him about taking me on to study as a hide preparer. That means, that "we" was really my sister and I only listened. He gave me a looking over and announced that he would take me on as a student and would pay me two rubles a week.

It seemed reasonable to me and I was in seventh heaven: I would become a hide preparer, under a master, my own person and eventually a member of the revolutionary party, this former yeshiva student.

When I arrived at the factory in the morning, with the first look that my master had of me, already he was not as friendly as he had been at the house. His first greeting, out loud: "Good morning, *Rav* Zelman Sender!" (The name of the Krynki rabbi at that time was Zelman Sender). That made it clear that this was not going to be easy. In later years I began to understand that the bad relationship between us was a result of a misunderstanding. He was a revolutionary, a free thinker and a dedicated fighter against everything that had to do with religion and its various symbols. In me he still saw the yeshiva student. So, he already understood that it would be a sort of good deed to laugh at me a little. I saw the embodiment of the wicked capitalist in my master and thought it was my holy duty to go against him in every way.

After the first welcome he ordered me to clean up and sweep the factory. I got down to work without much enthusiasm and it took longer to do than it should have taken. Therefore he scolded me with a "*Rav* Zelman Sender, move a little faster!"

When I was finished cleaning – I was ordered to mix the "rutcher." This meant to mix the standing water with whetstones, with which one would grind the hair from the hide. It was enough to give it a little mix, in order to spread an odor that was impossible to endure. At first I did not understand that he only meant to make fun of me, but as I realized he was up to one of his "tricks," I began mixing as if I would rather perish than give in to my enemy. Soon the stench spread throughout the entire factory, and the previous grins on the lips of my master and the other workers were transformed into grimaces and they all grabbed their noses. But I heartily continued mixing as if it made no difference to me, until my master ran to me and ordered me to stop. I played innocent and remarked that I had not finished the mixing. That was my first clash with my master.

[Page 199]

Several days later, I hung the hides to dry. The rope was very high and even though I was one of the tallest, it was very difficult for me to reach the rope. I climbed onto boxes and crates, in order to be able to hang the hides. But my master had to notice that a hide had fallen down. So, he screams at me – "What are you doing? Do not step on the hide!" I grabbed it from the box and stepped on the hide and my master turned away grinding his teeth.

Another time I remember was when I was carrying in a tub a little degraded material from one pot to another. I was not paying attention to carrying it straight and with two hands. I carried it with one hand and a little crooked and there was a little bit on the bottom. This my master noticed. He screamed at me: "Zelman Sender, pour it out!" So, what did he think I was doing? I got rid of it just fine. When he went to have his teeth filled, the fillings were sure to fall out because he ground his teeth so hard. I am sure, that only the thought that he had to meet my sister saved me from a slap in the face because then I truly deserved it.

Who knows how long we would have managed in future years if Judel Volkovisker had not arrived in Krynik to do organizational work for the "Bund". We had to change his job to a place in a small factory where the eyes of the police would not be on him. The situation occurred where I worked and I changed my job according to instructions from the "Bund" – this was the first good piece of work that the Krynki "Bund" had, according to me, carried out.

My Journeys to Krynik

Sam Levin

My first trip to Krynik was made at the beginning of 1890 when I was still in grade school in Horodok. I was then sent to Krynik as a representative of my younger sisters and brothers, to get hazelnuts to play with during the latter days of Passover.

I began the voyage during the Passover holiday with the Krynker driver, Chaim Fesl, who would drive passengers from Horodok to Krynik. Chaim was a short man with a fat stomach around which would always be tied a rainbow colored, wide belt that fit his stomach well.

He seated his passengers according to rank and lineage, some in the back end, others on sacks of oats mixed with chopped straw, that were laid out in the foremost part of the wagon. He rolled into the wagon by putting one foot on the end of the axle and the other on the shaft and the journey began.

There was a noticeable scowl on his face when he looked at his passengers. There were too many women and children. Who would help him to push the wagon uphill or out of the mud on every road?

I made this trip, the first time in my life I traveled alone such a long way, sitting absorbed the entire time in my childish fantasies about the nuts my aunt would give me and how I would bring them back to my sisters and brothers at home.

Arriving at my aunt's, she began to ask about everybody in the entire family. I kept my hands in my pockets measuring them to see how many nuts would fit.

And so hour after hour passed and I continued to measure my pockets. I was embarrassed to ask and she did not offer. She gave me only a piece of *matzah* [unleavened bread] smeared with chicken fat, that in one bite was gone, because I was very hungry…As for my nuts, the result was none.

[Page 200]

My second journey to Krynik was from Bialystok ten years later. I was already a young man of twenty-one and had come a long way from my Aunt Deborah's hazelnuts. I was already carrying about ideas of freedom, sang revolutionary songs and was active in the *"Bund."*

After a secret meeting that Krynker revolutionaries in Bialystok had held (among them was Yankl Katchke, Shmulke Rubinstein, Hershl Pinkes, Shmulke Terkel and others), – it was decided to send me to Krynik with a certain task in mind.

I began the trip from a tavern that the Krynker wagon drivers used as their rest stop and their passengers would gather there.

The short ride took an entire night, and first thing in the morning we finally arrived in Krynik. I lodged with my aunt Henia, who received me in her usual friendly manner. She asked me questions without end, what, who, when – then prepared food and drink for a good meal. Later, in passing, she asked what had brought me to Krynik on a simple Wednesday.

When she heard about my secret mission, she sighed. "Yes child," she said, "I have already lived through this, my people taught me the Torah. So, God should help you and you should not be deceived because of your foolishness."

The Krynker revolutionaries received me in a hearty, brotherly manner and before my return to Bialystok they made a farewell party at Shoshke Zelman the kettle maker's house for me. All of the Krynker youth from the sisterhood and brotherhood were there, fiery speeches were given, and everyone from the choir sang revolutionary songs. It seemed as if the government throughout Russia already lay in the hands of the proletariat. They made fun of the Tsar, like at Purim with Haman.

I asked them if they were not in too much danger and they answered that as long as Abrahamel Fortze stood guard outside they were not afraid. He had, they said, a pair of healthy iron shoulders with steel fists that were sufficient to defend our revolutionaries when necessary. The evening ended without any problems.

The Attempted Assasination of a Manufacturer

Betzalel (Alter) Potchebutski / Nachum Anschel Knischynski

Acting on the propaganda against the work givers, that they were the main cause of the existing slavery of the people and the working class – several Krynker "revolutionaries" [from among the youngsters] organized the attempted assassination of Nachum Anschel Knishynski, then the richest man in the shtetl.

Nachum Anschel came from Kobrin, used to trade in Krynki, driving flour to the bakeries. Later he was the bookkeeper for the Krynker, David Moreynu. Some time later he opened a tannery in the shtetl and he built it up until he was the richest man in Krynki. His factory had the largest number of workers. The initiators of the attempt were Leybke Noskes and David Yankl the blond's.

[Page 201]

On a wintry Sabbath night, when everything was covered with snow and no stars could be seen, Nachum Anschel left the *besmedresh* [house of study] for home with several other men from the shtetl. There Yankl the blond's pressed the trigger of his revolver, a shot was heard and immediately after that Nachum Anschel was stabbed with a knife by one of two conspirators and wounded.

Leybke Noskes was arrested, but a short time later was freed thanks to the intervention and endeavors of Nachum Anschel. A gentile was discovered as part of the plot and arrested. He was also released thanks to Nachum Anschel.

There was another incident involving Nachum Anschel shortly after the assassination attempt. Three Krynker young men, Herschel the Mangy, Chaikel Mutz and Meyer Yankl Bunems stopped Nachum Anschel in the street and begged him for money. He talked to them while approaching his factory. There, he asked why they needed the money. They answered him and he told them he would return with the money. Meanwhile he went into a room and from there called his workers to help him. They grabbed the three comrades, gave them a beating and threw them out.

"Niomke Anarchist"
(As told by his older brother)

Lipa Friedman

When my brother Niomke joined the anarchist revolutionary movement he was only fifteen years old. One time his comrades in the Bialystok movement decided that he should throw a frightful bomb in Krynik. It was thrown from the balcony of the women's section of the synagogue and exploded with a loud crash but there was no damage. A policeman caught him and arrested him, sending him to jail in Grodno. There he was turned over to the district court.

The people, on whom Niomke threw the bomb, hired one of the best lawyers to defend him and were witnesses at the trial. They said that it was not Niomke who had thrown the bomb. Furthermore the lawyer had worked with my father about what he should say and encouraged him so that he would not be afraid of the prosecutor, even if he would be yelled at. The witnesses swore that Niomke was religious and went every day to pray at the synagogue. The judge wanted to free him. But the chairman asked Niomke what he had to say in his defense.

Niomke answered that he threw the bomb and that the witnesses defended him only because they were afraid that his brother would take revenge on them and then he screamed: "Long live the social revolution!" Because he was so young he would not receive the death penalty. He was only sixteen years old. His sentence was to be sent in penal servitude to Siberia.

Part of the way was on foot with a company of political prisoners who had been provided with revolvers, in secret, by their comrades and before the departure they put them in their packs. At a rest station where they were eating their evening bread, the political prisoners revolted and shot the convoy captain and two soldiers, and forced the other convoy soldiers to unlock their chains. First they ran and hid. Comrades had provided them with money so that they could escape abroad.

But Niomke did not want to take any money and did not agree to go abroad. Instead he achieved his goal. He traveled to Grodno and there stood near the gate of the prison waiting for the "official" to take revenge on him. Before, while Niomke was sitting in prison, a group of young girls were brought there. They had been arrested for a strike in the Grodno tobacco factory.

[Page 202]

One of them was a young girl who Niomke went around with. The above mentioned "official" ordered them beaten until their execution. Their cries were heard throughout the jail. Niomke had decided to take revenge on this cruel man at the first opportunity. And he did. When the official left the government office Niomke shot him. He tried to hide, but the police ran after him. He ran into a house and from there managed to shoot a policeman. But the police had alerted the firemen, in order to take him alive. He continued to shoot until he had only one bullet left and then he shot himself leaving behind a message: "I fought for freedom!"

Krynker "Revolutionaries" Who Went Abroad

Betzalel (Alter) Patchebutzki

Menachem Motl was known as one of the organizers of the "oaths" on a holy book and prayer shawls and phylacteries for those gathered in the forest the night before the first tanner's strike in Krynki in 1897. During the strike he ran away from the shtetl, later did his military service and then soon returned home, for the second strike.

Then one day he saw how a policeman beat a striker so he cracked opened the skull of the policeman. People were searching for him everywhere, but he had left the country and settled in Chicago. There he came to understand that the American reality was a far cry from his ideals and he took his life.

Moshe Berl was among the leaders of the first strike and was arrested during the second strike. For five days he was beaten and tortured. He left prison with damaged lungs. Then he traveled to London and there resumed his revolutionary activities as a follower of Peter Kropotkin.

Socialist Activities
of a Proletarian High School Student

Sarah Fel-Yellin

My parents were among the enlightened in Krynki and I would hear discussions at home about exploitation and the injustice of the rich men. My father was a tinsmith and indirectly was involved with the factories – he made tubes, lamps and lanterns for them.

I remember, as if it were today, the Revolt Day of January 1905. I was then barely ten years old, the last child, and my parents took me by the hand and we all went to the demonstration on *Schischlevitzer* Street, together with the raging population. Young men had confiscated weapons from the police, dressed up with "swords" over their civilian clothes and together with several young women revolutionaries led the march. They also carried banners with messages. The monopoly had been captured, bottles of liquor were tossed out and then they left for Yenta's courtyard.

This was a beautiful May outing, surrounded by a large park, a little further was the Garden of Eden for the poor – Yenta's forest, where every Sabbath the shtetl population created a colorful scene – Parents with children, with packages of food for the day. At the springs people would refresh themselves with a cold drink and fill their bottles. Those who had the strength would go as far as the mill. In the forest there would be gatherings, picnics with speakers who, along with the news from the large cities, also brought courage and inspiration to the overworked of the factories, to the artisans.

[Page 203]

The Great Fire

I see the great fire in front of my eyes. Half the shtetl – the poor section – went up in smoke: from *Potchtove* Street, *Plantanske* (my street) up to "*Kavkaz*". The houses were wood and dry. The wind carried the blaze from street to street. The volunteer firemen could do nothing. My father was a captain with epaulets and brass buttons – I was always so proud of him, when he would march with the brigade on the market circle near the firehouse. But this time he abandoned my mother and me and left with the brigade to fight the fire. My mother cried, pleaded, but he left to do his duty.

After the fire people settled in with rich people in *Garbarsker* and *Shul* Streets and in the *Tzerkovner*. There in that house, of a good, rich man I first began to understand the difference between rich and poor.

Years later I would often, already like an equal, go to the rich houses to visit my friends from high school. I was the only working class child to go to the high school in Grodno (to my good fortune I was the last of the children and my mother liked education and culture). I would visit the Grossman's, Buak's and Nachum Anshel's children because I was very bright, received the best marks and often helped them. Their houses were beautifully furnished, with trees and flowers, surrounded with leather closets, with the unmistakable odor of wet skins. My poor nose in no way was able to take it, but for them this was perfume, the promise of riches!

A Worker's Reading Circle

1905 left its mark on our shtetl and on all its inhabitants. The workers felt proud and worthy because the first proof of freedom had arrived and broke the pessimism. I was then a young girl of thirteen – fourteen. I already belonged to a socialist circle, fought against "*saninshtchina*" (to devote oneself to sexual affairs) among the young students. During summer vacations I worked in a reading circle for workers; the partnership was a success. I read (the others did not know how to) and the workers then discussed what was read. I became more knowledgeable as well and proud of my father, the tinsmith, and of my mother, the cigarette maker.

In our home there was already some worker tradition: a father who ran to America because he led a tailors' strike in Lodz; an illegal library hidden in our wood stall. I would devour the books that opened new horizons for me.

Translator's Footnotes:

1.   From "My Memories" Volume 2, Warsaw 1913
2.   This collection of the obligatory tax on kosher slaughtering and meat, wine and other food products was held as a lease. The meat tax was created for the Jewish community to cover obligations that the community was responsible for to the government.
3.   "Kavkaz" means mountain, and is the name of a section in Krynki. A "Kavkazer" is someone from the Kavkaz section of Krynki.

<u>Descriptions and Memories</u>

[Page 204]

Descriptions and Memories

Translated by Judie Goldstein

My "Kavkaz"

Wolf Ekstein

In order to have an idea of the Krinker "*Kavkaz*" [mountain], one must imagine the Bialystoker "*haneykes*" or the Grodner "*yurzike*" [areas of the cities]. In this "*yurzike*" I spent a year, while I studied in the Grodno Yeshiva. I supported myself at the *yurziker* owners and ate "days" [boarders at the yeshiva were given meals by local families as a good deed] at their homes and I felt as if I was in "*Kavkaz*". This was also an area settled by the poor, in houses built without any planning, one large confusion of narrow streets, mixed up with a few underworld characters.

The Krynki fire broke out on a Friday morning in 1904, on a hot summer day. Yenta's forest burned, and the kids ran to see the fire. First going outside the shtetl, we noticed that Krynki was burning. Engraved in my memory is the image of how the "*Kavkazer*" poor were arranged on "Vigon", each with his bundle, at the river that ran past Alter Ayon's water mill and that it was late, just before the Sabbath. The wives did not have anything to bless the candles with and they were stretched out along the river and cried aloud.

From the time of the fire our parents started a new chronology and designated each event according to how many years since the great fire.

This was the time when various political organizations began that later had such a great influence on the masses. In the evenings dreamy young girls sat out on the balconies and sang their folk songs, such as: "You Love Me But You Do Not Take Me As Your Bride." The "*Kavkazer*" young boys were still busy chasing pigeons or directing wars against each other.

Since 1905 these youngster had become unrecognizable. My uncle, Moshe'ke Shmuel Abrahamel the *Melamed's*, would come to my father, Chaim the carpenter, to discuss overthrowing the Tzar. After the fire "*Kavkaz*" revived. Our famous *Zshabieh* Street was made wider and there were already brick houses there whereas previously no such thing had been seen on those streets. And later, after a long battle between David the Lapinitzer baker and Cheykl Olean, David won the lawsuit and broad Sokolker Street was opened and cut through *Zshabieh*. Lastly, before the Second World War, the Town Council renamed one of the *Kavkazer* little streets after I.L. Peretz.

I also cannot forget the constant wars that the Kozoltchik family carried on with the Akhims, a branch of the Kirschner family.

And although "*Kavkaz*" was marked with its poor, when the Sabbath or High Holidays arrived, "*Kavkaz*" was indistinguishable from the rest. Combed, cleaned up, the "*Kovkazers*" sat down at the table as equals with the rich. What they might not have to eat – they had in holiday spirit.

I remember my grandfather Shmuel Abrahamel the *melamed* [teacher], of blessed memory. He always taught about ten to twelve children, from "*Kavkaz*." There was no contract stating when tuition was to be paid. This was not how things were done. My grandfather was forced to go a little hungry. But that is during the week. Should his Sabbath really be so bitter – we still have a great G-d, who performed a miracle. My grandfather had the concession for the city *eyrev* [wire strung around a town to classify it as enclosed private property so object may be carried on the Sabbath] and therefore also the right to go around the city on Friday to collect *eyruv* money. He would come home tired out just in time to bless the candles but still in time for the Sabbath.

[Page 205]

"*Kavkaz*" also had its own *besmedresh* [synagogue, house of study] where almost always the trustee was a wise man. He did not live in "*Kavkaz*". The sexton of the "*Kavkazer*" *besmedresh* was Chaim Ascher. Everybody respected him because he was a scholar. There was a cozy feeling in the *besmedresh*, not the snobbishness of the large *besmedresh* of the rich men.

Chaim Ascher Prizshanski Sexton
"*Kavkaz*" besmedresh

In that atmosphere I spent my childhood and perhaps it left its mark on everything I did later.

After the Krynki fire "*Kavkaz*" grew larger and became nicer. But after Hitler's fire there remains only to say: *Yisgdal vyiskadash* [two first words of the prayer for the dead] – mighty and holy is your name, our Krynki.

Our Shtetl In The Past

Avram Miller

The Waters In Krynik

Krynik lies in a fertile valley, surrounded by crystal clean springs from which a passersby would bend down to drink the refreshing water. *Kvaln* [springs] were called in our language *krenitzes* [springs] and from that word came the town's name, Krynik, just as Bialystok – because of its white ground, or Halinke – because Matys Halinker lived there…

Around the shtetl were spread out Prince's Courts. I cannot forget Virion who owned the spring where we would go during the summer. Saturday after *cholent* [slow cooked stew that was served on the Sabbath for lunch after being kept warm overnight in the bakery oven] we went there to drink and wash our eyes and make bets as to how long we could hold our hands in the cold water. For hours at a time we children would stand around the spring and wonder how it could boil and boil and yet the water was still cold. The Hasidim would go there every *Erev Pesach* for *mayim shelonu* [water left standing overnight to be used to knead matzos for Passover] and on the road back they sang Psalms of praise. Ayon and the aristocrat from the city would allow themselves to send even the madmen to the spring to get water for tea.

From the above mentioned spring and from other springs in the area, wound the crystal rivers and spread like a wide lake whose waterfall carried to the Krynik mill – the new mill (although a dozen years ago it was already old) – and still a lot of mills. It is impossible to calculate the number of ways that this small river would be used. It was used into wash Viryon's sheep and to whiten the gentile's linen; besides them, all the women rinsed their laundry there and my mother would beat my shirt against a rock with a large wooden "*prianik*" [Russian: stick].

I still remember the large pack of things that Yankl the dyer would carry to the river to rinse. Quiet, without noise, the river flowed, never raging, never protesting, swallowing everything and going on its way. Even when my grandmother went to wash out a curl, the river did not refuse her. All the filth from the one time dye factories and later the tanneries would be thrown in the river and it would swallow it and continue to flow.

[Page 206]

Only once a year, in the spring, would it get angry and over flow its banks and rage with tumult and commotion, and this – because it was not able to take in all the water from all the surrounding mountains.

The Marketplace And The Streets

The map of Krynik looked like an inkstand with the ink spilled out onto a sheet of paper: The round marketplace in the center with a row of stores, that lay like a twisted loaf on a large white loaf. In the middle of the stores, a gate. On market days the pickpockets made a living there. The stores, made of clay and twigs, all in the same style, a door with a shutter always open, summer and winter, the roof, with a large overhang with heavy wooden posts to protect the people from rain during markets days or fairs. On both sides of the stores, stalls. From there all kinds of things were sold, from food to ceramic bowls. Around the marketplace – taverns, which means large house with still larger stalls in front of the house – a rail to tie up animals that the gentiles brought to sell on market days.

"Bialystoker" Street

From the marketplace the streets and alleys went off in various directions. At the end of every street – Christian houses. The street certainly had Russian names, but they were always called by their Yiddish names and nicknames, such as: Mill Street, Sokolker Street, Pottery, Blacksmith, Shishlevitzer, Church Street, The Halinkerkers Street, Government Office Street, Tannery Street, Bath Alley, the Narrow Street, etc.

Krynki also had a "*Kavkaz*" and a "*Tiflis*" where the palaces were located in our shtetl.

Count Varion Stacks Tree Bark For Krinik

As known to tan leather, tree bark was used. And to get the bark a lot of raw material was used in Krinik. When the factories became larger and a lot more bark was needed, Varion went into business. He bought a strong steam engine, built a large structure and a gigantic stable where there was enough room to store bark for the entire winter. The manufacturers would pay Virion for bark by the pound.

A Cloud Burst

There were not only fires in Krinik – I also remember a flood. It happened in the summer of 1902. The weather was beautiful. The wives were rinsing their laundry in the river near Nashelnitze. Suddenly there was a cloud burst from the castle side. This was not just any rain, but a wall of water that went to the mill and took everything with it. The women at the river barely escaped with their lives and the roof of Virian's large stable that was full of bark for the tanneries, was dragged away lying on its side as if it were a hat. Also the bridge near the mill collapsed. For me, then still a small boy, as well as for my friends – this was an extraordinarily interesting event, but for Eli the Miller it was destructive. Also for Count Virian this trick of nature cost him money.

[Page 207]

The Tanneries In The Past

The workday in the leather factories, in their first years, would begin at five o'clock in the morning and end at dark during the summer, and nine or ten o'clock at night during the winter. Five minutes after five o'clock in the morning the entrance gates were already closed. This was called "*farshlofen a frishtik*" [missing breakfast by sleeping late]. This happened once to me when I worked for Aizik Krushenianer in the factory at Abraham Moshe the mirror "*faltzer*."

I was 11 to 12 years old. One winter night I awake and notice that it is light outside (from the newly fallen snow). The wall clock says, and I think, that is already late. I quickly get dressed and do not even pour water to wash my hands. I run through the deep snow (there was no footpath) to the door of the factory. The door, I see, is closed. I go back home with my head hanging: "*farshlofen a frishtik*". I run into the synagogue and to my surprise the clock says only two o'clock. I put my ear to it – the clock is working. I turn back towards home and go back to sleep.

The Artisans

Krinik was an industrial city and as was customary, the factory workers occupied the "seat of honor" among the laborers in the shtetl. But in Krinik there were also artisans of all kinds: shoemakers, tailors, cabinetmakers, carpenters, masons, blacksmiths, locksmiths and so forth.

This is in order to mention some of them who, before my time, were famous for their great talents. I will begin with the foundation, that is, with Pinchus the mason. His foundations of natural fieldstone were amazing, beautiful and strong. His vaulted cellars were famous throughout the Krinik area: no blazing fire would ever destroy them. While plastering the outside of the Krinker synagogue, he fell along with the scaffold but landed on his feet. During the winter he would drive around as an agent from Israel, on his head a *shtraymel* [large round hat edged with fur] like a Hasidic rabbi. He was truly a nice man.

The rebuilding of the shtetl after the fire was achieved by a lot of masons: Aizik Herschel, Eli Chaim, Michel and Alter Lantz's, Israel Elisch's etc.

And some of the carpenters were: Shmuel Azshar's, Yosel Motch's, Eli, and the best carpenter in the shtetl, - Meyer Fischel's, a short man with bent shoulders, but a clever craftsman.

Levi the cabinetmaker (Saroki) was the best in his trade in Krinik. He was also an inventor.

The second best cabinetmaker was Eli Meyer Fishel's (Eli Masoliner). His work was fit for a museum. Their names were perpetuated through their work in the Krinik synagogue.

Levi's son, Efrim, was famous in Grodno Province for his ability to draw – a rarity among cabinetmakers. Boruch Stoliarski was smarter and had more work than the others.

Israel the blacksmith was the best in his trade. And the best tailor was – Itche Vigdor Mendel's. Nachman Velvel Itche's had for dozens of years led the large tailor's trade in Krinik.

[Page 208]

The shoemakers Sheyma and Moshe Meyer were artists of their trade. There were also shoemakers in the shtetl that had a name not only as good craftsmen but also for their sense of humor and to play a trick on somebody, so that people would derive pleasure from them.

Nice Citizens, Preachers, Hasidim, Cantors

In olden days the aristocrat and nicest business owner in the shtetl was David Todros's (David Mareyni). His wife, Eda Liba was a daughter of *Reb* [Mr.] Israel Salanter, the founder of the *Musar* [19th to 20th century Jewish religious movement that stresses moral edification] movement. *Reb* Israel, while searching for a son-in-law, would also preach in the Krinik synagogue. Once the brass chandelier that hung from a rope over the *bima* [pulpit] made him so nervous that he shortened his speech.

The city had once gotten its preacher, Hershele Dubrover, excited. The common people had him really sacrificed for him. One of his students had once in the large *besmedresh* yelled out loud:; "So, will the rabbi not question our decision?" What he meant was, "decide the question."

Krinik also had a pious man, *Reb* Yosele, of blessed memory, and a "miracle worker" – Aizik Benyamin Zelig's.

There were a lot of Hasidim in our shtetl, followers of a variety of rabbis such as Slonimer, Kotzker, Cobriner, Carliner, Novo-Minsker and Stoliner. The Stoliner Rabbi, *Reb* Smuel'ke would visit Krinik twice a year, as well as the Kobriner, *Reb* Machum.

Cantors did not have too much luck in Krinik. The shtetl always paid good wages to the rabbi and the ritual slaughters, but a cantor was like a firth wheel on a wagon. When one would arrive in Krinik for a Sabbath, everyone would pray at the first *minion* [quorum of ten men] make *kiddush,* [benediction pronounced on bread or wine on Sabbaths] eat well and go to hear the cantor. He might have been the best cantor but they all ruined it going "feh, feh!"

In Krinik there was a custom that Friday before the evening *parshe* [portion of the Pentateuch] "bhelusach", the holy tunes would be played in the synagogue. The custom went back a long time, but the Rabbi *Reb* Boruch annulled the custom, because it made the women late for candle lighting.

Krinik was the only shtetl that owned a chapel, and everyone in the area would make use of it.

From The Respected Citizen Of The Community

The revolutionary movement in Krinik drew young people as members. People would laugh at these revolutionary youth and tell several funny stories about them. For example, young girls would not scrape potatoes, because Nikolai is the Tzar, or that one called for the freeing of the hens from the hen house, and other stories like this.

The Krinik community leaders scarcely thought about the working masses. So they would not invite the artisans to the meetings about city business.

But the shtetl had "common people" who would not be led by the nose. They would prove that the community leaders were arranging city business in a way that was liable to be unjust to the labor masses, for example by taking over the meat tax, the yeast tax, or the bath - soon there was an outcry, as if the heavens had opened. They already called a stop to the reading of the law in order to call the attention of the worshippers to these grievances and created a terrible scandal. Leading them was Yosel Yekels and after some derision, Krinik became happy.

Types From Among The "Common People"

"Yankl Yehuda" the blacksmith was especially distinctive. It was his custom to immediately turn to the rabbi. He prayed with the first *minion*, ate a large onion or garlic and left for *Reb* Boruch's. The rabbi, only just awakened, wrapped in his morning gown, sits down in his armchair – to receive Yankl Yehuda. He yells "Good morning, rabbi!", reaches with both his hands for the arms of the chair and loudly rattles off the entire story for the rabbi. *Reb* Boruch begs him: "I am a sick man, leave me alone!" But Yankl Yehuda does not quit: "Rabbi, you must listen to me from a to z!" And that is what he did day after day.

[Page 209]

His son Lipa, was a different type: He did not get mixed up in community business. He would drink liquor and go to sleep.

One winter morning, when it was burning cold, he went intoxicated from the monopoly [a place that sold liquor], to creep near Motl Staike's on the large stone, took off his boots and called out: "Thank G-d, at last I am home on the oven!"

Also Leyb "the writer" (Leybe Furie) was a modern kind of man. In the course of a dozen years he taught the Krynki young boys and girls to write Yiddish letters. He was the Yiddish writer in the shtetl. People would say: "Writing is good in this world and studying is for the world to come".

About Yudel Bertchekov's, the joker of the city, one could write an amazing book. His witticisms were heard everywhere and all of Krinik delighted in them.

Triple Storied Names

In Krynki one would call a resident, even a respected citizen, by his original, private given name. At least one and perhaps two names would be added. So, for example, the writer of this article was called Avrahamele Itche Schachne's. Almost everyone was called by three names and not necessarily with a surname. Take for example my neighbors. They were called: Abrahaml Herschl Berl's, Niome Velvel Itche's, Moshe Chona Faivel's, Chatskel Abraham Tzale's, Zelig Shlomo Rubin's, Leibe Mordchai Shimele's, Zeydke Libe Rashke's, Shimon Jankl Alik's, Yankl Mordchai Slomo's, Yankl Moshe Avraham's, Avrahaml Mote Irye's, Shiya Shmuel Moshake's, Avrahaml Meyer Leyb's, Chatskel Leybe Esterke's, David Avraham Leybl's, Velvel Chona Paya's, Efrim Leybke Shmaya's, and Toybe Chana Chaya's. Others were called by four names like Pinie Minie Faygel Yehoshie's.

The Pastimes Of The Children

How did Krynki children spend their free time? Friday, for half the day and on the Sabbath after lunch, they went to Virian's forest, the woods, and Yenta's orchard. Summer – they bathed in Virian's pond and during the winter skated on the lake and then went to the *besmedresh* to warm up. At the end of the summer they would pick chestnuts near Yenta's courtyard. Sabbath evenings the children would go for a walk on Shislevitzer Street – to welcome the sheep and animals during their return from their pasture in the fields.

Krinik Flourishes Anew (During The Reconstruction Of Krinik)

The last years before the First World War Krynki blossomed with its leather industry and with its great rich men. But the greatest honor was obtaining for our shtetl the Maltcher Yeshiva that was located in the *"Kavkazer" besmedresh*. The *gemore* [volume of the Talmud] tunes resounded from there day and night. Krynki on one side was then full of freethinking young men with shaved chins who were full of revolutionary ideas; and on the second side, religious young men, growing beards. A lot of them later went over to the tannery camp, having been infected with mutiny and left their studies.

[Page 210]

"Disturbed," Mentally Ill, Dark Souls (Underworld)

Krinik had a large number of mentally ill. The most intelligent of them was Meyerim (I will explain about him separately). There were also other types in the shtetl that during Purim or Simchas Toyrah would be in a jolly mood. Leybe Motche's and Shmuel for example, would turn over the *kapotes* [long, black coats worn by Orthodox Jews] to the left side, put on hats, creep up onto a stall and call into the synagogue. Leybe Motche's would then use the opportunity to talk to the rabbi or the wealthy men about a scholarly matter.

Dark "Souls"

Krynki, like other towns, had its share of dark people, the inferiors of the Jewish community, operators and thieves who would steal anything from a hinge to a horse. The thieves were grouped in gangs, each with its "rabbi" and they never betrayed each other and never took over each other's "living."

One of the famous ones was Henoch Hillke's. Once he arrived in Zelve for a fair and made good "business," filing his pockets with the merchandise. In the end people looked around and knew that a Krinker was there at the fair. They immediately chased after him with a couple of good horses and Henoch was brought back to Zelve to the rabbi. They would not give a Jew over into gentile hands, unless they were absolutely certain that he was the thief.

The rabbi ordered a hearing. So he was brought to the synagogue so that he could swear on a Torah scroll. Henoch went up to Holy Ark, opened the curtains and in a loud voice screamed: "Torah! Torah! Defend your honor! People want a hearing for *Reb* Henoch son of Hillke – he is accused of being a thief!" The people heard it all and they were very frightened and *Reb* Henoch son of Hillel was set free. From then on the name "Krinker Thief" meant smart.

These dark people would be the Purim actors in the shtetl and in other presentations. Who does not remember the King with the Horse, Rabbi Refol with the paper crown, and Mayer Aba with the drum?

We also had informers who would betray the revolutionary activists to the government. Several of them were active on the Tsar's side at the beginning of the twentieth century. One of them, made his living from freeing those arrested – after he had betrayed them.

Also in the twentieth century there was in Krynki a nasty informer, Yankl Kopel the *"ozshiranktchik,"* who served as a secret agent for the police. He would get money from everyone he could and if people did not cough up he would inform on them saying this one is a Communist and he would be taken off to jail. Later when the Polish government found about his antics, he was arrested and they wanted to be rid of him. But he managed to escape and hide.

Krinker Healers· Doctors

The only doctor in the shtetl was *Pan* [Polish: lord] Jejkovski. He thought of himself as a professor and his practice also included the surrounding towns, such as Brestovitz, Amdur and also all the courts and villages.

A sick person would turn to him when all the other healers and remedies had failed. It would often happen that it was already too late and the doctor could not help.

When the Krynki population grew and Dr. Jejkovski was older, the government built a hospital outside the city. Naturally, Dr. Jejkovski moved over there and it was too difficult for him to make house calls in the city. Krynki found a doctor, a young man, but the people did not have faith in an untried doctor and so they would run to the old one. Very often he would tell them to go to the doctor in the city.

[Page 211]

You have a doctor – he would say – it does not matter, he is good; when he will have put a few people in the cemetery through his mistakes, like I did, then he will be an even better doctor.

In Krynki there was also a Jewish doctor – Goldberg. He was called the *lupatch*, because he had thick lips. He was a pious Jew, and would pray everyday in the *besmedresh*. But "he did not make a living" and he left Krynki.

While he was packing his furniture and piano, I got the courage to ask him why he was leaving us. His answer was that a doctor in Krynki was like being an organ grinder: he stands in front of the house or a courtyard, and plays various melodies. Whoever has God in his heart, waits for a penny and if not – then the organ grinder gets tired of playing and goes away.

"You, Krinkers," he claimed, "wait until the Sabbath for a visit when I must not take any money and you must not give any. So if somebody has God in their heart they would pay me during the week. But some pretend they do not know, and others forget entirely. So I must say 'adieu' to your Krynki."

Pharmacists And Midwives

The city also had a pharmacist and a pharmacy but at Cyvia Mzik's stall there were more medicines than at the two pharmacists together.

There was also a midwife who had finished a course of studies, the Polish Stepanovshtchikhe. Also there was a grandmother, Miriam Reyzel, Moshe the cantor's wife. Every Purim she would send "her" children a lollipop as *shalakhmones* [gifts exchanged by friends and neighbors on Purim]. She was always afraid of a Jewish competitor. As it happened one of Eli the miller's daughters went to Vilna to study and came back a certified midwife with a diploma, dressed in a nice cape and a hat.

Miriam Reyzel saw her as a strong competitor, so she played a dirty trick and the young woman had to run away from the city in the middle of the night without her cape.

Healers, Exorcists And Other Healers

Also no branch of medicine was missing in Krynki: from exorcising the evil eye, to getting rid of a toothache, fear, swellings and doing cupping (drawing blood).

A patient used all these old wives' remedies and if they did not help then the patient would go to a healer. There were a lot of these healers in Krynki: Piave the healer, Abraham Meyer Piave's, Motl the healer, Yankel Motl, Shimon Ber the healer, Simcha the barber-surgeon and Feyshke the barber.

More About The Polish Doctor

D. Selkof

Pan Jejkovski, the Krynki doctor was a tall Christian with a thick Polish mustache and a fat, red nose. Exactly how old he was, nobody knew. Old Jews claimed that he was a specialist, only G-d help us, nobody should need him. He was never alone and walked slowly.

[Page 212]

Dr. Jejkovski

On a summer, Sabbath during the day, while walking through the Jewish streets, to call on a Jewish patient, all the children would welcome him with a "good *Shabes*" The children would take off their hats and he would give them each a pat on the head to inspect them to see if a child is clean or not. He always got along well with them.

For a visit he would charge thirty kopecks. He would not take any money from a patient who he knew could not pay this amount. Furthermore, in the *besmedresh* it was said that for poor women who had given birth he brought a hen and a bottle wine. And people delighted in telling these stories and to be sure the *Pan* Doctor is one of the pious among the gentiles and after his death he will be allowed into the Garden of Eden.

The Krynki Jewish Community Council paid him one hundred rubles a year as a reward for his unpaid visits to the poor. Customarily at the end of the year the Council would pretend that they did not have any money for him. This would start a lot of trouble in the shtetl. Poor Jews would stand for hours, with hats in hand, at his closed door. Jewish women would be screaming and crying that their daughters were having a difficult labor and he had to come to save them this minute. But the *Pan* doctor would not move. He would only say: "Go to the Council. They have to pay me what they owe." There was turmoil in the shtetl. Some ran to the rabbi and others to the councilmen. This did not help. So they used an old Jewish solution: that means they did not allow prayers and readings on the Sabbath; The men did not leave the *bima* [pulpit] until the rabbi and several responsible men said that they would settle with the *Pan* doctor the next day.

The majority created such a tumult even during the cold, dark winter days when the wet penetrated the small, poor huts and one could not get rid of diseases. After the obstacle of reading the law, the next evening, Jews were seen going out in the deep mud with large lanterns in their hands and behind them, in high galoshes, was the *Pan* doctor, singing quietly a Polish song, on the way to visit the poor.

With the outbreak of the First World War, the *Pan* doctor was activated and we never saw him again. People said that he died in Russia alone. If he went to the Garden of Eden, nobody knows to this day.

[Page 213]

Krinik Of My Memories

Berl Zakon (Berlartser)

Translated by Judie Goldstein

As it was told

Krinik lay in a valley surrounded by springs, from which the name Krinik comes from, and therefore during the autumn there was always a lot of mud.

It was said that during the Polish uprising in 1863, Polish agitators arrived in Krinik and spoke to the population about "how good and nice it will be for you when you belong to us, instead of to the Russians. With us you will have everything in abundance." Kelman the butcher asked them a question: "And will you give us pasture for our goats?" (Jews did not pasture any goats, especially butchers). At the time they answered: "Yes." But that night they came with rope to hang him for making fun of them[1]. (Kelman knew that he was allowed to make fun of them, because he was not dependent on the *porets*[landowner, noble] like other Jews who therefore had to hide their thoughts, and doff their hats for him). But Kelman was smarter than the Polish rebels and he did not go home to sleep. But there was another Jew staying at his house at the time and they took him for Kelman's father. They already had the rope around his neck, but at the last minute they realized they had made a mistake and let him go.

There Were Times

Krinik had a large synagogue, 4 large *botei medrashim* [houses of study], Hasidim *shtiblach* [houses of prayer] and *minyonim* [minions, ten males necessary for public worship] (in private houses).

Besides rabbis, ritual slaughterers and judges, the shtetl also had enlightened men. I remember one of them – Motl Arje the *Staroste* [village head in Polish, Governor in Russian]. First he would read "*Hamelitz*" and later "*HaZfira*" [both Hebrew newspapers]. Hebrew was the holy language for him. He would search through the newspapers from the first to the last line, including the price of the advertisements.

Krinik was in Grodno Province and was considered a city but only because of its industry and it revolutionary zest, it still did not belong to this sort of community.

When the "*Bund*" [socialist labor party] put up a candidate from our Grodno Province for the second "*Duma*" [Russian parliament] (the first was boycotted by the Socialists). The candidate was the renown, at that time, Bund activist Shmuel Goshanski, who was famous under his pen name "*lanu*" [ours] but he was not elected - so in Krinik we decided, "*lo lanu*" [not ours] (a prayer in Hillel).

Before the First World War there was "prosperity" in Krinik (a flourishing, good times): whoever wanted and was able to work made a good living. There was even more work than Krinkers could fill. People came to work in Krinik from the surrounding villages and towns. The relations between Jews and Christians were friendly.

Krinker Manufacturers

Krinik had rich manufacturers, two of them were distinguished: the first, Nachum Anschel Knishinski – with his wealth, knowledge and practical wisdom.

[Page 214]

Once Itche Nathan's –the *shames* [sexton in a synagogue] in the rabbinical court and the *shames* in the large synagogue in which the factory owners prayed, came to Nachum Anschel for Chanukah *gelt* [money] (this is what it was then called). Both of them were scholars, had studied in the famous Volozhyn yeshiva. Nachum Anschel bless the Chanukah candles and said to Itche Nathan's: "I will of course give, but one must not make use of the light from the Chanukah candles ". Itche Nathan's answered him: "But for a *shames* one may". (A scholarly word game).

Itche Nathan's -- Rabbinal court shames
and high shames in the large synagogue

The second manufacturer, Leybe Matus's was a distinguished for his scholarship and benevolence. When a poor man did not even have the smallest of coins for the Sabbath, he would go to Leybe Matus's to beg for his help. And it just happened that there were two weddings taking place the same evening and there was only one hall in Krinik. So they went to Leybe Matus's and he made place for the other wedding in his own large house.

There is another manufacturer worthy of mention, Gamliel Levin. It was said that when he was young he sang in the St. Petersburg Royal Opera.

Fires

One of the large fires that broke out in Krinik burned down most of the city: Meyerim the *melamed* [teacher] was burned in that fire. Very few houses remained, but as the factories still stood, everyone worked and in a short time people rebuilt and Krinik looked better than it had before.

Great Men Of The Torah

Our shtetl was proud of its great Jews and with its noted rabbis. And so it was with *Reb* Boruch Lavski who was the author of "*Mnoches Boruch*" a book for scholars that was very current for them. He was greatly respected in the city and when he would walk through the synagogue, everyone would stand up and make room for him.

Reb Zelman Sender Shapiro, known in the world as a sage and pious man to whom men would come from every region for a blessing, brought his famous Maltcher yeshiva to Krinik. But here he did not get much pleasure from it. Krinik was an industrial and revolutionary community and a yeshiva student only had a ruble and fifty kopecks a week for sustenance, and therefore a lot of them needed help. Evidently being lenient in interpreting the article of our sages, blessed be their memory, not to finish eating and not to finish drinking. Not one yeshiva student rebelled, violated a law, left the lectern to work in the factory or exchanged the rabbis of the 3rd to 5th centuries C.E., whose discussions of the *Mishnah* [post biblical laws and rabbinical discussions of the 2nd century, B.C.E.] are included in the *Talmud*, for Marx and Engels. Several would call the workers by names from the *Gemore* [part of the *Talmud*[2] which comments on the *Mishnah*] such as: "Rabbi Pappa", "Rabbi Chuna" and so forth.

[Page 215]

In Krinik *Reb* Zelman Sender got as much attention as in tiny, poor Maltch, where besides respect, for such a rabbi, a sage and pious man, he created the shtetl-- his yeshiva almost brought a livelihood. So, Jews blessed with girls would board students in their homes and with after several years, depending on the conditions and the dowry they would marry the daughters.

But industrial Krinik was in need of a rabbi, a judge, who would treat and judge business disputes. *Reb* Zelman Sender would have nothing to do with lawsuits and would send those who did not have the necessary authority to the person who decided matters of rabbinical law. The manufacturers were not too happy about this.

Reb Zelman Sender's wife would ask the parties to a lawsuit a puzzling question: "Why do you have so many lawsuits? I lived in Maltch for forty years and I never sued anyone!"

Luminous Figures (Beautiful Images Of People)

From among our luminous figures I would first like to mention Moshe Yehoshe the *Teper* [potter]. He was a Jew who sat and studied day and night and at the same time was a spreader of Torah publicly. He studied with friends. He was a poor Jew in a community with so many rich manufacturers – all the city money lay with him and it was safe and secure. The breadwinner was his wife who had a pottery store on the marketplace. Only on Thursdays, the market day in Krinik, would Moshe Yehushe leave the *besmedresh* and go help his wife sell pottery. A peasant woman haggled forcefully with him and wanted him to give it to her at less than cost price. He answered her by paraphrasing the *gemore*: "You do not want to buy the pot – then do not buy it.

When he left the marketplace he went back to studying with his friends Velvel the Kvasnik and after him Tzalke the Tailor who later became a teacher. He was a Jew who in his youth had studied very little and knew even less. Therefore when he was older, like the *Mishnah* sage Akiva, he began to study Torah with such diligence that he had reached the same level of study as his friends.

The *heder* of *Reb* Shmuel the *Rebetzin's* [rabbi's wife], who was the *gemore melamed*, in Krinik was esteemed like Harvard or Princeton Universities in America. If parents did not care for their son's behavior, he would be reproved and told that it was not suitable for him to do this. He studied this at Shmuel the *Rebetzin's*.

Special Common People (Special Characters Of The People)

There were in Krinik Jews penetrated with deep religious faith. One of them was Zundel Ite's. His entire life he had a lawsuit with Monye the Dyer. When he became very ill, my uncle went to visit him. Seeing as his days were numbered, my uncle said to him: "I will go to Monye for you and beg him to forgive you.". "Oh, no" answered Zundel, "I will end my lawsuit with him in the celestial court."

There were also feeble believers. One was Yudel Berchekov's. From the *Elul* [August] on and especially during the ten days between New Year and the Day of Atonement, he would say only one thing: "Already it will soon be the Day of Atonement and I have not committed any sins."

[Page 216]

During the First World War, due to the then difficult economic situation, a lot of Jews took to horses and wagons as a livelihood – even some who were better suited to be teachers than wagon drivers. These were Jews who knew how to teach but did not know anything about horses. One of those was driving me to a nearby shtetl. As soon as we were seated in the wagon, the horse did not want to go. I said to the wagon driver: "The horse wants to get into the wagon. That should give him a sense of justice. He should sit in the wagon and we should pull him." The drive answered: "When I say ey-no! (a command to the horse that he should start moving) this makes the horse go." The horse answered: "My strength, I have no strength, my days are short" (paraphrased from Psalms Chapter 102, line 24 "He drained my strength in mid-course. He shortened my days.")

As everywhere, there were types in Krinik like the "*kapitzes*" for example who would speak together in their own idiomatic language. That was the case with Smuelke and his buyer Leybke. Shmuel would give him money to go to the markets and buy horses for him. Once Leybke brought back from Amdur a mare that was not worth what he paid for her. Shmuel said to him in these words: "You Leybke-eybke – for such a mare you paid twenty rubles-ubles. Oh, oh, you should fight this misfortune!"

This same Shmuel once while walking home, suddenly fell down near our house and it looked as if he was dead. I quickly ran to get his wife. Perhaps he was suffering from apoplexy. But his wife, from the smell, had soon figured out that this was simply a *shnaps* [liquor] attack. She gave him a slap on his cheek and the "dead man" Shmuelke suddenly got up from the ground and stood on his feet, as if there was a spirit in him.

On the Day of Atonement he would come to the large *besmedresh* [house of study, synagogue] and scream the entire day: "Repentance, prayer, charity!" It never went further than this with him, poor thing.

There was a Polish doctor, Jejkovski, in Krinik. He liked to joke with people. Water was brought to him by Yudel the *Waser-treger* [water carrier]. Once the doctor treated him to a glass of tea "no sugar" and *shnaps*, because after dragging the pails old Yudel had fits of coughing, sneezing and who knows what. When Jejkovski asked him: "So, Yudel, how is the liquor?" "A little water should not get into to it" answered Yudel quite ready for a refill.

The Nazi animals cut down everyone. Once upon a time there was a Krinik – a kind and dear Krinik and it is no more.

I Remember

Moishe Weinberg (Pinkes)

During my childhood there were two blind men living in Krinik: Itche and my *zeyde* [grandfather] Yankel. I remember him and will describe here several of my zeyde's mannerisms.

He was a carpenter and once he fell from a scaffold, split his head open and became blind. His house on the synagogue courtyard was close to the large *besmedresh*. He sold it to Michel the tailor and had a contract with him that he keep one room to live in, for as long as he lived so that he could go by himself, despite being blind, to the *besmedresh*.

[Page 217]

Some mornings before going to the *besmedresh* he would leave out a saucer with a little milk for the cat, a constant visitor in his room. He never spilled any of the milk while he was pouring it.

He knew a lot of stories by heart and I would look in the book and pay attention to make sure that he did not miss a word.

Also I remember: Yudel Berchekove's who would read "*HaZfira*" [Hebrew newspaper] told my zeyde he had read that in St. Peterburg there were doctors who could operate on the blind and restore their sight. So, Yudel advised my zeyde to write his two daughters in America and tell them that they should send money for this operation. My zeyde answered him: "No, Yudel, I will never see again and begin to sin anew!"

And so he continued his G-d fearing, religious life and then he left for Israel, still blind, in 1903. He died there and is buried in Jerusalem.

And a couple of words about Michel "belartser," my rabbi who was murdered by the Nazi animals with all the Krynki martyrs. He was a kind Jew who would be greatly vexed when he would have to slap a student for bad behavior.

His wife Rachel-Leah was not careful about her language. He would beg her with a cry: "Gracious, Rachel-Leah, why must you curse everybody – it is better to bless them!" Often he would try to influence her to be good.

Krynki Life-Styles

Not A Fanatical Community

Berl Zakon (Belartzer)

There were religious Jews in Krinik but no fanatics. They did not shave a woman's head after the wedding. Marrying two orphans and putting up the marriage canopy in the cemetery in order to stop the appetite of the Angel of Death [to stop an epidemic] – that these things happened, I first found out from Mendele Mocher Sforim's book "*Fishke Der Krumer*" ["Fishke the Crooked"].

A wedding was an important event. Many years ago the *khupa* [marriage canopy] stood in the synagogue courtyard. The bride and groom would be accompanied to the *khupa* by masses of people. They were led there from the farthest houses. At the front were the musicians with their leader Moshe Kreyne's. The last thing was to put up the *khupa* near the "hall."

The Sabbath And High Holidays: The Holy Sabbath

From Thursday on, the Krinker wives would work to bring the Sabbath into the house. Friday afternoon one could already smell the fresh *challah* [bread, braided egg loaf]. The *cholent* [stew eaten Sabbath at lunch] in the oven, the houses set in order, the candlesticks polished, the Sabbath feeling had taken over. A little later, the traditional Jews having washed will put on their Sabbath clothes, go to the synagogue to welcome the Sabbath. The pious women have already said the blessing and lit the Sabbath candles and the Sabbath already ruled in all its magnificence. With the Sabbath spirit – the men went home from praying, with echoes of "*gut shabes!*" [a good Sabbath], the "*Scholem aleichem malachey hashores*" [peace be upon the ministering angels], the benediction on the wine and bread and later – Sabbath songs.

[Page 218]

Sabbath morning, coming from praying, the men receive a veritable feast for lunch, which they look forward to the entire week. Here in Krinik the Jews knew nothing about dieting and people ate as an appetizer mashed eggs with onions, radish with chicken fat; after that – fatty meat (people would complain that the fattest meats would be sold to the wealthy, not to the poor) and a *cholent* with noodle pudding (even with two puddings), *Tsimmes* [vegetable/fruit stew] and so forth. The Krinik revolutionaries were freethinkers. But as for the resurrection of the dead, they believed a sign, they would say. The men lay down for a nap after such a heavy meal, and later got up and were healthy.

After their nap, the older Jews went to the synagogue to study as a group, or to recite a chapter (summer), "*borkhi nafshi*" [bless my soul] (winter), or perhaps a couple of chapters of Psalms.

The Holy Sabbath is passing, and it will be missed. The women say "G-d of Abraham, Isaac and Jacob" . Out with the Sabbath spirit, the gray weekdays are coming.

The revolutionary youth lived with its *oneg shabat* [enjoyment of the Sabbath] – by going to the woods to a meeting or to lectures and discussions and these voices would not be silenced by the leaving of the Sabbath.

Days Of Awe

From the beginning of the month of *Elul* [August] the women went to the cemetery. A lot of women would take Sarah Rachel the Fat as their intercessor, so that she would plead for them.

During the Days of Awe [from New Year through the Day of Atonement] the synagogue would be packed, even the old men, who during the week could not be counted on to form the ten man quorum needed for public prayer.

The eve of the Day of Atonement during afternoon prayers the choice honors would be auctioned. The straw had already been spread on the floor. And for *Kol Nidre* [declaration on the eve of the Day of Atonement concerning vows] all the synagogues were full of people. (When *Reb* Zelman Sender decreed, because of the fires and the unhealthy times, that the women's section should be closed, the Krinker women considered it a great decree that not even a ruler would try to pass). The men were wrapped in prayer shawls and a lot in white caftans. Solemnly, in a fear soaked silence, everyone listened to *Kol Nidre*. And after the evening prayers and the *"Yeyles"* [prayer on the Day of Atonement], a lot of men stayed to say *"Shir Hayekhod"* [hymn of the unity of G-d] and Psalms. My father would not come home to sleep that night. He would not eat all day, so that he would not be thirsty during the fast on the Day of Atonement. His health was not good and was sick for a long time.

Sukes

At *Sukes* the young boys would carry the *lulav* [palm branch] from house to house so that everybody would be able to bless an *esrog* [citron, an expensive fruit which is blessed during the *Sukkoth* holiday]. On the intermediate days, vacation time, proposed marriages were finalized, and teachers would attend to enrolling students.

The night of *Hoyshayne rabeh* [the Great Hosanah, the seventh day of Tabernacles] religious Jews sat the entire night studying Torah and saying Psalms. That night the sky would split and all petitions would be granted. It was said that somebody had pleaded the entire night for *kol tuv* [all manner of good], but it came out as *"koltun"* [a tuft of twisted hair] and the Master of the Universe really fulfilled his petition.

Simkhes Toyre [holiday on the day following *Sukkoth*, celebrating the completion of the year's reading cycle of the Torah] was the most joyous day of the year in Krinik. Nach Keyle's would scream out *"tsone kodoshim!"* [holy flock, the Jewish people] All the children would answer: *"me!"* [baa, bleating] – like lambs. After prayers everyone would have honey cake and liquor.

[Page 219]

Hanukah And Purim

Hanukah [feast of the Maccabees] was a national holiday [not a religious holiday]. But, dedicated to the miracle that came to pass, everyone would eat *latkes* [fried potatoe pancakes] and play with *dreidels* [a spinning top with Hebrew letters on each side].

The second happiest holiday of the year was Purim. After reading the *megillah* [book in the form of a scroll] money would be given to the poor. Today people send *shalakhmones* [presents exchanged by friends and neighbors on Purim] to each other! Purim actors would go around to as many houses as possible to entertain people and get a couple of coins for Passover.

The Dear Passover

Soon after Purim, Passover eve would arrive. After the hard winter with its cold and snow, came the season of our freedom together with the rebirth of nature. The contractors were busy baking matzah. The porter carried the first baked pieces of matzah to the wealthier citizens (each of them had paid well and he would wish them: "all manner of good"). Passover eve, when the contractors would be extra strict as they were baking matzah *shmurah* [watched with special care]. All the work, from the flour to putting them in oven – they would do with their own hands.

The children had new clothes and shoes for Passover. A child would be filled with grief if the tailor or the shoemaker could not manage to finish the clothes or the shoes.

Us schoolboys derived a special pleasure at Passover. After the hard winter with the deep snow, going home at night from school with a paper lantern (not once did paper catch fire on the way) we would, with the coming of Spring, feel like those arrested on being freed from jail. We ran straight away to Yenta's courtyard and Virion's forest and of course not forgetting playing with the nuts.

Shavues

Shvues although people ate dairy foods it was a much appreciated holiday. First because of the gift of the Torah, and second because on *Shvues* people are freer. It was said, "During Passover one can eat as one will, but must not eat what one will. However on *Shvues* one may eat what one will and as one will".

Tishebov

Tishebov [the ninth day of Ab, a day of fasting and mourning to commemorate the destruction of the two Temples in Jerusalem] is a day of sorrow, but in Krinik people did not make a big fuss about it. But *Tishebov* 1914 there was great sorrow in Krinik because the day before the "reserve" had been mobilized and sent to the front to fight the Germans.

"Linat HaZedek"

Since the end of the 18th century there was a *"Linat HaZedek-Bikur Holim"* [staying overnight with the sick and visiting the sick] Society in Krinik whose members were young unmarried women. They took the place of nurses staying overnight with the sick and if possible giving the patient needed help. Whereas making banquets for women was then not done, they would once a year bring a cake to the house. Poor patients would be given medicine without charge and during the First World War – dairy products.

Medicine bottles would be left out as they were needed. All year long the bottles were at our house. In the middle of the week there was very little demand. But Friday night there would be a run on the medicine. Krinik was an industrial city and people could not take to their sick bed during the week, but they could on the Sabbath.

[Page 220]

The Mentally Ill, Confused And Nicknames

Betzalel Patschebutski

A Disturbed Person

Meyerim Shveygidiker – a tall, nice man with black hair and beard, who would keep silent, would have fits of wild laughter. He was the water carrier and slept in the *besmedresh* and during the summer he went around barefoot.

It was said that he was from a great lineage, graduated a university and could speak. He would write addresses for letters being sent abroad, would help the externs study mathematics, algebra, geometry and languages – English and French.

Nobody knew when he had come to Krinik and when he left. It was said that in 1920, when the Bolsheviks arrived in Krinik they found him alone in the *besmedresh* and wanted to question him – he remained mute. When they found out that he could speak they beat him so badly that he never recovered and died soon afterwards.

It was also said that one of the Krinker city leaders once asked Meyerim why there was so much mud in Krinik? – Meyerim answered: "that the Mast of the Universe gave a look and saw that you are a leader in the city, so he spit on this place and since then there is mud here".

Motke – His craziness consisted of talking to his dead father. He beat his mother, a small, stooped woman (had a hardware store). They would both yell and scream and create such fusses that the shtetl would shrink from them.

Motke would take food to his father's grave and scream that it is dinner. He would attack his mother when she had not prepared dinner or forbid him to the cemetery.

Meyer "Tzitzun" – always filthy would say that his mother had weaned him "too young".

Shimon a "wife" strong man – had broad shoulders and a thick, blond, curly beard. He would beg for an arranged marriage, a "wife." He would say "I am insane, completely insane!"

Itche Kugelach or "Angel of Death" – always unbuttoned, in a unbuttoned shirt, with disheveled hair and pop eyes; would yell in the shtetl that somebody was going to die.

Yenta Kleinkepele had beautiful red cheeks and would speak with half words. Her parents kept her in the house but she would sneak out from time to time. When she became pregnant she said that the "ardent one" did it.

Seasonal Disturbed People

Kutiel – Was a quiet man with a family, a teacher, a tanner and a Kobriner Hasid. In the month of Tamuz he would say that the shtetl could only be cleansed of sin by immersion and he would run barefoot to the river.

Simcha Rachel Motchke's – was a scholar and had a rabbinical and ritual slaughterer diploma. But he was not allowed to devote himself to this so he killed himself.

An Exorcist

People "possessed by an evil spirit" were brought to Krinik – to the Tarars from Krushenian, where the evil spirit was exorcised.

Nicknames

Itke-Kitke, Alte Sabbath loaf, the *botchkes* [half boots], the *Bebelach* [small beans], the Gimzlach, Drotch, Lapontz with the Bells, Leyzer Drole's, Match-Patch, Mukholap, Mitl-Shtikl, Moth, Slavic, Skreytchik, the Ardent one, Braid, the Kugelach, Pumpkin.

[Page 221]

Nicknames According To Chaim-Opstam

Amstobover, Grodner, Lapinitzer, Spodviler, Shchuchiner, etc.

An Error

A. Fridenstein

The first time I heard about Krinik was when I was studying at the yeshiva in Brestovitz. I heard some Jews in the *besmedresh* talking disparagingly about the Krinker factory workers who were mainly Socialists and committed sins to hurt other Jews. They ate in the open on the Day of Atonement [a fast day] and on top of that non-kosher kielbasa [Polish sausage]. I thought that the Krinker young men were licentious and had no feelings for their fellow Jews.

Brestovitzer young men were the exact opposite – the middle class children were students. Many of them were enlightened. They were truly infected with apostasy – from the "secular books" they read, but they were respectful, well behaved children. They did not trample on Jewish laws and traditions and the feelings of their fellow Jews.

The first time I met Krinkers face to face was about a dozen years ago in America – in Chicago. Then I realized that the impression I had of them was false they were exactly the opposite of what I had heard. At that time not one of the former Brestovitzer middle class young men heeded my call to do something together for the needy in our shtetl. The former Krinker young men, the non-religious, arranged to assist all the Krinker institutions, including the religious ones, fulfilling the needs of all the Jewish elements in Krinik. I joined the Krinik Relief Union and even became an active member.

I corrected my error.

A game of croquet in the day home for orphans

Footnotes:

1.   Kelman's son, Shiya, also loved to joke. When the Catholics walked through Mill Street with a priest in the lead and they all sang the prayers (as was their custom, in Latin) Shiya said to us in all seriousness: "he already made a mistake!" and then "Oy, he has made more than one mistake, he knows nothing about Hebrew!…"

2.   Talmud – There are two Talmuds: the first known as Bavli or Babylonian is the most famous, completed about the 5th century; the second is Yerushalmi or Jerusalem, edited around the early 4th century. The core of both is the *Mishanah* and *Gemore* and has become the term used for the Talmud.

Notices and Lists

[Page 222]

Notices and Lists

Translated by Judie Goldstein

Yiddish Names Of The Krinik Streets

Amdurer Street, Bath Street, Bialystoker, Community and Grodner Streets; Halinkerke Street; Chaykl's (Azheshkove) Street; Pottery Street; the Market and Marketplace; Mill Street (*Koschelne* [Church]); New and Sokolker Streets; Post Office and Currant Streets; Peretz Street; Tzerkve [Russian Orthodox Church] Street; Police Station Street; Synagogue Street; Synagogue Courtyard; Shishlevitzer and Blacksmith Streets; Narrow Street (Wonske).

Names Of Regions

"Tiflis", "Kavkaz", Yenta's Courtyard, Forest and Orchard.

Jewish Farmers in Krynki

During the time of the German occupation during the First World War, many Jewish families started to become involved in agriculture, especially at the edges of the town and the surrounding areas. Even after the war, there were some who continued working in agriculture, especially in growing potatoes.

Similarly, we find (according to the census of Dr. Lipowski of the JOINT), that 37 Jewish families in Krynki farmed 10 Dessiatin[1] (more than 100 dunams) of land. 135 people were occupied in this, and 246 individuals were sustained by this. In 1927 as well (according to the accounting of the Y.K.A.), two Jewish families in Krynki farmed an area of 21 hectares (200 dunams).\

Translator's Footnote:

1.   1. An old Russian unit of area. See https://en.wikipedia.org/wiki/Dessiatin

Jews On The Krynki Town Council

In 1927 the Krynki Town Council, according to a proposition from a member Bendet Nisht, and with a majority of 19 votes to 15 – decided that all official announcements and orders of the Town Council will be printed not only in Polish but also in Yiddish. Also that at the meetings of the Town Council one may speak and make speeches in Yiddish.

To carry out this order it was necessary to get the agreement of the District Governor.

(According to "Grodner Moment" of 25th November 1927)

The Community of Krynki Declares a Boycott of Nazi Germany

In the spring of 1933, the leadership of the Jewish community of Krynki sought to organize a boycott of Nazi Germany. It appointed a special committee for this purpose. They declared a public fast day on May 8, and posted large placards calling on the Jewish residents to close their stores and stop their businesses that afternoon, and to gather for a public meeting in the Great

Synagogue in the evening. A prayer service would be conducted, and speeches would be given, including from the rabbi of the town, about the situation of the Jews of Germany and the Soviet Union.

Dedication Of The "Public Heder"

The "dedication" of the "Public *Heder*" in 5690 [1930] was a "city event" in Krynki. Rabbis, social workers from various cities and towns, gentiles and also *Reb* Meyer Karelitz from Vilna were invited and came to the celebration.

An orchestra played and the Sokolker cantor sang synagogue music.

[Page 223]

Moreover greetings – first to B. Ayon, Chairman of the *Kehila* [Jewish Community Council], that gave the "heder" 500 zlotys and even promised support; then Zev (Velvl) Weiner in the name of the "Building Council", Shalakhovitch – from the "Council," Segal – from the workers, Rudy – from "*Linat HaZedek*" [staying overnight with the sick], Tarlovski – Chaiman of the Loan Without Interest Fund, Yitzhak Slapak – from the retailers, Melamed – from the *besmedresh*, Lublinski – from the Zionist organizations. Then the non-Jewish representatives of the government; and then rabbis and other prominent guests and especially the "host", the initiator and manager of the "Public Heder" – Rabbi Mr. Hezekiah Josef Mishkovski.

The second part of the program that went on until late at night, was dedicated to "calling down blessings" and this brought in over seven hundred dollars, a large sum in those days.

"It was joyous to see how the men and women carried their contributions to the building of the *heder*" writes "e'n" (the Kuznitzer Rabbi Mr. Nissen Ekstein) who took part in the celebration. In the Vilna "*Dos Vort*" [The Word] (delivered according to M. Tzinovitch). "And it was a beautiful moment" (writes there "Abraham ben HaChaim", son of Rabbi Mr. Kh'I Mishkovski), when "a poor man who goes around to houses, brought his contribution of eighteen zlotys". "Even those only concerned with the leftist groups had - - under the influence of the celebration gave significant contributions, above their means". And further "women" due to the initiative of the native rabbinate Breyna Miskhovski, brought their contributions, not satisfied with what their husbands gave."

At the end the people, young and old, Hasidic rabbis and ordinary people, in ecstasy sang and lost themselves in a "festival dance". And with the singing they went to the dance "Preparing for Tomorrow".

"Krinker Vakhnshrift"

A Zionist publication, "Krinker *Vakhnshrift*" [weekly] appeared in the shtetl in 1918.

"Funken"

Several books under the name "*Funken*" [sparks] - "organ of "Poalei Zion" and "Freiheit" in Krynki – appeared in the summer of 1927.

Editors of "Funken" Krynki 4 Jun 1927

"The Young Revolutionaries"

An illegal communist publication "The Young Revolutionaries" appeared in Krynki in September 1928.

[Page 224]

A Book About Krynki And Krynkers

An important memorial book about Krynki (118 pages printed on glossy paper) was published in 1930 by *landsleit* [compatriot] in Chicago (United States) for the 15th anniversary of the founding of the "First Krynker Relief Union".

The book, written in soft, homey, Krynker Yiddish, was edited by the Heiman brothers and Ab(raham) Miller who published an important work. Ab(raham) Miller described life in his hometown, studies of Krynker economic development since the 18th century, the raging struggle of the Krynker Jewish workers for freedom and better working conditions, daily life and the various figures and characters of the shtetl and the ordinary people.

The book, to this day a rarity, contains memories of other participants, material about the Jewish Public School and institutions and a lot of rare photographs.

A considerable amount of this Krynker literary treasure of this new elaborate edition was used here for our "Yizkor Book."

Investigator, Man Of Letters And World Scientist

A Krynker

Hersch Mintz was born in 1906 in Krynki, went to *heder* there, later graduated from High school in Grodno and in 1927 from the Polish Teacher's Seminary in Lemberg. Since 1928 he has been in Australia where he continued his education at the University of Adelaide and Sydney. Later he became a lecturer of European literature.

During the Second World War he took part as an officer in the Australian Navy and settled afterwards in Melbourne and was active in Jewish community life.

In the scientific field Mintz helped in the evaluation and theory about wool – as a part of its basis. He was the first university wool investigator who divided the original quality of wool and put it in table format that is now used throughout the world. His work about wool and sheep serves as a handbook in the universities and his work is acknowledged as the greatest contribution in this field.

[Page 225]

He is well versed in literature in several languages, write Yiddish, Hebrew and English, is a contributor to the "*Australishe Yiddishe Neyes*" [Australian Jewish News] newspaper and of this Jewish-English and English press, where he publishes in succession works about Jewish literature, theater and culture. In the Australian Jewish "*Kdima*" [priority] Almanac he published works about the history of the Jews in Australia. He is the author of books in English and Yiddish about the history of Jewish communities in Southern Australia (English) and Jakob Spears journeys and visit in Australia as a travel agent from Israel in 1861 (published by "YIVO").

Hersch Mintz is especially active as a Jewish cultural worker for the Zionist pioneer youth movement and for the "*Histadrut* [labour] campaign".

During his second visit to Israel in 1964, Mintz led negotiations concerning preparations for a movie about the sheep in ancient times in Israel due to archaeological discoveries. The agricultural faculty in Rehovot invited him to lecture about wool science and the possibility of raising Merino sheep in Israel.

Translated by Jerrold Landau
Great responsibility, ideas and a sense of justice demanded of a judge

Master Sergeant Chaav Inbar, native of Krynki, seated on the judge's chair of the Israel
Defense Forces. She is the daughter of Hindka, the sister of Bendet Nisht. She is a judge in the
military court of the Israel Defense Forces.

The only female judge in the Israel Defense Forces, and apparently the only one in the world, is the young woman, filled with humor – Chava Inbar, the daughter of Hindka, who is the daughter of Shmuel Nisht, the father of Bendet Nisht. She studied law at the Hebrew University of Jerusalem. Before her appointment as judge, she served for ten years as a defense lawyer in the advocacy of the northern command, in thousands of cases of absenteeism, refusal to fulfill duty, careless use of weapons, etc.

(From B. Landau, *Bemachane* [In the Camp] newspaper of Israeli soldiers, 2 Cheshvan, 5730 [1969].

Additions

[Page 226]

The Fundraising campaign in Krynki in 1903 for those injured in the Kishinev Pogrom

As in many Jewish communities in Russia, Krynki conducted a fundraising campaign for the benefit of those injured in the Kishinev Pogrom. The campaign took place in the spring of 1903, a short time after the slaughter of the Jews of Kishinev. This was an expression of Jewish fraternal feelings. In *Hatzefira* of Warsaw from 23 Sivan 5663 (June 10(23), 1903) [1]), a list of approximately 300 donors from Krynki, the majority being businesses.

Let this also serve as a list of testimony to the names of those families by including them in Pinkas Krynki. (In general, the names are written as they appear in the list. The kopeck amounts are noted only with numbers.)[a]

Sent from Krynki to the government authorized committee in Kishinev to support those injured by the disturbances:

Collected by L. Garber, B. Hirszowicz, B. Kniszinski, M. Swarcman – from the local rabbi and head of the rabbinical court 5 rubles; N. Kniszinski 10 rubles; Grosman-Lewin Co. 8 rubles; L. Garber, B. Hirszowicz, Tz. Fabrikant, Y. Margolis, Y. Garber, D. Kniszinski, P. Onuszewicz, Garber brothers – each 5 rubles; Iwenicki brothers, A Brustyn, M. Szwarcman, V. Ch. Nakdimon, Y. Torlowski – each 3 rubles; Sh. Wiener 2.50 rubles; Dr. Halbert., M. Szimshonowicz, Y. Slower, B. Kincler, B. Stolarski – each 2 rubles; M. Chazan 1.30 rubles; A. Garber, H. Garber, M. Garber, A. Zalkin, B. Kalinowicz, N. Ostrowski, B. Y. Iwenicki, A. Gotlib, A. Mordechilewic, Dentist Awerbuch, Sh. Goldberg – each 1 ruble; A. Bajdel, W. Slapak, Krupnik, Sh. Nisht, Ceszler brothers, A. Listokyn, W B. Fink. A. Lazicki – each 50 kopecks; D. Okun – 35; A. Fajnberg, M. Kuzniec – each 30; W Gurawic, Ch. Bunimowicz – each 20; A. Braude, Y. L. Chajes, Z. Szajnberg, Y. Broneg – each 1 ruble; P. Kohen, Laszer, each 50 kopecks.

From Factory Workers

Tannery of N. A. Kniszinski: Z. Otwezski 1 ruble; N. Trachimowski, Y. Gel, Ch. Finkelsztejn – each 20 kopecks; Y. Ajlin, Y. Borkowski, M. Janowski each 15; L. A. Lampert 50; Sh. Tewel, E. Gering each 30; Ben-Tzion Kantor, S. Surowicz, Walenti, A. Wiener, Zajdka each 25; Kohn, A. Bunim, Sh. Y. Rachkin each 50; P. Moszcanski, W. Melnyk each 25; W. Kac, Ch. Z. Kaplan, A. Kroln, A. Lider, A. Lopote, M. Lejbrowicz, L. Ostrinski, M. Farber, Y. L. Kundzic each 50; B. Szturmak, S. Tryzwa, A. Pandera, Y. Brzeszowski, Y. Sh. Ajnszmid, M. Bortnowski, Sh. A. Goldszmyd each 25; S. Reizen 20.

B. Kniszinski Tannery: Ch. Morani, A. Szkilewski, A. Szyf each 1 ruble; A. Mendelson, A. Y. Krynker each 50; M. Chirig 30; M. Lebendik, W Kopel, D. Krinski, Y. Charas, A. Ch. Krynker, Ch. Judelewic, W. Goldberg, Zisl each 25 kopecks.

[Page 227]

Grosman-Lewin Tannery: A. M. Sikorski, D. Stambler, M. A. Zonenberg, each 1 ruble; Sh. Chowski, M. Lesnik, each 50; A. Y. Seliber 36; Sh. Adinak 30; A. Roitbart, L. Gercowski, Z. Birnbaum. G. Nowyzak, L. Slower, Y. Gershuni each 25; M. Szepjocki, F. Bordon, N Langerfajgn each 20; H. Kurkyn, A. Czyk, A. Grecowski, M. Eksztejn each 15; N. Chawer 10 kopecks.

A. Brustyn Tannery: Grobsz, Y. A. Fajnsod, Sh. Wilenski each 5; A. Charo, Tz. Gendler, A. Kohn, Y. Kalia, Y. Gordin, Y. Charo, T. Lew, A. Gliman each 25 kopecks.

L. Garber Tannery: L. Lew, H. Lew each 50; H. Szturmak, Y. Grynberg, Sh. Wajsman each 25; M. Kotlier, Charanzaj each 20; Sh. Kozelczyk, E. Epsztejn, M. Zev, H. Bobor each 15; L. Charst 10 kopecks.

Y. Garber Tannery: M. Epsztejn, Y. Slapak, L. Nemirowski, D. Szoszan each 50; Sh. Chaszkes, R. Morber each 40; M. Liakow 25; Y. Hant 15 kopecks.

Garber Brothers Tannery: Sh. Elizerowicz, H. Stoliar, P. Szklorski, Y. Pruzhansky each 50; B. Orenowski, A. Tykocki, Ch. H. Gendler, Y. Eplbaum, M. Tykocki, Z. Boszniak each 25; Iwoszkowski 10 kopecks.

Y. H. Nakdimon Tannery: W. Gurewic, M. Kaplan each 50; Y. Glembocki, Y. Aleksandrowicz each 40; Sh. Kaplan Y. Ch. Griszcinski, Y. Terkel each 25; M. Kozelczyk, Sh. Zolto each 15 kopecks;

Ivenicki brothers tannery: B. Szkolnyk 50; Sh. Grosman 30; W. A Studnyk, M. Terkel, Ch. Tresczan, L. A. Brewda each 25; Sh. Socharewski, P. Grosman each 20; B. Belicki, D. Tykocki, Ch. Leibowicz, W. Szurmak, Bojlmat each 15.

M. Margolis Tannery: A. Zylberblat 25; Y. Wajrman, H. Lipski each 15; B. Szturmak 10 kopecks.

Tz. Fabrikant Tannery: Y. Szajnberg, W. Leibowicz, P. Rabinowicz each 50 kopecks.

A. B. Frajdman Tannery: A. B. Frajdman 1 ruble; B. Done, Sh. Slower each 50 kopecks; L. Feldman 25 kopecks.

N. Epsztejn Tannery: N. Epsztejn 50; Y. Yatom, A. Brewda each 25; N. Najman, Sh. Lezjorowicz each 15; A Polk, Z. Majster each 10 kopecks.

Dubinski-Kirzszer Tannery: W. Sikorski, M. Kirzszner, M. Dubinski each 50; Y. Gozszanski, Y. Ch. Zubowski, N.Barkin each 25; Y. Poliak 15 kopecks.

From a Special list:

A. Yatom, M. Lublinski, Sz. Jacewlan; Y. L. Zaleski, Y. Limder, M. Lubelski each 2 rubles; Karpowicz 1.25 rubles; Mordchilewicz, Sh. Mordchilewicz, Y. Wilenski, A. Jacewlan, M. Chackel, Y. Cackel, A. Lowski, A. Paczewocki, Sh. Yacewlan, A. M. Yatom, M. Pruzhanski, Y. Lew, N. Edelsztejn, M. Margolis each 1 ruble; Sh. D. Sapirsztejn 75; A. Gendler, Sh. A. Chait, M. Polewocki, L. Rotbart, M. Afrimzon, Sh. Kotlier, A. Farber, N. Borowski each 50; M. Pivka's, B. L. Drajzy, Y. Lezjorowicz, A. Fel, A. Perlman. A. Puria, Sh. Edelsztejn, Y. K. Tewel, A. Furman, Ch. Y. Zalkin, Ch. R. Marac, T. R. Grosman, A. Galiant each 30; Ch. Alian 35; N. Polanski, Z. Szynder, Tz. Hercberg, M. A. Sochen, Y. D. Melamed, Sh. A. Temkyn, M. Gabai, Sh. Wajn, Y. Becalel, R. Gozszanski, A. Klotnicki, A. Mordchilewicz, D. Elkan, A. Najman each 25; M. Szolker, M. Zalkin, Y. Z. Chait, Sh. Glembocki, A. Kugel, Z. Sapirsztejn, Y. Kapoler, N. R. Rojtbard, A. Efron each 20; Y. Morn, W. Mosztowlianski, Z. Kapica, Ch. W. Leiber, Sh. Toker each 15; T. Kohen, Y. Lewin, B. Z. Nisht, D. Prenski, Y. Szafer, Y. Tewel each 10 kopecks.

[Page 228]

Small donations 20; Menchenewicz 50; A. Walker 29 kopecks.

Ancis-Listokin Tannery: A. W. Wiener, Sznajder, Kos each 25; Listokin 50; Tz. Mordechilewicz 15; Ancis-Listokin 2 rubles; A. Kugel 1 ruble.

Assistants of the Sh. Priwes company – 31 ruble.

Total transferred: 188 rubles, 30 kopecks.

Beis Yaakov Girl's School

Students in the General Chede

Translator's Footnote:

1.   The two dates were given in the original text. They seemingly represent the discrepancy between the Gregorian and Julian calendars, as the Julian calendar would still have been in use in Russia at that time.

Original footnote:

The arrangement of the names is as it was in the aforementioned newspaper, by donor and company. The kopeck amount is listed only with a number, without specifying the currency.

At the outbreak of the Storm 1939-1941

[Page 229]

During the Time of the Storm
1939-1941

Translated by Jerrold Landau

At the Outbreak of World War II
Fear and Terror

The devil, Hitler may his name be erased, attacked Poland on September 1, 1939, and the Second World War broke out. A draft of men of age 18 and over was immediately called. Some of them immediately became German prisoners, and never returned.

Quickly, the buzz of airplanes was heard over Krynki. They began bombarding the [market] square unimpededly. The youth went to and for trying to reach the front, for which nobody knew the whereabouts…

On the 8th of the month, the Nazis already reached Grodno, having passed over Krynki. Fear and terror took hold of the Jews. The elderly fasted and recited Psalms. The Polish police and city leadership did not even have time to escape. The confusion was great, and everyone hid in the houses, without even sticking their noses outside.

In the meantime, the German troops arrived, wearing their clunky helmets. They revealed the secret that the Russians were about to enter the town. The news quickly spread through the community, and aroused sparks of hope in their hearts.

22 Months Under the Protection of the Red Army
Temporary Rescue and Anxieties

On September 15, an airplane appeared in the sky with the red star clearly visible on its wings. It dropped flyers on the town, informing the residents that the Red Army was approaching, and would reassure their lives and property. While the Soviet troops were approaching Krynki, and the Polish police was still present, the local laborers did not wait. They grabbed the rule into their hands, and raised a red flag over the town hall.

The Jewish residents welcomed the Red Army with enthusiasm, good wishes, joy, and flowers. Veteran Communists even jumped atop the Soviet tanks and kissed the soldiers. Our Jewish brethren breathed a sigh of relief. Even the wealthy people and manufacturers, who had reason for concern, were satisfied, for at least they were saved from death.

Not many days passed before the Soviet authorities began to impose their rule upon the town. Factories and real estate were nationalized. Private ownership of businesses was liquidated. They reorganized the foundations of the cooperatives.

Enthusiasm for the regime was dimmed with the passage of time among those who had awaited it. For some reason, the new authorities did not place any trust in the members of the Communist Party. They even suspected them of being Trotskyites. On the other hand, the authorities did not refrain from relating with more trust to those who were not among the ranks of the party, for example, to the physicians and pharmacists.

In the interim, life in the town found its routine, and a Soviet way of life spread through.. The wealthy, especially the manufacturers, were for the most part arrested and deported to Siberia. Thus, they were saved and remained alive. Those who remained in place found themselves in a very bad situation. Everyone made efforts to find some sort of employment. On the other hand, many Jewish families who had been previously unemployed found employment as officials and laborers, and were satisfied with the change of times.

The situation of the refugees who had escaped and arrived in Krynki from central Poland, which had been conquered by the Nazis, and who were unwilling to accept Soviet citizenship, was very serious. They were deported to the interior of Russia. However, in general, the population worked, and the Jews waited for better days.

The saying that was then common among those going through the town, attributed to the Slonimer Hassidic rabbi, was "German conquest means certain death, whereas Soviet rule is life imprisonment."

[Page 230]

Teaching in Krynki During Soviet Rule

by Arnold Rozenfeld

Translated by Jerrold Landau

I spent time in my native city of Radom, and more than once I recalled far-off Radom , where I had spent such happy days in my life when I served as a teacher in the Hebrew school there.

Then the Second World War broke out. Within eight days, Hitler's troops took over all of Poland. Anyone who did not succeed in escaping on the first day of the war could not leave the place. I was among them.

I wrote about the suffering that I endured during the first three months of Nazi rule in Radom in my book "Three Months in the Nazi Hell of Radom." However, I did not despair, and I hatched all sorts of plans to escape from the talons of the Nazi murderers. One day, I was prepared to set out on a journey, and the question stood before me: to where? In my predicament, I recalled Krynki, and told myself: "If I can only get to there – I will not fall. I will live!" However, the distance was far, very far. I wrote some things about it in the aforementioned book. However, I reached Krynki.

It was no longer the small town that I had left many years previously. There were already hundreds of Russian Communists there, including Jews, under the rule of the Soviet Union. I could no longer see any signs of joy, or happiness in the eyes of my few acquaintances, as it was many years previously. Already on my first day in Krynki, I found a group of my former students, including Eli Gozanski, Mashka Kaplan, Chana Rubinsztejn, and Rachel Aharonowicz. When I arrived, they looked after me like an older brother. I will never forget all that they did for me during those days so that I would feel good. They did this with all their heart. I was never particularly fond of the Yiddish language, and did not know it well, but nevertheless, "*vos tut men nisht for parnassa*?" (what does one not do for a livelihood?) When my former student, Chana Rubinsztejn, came to me to invite me to teach in her Yiddish school (with Yiddish as the language of instruction), at which she was the principal – I did not refuse. However, despite all my good intentions, I could not adjust to teaching in this language that was strange to me. This was despite the fine manner with which my principal related to me, and her request that her husband, comrade Perlman, work with me to prepare my lessons. I felt that I could no longer continue there. At that time, my dear friend, Eli Gozanski, made every effort to pull me out of the "mud." The supervisor of the Russian school knocked at my door every day, and did not let up until he set me up in the Russian school.

I was offended that my role was an unimportant teacher during the first month. However, it quickly became known there that I could give a great deal to that educational institution, which was a high school with a very large number of students. Most of the teachers were Russians, and it was headed by a Jew from Minsk whose name was Lewin, if I am not mistaken. He was a dedicated Communist, but an upright man with a good heart. He found out by chance that I had a high level education, and was an expert in German, with a great deal of experience. One day, he transferred me to teach German in the upper grades. I demonstrated my knowledge of that language, and I quickly became the sole expert of it in the town. Every important examination in German was conducted by me, and I was the only one who taught it in any important government institution. My financial situation flourished from day to day. It is worthwhile to note that in those days, the two Kozlowski brothers had an honorable position in the education network in Krynki. The younger was the vice principal in the high school, and his older brother was the supervisor of schools. I do not know what their fate was after I left Krynki for the second time.

Incidentally, I benefited from full room and board in the home of Rachel Aharonowicz, my former student in Krynki. She was like a sister to me. I never felt lonely if I had anyone close.

Who knows if I would have survived the war had I not become a "person of Krynki." At the end of the school year, a few days before the outbreak of the war between Russia and Nazi Germany, I was stricken badly by a stomach ulcer. My situation was particularly bad, and the doctors recommended that I be sent urgently to Zheleznovodsk for convalescence. To my good fortune, I went there to convalesce, and thus was I saved.

From Krynki to the Land of Israel
via the Soviet Union and Syria

by Yehuda Eckstein

Translated by Jerrold Landau

I recall that during the time of the outbreak of the Second World War in September 1933, when the German scouts entered Krynki, they left it within a few days, and the Red Army entered, the Jews exited the synagogues enwrapped in their tallises to greet the redeeming army. How great was the joy among the people.

[Page 231]

I, whose longing and pining for the Land of Israel disturbed my rest, left my family and town, and set out in October of that year to Lithuania, which had not yet been conquered, with the intention of reaching my desired destination. I reached Vilna, and joined the *hachshara* kibbutz on 37 Sovoch Street. This was a refuge for many *chalutzim* [Zionist pioneers] who escaped to Lithuania from Poland with the hope of going from there to the Land. Among them were the Krynki natives Avraham Dranicki, Berle, and others who were together with me in Hechalutz Hatzair [Young Hechalutz], and who did not succeed in coming to the Land. May their memories be a blessing.

News spread through Lithuania for some time that the British had placed the Land of Israel into the hand of the Jews, who had established a state. We all knew that, to our dismay, this was not true, but rather a tale. I spent approximately 16 months there. When we visited the YIVO (Jewish Scientific Institution) there, we registered in the guestbook: "Our aspiration – to the Land of Israel. Krynki natives, December 10, 1940." Yehuda Eksztejn and other signed.

I left Lithuania on the 18th of that month, and I arrived at my desired destination, the Land of Israel, on January 5, 1941, after journeying on a difficult trip through the Soviet Union, Turkey, and Syria. I went to Kibbutz Ramat Hakovesh.

The Remnants of Hechalutz Hatzair

by Chaim Sheinberg

Translated by Jerrold Landau

When the Soviet army entered the town at the beginning of the Second World War, our movement knew to begin clandestine work. A group of members made contact with workers who arranged the smuggling of *chalutzim* across the border of White Russia to the "independent" Lithuania of that time (region of Vilna), from where there was a strand of hope that one might be able to set out for the Land of Israel. Some indeed arrived in the Shacharia Kibbutz of that city, including the late Yehudale Eckstein (of Ramat Hakovesh), and Lea Sapir, who succeeded in making *aliya* to the Land during the years 1940-1941, at the beginning and at the height of the Holocaust.

Other Krynki natives of that kibbutz found their way, at the time of the invasion of the Nazi brigades, into the pioneering clandestine resistance at the ghetto. Let us remember here our comrade Avraham Dranicki (Walutiner), who fell in his resistance against the Nazis in a town near Kovno.

I myself, the final secretary of Hechalutz Hatzair of Krynki, encountered the war as I was preparing for *aliya* in the kibbutz in Baranovichi. I had good fortune, in that after going through ghettos, forests, and camps, I earned reaching the shores of our Land. May these few lines serve as a form of a memorial monument to the memory of those enthusiastic and dedicated pioneering youth from our town who dreamed of being with us here, but were cut off and did not make it.

[Page 231]

At the Outbreak of the Storm

(1939 – 1941)

Translated by Judie Goldstein

Jews in Krynki under the Soviet Regime

Kushnir Eliahu and Friede (Zalkin)

The Jewish population of Krynki impatiently awaited the arrival of the Red Army, and as soon as our workers heard that the Soviet military crossed the border, they did not wait long before taking over the government in the shtetl. Before the Polish police had managed to leave Krynki, there was already a red flag flying from City Hall.

Jews welcome the Soviets with an outbreak of joy and enthusiasm. Communists jumped up onto the tanks and kissed the soldiers. The people were just plain happy.

Shortly the enthusiasm on the part of the followers of the Soviet regime began to cool. But to them, after the Polish regime, they wanted to try communism. The government quickly suspected those, for example the doctors and pharmacists, who did not declare party affiliation.

[Page 232]

Generally the Jews were happy. The factories, other enterprises, and fixed property were nationalized. But even those who spoke out against the Bolsheviks, such as wealthy men and manufacturers, gave thanks for escaping the peril, knowing that they had at least been saved from a sure death by the bestial Nazis. The Soviet government very quickly forced them to go to Siberia and in fact thanks to this they survived. But for those who were not sent away, their material situation worsened and some tried other occupations. However, a lot of Jewish families that previously could not make a living, now had positions as officials or other work and they were happy.

The situation for the refugees, who arrived from Central Poland and did not want to become Soviet citizens, was very serious. They were sent deep into Russia.

The regime in the shtetl stabilized with time and instituted a Soviet way of life. People worked, the Jews lived and hoped for better times. A typical witticism in Krynki at the time, attributed to the rabbi of the "Slonimer" Hasidim, was "the German occupation is death, but the Soviet – an eternal prison."

The Beginning of WWII

Beyl'ke Shuster-Greenstein

The first of September 1939 the terrible murderers of Jews, may their names be erased, attacked Poland and the first call up of the sad war was announced. Immediately, all the young men eighteen and older were mobilized and my oldest brother, Heshel, was among the first. Later, he was captured by the Germans, became a prisoner of war and never returned.

These were difficult days when one had to bid farewell to so many acquaintances, comrades and neighbors. Everyone knew how serious the situation was and who knew when the war would end?

Everyday new information arrived, as the Jew-murderers crept further and further into the center of Poland. A heavy sadness, like a dark cloud, overcame everyone. There was one remaining hope: that America and England would come to help and things would once again be good.

But the world was busy with politics while people were falling like flies. Everyone's ears turned to the radio and then great bitterness. The latest information brought fear and all around there was darkness. We were not allowed to move around later than nine o'clock at night –a condition of war.

We quickly heard the hum of airplanes. We ran out and the metal birds already flew unhindered, shooting up the square where the young men had been gathered together to march off to the front. Already nobody knew where the front was.

On the eighth day it had already reached Grodno, bypassing our shtetl. We were terrified. The orthodox fasted and said Psalms, but to no avail. The police and the leader of the shtetl were ready to flee. There was a great panic. People hid in their houses and were afraid to stick their noses out.

Meanwhile the murderers, on motorcycles wearing large metal helmets, drove into the shtetl and secretly told us that the Russians were coming to our town. The rumor quickly spread and there was hope again in everyone's heart.

[Page 233]

On the Eve of the Russians Entry

Avraham Sofer

On the tenth day after the war broke out, the police and all the Polish government officials fled Krinik. The entire population was frightened and terrified. We received information that the Germans were ten kilometers from us. We could already clearly hear shooting from heavy artillery and tanks. In the sky was the noise from airplane formations. The sirens, indicating that people should hide, had already stopped. Everything was dead. The streets were empty; a deathly stillness lay over everywhere. From time to time the heavy steps of Yakov Kozoltchik (Jankel Khazir), who was alone, with a stick in his hand, walked the dead streets. And every step resounded with an echo. We sat in the house with the windows shuttered.

From time to time we would hear heavy artillery and the sound hung in the silence. I crept up to the attic and looked through a hole to see the highway that went from Sokolke to Bialystok. I saw Kozoltchik walking alone in the street, holding a loaf of bread with salt in his hand. With long strides he walked out to the highway. I saw two rows of metal helmets. They came closer. There was a loud yell: "hands up!"

Yakov put down the bread and salt and raised his hands over his head.

Several minutes later the heavy steps of the Germans were heard. They were going back to the road they had arrived on. They were a reconnaissance group – about twenty people.

The fifteenth day of the war. Nobody knows anything about what is happening at the front. The majority had hidden their radios and the shtetl was cut off.

Suddenly we hear the drone of an airplane. It circles several times. A red star can be clearly seen on the wing. We see two hands tossing out paper that flew in the air. Notes fall on our heads. People run out to catch one. So do I. I catch one and quickly run home with it. My father takes it with trembling hands. Everyone stands around, as my father reads:

"To the citizens of Western White Russia:

"You are a member of our people and we going to help you. Our government and Comrade Stalin have ordered the Red Army to cross the border of White Russia to ensure your life and well-being.

"The Foreign Commissar of the USSR
V. M. Molotov"

There was joy in Krynki. People hugged each other with tears streaming down their cheeks, tears of joy and luck.

Under the Rule of the Red Army

Beyl'ke Shuster-Greenstein

The shtetl was truly dancing in the streets. Everyone was beaming as they met their friends and chatted and talked politics. Everyone was in a holiday mood.

People took flowers and called out to welcome the Red Army. My brother Heykel ran around beaming with joy and my mother cried from joy and sorrow because their eldest son could not be with them. She ran to get some information about our eldest brother who had not returned – but to no avail.

[Page 234]

Meanwhile a new life began. All private enterprises were liquidated and cooperatives were formed. The factories were nationalized and my father went to work in a shoe-making cooperative. Life returned to normal.

The banishing of the manufacturers (our next door neighbors with whom we had lived for so many years) began. People were depressed and nobody knew what tomorrow would bring. Our neighbors, Potchebutski, were banished. And because of this a few from our shtetl survived, even though they were tormented and a lot had their health was destroyed. But they lived to take revenge.

Depression ruled in our house: we expected to be sent on our way because of our relationship to the party. My mother was brought in but only to frighten her. Oh that they would be sent away so that somebody would survive!

Meanwhile a crowd of people from Poland, refugees, among them my young man from Pabianitz arrived. All the strangers were ordered to leave Krynki, which was then a border city, in three days. We decided to travel together [my young man and I] deep into Russia, having the privilege of choosing a place because my uncle, Ayzik Tsigel, was one of those in charge of transport. We traveled to Minsk thinking that we would be able to return. A childish fantasy!

The Destruction and end
of the Jewish Community of Krynki

[Page 235]

Destruction and Might

Translated by Jerrold Landau

Earth, do not cover my blood. (Job 16:17)

[Page 237]

By the editor

Killing and the Ghetto

At the Beginning of the Nazi Invasion

On Sunday, June 22, 1941, at 10:00 a.m. several airplanes were seen in the skies of Krynki. An air raid siren was heard, and shots were fired. A mood of perplexity immediately overtook the city. Many thought that this was a military exercise, however some immediately figured out what was happening. The speech of the Soviet Foreign Minister Vyacheslav Molotov, broadcast in the afternoon, clearly outlined the situation. He stated that Germany had opened a war against the Soviet Union. The Red Army command declared a sudden draft of a certain number of the population.

The next day, Monday morning, airplanes appeared over the skies of Krynki once again, and bombarded the center of the city. The confusion of the hasty retreat of the Soviet army pervaded all around.

At dawn on Tuesday, June 24, Krynki itself was bombarded heavily, especially the Jewish quarters, and including the synagogue, which was known for its beauty and esthetic architectural structure. The Kavkaz neighborhood and several streets were completely destroyed. Other areas were partially destroyed. The first Jewish victims fell. The Soviet leadership and police arranged themselves for immediate departure. Soldiers ran about barefoot, with their shoes on their shoulders, in their haste to flee eastward, to Minsk, even though nobody knew where the front was.

Flyers were dropped from the German airplanes calling on the residents to go out to the fields. The Jews were commanded to cover their heads with white cloths. Masses of people therefore left the town without taking anything along. Their destination was the valleys and pasture areas several kilometers from the settlement – relying on the assumption that the civilian population was moving about freely and honorably in the fields, and would not harm them. Immediately upon arrival, the Jews sensed that a polar change had taken place with respect to their relationship with their Polish neighbors, with whom previously, during the time of Soviet rule, they literally had an idyllic relationships. Now, it had become the epitome of hostility. Our fellow members of our people realized for themselves that they must separate immediately from these neighbors and band together in the public pasture (the Wygon).

Flames and the First Murder

The Nazis entered Krynki in the afternoon, as it was engulfed in flames on all four sides. It took several days of effort to put out the fire. Some form of calm pervaded during those days, and the panicked people continued to remain in the valleys outside the town. Then on the morning of the Sabbath, June 28, several low-flying airplanes were seen. When they figured out the place where the Jewish masses were congregated, they signaled the German gunners who were stationed around. They immediately started firing, and about 50 people, including the elderly, women, and children, were killed. The innards of some of them were crushed and scattered about. Many others were injured.

Now, the murderers did not hesitate any longer. They began to pillage the town itself. Ch. Weiner, a Holocaust survivor, relates that the S.S. men broke into the *Beis Midrash*, gathered the Torah scrolls and other holy books, and set them on fire. They only permitted the Jews to extinguish the fire once the smoke began to burst through the roof. By risking their lives, the Jews succeeded in saving the Torah scrolls.

On the morning of Monday, June 30 (according to Ch. Weiner, this took place on July 3), a group of S.S. men surrounded several streets, arrested about 15 Jews, brought them to a grove (Szolker Wald) about two kilometers from the town, and shot 14 of them. Another two, Hershel Leib Shachne's and the dentist Tajchman, were brought to Lesser-Brestowice where they were shot to death. One youth, Berl Tewel, who had been shot in the grove, was badly injured and fainted. After he woke up. from his unconsciousness and the murderers were no longer seen in the place, he succeeded in raising himself out of the pile of corpses and reaching the town in the darkness of the night with his last strength. He said that the prisoners were prepared to attack and kill their four murderous guards, but their friend Aharon Wolf (Munchik) urged them to not do so, for it is better to give up one's life for the entire Jewish community than to place it in danger of destruction - heaven forbid, if even one of the four German Nazis was killed.

[Page 238]

Polish Jew Hatred, Decrees, and Degradation

At first, the Germans announced in town that they had come to rescue the Poles from their Russian Bolshevik tormentors, and that the authorities therefore demanded that they turn over to them the Jews who had collaborated with the Soviets. Indeed, a town leadership council was immediately set up, composed of Polish Jew-haters. The local government was in fact given over to them during the first month of the Nazi occupation. They now added poison to the German murderousness. As well, a committee of Poles who had just been released from the Soviet prisons in the area was set up. They began to storm after the Jews without discrimination, and slander them – especially regarding anyone who had formerly been employed in any Soviet business – stating that they were Bolsheviks. Thus, tens of Jews, not only Communists, were taken outside the town and killed. Their place of burial is not known.

Now, the period of various anti-Jewish decrees began. First, the obligation of forced labor was imposed on all Jews from the age of 14 and above, to 60 for men and 55 for women. They were ordered to appear in the market early in the morning every day for "labor brigades." Polish bullies along with a number of Germans would direct them to pave roads, plant grass, collect the dead from around and bury them, and perform various other tasks.

After a few days, additional decrees were announced: wearing the Magen David patch, the ban on coming into contact with and doing business with gentiles, the ban on owning a horse or cow, and other such tribulations. Among other things, Jews were obligated to remove their hats in front of any German they encountered on their route, and to be the first to greet them.

Anyone who was not careful about this or did not do this properly, women included, were taken to the police and were administered 25 lashes with a whip. There were cases where Jews even paid with their lives for a "transgression."

The Judenrat and its Tasks

At that time, the Jews were commanded to set up a Judenrat as a form of "representation" that would be responsible for carrying out the commands of the German authorities. First and foremost, they had to provide various workers for the needs of the Nazis and their offices. Of course the work would be without pay, and to work at various backbreaking tasks, as will be described. Second, the Judenrat had to collect all kinds of contributions and fees from the Jews, the vast majority of whom were impoverished – in accordance with the wishes of the Nazi thieves. Every one of their edicts was accompanied by the threat of a personal or collective punishment for the members of the Judenrat, including death, if it was not fulfilled, or was not fulfilled properly. This was the situation with respect to other demands of the murderers, such as: immediately providing gold, jewelry, expensive items, fine furniture, furs, expensive clothing and drink, etc. – to satisfy the appetites of the extortionists, who knew no satisfaction. Demands and edicts of this nature grew and became stronger from day to day.

In the autumn of 1941, rumors spread through the town that they were about to lock the Jews into a ghetto. At once, and frequently, frightful news, each piece worse than the previous, began to arrive about the bitter fate of our Jewish brethren in various cities and towns in which ghettos already existed.

The Jews believed that if they could be productive and worthwhile for the German war economy, they would be able to endure the era of tribulations in Krynki in peace. One tanner, Yankel Szinder, even operated a tannery in the town that employed Jews, and operated until the final liquidation of the community of Krynki.

Imprisonment in the Ghetto

The Judenrat was quickly commanded to lock the Jews into the bounds of the ghetto that the Germans had designated, with an area of 1-1.5 square meters as a "living space" for one Jewish person. Hundreds of Jews were enlisted to erect the high fence to lock them in. It had two gates: one in the marketplace, entering Garbarska Street, and the second next to the river on the same street.

[Page 239]

On a December day in 1941, the Jewish residents were given the order to move to the ghetto within a single day on the designated day. A commotion overtook the community, for everyone hastened to move quickly to the narrow confinement, and to find a corner for their family. They only managed to bring with them the most vital necessities. Not everything was allowed to be brought there. Polish police were the first to go out to the Jewish houses and choose for themselves the choicest objects. Anyone who attempted to take such a thing to the ghetto would be fined, beaten with death blows, or even shot. This is the bad luck that came to Sheimel Szajman (from the Bubickies) when he was caught carrying his shoemaking equipment to the confinement. He was shot to death.

The market square of Krynki was bustling with a crowd on that terrible day when the thousands of its Jews went into the confinement of the ghetto. Many Christians wandered about: a few who expressed their agony at the scene that was unfolding before them, and so many who were filled with joy and gladness, and even mocked the crisis of their *Zyd* neighbors. Not only would they be finally freed of them, but they would also inherit the best of their property. Now, S.S. men were standing together with Polish police at the entrance gate of the ghetto. They were searching the belongings of the Jews, checking and examining each package, packet, and article of clothing. They took for themselves the best of what they found. German photographers and journalists were also standing there, perpetuating the great victory of the murderous "master race" with photos of the perplexed Jews, as they were beaten and forced to enter the gate of hell.

During the Time of Confinement

Slavery, Crowding, and Hunger

When the gates of the ghetto were locked, a guard was placed over them, and nobody was allowed to leave without a work certificate or a permit from the secret police. A Jewish militia (ordnugnsdienst) was set up in the confinement, and the number of members of the Judenrat was reduced to seven, namely: Yosel Golc as head, Yisrael Kalinowicz, Talia Goldschmid, Yankel

Grosman, Yankel Lewi ("The Clearer"), Natan Mostowlianski, and Meir Kaplan. From that time, the Judenrat, with the help of the Jewish police, was a form of government within the realm of the ghetto. It even had its own jail, in which those who transgressed the stringent work orders were imprisoned. Yankel Kozolczyk (nicknamed The Pig) was appointed as head of the Jewish police militia, and his deputy was Yosel Mostowlianski. The witness Eliahu Kuszner said the following about Kozolczyk, who was now the ruling force of the Judenrat:

"He was a tall person, broad shouldered with unusual physical strength. He had immigrated to Cuba during his youth, where he gave himself over to suspicious businesses, and was involved in acts of murder. He returned to Poland, and became a boxer.

"He appeared in Krynki during the time of the Soviet occupation. When the Germans invaded, he volunteered, solely on his own accord, to move with his own hands a 100-kilogram shell that had not exploded, to which the Germans were afraid to approach. It is said that he helped people. On the contrary, however, by nature he had no conscience, and he caused ill to many people. He emerged alive from the tragedy of the Holocaust, including Auschwitz, and reached Israel, where he was known by the nickname "Shimshon-Eizen" (Shimshon of Iron). He died in 1950."

Ruling over everyone, however, was the cruel, bloodthirsty Nazi, Amts Komisar (Town Ruler), who instilled fear and terror upon everyone. When he entered the ghetto several times a day to make their rounds, the narrow alleyways immediately became empty of people – to the point where no living being was found there.

The south-eastern portion of the city, with Garbarska Street at the center, was within the bounds of the ghetto, that had been surrounded by a barbed wire fence. It continued from the market square until the river on one side. On the other side was the street of the bathhouse and Gmina Street. Within this area, the Nazis took the synagogue courtyard for themselves as a field for the repair of tanks.

Three or four families were crowded into each dwelling in the cramped confinement – due to the intention of the Nazis to destroy the Jews in a variety of ways, including "natural causes" such as suffocation and epidemics. Eyewitnesses relate that three or four housewives would stand beside the chimney fanning the flames, with their eyes tearing from the abundance of smoke and suffering.

Already at 6:00 a.m., in all weather, the residents of the Ghetto – men, women, and even young children – were commanded to appear next to the gate and arrange themselves into their work groups with their leaders. They would go out to work accompanied by a Polish guard. Anyone who disobeyed this command would be imprisoned. The only ones exempt were those with special permits such as the militia commander and his deputy, several policemen, as well as the Judenrat members and their families.

[Page 240]

At the time of labor

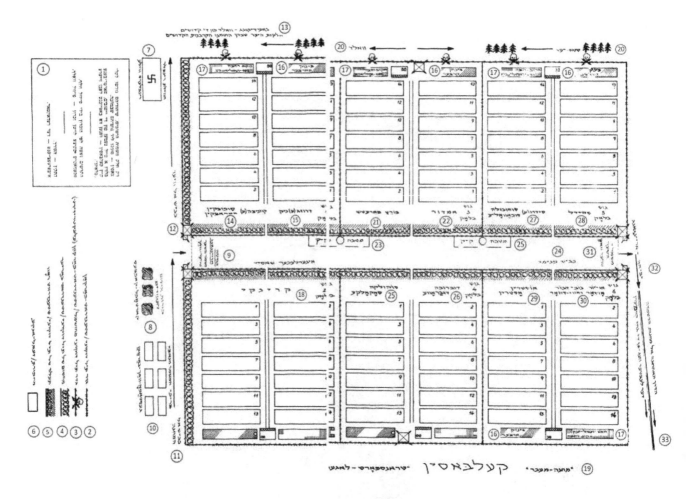

The Kelbasin Sketch

Translated by Jerrold Landau

The Kelbasin (Kielbasin) sketch appears on two unnumbered pages following 240, with the right to left orientation reversed. The key is as follows:

1. Only a portion of the place names from which Jews were deported to Kielbasin are noted next to their blocks in the camp. The chart was prepared by memory by Feivel Wolf. It was edited by the editor.
2. Barbed wire fence
3. Electrified barbed wire fence
4. Barbed wire barricade
5. Barbed wire gutter
6. Excavation
7. Reinfeller's villa
8. Potato pits
9. Entrance. Gate guard.
10. Gestapo guard barracks
11. Road to the camp
12. Road to the forest
13. Location in the forest where the martyrs were hanged.
14. Kozińce, Sapockin
15. Block 1. Drozgenik
16. Dungeon
17. Washing area
18. Block 2. Krynki
19. Kielbasin Transit Camp

20. Forest
21. Moroch
22. Block 3. Amdur
23. Kitchen
24. Internal road
25. Sokółka
26. Block 4. D'browa
27. Sidra. Suchowola
28. Block 5. Skidel
29. Ostryna
30. Block 6. Ożary. Nowy Dwór
31. Gate guard
32. Exit
33. The last way to the death camps and gas chambers.

[Page 241]

The arrangement concluded with people in groups of four. The crowd of forced laborers, wearing torn, worn-out clothes, and freezing from the cold (their "proper" clothes had been stolen from them by the Nazis) marched to the workplace, to various German operatives in the town itself or to the roads outside of the town. Anyone who did not march properly or who stepped out of line would not only earn a shower of "compliments", i.e. loud mockery, but also lashes from a whip or angry beatings with batons.

A. Sofer writes that the food ration for the people of the ghetto was 100 grams of bread per day and a similar quantity of potatoes. The Judenrat would attempt to provide, to the extent possible, a food supplement to the workplaces of the workers with the most backbreaking labor – a bit of fat or some other additional food items. They could provide this only for those who worked outside the ghetto. Some were able to obtain a portion of butter or some other food from gentiles through purchase or barter in exchange for clothing or some other piece of merchandise. However, they would have to smuggle the product through the ghetto gate, hidden in a broom, the hair of a woman, or some other hidden place. Therefore, everyone who returned from work in the evening would be checked carefully by the Polish and German guards, and if someone caught with "his transgression" – the smuggled food would be "confiscated" and he himself would be "treated" to curses and kicks. If he succeeded in getting through without being caught, he would have to give a "tithe" to the Jewish policeman who was stationed inside the gate.

The Judenrat was also obligated to provide a workforce to the farms of the area, which were now directed by Germans. Approximately 40 Jews worked in this manner in Jaszmonta, Stajnow, Szolka, and other villages. They would return to their homes in the ghetto once every week or two – tired, dusty, hungry, and weakened from the backbreaking work, the beatings, the thrashings, and the suffering. They were also broken and crushed from everything that their eyes saw, including the torment and murder of their fellows.

Torment and Evil

Those who worked in Jaszmonta related that one evening, when they returned tired out to their tents, a command from their director to arrange themselves in a row was suddenly heard. A group of S.S. men immediately appeared. They were passing through, and they desired to torture Jews. They commanded the tired Jews to start running while singing Hatikvah without stop – and with falling down to the ground and rising again and again. Anyone who could not stand up to the test and failed was shot on the spot.

A second incident took place in Stajnow, approximately 10 kilometers from Krynki, where 24 Jewesses were working. During a party at the home of the German director of the area, the drunk gendarmes wished to "enjoy themselves" with the Jewish women. At 4:00 a.m., they ordered them to strip naked. Anyone who did not obey was beaten with death blows. Then they made them run naked for hundreds of meters into a stream of filthy water, and they were forced to fling handfuls of mud and stones at each other, as the tormenters mocked and beat them.

The murderers knew no bounds with respect to forcing the Jews to work at backbreaking work. At times, they burst into the ghetto in the darkness of the night, and took the Jews, broken from hard work, out of their beds, and forced them to run in the cold for 12 kilometers outside the town and to clear the snow from the roads.

On January 14, 1942, the Polish policemen arrested 20 Jewish butchers in the ghetto due to the rumor that reached the German gendarmerie that they had smuggled a cow into the ghetto to slaughter for meat. For three days, they were interrogated, beaten, and tortured to the point that their blood flowed. They were then taken to the prison in Bia³ystok. All efforts of their family to save them, including with the help of bribes, did not help. They were shot to death in pits which they were forced to dig themselves, six kilometers from Białystok.

One day, the gendarmes suddenly ordered that Garbarska Street be excluded from the bounds of the ghetto, thereby dividing the confinement area into two separate, unequal areas. One was now called "The Small Ghetto." Through great effort, they succeeded in getting the Germans to agree to allow a connection between the two parts of the ghetto on the Street of the Bridge, through a water conduit.

The Terrifying "Feldwebel"

"That stormy winter, the Feldwebel (Sargent), a tall, fat German with piercing eyes, responsible for ensuring that the road to Białystok was cleared of stone, was particularly infamous in Krynki for his cruelty. He was a sadist for his own enjoyment, evil, and a wild beast" – Lola Wolf-Reznik of Krynki relates. "At 5:00 a.m. he would burst into the ghetto with his murderous friends, break doors and windows, take out men, women, and children who were half naked, make them go outside, make them run fast on 'his' road, as he drove behind them and prodded them on with his thick whip. Now, in the strongest cold, he would work them hard at clearing the snow, without a break, and while fasting, until a late hour of the night, and until they were drained of their energy. The fingers and toes of many of them were frozen. Others contracted pneumonia or tuberculosis."

[Page 242]

Feivel Wolf relates: "At the end of February, we were drafted by the Judenrat to daily clean the street leading from Krynki to Sokolka. Our taskmaster was a fat German sergeant in his 50s, with a long mustache. His deputy was Tall Max.

"On Sunday, March 1, he forced us to run almost to Sokolka, a distance of approximately 22 kilometers, and held us there until 9:00 p.m. It was already an hour after midnight when we returned to Krynki. I found a note on my table at home demanding that I be prepared to present myself again at work at 5:00 a.m. I and many others like me did not go out. Therefore, the aforementioned fat pig entered the ghetto with about ten Germans to hunt for people. When they entered the house of Mosheke Schmid Traszcan, they took his pretty daughter from her bed naked, took her outside in the 30-degree cold, and whipped her. Then they snatched the daughter of the midwife, took her out, whipped her, and held her in the cold. They snatched Rabbi Kwiat for work.

"When word of the rampage of the murderer reached me, in the small ghetto, I and 17 others presented ourselves for work. Then the evil one cut and burnt before our eyes half of the beard and mustache of the tall rabbi. The German assistant next to him grabbed me by my head, shook me up and down, and gave me seven lashes with a rubber whip, after they tortured and beat the other Jews. They made us run ten kilometers on foot to clean the road next to the village of Szudziałowo."

A. Sofer writes about the same "event" that the Feldwebel also raped several girls, and sent them back to the ghetto with barely their lives.

The Bloody Day of Passover Eve

The Hymn of the Murderers, and "Business"

Even in Krynki, as in many other places, the murderers made sure, in accordance with the plans and directive of those "knowledgeable" in Jewish matters from among their upper command, that the Jews not be allowed to remove their attention, even one bit, from their bitter fate on the days of their holy festivals. Furthermore, they must suppress their special times and their souls completely. The day of Passover eve was a day of of murder of Jews for the workers of the Nazi devil.

The eve of Passover 5702 [1942] approached. Those imprisoned in the Krynki Ghetto baked matzos, koshered their vessels, and attempted to prepare as much as possible for a kosher Passover in secret, hidden from the Germans.

On Friday morning, the eve of Passover, the commander of the ghetto ordered the Jewish police to send out all the youth for work. He and the ruler of the town did not permit anyone older to leave the ghetto. After several hours, the gate of the confinement opened, and approximately 200 Gestapo men entered with their uniforms and black hats, bearing their symbol of the skull and two crossbones below, singing their hymn "Horst Wessel."[1] with the words "When the knife is sharpened, Jewish blood flows." They invaded and burst into the alleyways to pillage the homes, beat and tortured. Volleys of shots burst out, accompanied by screams and calls for help.

Abraham Sofer writes, "At that time, Yaakov Kozolczyk ran outside, with his cloak ripped and his eyes full of tears, calling out incessantly, 'Jews, hide – they will shoot you!'

"The shooting did not stop. At that time, the Judenrat conducted negotiations with the murderous captain of the Gestapo brigade, who ordered specifically that 300 people be shot. In exchange for a bribe of a great deal of gold, hides, and other valuables, the robbers were 'placated to lower the price' – that is to only kill those with beards."

The Slaughter

The terrible slaughter of the "tens" lasted for two hours. Among those murdered was the local rabbinical judge Leibel Segal, and the rabbinical judge and rabbi of the Hassidim Reb Shmuel Leib ("The Yellow"). The murderers ignited his beard on fire while he was still alive, and then then nailed him to the wall of the Hassidic house of worship. Moshe Leib the baker ("Mosheke Mazik's, Chana the Baker woman's) displayed strong opposition to the murderers and fought with them. Women also perished in the slaughter, some of whom were pierced to death by swords. They were all hauled one by one through the ruins of the ghetto and murdered near the garbage bins of the destroyed tanneries. The wild beasts left the ghetto in the afternoon with the "Horst Wessel" song emanating from their throats.

They did not permit the victims to be buried in the Jewish cemetery. They were buried in their clothes, in the presence of the ghetto commander, in a mass grave on the Street of the Bathhouse, in an empty lot of Shmuel Hadwad next to the Linat Hatzedek building.

[Page 243]

The Absorption of Deportees: Epidemics

Following the ruined Passover holiday, the Jews of Greater Brestowice, approximately 1,200 souls, were transferred to Krynki on wagons. They arrived half naked, covered in rags, without food, bedding, or even a coin – for everything was stolen from them. Now it was necessary to arrange living quarters for them in the frightfully crowded ghetto, and to provide them with firewood, food, and clothing. They were housed in the schools, houses of worship, and in many houses.

Lola Wolf-Reznik relates: "The hunger in the ghetto increased from day to day. Epidemics, especially typhus, spread quickly taking many victims.

"An exemplary hospital and an infirmary in the premises of the General Cheder was set up in the ghetto. They provided medical aid gratis. Some medical supplies were available. This was perhaps the most important activity of the Judenrat in Krynki. It was better set up with its cleanliness, its medical staff, and its general principles than the local city hospital."

And They Tortured Them with a Pool

In June 1942, the commander of the ghetto desired to construct a pool outside the city for himself and his staff. Every day, they would force thousands of Jewish men, women, and children to run there, to drag pallets laden with heavy soil, under the whiplashes of the taskmasters, especially of the wild Polish policemen. They would also force those who were working in the factories to run there after a difficult workday. Rather than returning them home to their ghetto, the murderous commander and his gangs would be waiting for them at the gate. With the butts of their guns, they would force them to turn back – this time to the pool. There, they would be forced to work, accompanied by curses, until their energy was exhausted. They would return in the darkness of the night, weak and beaten, to the empty pot and table in their homes – relates A. Sofer.

One day, when the number of forced laborers did not reach the quota that was satisfactory to the Germans – they forced all the Judenrat members to run to work. They also beat them harshly, and ordered them to supply a number of Jewish workers.

When there was nobody else to draft, the Jewish police, having no choice, chased out all those who were in the *Beis Midrash* immersed in their fasting, and gave them over to the Germans to send to work.

Time passed, and the work on the pool in the lot of Wyryon was completed. Then they worked on clearing ruins. A German in charge of the economy opened a workshop for tailoring and hat making. This work was solely for the benefit of the Germans who were traveling to their homeland, taking their pillaged merchandise along with them.

In the Final Months of the Ghetto: Inclinations to Revolt

Life in the Ghetto became worse from day to day. Food supplies were completely exhausted. A public kitchen was set up, but it did not have the foodstuffs to feed the hungry community. At times, it would only distribute hot water. People went about pale and weak from exhaustion. The death toll rose. The field next to Linat Hatzedek, where the victims of the bloody Passover eve had been buried, filled up with graves. Hunger got sharper, and increased. Smuggling into the ghetto died down. The majority of the community lived with the hope that the day of redemption was not far off. There were those who preached about finding a way to free themselves through their own powers, to go out to the forests with weapons in their hand to fight the enemy. On the other hand, there were those who were against this idea, saying that they must continue to remain in the ghetto, and wait until the end of Amalek would be like the end of Haman – relates Sofer.

He further relates that Simcha, the son of Nachum Bliacher, set up a radio device in an empty barrel. Every day, he and Buma Frydman would listen to the news from London, Moscow, and Berlin. This was a deed that could bring the death penalty to many, so it was kept an absolute secret.

And again: They would send most of the youth to work on digging peat in Podbianika or to cut trees in the forest. It happened that the partisans of the "group" confiscated the axes and saws, but refused to take the youths with them to the Partizanka. In general, the partisans would take everything from Jews whom they encountered in the forest, and send the person away. They claimed that this was because the Germans sent spies to the forests wearing yellow patches, disguised as Jews, and these people could later disclose the partisan hiding places to those who sent them. It even happened that they threatened the Jewish youth who were digging peat, and who wanted to accompany them to the forest, that they would shoot them if they came with them.

Translator's Footnote:

1. See https://en.wikipedia.org/wiki/Horst-Wessel-Lied

[Pages 245-249]

Translator's note: These Hebrew sections on the Scroll of Kelbasin by Dov Rabin and Feivel Wolf are equivalent with 277-287. The Yiddish section by Wolf has more detail than the Hebrew. The Hebrew is not being translated.

[Pages 249-250]

Translator's note: The material from the Hebrew sections by Avraham Sofer is included in the Yiddish sections by Sofer that are already translated. Therefore, the Hebrew is not being translated.

[Page 250]

Our Krynki Holocaust Tribulations

by Eliyahu Kushnir

Translated by Hadas Eyal

The Border Pharmacy

When the Krynki Jewish ghetto was set up on December 13, 1941 it's barricade ran through the yard of my pharmacy. Jews who worked outside the ghetto and were able to somehow find food, would throw it towards the pharmacy and we would throw it over the fence into the ghetto.

Life in the fall all of 1942 was a nightmare of terror and constant fear of death. There were frequent rumors from neighboring towns of slaughter and "transports" of children and elderly to unknown destinations.

On November 1st, 1942 rumors spread that something "special" was about to happen and my family urged me to move into the pharmacy beyond the barbed wire. My wife and I crossed the barricade that night. We went up to the attic and laid there. At 6:00 a.m. we heard an earsplitting uproar of wild yelling, wailing and gun fire from the ghetto, followed by a commotion of moving carriages, an entire camp. We didn't know what was going on.

The pharmacy did not open that day. It was managed by a Polish professor brought in by the Nazi commissar but when I heard movement from there at approximately 10 a.m. I snuck down from the attic and peaked into the pharmacy through the back door. I asked the Christian intern to call the pharmacist professor and from him I learned that all the Jews were taken out of town. Among them, my entire family.

Jolted and shocked, we decided to end our lives. We were even able to obtain a box of poison but the pharmacist let us stay in the attic for one more night so I decided to wait for the next day.

[Page 251]

Early the next morning we woke to desperate cries in Yiddish: "Oy, where are my children?" We ran down and there was Yosel Goltz the Judenrat, running, crazed, wringing his hands, looking for his family that disappeared. He told us that some Judenrat and professional workers, mainly tanners, were left to work in Krynki. Yankel Shinder and others assumed that the Jews who could be of service to the Germans may be able to successfully escape hell.

Goltz also told us that the Germans, with whom he came into contact as a Judenrat and whom he regularly bribed, warned him in advance that the ghetto was going to be liquidated. He rushed to prepare his family a hiding place where he left them while he went to pay a ransom for their lives. When he was late to return, his family left the hiding place and asked a young acquaintance to lead them to the place where all the Jews were rounded up. By the time Goltz returned – he couldn't find them. We also found out that my mother-in-law, aunt and the children willingly left their hiding place because they heard the Germans "promised" that the town people would be moved to ghetto Grodno.

The Empty Ghetto

In order to maximize our chances of saving our relatives and the children we had to first become "legal" in the ghetto. We left the pharmacy attic and snuck into the ghetto to our apartment. The apartment was already taken over by other Jews who barely vacated a corner for us. The Germans we met told us we will soon see our relatives.

House gates and doors in the ghetto were flung open, lamps were on. You would go into an apartment and see before you a dish ready to be cooked; here a sewing machine with a shirt half-sewn; there bread dough with finger marks sunk into it; next to a grater – a whole potato; on the table – a crumpled tallit, an undone tefillin, and a Siddur open to "Shmoneh Esrei" in the middle the Amidah prayer. The beds are ruffled. Clearly the Jews were torn and snatched at dawn.

In the Tannery with the Remaining

We were lucky. The wife of the German tannery manager happened to our apartment to see the seamstress who lived with us. In return for silverware and Czech cutlery we were accepted to the tannery - I as a medic and my wife as a nurse. With time I befriended the manager. From time to time we would bring him gifts that were easy to find: anyone could walk into an apartment and take what they wanted. If a Christian would take a plate out of the ghetto he would be shot, but the Jews were uninterrupted because the murderers knew that sooner or later everything will remain in their hands.

The tannery manager, an SS man, agreed to at least return our son. This is when we found out that everyone taken from town was gathered in the transport camp in Kielbasin . A car was eventually sent to bring the child but returned empty – they were all sent to Treblinka the day before.

We stayed at the tannery camp 12 weeks. I bandaged and treated the Jews with a great deal of luck. Despite not being able to sanitize needles and lacking any alcohol, there were no inflections.

Polish people from town who were once communists and now dangerous hooligans also worked in the tannery. One day in January 1943, a Polish woman spotted my wife's felt boots. She suggested that my wife give them to her as a gift because "she will soon not be needing them anymore". We understood the hour of Jewish extermination is approaching.

Shortly after that day, the guard told me someone is waiting for me outside. It was Piotr Biganski, our former landlord. He came under the pretense of urgently needing a certain medication, asking me to concoct it. He then whispered that he was willing to hide my wife and I at his place.

There was tension in the camp those days. People would sneak out at night to look for a hiding place in the area, retuning disappointed. I therefore asked to send a message to Biganski that the medication I prepared for him is ready. He appeared and repeated his offer. Although I did not take him too seriously because I knew he was an unusual man, I got hold of a coat, two window drapes and several lady stockings that he asked of me and passed them to him when I had a chance.

[Page 252]

On Shabbat, January 23, the tools were taken from the craftsmen – a bad sign. When I asked the manager about it he said that "if anyone will be left here, you will be the first of them". The situation was clear. Not only did our Polish co-workers not express emotion or any kind of worry for us, they were outwardly happy they would be able to enjoy the things we leave them. We were so angry, we began to throw into the oven and burn everything we were meant to leave behind. The Polish raised a commotion about us burning "things that already belong to them".

Most of the Jews in the camp were young and sought life. However, we knew nothing about whether there were Partisans among us.

With us in the camp was a worker called Zelig Vacht whose wife I threated for open tuberculosis. She died in my arms. He became a close friend and tried to be in our company as much as possible. We told him and a few other close friends our secret of the possibility of finding a hiding place but that we do not trust the person willing to hide us and we do not have the money we will need for that. They all persuaded us to take the opportunity because there is nothing to lose, and maybe, if we stay alive, there will be someone to tell the story of the Shoah that fell on the Jews of Krynki. Vacht also took it upon himself to get us out of the camp that was now surrounded by the Gestapo with only a single section guarded by a Polish policeman. It was our last window of opportunity.

Hiding Underground in a Crate

We approached that fence section in the dark of night. Vacht whispered to the Polish policeman that he will show him treasures buried underground if he moves a bit from the gate to let us leave through it. The trick worked after we also shoved several money bills into the hands of the policeman. In pouring rain, we plodded through mud until we reached Biganski's yard. We knocked quietly on his window. A woman's voice answered that she is bathing and not open, so we hid in a cellar we discovered. Biganski found us there later by chance when he came down to check that the rain water didn't reach the potatoes in the cellar shed.

He was perplexed at first then greeted us. But he turned pale when he lit a match and saw another man with us. After pleading, he eventually agreed to hide Vacht as well. We took off our watches and handed them over along with all the money we had. Now he invited us into his house, fed us and led us to the cellar.

Our dwelling was in a crate that was 140 centimeters long and one meter in height and width. It was meant for two people laying with their legs bent. The third person was forced to stand in turn inside the chimney through which we were lowered to the crate. The chimney was covered on top with wood planks. On top of the planks, Biganski threw mounds of potatoes.

The first 24 hours we laid hungry and swooning until he returned home apologizing he did not bring us food earlier because he was busy slaughtering a pig at a party. He took us up, fed us dinner and gave us instructions we needed to obey without question because we were surrounded by enemies, especially his hating brothers who came into the cellar to take their food supplies.

Biganski also told us that all the Jews were taken including those from the camp and that eight of them who tried to escape were caught and shot to death in the cemetery.

Sheltered in Sodom by Two Righteous People

He would bring us food every night when he came down to the cellar to collect potatoes for his cows. He also took the bucket we used as a toilet. Once every two weeks he took us up late at night to bathe after a thorough inspection around the house and if no person was expected to visit. Only then would he command: Come up! We'd quickly sneak into the house while he covered the windows and locked the doors. Bathing night was a celebration. Mrs. Biganski, smart and infinitely generous – a true angle from heaven – would cook us food then allow us to use their beds to catch a human nap with our limbs stretched out.

[Page 252]

One evening, there was a knock on the window while we were bathing. We all turned pale but Mrs. Biganski did not lose her resourcefulness. She answered as she always did in these situations that she will not open because she is bathing. Turns out it was one of Mr. Biganski's brothers who was looking for his horse and came to check if anyone saw him. From then on we could no longer bathe.

In the spring of that year Vacht contracted tuberculosis and his coughing got continuously worse. Biganski moved him to the attic where he got worse, probably due to a cold, and the sound of his coughing could be heard in the street. Vacht begged Biganski to take him to Bialystok ghetto where he had friends. Putting himself in great danger, Biganski hitched the horse and took Vacht there. With utmost mercy he also offered Vacht to return when his health improves. After the war we learned that Vacht and five other Jews escaped from the Bialystok ghetto just before it was liquidated but they were caught and shot on their way to Krynki. Only Shteinspir survived – the sole living witness to this escape.

We stayed in the attic after Vacht left even though it would have been easier to discover us there. After harvest, Biganski installed a new crate under the hay and began to feed us better food to make us healthier and stronger. Moreover, our friendship with this family grew to the point he would even bring us the newspaper. *[Page 253]*

An additional man in the den of evil

Once it happened that a goy climbed to the attic to look for something and saw me crawling from the crate to get the newspaper. The man recoiled, pale as whitewash from what he saw, but left without a word. He was smart and kind because he did not even mention it to Biganski. He would bring our landlord a large portion of freshly collected honey from his bee hive saying: "Take, take, you need it!".

In the winter of 1943/1944 the Germans brought Ukrainian police. Two of the families were housed in our yard. They exposed their evilness straight away: they found two Jews hiding in the field, the first they buried alive and the second they gave over to the Germans. We found this out only later because our landlord did not want to worry us.

We were surprised one day by a baptism party in the attic. White sheets were hung around the walls and tables were set. Biganski's neighbor guests, brothers and the policemen ate and drank all day while we were in the crate beneath the hay, hearing the praying and partying of the Ukraine murderers. After the guests left that night Biganski served us schnapps, meat and candy as refreshments.

Approach of the Red Army

The Red Army was approaching us, delayed near the town of Svislach where the Germans displayed stubborn resistance for several days. Before they left Krynki the Germans set out to demolish the place. They blew up the factories and set the homes on fire. Our landlord Biganski moved around like a crazy man fearing more for his house than for our lives despite all the efforts he invested in saving us.

He came up one day and curtly commanded: "Out!" He led us across the field within the artillery range until we reached his plot. There, he commanded us to lay under the grain and he left. We laid there the whole night with the loud noises of the German command ringing in our ears.

In the morning after an additional night, Biganski came to inform us that the Soviets arrived and he left again. Fifteen minutes later we arrived at his house. The neighbors who saw us could not believe their eyes, that some Jews remained alive. Our landlord and his wife came towards us with a sly smile. We were given the same apartment the police had stayed in. We were swollen and our eyes blinded from being in the dark for so long.

The Goyim Take Revenge On Our Saviors

Word quickly spread in town that we were saved. Other Jews who hid in the nearby forests also survived but there were no acquaintances of ours among them. The town goyim now began to go after our landlord, snitching on him to the Soviet authorities.

We ran to the Russian officers and high rank Soviet clerks to beg for his life and telling them about his total devotion and self-sacrifice. Our efforts were unsuccessful until a high ranking NKDV commander who happened to be Jewish passed through town. After hearing our story, he asked to meet our savior to thank him personally.

Biganski returned home. The next day the commander arrived with an entire battalion. Biganski was called outside and once in view, the commander gave a command of "Attention!", took his hat off as a sign of respect as Russian custom, kissed our savior and his wife's hand, and thanked him for saving our lives. From then on all the high officers and clerks who passed through Krynki treated him the same way.

We stayed in Krynki several more months. The other eight surviving town Jews moved in with us and it was much more pleasant for us. However, the hatred from the goyim continued to increase. They were unable to forgive us for surviving and our landlord for saving us.

We therefore moved to Bialystok. Although there were few Jews left there, mutual ahavat-yisrael (love of one's fellow Jews) was everywhere. Even Jews who did not know each other before would hug, kiss and cry when they met and realized they are not the one and only Jew left in the world.

Biganski came to visit us in Bialystok several times. As long as we were in Krynki, no harm was done to him. But when we left – the goyim constantly harassed him. We received no response to our last letters to him. We do not know the fate of this Righteous Gentile and his gentle kindhearted wife.

In November 1945 we miraculously managed at long last to get to Eretz Israel.

To Auschwitz with the Krynkiers

Jumping from the Death Transport

The people of the work camp in the tannery of Yankel Szinder and I were sent from Sokolka in a train car. Among the others were my uncle Yisrael Skobronik (Afrikaners), his wife, and his two lads, as well as the director of the camp Yaakov (Yankel) Kozolczyk ("Pig"). Some Jews recited chapters of Psalms, and the women wept. The remains of the Jews of Sokolka were included in our transport, about 1,200 people. Everyone was certain that we were being taken to Treblinka. Yaakov broke the window, and a group of youths prepared to jump out through it. We set up a row among ourselves. Moshele, Shepsl Kusznir's son jumped first, and then he himself jumped. Others slipped out one after the other, as the train was traveling at full speed. One mother urged her two sons to jump, and helped one of them next to the window. Yaakov was standing next to them, helping them push themselves out. Yosel and Chaim Brawerman, Leibel Naliber, Hershel Abramowic, Sonia Funk, Avrahamel Klajnbort, Zeidl Jakobinski, Dora Kirpic, and her brother the lad Zundel all similarly jumped.

When my turn came, my aunt begged me, with tears in her eyes, to travel with them. She even hung on to me to prevent me from jumping. Yaakov stripped down to his undergarments and threw his clothes out the window. But he did not succeed in trying to push himself outside, due to his clumsy body, despite all his efforts. He then took out a vial of poison and swallowed it, but his heart overcame the poison. He lay down and growled like a slaughtered animal. A white froth covered his lips, and there was no water in the wagon. We scraped off ice from the walls and we thereby restored his soul.

When the transport approached the Malkin station, close to Treblinka, some people on the train began reciting Psalms. Filipski donned his tallis and tefillin. Everyone's arms and legs were trembling. However, the transport flew by Malkin and sped on. We became calmer. The Orthodox among us claimed that the recital of Psalms was what saved us, and that they were taking us to work, as the director of the factory had promised.

[Page 255]

Night fell. Groans and the knocking of frozen legs swelled up. Everyone was thirsty. People scratched the frost off the walls with their hands and relieved their thirst a bit. The next day, while we were still traveling, the cold subsided and the walls dried. They were tormented by thirst. The guards agreed to bring a cup of water in exchange for a ring or a watch.

On the third day of our journey, we passed by a railway station where Jews and Christians were working at clearing snow. Some of them warned us out loud that they were taking us to be slaughtered, and that we should escape to save ourselves. Inside the train, people burst out weeping, and started reciting Psalms fervently. A shout was also heard from outside that they were transporting us to Auschwitz, a name that none of us had yet heard. We wondered: is this a second Treblinka?

Night fell, and Yaakov ordered that we burn everything that we had with us. Izik Brustyn was the first to set his bit of money on fire. Tears fell from everyone's eyes.

The next morning, January 24, 1943, we arrived in Auschwitz.

Krynkiers Who Jumped from the Transport Arrive in Białystok

Translator's note: This section is equivalent with the Yiddish article: "Jumping From the Death Train and Arriving in Białystok" on page 297.

In Auschwitz by Abraham Sofer

Translator's note: This section is equivalent with the Yiddish article "In Auschwitz" on pages 298-304 by Abraham Sofer. Some of the headings are different, but the material is equivalent.

[Page 259-260]

Translator's note: The sections from 259-260 regarding partisans are equivalent with the Yiddish sections from 311-315. They are not being retranslated.

[Page 261]

In order that the later generations should know,
The children who will be born;
They should tell it over to their children

Psalm 78:6

The Holocaust

Translated by Judie Goldstein

The Poem of the Murdered Jewish Nation

Yitschak Katzenelson

Cry out from every grain of sand, from under every stone,
From all of the houses, cry, from all the flames, from every chimney---
It is your blood and sweat, it is the marrow of your bones
It is your heart and life! Cry out! Cry loud!

Cry out from the furnaces, cry young and old, a cry, a lamentation—
Cry out murdered Jewish nation, cry, cry out!

[Page 262]

<u>Destruction and Heroism</u>

[Page 263]

Holocaust and Heroism

A Dream

Sarah Fell Yellin

Somewhere in a far off, yet near land,
Is a field with graves covered in green.
In a cloudy rainy dawn
I stand …
How could it be? I do not comprehend: why has it happened?
Alone, standing on foreign pasture
Alone in a deathly, green world?!
I delight in the living grass
And the dainty white flowers upon the nearby grave….
All my limbs cling to me for dear life:
What am I doing here?
How did I get here?
My thoughts are as quick
As a whirlwind groping, searching for that which is mine…
How dare I come to the death field alone?!

A luminous eye shines through the cloudy grey
A spot of blue sky
A gentle breeze passes through my hair…
And I was incapable of comprehending everything
To where shall I go from here?
I shall inquire of the birds:

"Hey, over there, tell me to where do the green paths lead?"
Barely had the sounds left my mouth
A strange shudder fell upon me
It wasn't my voice…
It came forth from the graves in the valley
An echo, half muffled coming from a holy place
Each word like a shofar sound
Hopelessly it innocently asked:
"To where does this green path lead?"
From far afield I see the old water mill
Younger days quietly fluttered by…
Something had jarred me
Inside my uneasy soul…
At the doorstep of my home….
The breath of my father and mother
The sweet flavors of growing up
and….

From the field of graves
I take my leave to go
And immediately…as if alive
Before my very eyes
The town of Krynki stands:

Yenta's forest
Virian's forest
Sislevitzer Street strolls around
The shtetel…
Plantanska…my father's house…

As if Garbaska Street and the "Kavkaz"
Greet me and the trees in the orchards
Sokolker and Patszava
The market with each and every street…
Foodstuffs arranged in a circle
The bath street, the city gate, the many shops…
So was there then a name
For home where your cradle stood?
I finally understood.

~~~~~~

I felt a gentle hand, a warm touch upon me
"Get up…it is late…"
A dream! A claim from the past…graves of green…
In such a bright and splendid valley...

[Page 264]

The Cataclysm · Nazi Germany Attacks Russia

Avraham Sofer

The Russian Army Flees

On Sunday, the twenty-second of June 1941, suddenly one heard the sound of the sirens from the tallest wall of the town. It sounded like interrupted sounds of crying, throwing fear into the hearts of the population of the town. The planes flew two times around the town and turned off to the direction of Grodno.

The streets were black with people; automobiles were going back and forth throughout the town. The Red Army was worried and upset. They had received orders from army headquarters: mobilize the population!

Everyone received a draft notice and was already required to stay by the staff headquarters. The crying and commotion was great: "My husband! My child!" It was just like a year-and-a-half earlier. Those that were mobilized went to the town of Gross-Brestovitz, fourteen kilometers from Krynki. The commander of our group also left.

There is no discipline or order anymore. What has happened to the strong Red Army? Where are all the airplanes?

Monday, the second day of the war, there is a stream of tanks, automobiles and pedestrians leaving the town. Soldiers ask about the way to Minsk. No one stands still, everyone is running around.

On Tuesday, the militia and the N.K.V.D. are all packed and ready to leave. No one knows exactly where the front is located. Soldiers are carrying their boots on their shoulders and flee barefooted. The youth of the town gather in the market place, create and attach themselves to the fleeing army units. I am also counted amongst them.

The Downfall of the Jewish Community of Krynki

Lola Wolf-Reznick

No Maneuvers This Time

On Sunday the twenty-second day of June 1941 at ten o'clock in the morning a number of airplanes appeared in the skies over Krynki. A number of shots were heard and an unquiet spirit already pervaded in the town.

Many thought that it was only military maneuvers they were witnessing. Others had already grasped the reality of what was actually taking place. The speech Molotov delivered on the radio at twelve o'clock made clear to everyone the true situation at hand.

The Jewish Quarter Is Bombed And Destroyed

Early Monday, airplanes again appeared over Krynki and bombed the periphery of the town. Very early on Tuesday, a strong bombardment commenced on the town of Krynki itself, especially of the Jewish quarter. In that bombardment the "Kavkaz" quarter and Zhabya Street were totally decimated with Bialistoker and Mill streets meeting only partial destruction. Also other areas such as Garabska and Elekrovnia Streets were damaged in a number of places. A number of Jewish inhabitants had already been killed such as Leibel Zak, his wife and a few others.

The vast majority of the Jews abandoned Krynki heading for the mountains and town pastures, fleeing and resting when necessary. They believed that no one would shoot at an innocent civilian population hovering in an open field.

The town was burning on all sides. It took a number of days to extinguish the fire and for a few days the town was quiet.

[Page 265]

The Russian inhabitants were the first to evacuate the town. Together with them, many Jews also left. To this very day I have no knowledge of any of them surviving the war except for Reval Rotbard.

The Mass Murder At The Town Pastures

The terrified populace was still huddled in the mountains and in the town pastures. Shabbos, the twenty-eighth of June, at nine o'clock in the morning, heavy German artillery, positioned only a few kilometers away, fired at the town pastures, which were filled solely with Jews. Fifty people were killed, and many others were wounded. Amongst the victims were: Borovsky; Chana and Necha Kirzhner, together with their mother: Zhukavitzky, the druggist, with both daughters, Roza and Tanya: L. Golinsky, the engineer: Dinah Rachkin, the wife of Shmuel Yitschak Rachkin and her three children: Feige, Esther and Abele: her sister, Mrs. Melamed with her husband and two children: and her second sister, the wife of Motke Amdursky: Mashe Kaminsky, the wife of Yisroel Kaminsky with her little son: Sloer's entire family except for the father, the wife of Dr. Lichtenstein's brother and many others. Also many Jews from Sakalke, who had fled from the front lines to Krynki, met their death in the town pastures.

Around two in the afternoon, the Germans entered the town. Soon all inhabitants were ordered to assemble in the market place where a number of Poles (German spies) together with the Germans, gave speeches concerning martial order and future "arrangements" in the town.

"Better We Should Be Sacrificed For The Sake Of The Town Rather Than The Town Be Sacrificed For Us."

Early Monday morning a number of S.S. troops suddenly surrounded a number of streets in the town and grabbed 16 Jews. They took them in the direction of Grodno, but around two miles from town they shot 14 of the captives in a small forest not very far from the way leading to the village of Shamianitza. The two remaining captives, Hershel Leib Shachnas and the elderly dentist Teichman were led to Klein Brestovitz and were shot there. Amongst the martyrs that day were: Daniel and Moshe Levin, from Grodner Street; Yaakov (Yankel) Novik, the accountant for the mayor; Ahron Wolf; Montshik the Smith's son together with his wife and brother; Berel Tavel; Zaydel Lash (Velvel's son); Shmuel Shachnas; Hershel Leibel; Noach Kayle's son; the son of Yosel Simcha Grosman from Mill Street and others.

Berel Tavel was only been wounded, and, not noticed to be still living, was left alone by the murderers. As the Germans moved further on with the two remaining Jews, Berel picked himself up from amongst the dead and, barely alive, reached the Shtetel, where he received medical help.

When he came back to himself, he related how on the way the group of Jews wanted to attack the two S.S. men who were leading them and thus saving themselves. However, Ahron Wolf, Arel Munthchkes begged them not to attack the S.S. claiming that: "It is better that they should be a sacrifice on behalf of the entire community rather than the Shtetel be a sacrifice on their behalf."---for everyone was aware of the consequences to Jews for killing a German!

In the morning we were given permission to bury in the town cemetery those who had been shot.

A terrible mood of panic prevailed in the town. Those Jews who the Germans conscripted for labor took leave of their families not expecting to see them again. When they came back from work in one piece they would be mighty grateful for one more G-d-given day of life.

[Page 266]

The Polish Anti-Semites Take Revenge On The Jews

A city government was quickly established, made up of Polish anti-Semites who whole-heartedly supported the incitement of the German murderers. Additionally, Poles who had recently been released from Soviet detention organized themselves into vigilantes and would carry out sentences against Communists, of course only according to their own discretion. Understandably, ninety percent of those that they accused of being Communist were Jews! It was sufficient to be an outstanding worker, a watchman of a factory, or an employee of a Soviet establishment in order to be labeled a Communist. Any Christian could kill a number of innocent Jews by just pointing them out as once having been an alleged Communist. In such a way tens of innocent Jews perished.

Such was the fate of sixty-year-old Yerucham Lavendik. He was a simple worker whose only sin was that during the Soviet occupation, he was dubbed as an outstanding worker, a "Stachanavitz" as such workers were called. Other victims were Alter Pinia Weiner, Meir the tailor's son amongst many others whose place of burial remains unknown until this very day.

Edicts And Persecutions

Within a short time, a number of edicts were issued against the Jewish population, the first being forced labor. Ladies from age fourteen until age fifty-five and men until the age of sixty were forced without exception to appear very early in so-called work columns at the market. The Polish bandits together with a number of Germans would send the groups to various work destinations.

The work consisted of public construction of roads, ripping out grass, gathering up the dead from the streets and burying them and cleaning up various public areas.

A short time later, an order was issued which obligated all Jews to wear on the right arm a white band 14 centimeters wide with a yellow Star of David in the middle. A few days later a new decree came out which ordered the wearing of a yellow band with a white Star of David. Not much later another decree demanded the wearing of a yellow Star of David attached on the front on the left side and a second Star of David sewn on the shoulders of one's coat. All this was done in order to be able to recognize Jews from kilometers away!

Jews were obligated to take off their hats when a German passed by them. And if one was not quick enough to do so, he was brought before the German police and was mercilessly hit with hard rubber police batons. Many Jewish ladies were not able to avoid this particular punishment. In some cases, Jews were actually shot to death for this "crime". So was the fate of Chaim Kotlier, the son of Betsalel Kotlier. Chaim, as a result of his serving with the American forces fighting in France during the harsh campaigns of World War One, had lost his mind. He had been living under the care of his parents in Krynki. While standing with his father next to their home, the feeble-minded son was not able to take his hat off for the Germans to their liking. Therefore, he was immediately shot to death on the spot!

We Are Closed Up In A Ghetto

In September 1941, rumors began to circulate about the imminent construction of a ghetto for the Jews of Krynki. From day to day it became very evident that the rumor was not groundless. Terrible stories were related concerning towns and cities where ghettos were already in existence.

In the end of November 1941, the Jews were authorized to establish a committee which would handle all contact with the German authorities and be responsible for carrying out all the German orders. Soon an order was issued that stipulated that the area on the left side of Mill Street until the right side of Rinkava Street up to the power station; and Garbaska Street until the river should be fenced in all sides with a barbed wire fence in order to demarcate the boundaries of the ghetto. The Germans had calculated exactly, not allowing - heaven forbid - more than one to one-and-a-half square meters of living space for each individual Jew in the ghetto. Seventy percent of Krynki's population, meaning Krynki's entire Jewish population, was required to live in such a narrow and confined space.

[Page 267]

Very soon the actual decree to build the ghetto walls was announced. Hundreds of Jews were actively engaged in building the high walls of their own prison. Two watchtowers were built. One was situated at the market at the entrance to Garbaska Street. The other tower was erected before the bridge over the river, also on Garbaska Street.

Guards were posted outside and inside both towers, and no one was allowed to enter or leave without a special permit.

A representative body for the Jewish community was selected, the so-called "Judenrat". Its purpose was to deliver into the hands of the Germans the various valuables that were regularly confiscated by them. These items included: clothing, footwear, fur, gold and jewelry. The Judenrat was to pay special attention to insure the quick construction of the ghetto fences and also to provide the daily quota of laborers for various work projects.

Around the twentieth of December 1941, a decree was made that the Jews should move into the ghetto area in a matter of a few days. Not everything was permitted to be brought into the ghetto. Polish policemen would look over the Jewish houses and choose for themselves the best things, whether in order to confiscate them immediately or to command that they be left for them later. The Jews therefore had to transfer to the ghetto a number of necessary household items, in a timely fashion. However, often one would be caught and "honored" with serious beatings, ordered to pay huge fines or even be shot. Shimel Sheiman (of the Bubitsekes) was shot under such circumstances, as he was moving his shoemaking equipment into the ghetto.

I recall those days when we moved into the ghetto: The market place was filled with people, with many Christians walking about. Many of them were sad yet the majority was happy—finally they will be finished with the Zhids and even inherit their possessions!

Many S.S. men and Polish policemen stood by the entrance to the ghetto, and every package and parcel was checked. The best items, over fifty- percent, were confiscated. One heard the yelling, crying, fighting, and above all the cruel bandit like voices of the S.S. men, their orders, ironic laughter and most of all their terrible beatings!

The Judenrat

Approximately a few days later, the ghetto was sealed. None of the Jews could leave the ghetto confines without a special permit (a piece of paper written in German with a stamp showing one's place of work). The previous Judenrat was reduced to seven members.

The Judenrat of Krynki Ghetto was now composed of: Yisroel Kalinovitch, Talya Goldshmidt, Yankel Grossman, Nota Mostovliansky, Yankel Levi (the clear one), Yossel Galtz and Meir Kaplan. Immediately an internal security service was organized, composed of twenty-five policemen with a commander—Yankel Kazaltchik (Yankel "chazir" from Kavkaz) and his deputy—Yossele Mostovliansky.

The activities of the Judenrat did not always correspond with the interests of the community as a whole. Stemming from a background of Jewish 'tsores' pain and suffering and unrelenting struggle for survival, very often the Judenrat would act on superficial instincts, egoistic and personal interests, sympathies and antagonisms etc.

The members of the Judenrat were taken from organizations and partially from men who submitted freely to the Germans and were certified by the German authorities in Krynki. Only the ghetto police commander, Yankel Kazaltchik, who with his strength, vulgarity, wild appearance and brutality impressed the Germans, was nominated via the S.S. men! However, the brutal, sadistic, bloodthirsty German commissar ruled over everyone!

[Page 268]

Life And Scenes Of The Krynki Ghetto

The scenes of the Krynki Ghetto were appalling. Beginning at six o'clock in the morning the workers were assembled in lines. Amongst them were many elderly men, women and young children, who were actually supposed to still be attending school. They would now wait for their work leader and for two Polish policemen, who would lead them to their place of work. I remember the terrible scenes of the men in the winter:

They would go wrapped in rags full of holes (the Germans took the best clothing), everyone shivering from fear and cold! Imprinted on their faces was the great trouble and hurt caused by the horrible fight to survive and by the dread of now and the coming dawn.

Here is a woman who left her small child at home and went by herself to earn some money. She suddenly begins to have a fit when thinking of the possibility of not being able to pass through the ghetto at the gate with the small amount of milk for her child, promised her by the farmer.

There is a thirteen-year-old girl, in ripped shoes. She holds in her hand a kerchief in which she hopes to bring in a few beans received yesterday from a Christian friend who had brought them to her work place. The non-Jew, she relates, shared the same desk at school and now wants to help me a little.

There a Jew with sunken cheeks and an out-stretched nose looks constantly in one direction - - What kind of image does he see there and what is he wondering about?

In my brother's boots and with my mother's shawl wrapped over me, with a little rye bread spread with beet marmalade, I stand together with the factory workers. Suddenly I hear the scream of the work leaders: "Arrange yourselves in lines of four!"

The factory workers' column is already in order. I bid goodbye with my eyes to my little brother and my cousins who I can see, already standing in other work columns, also ready to march.

We go out from the second gate near the river on Garbarske Street. Five meters out of the gate, we are suddenly stopped. Two gendarmes drive toward us from a village and they "amuse" themselves checking the crowd—whether our badges are sewn on right, or whether someone has concealed his badge, G-d forbid, etc. Soon we hear screaming and crying, the crack of whips and rubber batons and the cynical laughter of the Germans. We march further. The Poles run after us, demanding clothing, shoes, and underwear. They claim they will pay—exchange a few eggs for a dress, a liter of milk for a pair of shoes. They don't want it for free. A woman throws a blouse at a Christian friend. She asks her Christian acquaintance to prepare a half liter bottle of milk for her child. It should be ready for her when she returns from her day of labor at five o'clock. The Christian promises her quietly that everything will be ready, so that the Polish police who firmly guard the workers should not notice anything.

I work very hard operating a cutting machine in a leather tannery with three other Jewish girls. The machine stands in the "damp" tannery next to the vat where the hides are placed in lime. The air is intolerable. The hides go directly from the vat into the machine without being rinsed of the lime, which eats away the skin of our hands. We wear no special work clothes. It is winter. Our clothes are soaked with water and lime; our hands are all cut-up and bloody.

We have an hour lunch break from twelve to one o'clock. At five o'clock in the afternoon we organize once again into rows of four, and we march with the police escort back to the ghetto. The Poles again run after us and ask for various items. A Christian carries a small bottle of milk, another piece of bread. Suddenly the police grab a Jewish woman for some infringement, accuse her of dealing with the Christians and take her immediately to the gendarmes. No one will be envious of the beating she will receive at the hands of the Germans. By the gate of the ghetto there is a very strict inspection. Polish police hooligans carefully inspect every worker. If anyone is found attempting to smuggle the minutest item into the ghetto, he is beaten immediately.

Besides this, the Judenrat was forced to provide Jewish workers to the courts of the "Paritz" (minor Polish nobles) located close to Krynki, where Germans had taken over from the Polish nobles. Jewish workers worked in Yeshmanta, Shtinef, Shalk and at other courts. They would come home only once a week or once in two weeks, on a Sunday, dirtied and completely worn out from very hard labor, hunger, beatings and the terrible troubles they had to endure.

[Page 269]

Jew-Baiting And Murders

Dreadful things happened to the workers outside the town. It so happened once with workers from Krynki who worked in the village of Gross-Yeshmante, where they were resting in their tent after an exhausting day of work. At six in the evening they suddenly heard their work leader shouting orders to gather in a nearby place.

A group of S.S. men who were passing by had appeared, and when they found out that there were Jews working in the vicinity, they desired to "play a bit." They ordered the Jews to arrange themselves three in a row, run, bend down, run, bend down, scream, sing, sing "Hatikva" etc. They made the Jews wear themselves out in such a manner for two hours. Three Jews who fell to the ground exhausted were shot dead on the spot.

Another horrible incident occurred in the village of Shtineff, ten kilometers from Krynki. Around twenty-four Jewish women were on work detail there. During an evening party, while the Germans were enjoying themselves in the court, two drunken soldiers managed to "amuse" themselves with these Jewish women. They ordered them to strip themselves completely naked at four o'clock in the morning, forced them outside into the yard and chased them a few hundred meters. Then they ordered the women to go into a muddy river and pelt each other with mud and stones. For the next half-hour, the scene was accompanied by wild laughter, shouting and incessant beatings.

Beatings, fear and pain were also the lot of workers in Krynki itself, whether in the factories, outside while paving Krynki streets, or doing other work. Every Jew, whether old or young had to work in forced labor. The only Jews freed from this work were the family members of the Judenrat, of the police commander and of active policemen.

Every week, one would receive a portion of bread and potatoes. The sick would receive a half-liter of skim milk, which was brought in from outside the ghetto.

In the first half of January 1942, the Krynki gendarmes suddenly arrested twenty Jews, some of them members of the Judenrat. No one knew the reason for the arrests. Around six to seven hours later, one of the arrested men returned, pale, frightened and not able to answer anything in response to the questions of the families of the remaining detainees. A few hours later the rest returned, all of them silent.

I happened to know from my uncle who was also amongst the arrested that the gendarmes had interrogated them, accompanied with terrible beatings and tortures demanding that they should "reveal" what they know about a certain partisan group on the verge of formation in Krynki. This was, by the way, the first case in the entire area, in which arrested Jews were returned alive.

The "Twenty Men Action"

On the fourteenth of January 1942, twenty men were suddenly arrested in the ghetto.

The reason for the arrests was not known. According to one hypothesis, it was all a provocation by the Polish police. Amongst those arrested were: Zalman Lash, Laizer Kugel, Moshe Gabai with his only son Motele, Dovid Shushansky, Kapel Zalkin, Ever the butcher's two sons: Chana and Moshe with son-in-law, Abramovitch's two brothers (both shoe makers), Yankel Geller, Asher Shain, Avramel Labendik, Yudel Lopatta, Yossel Gabai, Itsche Slapak with my father Zalman-Nissel Wolf and another three Jews whose names I do not remember. For three days, they were held in the police station, tortured, tormented and bloodied. The Judenrat did not do enough to rescue them. After three days they were taken to prison in Bialistok. The families of those arrested spent much money and time trying to save their loved ones, but unfortunately without success. On the fifteenth of May 1942, they were shot to death, approximately six kilometers from Bialistok, only after each one was forced first to dig a grave for himself!

[Page 270]

The Murderous Sergeant

We then withstood a very terrible winter. Krynki survivors shudder just thinking about the "sergeant," a sadist and merciless murderer, who cast fear and dread upon the ghetto. At five in the morning he and his German "helpers" would enter the ghetto, break down doors and windows and drag out half-naked Jews to the Bialistok highway to clear the snow. His wild cries of "schneller, schneller" ring in my ears to this very day! Without a break, without eating, the Krynki women, men and children would clear the highway of snow until late at night, also in the worst snowstorms. They would come back home with frostbitten hands, feet and cheeks, starving and completely exhausted from a grueling and cruel workday. And so it was the entire winter. Many came down with tuberculosis, pneumonia etc.

Hunger And Epidemics

From day to day we felt the hunger more strongly. Deadly diseases began to spread, mainly the dangerous typhus, which killed many, including Rochel Turkel with her little daughter, Nechtse Slayer with her son Moshel, and many others.

In the building of the "Main Cheder" in the ghetto, a hospital was established with a clinic and pharmacy. Help was given free of charge. Perhaps this was the greatest accomplishment of the Judenrat in Krynki, and it was more hygienic and better supplied than the local Krynki hospital.

The Pre-Passover Action

The Passover holiday was approaching. Our Jewish people had baked matzos and made their homes and dishes kosher for Passover. Quietly, and unnoticed by the Germans, we arranged as much as possible for a kosher Passover.

At nine in the morning on Friday, the day before Passover 5702 (1942), the doors of the ghetto were opened and two hundred Gestapo agents with black hats with their symbol of a skull and two bones underneath marched into the ghetto. They immediately spread out through the different streets of the ghetto and started to rob, hit, torture and shoot Jews. Tens of victims were annihilated in the most brutal fashion. On that horror-filled day the following members of the community were killed: the judge of Krynki Reb Leib Segal, Moshe Lev, (the husband of Chana the bakeress), who physically stood up against the Germans, Okun's mother from Garbaska street, who was slain with a sword while she was in her bed, and many others. (See detailed list of martyrs on page 318.)

People were shot one by one when they entered burned-out destroyed areas of the ghetto, near the general garbage disposal area, where the waste material of the entire ghetto was deposited. There amongst the filth lay the dead and bloody corpses, completely covered with human excrement and other filth. One was not even allowed to bury the victims in the Jewish cemetery. They were buried inside the ghetto itself near the "Linas Tsedek" facility, in a communal grave. The pogrom lasted over five hours. It was a real Pesach!

Translations by Judie Goldstein

[Page 271]

Brestivitzer Jews Are Transferred To Krynki

After the holiday, the Jews of Brestovitz were transferred to the Krynki Ghetto. A concentration camp remained in Brestovitz with around two hundred young men and women. About 1,200 practically naked expellees with absolutely no provisions were brought into the Krynki Ghetto. The exhausted, starving and completely overcrowded Krynki Ghetto now had to provide these Brestivitzer brothers with food, clothing and a roof over their heads. They were put up in synagogues, houses of study and any place available.

The diseases and epidemics spread even more quickly from day to day, and people were falling like flies.

The Ghetto Is Divided

In 1942, a new decree was suddenly declared---to exclude Garabaska Street and divide the ghetto into two parts. The decree was quickly enforced. Garabaska Street was fenced in and two gates were built in the fence. One gate was near Moshe Garber's wall and the other gate was placed opposite that, near Kugel's house. A great effort was made to convince the Germans to construct a bridge (like a viaduct) that would connect the two parts of the ghetto. It was similar to the infamous "bridge of tears" in the Venetian ghetto: after tribunal in the "Dozhen Palace" the convicted were led to the dreadful prison, not seeing anything around them while going through the covered bridge.

The Liquidation Of The Ghetto

Thus the first of November 1942 arrived. Sunday, at six o'clock in the afternoon, a tremendous panic suddenly overcame the ghetto. Rumor in the ghetto had it that the ghetto police commander, Yankel Kazaltchik was informed by a German that early next morning all the Jews of the ghetto would be shot. No longer was anyone allowed to enter or leave the ghetto. We knew from Jews who had just returned home that the market was full of Christian wagons, new soldiers and Gestapo men.

What happened Sunday night is difficult to describe with words. People endeavor to save themselves from death. We already knew about the "actions" and massacres that happened in Slonim, Vilna, and other towns and cities. Monday at six in the morning when we were lying hidden, another rumor was heard that people were leaving the ghetto somewhere, and were only allowed to take with them something to eat.

We got dressed, took with us a little bread, and went toward the gates. The streets were filled with soldiers, police, Gestapo and German civilians, all heavily armed. It was simply very hard to go through the streets. They were full of people; everywhere there was terrible congestion, people lost sight of their loved ones, a wife, her husband; a child, his mother; a sister, her brother. Everyone was screaming, crying, lamenting. It was a terrible scene! Going toward the gates, I lost my loved ones, my mother and my little brother, who were leading my blind uncle Avraham Shmuel.

Looking for them, I suddenly felt a strong lashing from a whip and heard a yell. At the same time, I heard someone hollering at me in Polish: "You should go back home where the factory workers have been separated to continue working; you, they will let you have a few more days!" cynically the Polish policeman shouted at me. No words could be of any help. I had to go back to the column of factory workers that had assembled on Garabaska Street at the synagogue yard. The street looked horrible, littered with leftover small packages, food and bloody corpses.

[Page 272]

We are under very heavy guard. None of those passing by can have any contact with us and we can't have any contact with anyone. A mother calls to her child for perhaps the last time, and receives a hit on her head from a thick rubber baton. She falls down weakened and bloodied. Jews who go by her pick her up and take her further. Everyone is so quiet, I communicate only by means of eye contact. At the market, wagons have been prepared for the women and children. Men go by foot, surrounded by hundreds of soldiers, S.S. men, Gestapo men, and Polish policemen.

So were our dear ones led to the town of Amdur. In the morning they were brought from there to the collection camp Kalbasin, near Grodno. There, they met up with Jews from all the surrounding Shtetels. From there, the Jews were transported to Treblinka and the gas chambers.

On the twenty-fifth of November, our beloved Krynki Jews reached the Treblinka death camp. None of those who arrived there returned, except for the single Jew, who succeeded in running away and survived: Feivel Wolf from the village of Spodvill.

The Work Camp And It's Liquidation

The Nazis did not expel approximately one percent of the total population of the ghetto! Some of those left were led back to work in the factories, and another part was left in the ghetto to clean it up.

The Germans quickly confiscated and sold the Jewish property, dismantled all the fences, settled Poles in the Jewish homes and uncovered secret hiding places of Jewish valuables.

The Jews who were ordered to clean up the ghetto lived in Grossman's factory on Geminia Street. Their camp was located there. For the factory workers, wooden barracks were erected on the factory grounds and in neighboring houses. Thus two separate camps were built, one for the men and the other for the women. Both camps were under strict surveillance by the soldiers and Polish police. If a Jew would appear in the shtetel, outside the boundaries of the camps, he faced a penalty of death lashes!

The "living dead" (as we were called) in the work camps were all broken by the terrible troubles we experienced. We were embittered, frightened and completely beaten down. We envied of the dead, who had already left behind all the suffering and torments.

We were aware that they would not keep us alive for much longer and there was no way out. Our Christian friends and acquaintances, our "good friends", ceased to exist. All of them turned away from us and did not want to help.

Shabbos afternoon, the twenty-third of January 1943, we saw that our end was already approaching. Polish workers from Sokolka were brought in to replace us in the factory. The guard around the camp was suddenly increased.

The night between the twenty-third and twenty-fourth of January, around fifty people escaped from the camp. Only six of them survived: Freidka Zalkin and her husband, Eliyahu Kushner, Motke Shteinsaper (killed in 1945 by bandits in Italy), Perl Levy (Yankel Levy's daughter) Chaim Weiner and I.

Krynki was liberated by the Red Army on the twenty-third of November 1944. For ten months thereafter, no one knew the fate of the remaining Krynki Jews from the above- mentioned work camps. Only after the end of the war did I find out that they were taken to Auschwitz. The majority were immediately gassed and burned in the crematorium. The rest were killed in the general work camp of Auschwitz. Those who survived were: Motel Kugel, Isaac Brustin, Avram Soifer, Rochele Zakheim, Reuven Kaplan, Pinia Klass and Motel Kirshner.

[Page 273]

Amongst Krynki Jews who escaped to Bialistok and from there to the partisans, survived: Herschel Roitbard, Molia Nisht and Reuven Kaplan.

In the Ghetto

Abraham Sofer

Deterioration and Overcrowding

The situation in the ghetto had deteriorated very badly. Every day brought new decrees and troubles. The Jews walked around like ghosts, becoming sicker and weaker. The ghetto extended on one half side of town, on one side starting out from Mil street, Bath Street until the river where the ghetto fence stood, covered with barbed wire. Further in the ghetto was Garbarska Street, over which a bridge was constructed, uniting both parts of the ghetto near Yoshke Garber and Alter Kugel's brick homes.

Further on was the synagogue courtyard, which the Nazis used as a place to repair their tanks. Gemina Street until Grossman's factory was included in the ghetto. Fences enclosed the length of the ghetto, until the power station. The Greek Orthodox Church was left outside the ghetto. From Tserkovna Street inwards and also a half side of Amdurer Street were included in the ghetto. The other side of the town was in ruins.

The ghetto Commissioner and the Officer Commissioner would patrol the ghetto a number of times daily. During those patrols the few narrow alleyways would be empty of people; no living person would be there.

The houses were utterly overcrowded. Three to four families lived in every apartment. Three to four housewives would stand at the chimneys and fan the fires. Tears would be flowing down their cheeks from the bitter smoke and difficult life. The synagogues and study houses were overflowing with the homeless. The sanitary conditions in the ghetto were very poor. The busy ghetto hospital was also over-flowing with the sick.

The food rations consisted of a hundred grams of bread per person and a similar quantity of potatoes. The only people that were able to enjoy small amounts of fats were those that worked outside the ghetto. And that was only when, with great difficulty, they were able to smuggle a bit of butter into the ghetto hidden in a broom or placed in the hair of a female worker entering the ghetto. Woe was to the one who was caught doing such a thing. By the gates stood the corrupt Polish Police together with a soldier. Alongside stood a Jewish policeman with a stick in hand who would take a percentage of the goods successfully smuggled into the ghetto.

The Judenrat was a total governing body, with police and even its own prison, in which one would be placed for breaking with the strict discipline of the ghetto, or for not being willing to go out to work. The children and wives of the Judenrat officials did not regularly go out to work. The commissioner of the ghetto, who welded dictatorial power over the Judenrat, was in constant confrontation with them.

[Page 274]

Bloody Friday

The day before Passover 1942, according to the orders of the ghetto commissioner, all the young people were sent out to work. No elderly Jew was let out of the ghetto, neither by the Town commissioner nor the ghetto Commissioner. At ten o'clock the ghetto gates were opened and one hundred and fifty German murderers armed from head to toe, were let into the ghetto singing the "Horst Vessel" song: "When Jewish blood is splattered by the knife." They scattered amongst the houses, and shooting mixed with crying and shouting was heard throughout the ghetto.

Yaakov Kazulchic, his shirt in disarray, his eyes full of tears, ran about the ghetto yelling: "Yidden, hide yourselves. They are going to shoot you!" The shooting did not stop. In the Judenrat, negotiations were taking place with a murderous officer of the death squad: He demanded three hundred Jews to be shot. For a large amount of gold, leather and other valuables, the Judenrat was able to cheapen the price: only those with beards were to be shot, only a few dozen men.

The massacre lasted two hours. Many were killed. (an exact list of the victims can be found on page 318.) Moshe Lev, the baker stood up heroically against the murderers. They took the rabbi of the Hassidim (who was nicknamed 'the Yellow') burned off his beard and then pinned him to the walls of the Hassidic synagogue with stakes.

The ghetto Commissioner forbade public mourning for the victims. They were buried with their clothes on with the town and ghetto Commissioners present. It was already the night of the Seder, a Seder full of destruction and torment.

When the ghetto Commissioner fancied to have a pool built for himself and his cronies, thousands of women, men and children were taken for forced labor. The slave laborers would drop dead from carrying the heavy loads of earth. They would receive harsh blows especially at the hands of the cursed Polish police, using their leather-tipped bludgeons. The factory workers were also not exempt from this special project. After ending their most difficult workday, they were forced at the end of rifle butts to work once more on the pool. Exhausted from working under duress, they were barely able to carry themselves home, only to come home to an empty table with nothing to eat.

Krynki Jews driven to work by the Nazis in the year 1942 *

"One Should Escape to the Forests"

Simcha, the son of Nachum Bleicher, "organized" in his cellar a radio set hidden in an empty barrel. Every day Boma Friedman would be there and listen to the broadcasts from London, Moscow and Berlin. This could have endangered hundreds of lives so it was kept top secret.

Most of the time, the young people were sent to work digging peat in Podbianka or cutting wood in the forest. It once happened that partisans confiscated from the work crews in the forest all their saws and axes, sending the Jews back to the ghetto, not willing to take them back with them to their partisan groups.

When a partisan would meet up with a Jew in the forest, he would take everything from him and say to him that he should go back from where he came. This was because the Germans would send spies into the forest disguised as Jews with yellow patches sewn on their backs. Allegedly these Jews and others would later reveal the whereabouts of the partisan bunkers. Once when partisans met up with Jewish laborers digging peat in the forests, a few of the youth, among them my brother, wanted to go with them into the forest. But they were adamantly refused and even threatened with being shot to death.

[Page 275]

Life in the ghetto deteriorated day by day. All reserves of food were used up. People became paler and weaker. The death toll increased greatly. The former field near the "Linas Tsedek", where all the victims of the Passover massacre were buried was already filled with graves. The famine only got stronger. The number of successful food-smuggling operations into the ghetto diminished drastically. Most people lived with the hope that the situation would not last much longer and one would be freed soon. When such people as Yudel Kaplan, Yeshaya Glezer and my father would say that we must search for a way to liberate ourselves, escaping to the forest and with weapons in hand, fight the enemy, others like Zaidel Philipsky for example would preach that one must sit and wait it out in the ghetto until Amalek will fall like the demise of Haman!

The Nazi Murderers and their Polish Collaborators

Chaim Weiner

Around the first of July 1941, the German S.S. troops started to quietly appease their thirst for blood. They entered the synagogue and gathered together all the holy scrolls and books and set them afire. When the smoke began already to spread through the roof, the Germans allowed the fire to be extinguished. A united effort was made by the Jews took in performing the holy work, to save the Torah scrolls and to put out the flames.

A few days later, the local Polish police force with a certain Polish spy on behalf of the Germans, named Aratzki, a person who "ate up Jews", began to undertake a murder "action" against former Communists. They were all gathered and shot a kilometer from town. Amongst the victims were: H. Schwietzer, M. Winak and others.

A brave Communist, Barkan tried to hide but was betrayed by the outcasts of Polish society and was caught and brought to a German lorry. Going to certain death, he proclaimed through out the entire market place, "Long live the Communist Party and down with Hitler!"

In June of 1942, the Germans commenced building a pool outside of town. Jews were forced to work there after their "regular" working hours until late at night. One day the required number of laborers did not show up, so the Germans forced the entire Jundenrat out to the work place, where they were very badly beaten. First the Germans commanded them to produce a ridiculously large number of slave laborers. Looking for a solution, the Jewish Police force dragged out fasting Jews who were sitting in the synagogue, to fill the quota!

Before the liquidation of the ghetto, in the beginning of November 1942, the local German authorities sent out invitations to all the pro-German Polish collaborators in the region that they should come and participate in the upcoming festivities against the Jews. They promised an official prize to each and everyone who took part.

On the second of November, at five o'clock in the morning, the invited Poles were already waiting at the gates of the ghetto. Together with German soldiers they appeared in the ghetto, armed with bludgeons and spikes to "greet" the Jews of Krynki in honor of their expulsion from their hometown forever!

The Liquidation of the Ghetto

A. Soyfer

Fall was approaching. The situation in the ghetto became worse and more despairing. The first of November 1942 arrived. The ghetto was encircled by machine guns. To escape the ghetto was already impossible. The ghetto Commissioner and the other Germans took back from the Jews all the

orders that were not yet finished. No one went out to his work-detail. Before nightfall, a rumor circulated that all the Jews would be sent to another town. The whole night, everyone made up knapsacks and prepared himself for the coming journey.

[Page 276]

At six o'clock the next morning, the ghetto Commissioner announced that in approximately an hour, all the Jews have to leave the ghetto. The prepared peasant wagons were already in the market place. At six-thirty, armed Germans entered the ghetto together with Gestapo officers. Around ten minutes later hundreds of people, young and old, were already standing ready with knapsacks on their shoulders. When they left the ghetto gates, a whole mob of Germans and Polish hooligans chased after them and hit them over their heads and backs with their sticks.

People fell down on the cobblestone pavement all bloodied, children screamed. The pavement was covered with pillow feathers. All of Garbaska Street was littered with knapsacks and wounded people. Children lost their parents in the tumult and were running among the feet of the murderers who were incessantly beating and screaming, "Quicker, quicker, get out!"

The officers were standing with their photographic equipment and were taking pictures and laughing at the same time!

Suddenly, a wild command came forth from the murderous director of the leather factory: that all the workers there should come over to the synagogue courtyard. The rest of the Jews went toward the Market place to the waiting wagons. The noise of the wheels of the wagons deafened the Jews. The director together with a Jewish representative, Yankel Shneider, sorted the remaining Jews. Those who were taken out of line ran to the market place, searching for their families. One hundred and seventy leather workers, all craftsmen, were kept back and with them, the Judenrat and the best shoemakers, tailors, and seamstresses, a total of three hundred and fifty people.

Arranged five in a row, we were led back to the factory. A few bloodied older people were still lying on the pavement. A deathly stillness was felt coming from the ghetto. The heavy steps of the murderers were heard in the air. The gates of the ghetto were left open.

We march with heads downward to Tarlovsky's factory. The shoemakers and tailors were taken to Grossman's factory, which was located in the ghetto.

[Page 277]

The Scroll Of Kelbasin

Dov Rabin

In October of 1942, the head German Reich security officer ordered the Gestapo Central Command of the Bialistok region to "evacuate" the Jews from their area. This meant the actual annihilation of all Jewish towns of the region. The annihilation of the Grodno district was put in the hands of the Gestapo Commander of Grodno, Criminal Commissioner and Deputy Sturmfuhrer, Heinz Ehrelis and his assistant, deputy Sturmfuhrer, Erich Schot.

Very early in the morning on the second of November 1942, in a sudden and simultaneous action by the Nazis, all the Jews of all the communities of the Bialistok region were mercilessly expelled from the homes they had inhabited for generations. However, due to the complicated logistics of transporting such large numbers at the same time, the evacuees were not sent directly to the death camps but first to "collection camps." In reality these were also extermination camps albeit generally without crematorium and forced labor. However, thousands of the tens of thousands of Jews who had been transported were "sentenced to death" there by hunger, cold, filth, lice, epidemics, persecution, beatings, shootings and a large array of other brutal and sadistic methods of murder.

On the other hand, although the Jews interned in these "collection points" were not so quickly murdered, nor were they so quick to put an end to their own suffering, these transfer camps served as preparation for the non-ending hell which faced the internees. The Germans constantly dulled and broke the spirit of their victims, breaking their will and bringing them into states of surrender and detachment from reality in order to prevent them from gathering any inner forces to put up any resistance to the Nazis.

The camp in Kelbasin was the most horrific of these "collection camps" in which tens of thousands Soviet prisoners of war had previously been interned and starved and tortured to death. This camp was situated around six kilometers from Grodno by the highway to Bialistok.

The Jews of Krynki were expelled to the Kelbasin camp together with the Jews of Brestovitz, a part of the mass of twenty-eight thousand Jewish victims originating from the Jewish towns in the area: Adelsk, Azher, Amdur, Ostrin, Dubrava, Druzgenik, Holnika, Yanova, Luna-Volya, Novy-Dovar, Sapotzkin, Sakolka, Suchavalya, Sidra, Skidel, Paretzch, Kaminka, Koritzhin, Kuznitza, Rotnitza and a remnant of the Grodno Ghetto. Only a few hundred able-bodied persons were kept for a short time in their previous communities (including Krynki) interned in work camps, which were still necessary for the Nazi war machine.

Translations by Judie Goldstein

The Chief Murderer and his "Court Sentence"

The evidence about the chief murderer of the tens of thousands of Jews of the Bialistok region, "Doctor" Altenlau, (director of the transports of Jews to the death camps) first came out in public when he was caught and brought to trial in the beginning of 1967 in the town of Bilfeld, West Germany. He was sentenced to eight years in prison! Concerning the direct murderers, the main slaughterers, the above-mentioned Heinz Ehrelis and Erich Schot, only the former was caught. The other had committed suicide a few years earlier. Apparently he surmised that the danger that awaited him if he had been caught and put on trial was not a great one, and he did not even bother to disguise himself. Nothing is known concerning the fate of the daily butcher of the Kelbasin Camp, Karl Rintzler (or Rintzer according to German sources), whose sadism and bloodthirst excelled even that of his Gestapo collaborator murderers.

[Page 278]

The "Criminal Commissioner and deputy Sturmfuhrer" Heinz Ehrelis held himself as an "intellectual" with aristocratic mannerisms. He was a lover of the arts and particularly music, and he preferred to conduct his extermination "work" behind the scenes. This however did not prevent him from boasting that one could "grind up" ten thousand persons in a wheat mill before his very eyes without him batting an eyelash!

However, this "hero", like his major commander "Doctor" Altenlau and the other haughty murderers did not display any outward heroism during his trial by admitting to doing any of his "good deeds," Nor did he at least justify the blood he personally shed, as he was judged guilty via eye-witnesses of his murderous behavior. Ehrelis lied outright declaring these things never happened. He was innocent like a dove....

And for all of his witness-established mass murders, the West German court sentenced him to six and a half years of prison with the right to appeal! And so the "verdict" handed down some two years later has never been imposed.

The bloodhound "on location," the Kelbasin Camp Commander, Karl Rintzler, and his gruesome actions are described later on by the only living Krynki survivor Feivel Wolf. There is also added confirmation of these actions as told by a number of other survivors.

Rintzler's Hell

"Rntzler used to go around like a wild animal with a big rubber stick"—writes the Suchavaler survivor, Simcha Lazar[2]. He particularly would detain women and strike them on the head and face for long periods of time. The blood running on their faces rendered them unrecognizable. This brutality would repeat itself day after day".

"One day a young man left the camp without permission. On the way to Sokolka, he was captured and brought back to the camp. Rintzler had his arms and legs tied up with a rope behind his back and put him under a table, suffering with unimaginable pain for twenty-four hours. The Jew was just choking with pain. In the morning the murderer untied him. The young man was not able to stand up because his blood had hardened all over him. Rintzler took four Jews and ordered them to dig a grave. He had the young man placed in the grave and shot him with a bullet. With a sinister smile on his murderous face he ordered that the grave be covered up".

"One time a young, eighteen-year-old man came late to head count at the assembly square. Rintzler saw this, called the youth over and had him put in the middle of the square. In the presence of all the assembled he shot him with a bullet in the neck".

"The murderer quietly put his hand in his pocket, took out a cigarette and started to smoke with a look of derision and contempt on his animalistic face".

"Two times daily a head count was taken at the assembly point of each barrack. After counting and recounting the assembled to make sure the number counted fit the submitted pieces of paper, Rintzler would order that we should run in our places for an hour. While running we had to sing Jewish songs. If we would not sing well, he would beat us murderously. A victim would fall to the ground; he would find another one. He was never satiated with Jewish blood. He had special delight in torturing Jewish women. So he would force them under threat of death, to clean with their bare hands the assembly point of the camp. He forced them to place some of the garbage inside their chests and to carry the rest in garbage baskets."

This is also told by a survivor from the town of Ostrin in "Sefer Zichronot L'kehilot Ostrin" [The Ostrin Yizkor Book], Tel Aviv, 5727 [1967].

[Page 279]

In reality, there was plenty of water in the camp. Nevertheless, the inmates were strictly forbidden even to come close to the water faucets. The women of Ostrin who were caught attempting to bring a little water for their babies, were tied one to another with rope and chased around the camp. This was all to put fear into everyone's heart not to "steal" any water. Compare this with others who were bludgeoned to death with rubber sticks for such a "sin"!

There were no restrooms per say in the Kelbasin Camp. For this purpose a pick pit was dug in the middle of the camp, where men and women had to relieve themselves publicly without any divisions between them. The women would be ashamed and would suffer terribly, holding back from relieving themselves with all their might.

A young woman who therefore waited until nightfall to relieve herself, met up with a German, while going out in the darkness. Trembling greatly, she ran back to her barrack. The German however, took her out of the barracks and seeing her beauty demanded that she strip naked for his pleasure. She begged him that she would prefer to be shot rather than take her clothes off. He took out his revolver and threatened her that if she did not do as he said, he would shoot everyone in her barracks. Not wishing to be the cause of the death of her friends, she was forced to follow the command of the German beast.

The Struggle For Survival (From Krynki Until Kelbasin)

I survived the Holocaust thanks to my birthplace, the village of Spodville, six kilometers from Krynki and nine kilometers from Gross-Brestovitz. There, I came into this bright world, born on the twentieth of June 1920 to my mother, Rivka and my father, Betsalel. Our parents had eight children: five sons and three daughters. Some of them are now living in Israel.

Our entire family lived in Krynki. My mother's two brothers—Avraham Niyeparszhnitz and "Daniel der Hoicher," Daniel the tall one, as people nicknamed him, and my father's brother Yankel and his sister Bashke de "Spodviller" (the one who comes from Spodville).

I served in the Polish army from the twelfth of April 1934 until the end of 1935.

On the twenty-forth of August 1939, I was mobilized to fight against the Germans. On the tenth of September 1939, I arrived in Lemberg with a group of other Krynki Jews and there engaged the Germans in heavy battle. Together with me in Lemberg, were: Yitzchak Stalarsky, Avraham Kleinbart, Leiba Lopate, Leima Shuster, Leizer Stotzky and others whose names I do not recall.

On the twenty-first of September, the Russians discharged us. With great effort, I then managed to get back to Krynki.

Early Tribulations

I worked for the Russians in the town of Amdur from the beginning of 1940 until the 22nd of June 1941.

On the Sabbath evening of the 22nd of June 1941, the Germans invaded the town.

Monday, the 23rd of June, I together with my brother, Itschke, Mates (Matisyahu) Paliyatchik and David Shalmuk, fled in the direction of Russia, eastward. However, on the road from Slonim to Baranovitch, I was badly wounded and it prevented me from continuing.

[Page 280]

On Sabbath, the 28th after midday, the Germans captured my brother and me. This was about six kilometers from the town of Zelva, not far from Slonim.

A German doctor, who examined us, obviously recognized that we were Jews. He however quietly promised that he would not surrender us to the authorities, because the Germans would shoot Jews immediately on the spot without any pretenses.

At dusk, at six o'clock, together with seven Christians, we were taken to a village four kilometers from Zelva. There, orders were given that we should be taken behind a barn, where we saw death before our eyes!

Speaking or even exchanging looks with one another was strictly forbidden and moving from one's place was certainly not advisable.

Within a few short minutes, four Christians passed by us with shovels in their hands. In accordance with the commands of the Germans, they started digging a grave. One did not have to be overly bright in order to figure out what had happened. When one of the Christian prisoners still had the courage to ask for a drink of water, the head guard gave him the following answer:

"We will soon make you drunk with blood!"

It started to rain and night fell.

As we stood there on the edge of the grave, totally pre-occupied with thoughts of death, a higher ranking German officer appeared and in a loud voice commanded:

"Do not shoot without an order!"

And so they led us back to the same barn that we were in earlier.

Early the next morning, when they led us out to the sunlight, an elderly Christian approached the head guard, spoke with him a little and immediately afterwards bread, potatoes and sour milk were brought to us. Later we were transported by car to Azernitze and from there to Roszhani. There, we were interned in a camp located in the "garden" of a White Russian priest. Jews were separate from Christians and the captured soldiers were also kept in a separate section. Altogether, there were 5000 men in the camp. Once a day we received a dead horse, which we ourselves cooked for our sustenance.

After being in that camp for six days, we were freed. What I witnessed there is a horror to describe!

A few days later, together with my brother, I arrived in Spodville. We found there our dear elderly mother together with my father's sister and husband. There a new series of terrible troubles began. At every step, they would shoot Jews dead for no apparent reason. My brother Itschke fled to Grodno, and I to Krynki.

And It Began Like This

Sitting by Yankel Spodviller and hearing all that was happening in Krynki, I noticed through the window a group of Jews with yellow badges on their chests returning from factory work. Soon my Uncle Yankel and cousin Shmuel came in with a few other Jews and ordered me to put on a badge so that the Germans wouldn't kill me.

That very same day I fled back to Spodville. There the situation was even more serious, because a number of Christians had been shot. In the morning I fled with a shovel on my back to Amdur.

I arrived safely but as I entered the town, a Christian recognized me and as it was told to me, the Christian immediately went about investigating what I was doing there. Accordingly, I was advised to hide and as soon as possible run away. Just a day earlier, sixty Germans had come to town from Grodno and demanded that all the Jews, old and young, big and small evacuate their homes. They were expelled to the fields, and according to a Christian eyewitness, thirty-three men were taken away. These were the first victims of the town (Himelfarb, the father together with his older son, two Eshkevitz brothers, Shimon Las, Moorshtien, Feldman, David Shalmuk, Hirshel the shepherd, Shmuel Intelegent, Motel Nachbi, Gronik, Zhupitza and others).

[Page 281]

Soon after my arrival in Amdur, I saw three Jews tied with barbed wire to the telegraph poles. This was their punishment for not arriving at work early enough.

Quite early the next morning I fled back to Spodville and in a few days, I was back as a steward on the estate at Klein-Brestovitz. The Germans considered him an important person. I had asked him to take me under his protection. I was left there with my uncle Shmuel working, but it did not last long and we soon fled for our lives back to Spodville.

In the morning, I was back again with my mother looking for protection by the Poles. We found a place for me by a certain Pole, and I was left working for him as a farm hand. One day as I was plowing the field a Christian came up to me and said:

"You foolish Zhid (negative Polish word for a Jew) , you are looking for a place to save yourself in these bad times? Here the Germans pass by and any small child will point you out to them as a Zhid and they will shoot you. Better you flee to a place where there are a lot of Jews!"

Seeing that the Christian was correct, I ran back to my mother in Spodville that day and the next morning, I fled to Krynki. There, they were in the middle of a shooting and I fled back to Spodville and from there, straight to Amdur. There, I was advised to go either to Grodno or to Bialistock. I chose to go back to my dear mother in the village of Spodville.

Time, meanwhile was not standing still. The Germans were advancing deep into Russia. For us in the village it became a bit calmer, so we stayed there. In the towns and cities around us, ghettos were being established.

On the 12th of February, at eight o'clock in the morning, in forty-degree frost, three Germans from Klein-Brestovitz entered our home and checked us for the yellow star. In just a few minutes, they stole our cow, twenty hens and all items of worth. They ordered us to abandon the village and to flee Spodville within an hour's time and go back to Gross-Brestovitz.

For the price of a liter of spirit they obtained from the Germans a permit for me to travel to Krynki.

In The Krynki Ghetto

That same day we arrived at the Krynki ghetto at the factory of Melech Zalkin.

Ten days passed and the *Judenrat* (a representative body of the Jewish community that the Nazis required Jews to form) took us for work cleaning the highway from Krynki to Sokola - twenty-two Kilometers. Our "employers" were a gruff German sergeant around fifty years old with long whiskers and his assistant Max "the tall one."

One time, on a Sunday, a market day, he drove us as far as Skolka, without eating and drinking and kept us there until nine in the evening. It wasn't until one in the morning that we returned to the Krynki ghetto. When I got home, I found a note on the table that notified me that at five o'clock the next morning I was to be ready again to go out to work at our fixed gathering point opposite the Judenrat.

I did not go out to work, nor did many others. The dirty *khazir* (pig) with another ten Germans entered the ghetto to grab men. Meanwhile they came into the home of Moshke (the smith) Trahshtshman, took their beautiful girl out of her bed and took her practically naked (in a thirty degree frost) out into the street and whipped her. After that they took out the Akusherkes' daughter and whipped her and kept her for a long time in the cold. They also seized Rabbi Oviat for forced labor.

[Page 282]

Meanwhile, in the "small" ghetto everyone heard what the murderer was doing.

Casually, as if no one was paying attention to me, I went to the gathering point and showed up for work. Looking at me, another seventeen men also came to the gathering point.

Right before our very eyes, the murderer tore out from the Rabbi's face, half a beard and mustache and burned them. Then his assistant grabbed me, hit me on the head, shook me up and down and gave me seven lashes with a rubber whip. At the actual time, it didn't hurt me too much, but later it bothered me. I was nicknamed "the whipped one." Then he tormented and bullied the rest of the Jews and also beat them. He drove them by foot ten kilometers from Krynki near the village of Shodzhialava to clean the snow.

The Massacre Before Passover

On the thirteenth of Nisan, we were three hundred men on the highway around three kilometers from town, cleaning the snow. At half past nine we heard shots coming from Krynki. About half an hour later, Christians came to us on sleds and whispered in our ears that they are shooting Jews in the ghetto.

At twelve-noon, the Germans took us for a mid-day break. We came into the ghetto and in front of us was utter bedlam. Scattered on the streets lay Jewish property, food and among all this lay the bodies of people who had been shot.

I ran to my house and on the street, I met the Zalkin family. When I asked them the whereabouts of my brother Itsche, I was told:

"He is alive."

"And where is my mother?" I added.

They did not answer. My mother was killed together with four other women and over twenty-five men. Among them were: Rabbi Qviat, Daniel the tall one, my uncle Manes with his brothers, Moshe the baker, (who resisted against the murderers and fought with them until he slipped near the well and only then was overpowered and killed), Mantshe Haikel Chazir, the tailor, the hump-backed, Moni Yaakov Kaplan and others.

The next day, Shabbos, they were buried on Bathhouse Street near the "Linas Tsedek" in a garden - men separately and women separately. Among the scenes at the funeral, I will never forget the grieving of Ephrayim Manes for his dead father.

At eleven-thirty, the murderers left the ghetto singing the song, "When Jewish blood spurts forth from our knives - the battle goes well."

Before The Destruction

After the great massacre, the Judenrat became more considerate of the mourning families and made an effort not to send them to dangerous work details. Thus they treated my brother and me. One day a young man from Bialistok by the name of Perlman who was a builder foreman for the Germans, came to my brother Sholke (he was a bricklayer) and took him to work for him. The next day he came and took me also as a worker. Sholke, Anshel Potshevutzky, Zeltchik, Chazkel Gandz, the son of the barber, and I all worked there on the Count's estate.

On "a nice day", soldiers from Krynki came and started to beat us for no reason. They forced us all to go back to Krynki and into the ghetto. I no longer went to work. I only looked for an opportunity to escape to a place where I no longer had to see the Germans before my eyes.

[Page 283]

After Passover, the sixth of May, I, together with twenty boys and two girls left Krynki and went to catch fish in the Refle Estate forty kilometers from Krynki - twelve from Resh and twelve from Volp. The remaining Krynki Jews worked in Yeshmenta at the highway to Luna and the station Brestovitz Zieliyana to Bialistock. At first the conditions in Refla were not especially good; only later did they improve.

Initially the Judenrat did not want to help us like the other workers. But Talya Goldshmidt championed my cause and once a month we were allowed to enter the ghetto.

On the first of November 1942, on a Sunday, at three o'clock in the afternoon, while I was on an errand for my overseer, catching carp for supper in the local fish ponds, they called me all of a sudden, saying I should come quickly because the Germans were asking for me. I was in a gloomy mood because I realized that something didn't smell quite right.

As I was running to my overseer's house, a Polish policeman in a German uniform took out his pistol from his hips and aimed to shoot at me. Only because of the employer's wife, a pretty and energetic Pole, who grabbed a hold of the policemen by the hands, started to curse him and told him that he was not worthy to carry the name of the Polish people nor come into their holy places if he dared do anything to me, was I saved. And she really did save my life. He told her that he had a duty to shoot me because I was not wearing the yellow badge.

I took the badge out of my pocket realizing that I had forgotten to attach it. Later, I heard how the lady asked him where he was planning to take me. He would have answered her: "Here, not far from where the Jews are found on the road." She did not let him answer until he had given his word that he would not harm me.

A meager two hundred meters from us, stood five Germans with a car and with them were nineteen boys, among them Sholom Shveitzer and two girls - all from Krynki, and they were waiting for me. In around fifteen minutes five wagons drove up and we were placed four or five people to a wagon and we were taken away accompanied by Germans and Poles.

At eight in the evening we arrived at Grois-Yeshmonta, and from there we went to the Masalin Estate where there were already assembled approximately three hundred Jews - one hundred and fifty from Krynki; and fifty each from Amdur, Grois-Brestovitz and Luna. They were quartered in a big school and worked on the Masalin-Luna highway. We were brought to them. A very heavy guard of German and Polish policemen was standing around us and no one had any idea what was in store for us.

Yosef Dvorkin from Grois-Brestovitz and Villensky from Krynki, both energetic young men, offered the German in charge a pair of nice boots, to induce him to tell us what was in store for us. He indeed did take the boots but didn't know a thing.

The whole night we did not sleep. At five o'clock in the morning, a hundred wagons drove up to the school and we were all ordered to take a spot in a wagon. Guarded heavily by the Germans, we began our journey. Monday morning we were already in Amdur. The Germans halted the first wagon at the end of Grodner Street in front of the Amdur Synagogue. I was sitting in the first wagon. An Amdur mailman passed by us and told me that only a few hours earlier, the Amdur Jews were expelled en masse in the direction of Grodno.

[Page 284]

Ten minutes later the convoy was on the move once again and at five kilometers outside of Amdur we caught up with a column of Jewish refugees from Odelsk and Amdur. The entire highway was filled with wagons of Jews from the district. Around ten kilometers from Grodno, we changed wagons and the new wagon driver told me that he knew me. He confided in me and told me that we were being taken to a starvation death at the Kelbasin camp. As we approached Grodno, the highway was even denser with deported Jewish.

It was already dusk and the Christian wagon driver advised me to jump off the wagon and to hide amongst the Christians for a certain death awaited me at Kelbasin. Accordingly, he told me how, around half a year earlier, thousands of Russian prisoners of war died of hunger and filth at the camp. I, however, did not follow his advice and at five in the morning we arrived at the camp.

Inside The Kelbasin Camp

We were commanded to go into block number five together with the Jews from Skidel. The night passed peacefully. In the early morning, I met a number of good friends from Skidel. Through a hole in the wall, we crawled into the third block where the Jews of Amdur were being held. There I met my sister who was married to a Jew from Amdur by the name of Shimon Ahkevitch. In Amdur, the rumor had spread that I had been shot. So everyone gathered around me, welcomed and wished me long life!

I already began to investigate what was going on. I asked, "Who was the commander of the camp and for what purpose were we brought here?" Gutman, a teacher from Amdur, a very capable former Judenrat official, with whom I began to talk, knew absolutely nothing.

Soon, a tall German, in his forties appeared before us and immediately it became clear that his name was Rinzler and that he was the commandant of the camp.

About an hour later, he came into the Amdur block, number three. Everyone started to run about. Yosef Karlinsky, the former head of the Amdur police, ran toward him. Rinzler commanded him to lie down on the ground and then whipped him!

The entire day was spent taking care of incoming Jews from the Grodno area.

At dusk, we were able to recognize Jews from Krynki near the barbed wire. I, Sholom Shweitzer and others from Krynki soon crossed over to them in block number two, bunk section number twelve. Some of the young men told me that my brother Velvel, Wolf and Avkas' son, a grandson of Zhidak, had fled the night before the expulsion and were with the Christians of the neighboring villages.

In Rinzler's Hell

A highway crossed through the middle of the camp. When the wagons would come inside the camp, the Germans would begin to hound the Jews. The Jews were forced to jump down from the wagons and to leave behind all of their possessions. Some good Christians however would throw down from the wagons the bundles that the Jews had brought with them. The Jewish police would hurriedly take down the elderly from the wagons. The nightmare that I witnessed there is indescribable.

The Kelbasin camp was located sixteen kilometers from Grodno, three kilometers from the plywood factory, three hundred meters right off of the Bialistock highway when traveling from Grodno to Kuznitza.

The Krynki Jews were expelled on foot with the Jews of Goshtiniatz through Makaravtza, Patshuvet until they reached Amdur where they spent the night in the emptied ghetto. Tuesday, at dusk they arrived at Kelbasin. On the way, between Makaravtza and Potshevut, the Germans shot Yudel Yudzhikan.

[Page 285]

Every day new transports of Jews from the surrounding areas would arrive.

For food, we received two hundred grams of bread with unpeeled potatoes, cooked with horsemeat.

The murderer, Rinzler, would be present in the camp daily from eight in the morning until twelve noon and from two until five in the afternoon. He had two Jewish assistants. One was a young man from Kuznitza and the other was from Dubrova.

They would wait for him until he came and followed him around like two dogs. During the hours he was present in the camp, everyone would stay in their bunk sections. Every day he would murder people with his blackjack. It was made of rubber with a piece of iron at its tip. He would for example, stand around in the middle of the camp together with his two assistants and look out to see whether some one was passing by with a jug or a quart container looking for some water. He would also check to see who was going over to visit a brother or sister in a bunk section. But when everyone knew to keep inside, he would command his assistants to find someone and bring him to him.

If at first, they would not give over his victim, he would take out from that bunk section twenty people to be shot. Soon enough the "guilty party" would come out on his own accord. He would then "honor" his victim with seven hits with his iron tipped club over his head. No medical help from the doctor (Gordon from Ozher, who survived) was allowed to be given to the victim. So would the victim expire from his wounds and pain within two to three days. In such a fashion, Rinzler murdered the wife of Moshe Lapinitz from Dubrova, a teacher.

And so he would murder people every single day. He would suddenly appear in the kitchen and see who was not working and kill him. He would receive letters or telephone messages from an officer in a certain shtetel that in such and such a village an expulsion order must be carried out.

Just hearing that Rinzler was in the camp, everyone would disappear into the bunk sections.

But even death cannot stop hunger and when the wagons with bread would arrive in the camp from the Grodno ghetto, everyone would quickly run to it, and Rinzler would already have something to do. He wasn't constantly around. The security services would also hit people, but not kill them.

The inmates would give the Jewish wagon-drivers from Grodno dollars in order they should bring or send over a loaf of bread, deliver a message in the ghetto, or bring letters. There was a wagon driver, Yudel Altshuler who would smuggle people into the ghetto in a hiding place he had in his wagon. I knew him very well in Grodno. I gave him twenty dollars and he personally brought me bread many times.

There were a number of Jews from Krynki who brought with them their own foodstuffs: chickpeas, onions, lentils, and barley. They would cook these in empty living quarters. I and Sholom Shveitzer would obtain cooking wood by taking up boards from the bunk sections. We would separate it with a knife. We would make holes in a pail, make a fire, put in a pot and cook. Half would be given to the "supplier" of the food and the other half would be for us.

The Jewish police had an order to arrest anyone found cooking, confiscate the food and bring him before the Judenrat for a whipping in front of the chief of police. Also the "guilty one" was not given bread for a number of days. I was whipped a number of times and deprived of my bread ration.

Early every morning, quite early, the dead would be gathered and brought to the gates, wrapped up in sheets or in blankets - thirty or forty every day. Under a heavy guard, we would take them out to the nearby forest and bury them in a grave, men and women together.

Twice a day, we had to assemble in front of the block for an inspection by Rinzler who was accompanied by his two assistants and Frankel from Druzgenik. He would always make use of his blackjack with the iron tip. Even having one's hat positioned on his head not according to Rinzler's liking was enough to receive a "sentence" from him.

[Page 286]

Frankel was the senior member of the Kelbasiner Judenrat and his assistant was Marek from Novy-dvar that was near Grodno. The overseer of the food supplies, (which were not received), was Arkin from Azher. Every town had its own representative on the Judenrat: Krynki - Meir Kaplan; Sokolka - Advocate Freidberg; Amdur - the teacher Gutman.

They were obligated to meet everyday with Rinzler in a barrack in the middle of the camp where he would whip people. The Judenrat officials had to bring to him the people who had to receive beatings or whippings.

On the sixth day, Friday he called the representatives of the Judenrat and demanded from them three hundred men to work on the station in town. For such a thing there were too many volunteers and one had to have substantial clout to be included in that group. Either a brother or a good uncle in the Judenrat or in the police would be sufficient to get you included. Near the gates of the camp they were commanded to get undressed and a thorough search was made of every worker. Gold and dollars were found during the search. Immediately, Rinzler had everyone brought back to the camp, called together the Judenrat and commanded them to confiscate all the gold and money.

On The Way To Death

Then he would proceed to fantasize with the representatives of the Judenrat, that he would send the Jews to Aushwitz, where they would benefit from "good conditions." There, one received five hundred grams of bread per day, cooked food three times a daily, a decent bed - a real spa!

On the eighth day, Sunday, the first transport to "good conditions" was sent - the Jews from Skidel. A few days later, Rinzler had in his hands letters that the Jews of Skidel had written to their closest friends in other towns describing how good all aspects life were in their new place! It appeared that the Germans forced their victims, before their deaths, to write these glowing letters! The same day after receiving those letters, fifty grams of sausage was distributed to every person. This was done in order to create an impression among the camp inmates that better winds were beginning to blow.

I did not eat the sausage and carried it back to the Amdur block to my sister's girl. There I, merely sat down in bunk section number fourteen and Nina Zelmanovitch approached us and said half jokingly and half seriously:

"Feivel, is the sausage from the Jews of Skidel?"

A conversation developed and more people came along. I said the following in a non-joking tone:

"If the Germans wanted us for work, they would not weaken and tire us out so much. They are bringing us somewhere only to annihilate us!"

For the word "annihilate" I received a slap in the face from Avraham Noifach from Amdur. My sister started to shout at me for speaking in such a fashion.

Very often members of the Judenrat of Grodno would come to take men from Kelbasin and bring them into the Grodno ghetto. It was all for gold and money.

After the transport of the Jews from Skidel there were eight quiet days without any new moves from Kelbasin. At that time in Grodno itself, the Jews of the second ghetto, the Slobodker, were moved.

One day, Shebsel Purim, Nachum Yeruchams Yankel, the blonde bakers' son, stood near bunk section number twelve and asked me a question:

"Why don't you escape? People are escaping."

I asked him: "Who are the men that are escaping?"

He answered: "Yankel the hatter's son-in law from Bialistock."

At that time, Sender Chaim Nisels from Shank came up to us. We started to talk and he blurted out that we "are sentenced to death" without any hope of rescue or miracle. I did not let him continue speaking and suggested to him that we should look for a way to escape. I added afterwards that the Christians of Spodville hold him in high esteem. He answered me bluntly that he had a child and wife and he could leave them. We jointly did not see any possibility of escape. He suggested to me that he would talk with other young men and that we should escape together on the same day, if I did not want to escape on my own.

[Page 287]

He brought me together with Feivel Talkevitzhener also from a village in a forest on the other side of Krynki. He reluctantly agreed to escape. He told other young men about the plan. I turned to my cousins, Shmuel Yankels, Mulya Zalmens and Pinia

Kravetzky. By day, they almost all agreed. However, when night came, and something had to be done, there was no one to talk to. Feivel Talkavatchner's sister, Avraham Kagan's wife, kicked me out of the bunk section when I came to talk with him.

Meanwhile the Sokolker young men were aware that in the Krynki block there was a person who wanted to escape. They came to me with the two Shtashur brothers, Mulya and Velvel. But they were also the types with whom no serious business could be done. One of them couldn't leave his father and the other could not leave his mother. Finally, a young man from Novy-Dvar, with a wide circle of acquaintances among the Christians of the area, together with a doctor from Sochovola made their way to me. The doctor wanted to flee together with his wife, who was also a doctor. We prepared a ladder and person to remove the ladder after our escape. Everything was ready, when the mother of the young man from Novy-Dvar warned him that if he left, she would take her own life.

On sabbath, the fourteenth of November, the fifth of Kislev 1942, three o'clock in the afternoon, an order was given: All Krynki Jews must leave block number two and move over to block number five. From there we were to be transported to the station at Lososna. In just a few minutes one had to move over into block number five. There I set my final plans and did not sleep the entire night.

Every few minutes new orders arrived from Yosef Manstavliansky. The last order was that at four in the morning, just before dawn, we were to be standing three in a row because at five-thirty the train would depart from Lososna. So the hour was drawing near and my heart began to pound. I did not give up on my cousin Pinia Kravetzki.

At a quarter of four in the morning we began to organize ourselves standing in the rows with our packs on our shoulders. Pinia did not take his place. He saw his mother standing with his father. Here is Shmuel Yankels with Motel with their mother. Then, the voice of Yosef Mastavliansky was heard screaming:

"Quicker, Rinzler is here in the camp."

Then Pinia said to me suddenly: "You want to be wiser than the entire world?"

And he was soon gone. I looked into the darkness and saw Pinia in his long coat go to his mother and father and took a place in the rows together with all of the Krynki Jews.

A quarter after four, Rinzler arrived, looked over everything, cut off the packs from the shoulders and gave the order to step forward. Immediately at the gates, the little children were separated from their mothers.

---

* Photograph kindly donated by Michel Jaskes who wrote: "This the original still picture that belonged to my grandfather who emigrated from Poland to Uruguay before WWII (1921), and that according to him, the picture had been sent to him by a Polish priest from Krynki. It was the only picture he had of his sister who like the rest of his family, they all perished during the Second World War."

[Page 288]

Do Not Forget, Remember!

By Chaim Sheinberg

Translated by Gloria Berkenstat Freund

Clench the fist, tighten the arm,
Harden your heart, suppress your spirit,
Forget your ego – look around you;
Do not stand baffled and do not remain motionless.

Remember for a moment
Your parents' small place,
The home in Krynki, the heartfelt one,
That appears in painful dreams.

Do not live in dreamland, look around you,
Your homey *shtetl* (village) no longer exists:
A *kehile* (community) of Jews for generations
Is buried in dispersed mass graves.

From the Shalker Forest [one hears] shouts and demands
An echo in the air.
The earth [as a witness] reveals the event: It demands and insists
In the name of the Martyrs who she hides.

A scream is heard from Kelbazin
Of pain and suffering and hunger,
There our kith and kin
Wrestled with death.

To you who hear the screams and demands
Of the six million murdered Jews –
Do not forget and never forgive,
Engrave on your heart [the word] remember!

From the ghetto's wire fences
And the gas chamber chimneys
The wind carries all along the roads,
Your *shtetl's* ashes toward you.

In Treblinka's fiery sky
Souls swarm in the clouds of smoke
As reported by asphyxiated and burned witnesses
Towns and *shtetlekh* (villages) totally annihilated.

Clench your teeth, devour your pain,
The world is deaf to your pleas,
She saw and she also heard,
And still turned away from you.

Do not ask, do not demand the reason from heaven, God
Why you deserve the fate of contempt,
Annihilated, erased,
The earth stained with your blood.

Your city vanished in fire and blood
Smoke and poison asphyxiated the house of Yakov,
As ordered by the beastly regime of killers,
That robbed, raped, killed.

Aim the fist, strengthen the arm,
Harden your heart, fortify the spirit,
Engrave the watchword from generation to generation:
Remember what Amalek did to you!

[Page 289]

After the Departure for Treblinka

By Feivel Wolf

Translated by Gloria Berkenstat Freund

Escape from Kelbasin

It was again quiet in the Kelbasin *lager* (concentration camp), and the Germans turned off the electricity.

I did not remain long in the Amdorer block with my sister.

On Tuesday, November 17th, at 4 a.m. the mud-hut was opened and Gutman along with Kopel Poliachek demanded that we stand up, because the Amdorers were leaving the *lager* in two hours and we were going to the train station. Gutman ordered us to remain calm.

I had been ill but immediately stood up. My sister Sarake stood and began to fix her knapsack. I had already firmly decided not to go along and to wait and see how things would end here. Finished with her knapsack, my sister saw that I did not intend to go and wondered why I was standing in place this way. I explained to her that I was not going. She cried,

"You are leaving me alone with a small child and instead you will travel with strangers?"

I further explained to her that I would not be traveling with anyone. She attacked me with sincere kisses and wished that at least someone from the family would remain alive and would start a new generation. These were the last words I heard from her.

All of the Amdorers went to Block No. 5 at 5:30. I remained all alone in the mud-hut No. 14 and I again looked through the little window. Rintzler came back to Block No. 5 exactly at 6 o'clock, went through, looked at everyone and ordered them to go to their death. After leaving through the gate, all of the mothers and children were taken away.

I already knew that after the transport this day would be calm, because Rintzler would not come. And I went to sleep for a few hours in the empty mud-hut where my sister had been for 16 days – in a corner, on the ground.

I walked around the *lager* at eight o'clock to see if perhaps someone from Amdor remained. Turning around I met Frenkle from Druzgenik. I ran to him to ask if he could add me to the people from Druzgenik (they were still in the *lager* legally). He looked at me, lowered his eyes to the ground and quietly said that he could not help me and advised me to try to go to the Suchowolers; perhaps they would take me in.

After several minutes I heard myself being called. This was Abraham Nyames of Amdor. The first thing I asked him was if he had already eaten. He was the cook. He invited me and gave me, perhaps, ten potatoes.

The day passed quietly. I crawled out at night to join the Suchowolers and slept through the night. Very early, a young man noticed me and began to scream, raising an alarm that a strange Jew was hanging around near them. They began to scream at me and demanded that I leave because I intended to rob them and I was assaulted with such curses that I had to leave.

I went to Abraham Nyames again, and again received potatoes. He could not help me. He remained legal, it turned out, because of the payment of money. He advised me to quickly search for an alternative, because any day he might leave the *lager* for the Grodno Ghetto with his wife and son, and I would no longer receive any food.

Walking thus with the potatoes in my pocket, I heard someone calling me by name. And I saw that it was Falye Lev from Krinek. He invited me into his mud-hut, where he lived with his sisters Manya and Yehudis, with Betzalel of Padbyaniki and his brother Artshik. Sonya Lev asked me immediately to which city I belonged and I told her about my situation. She told her husband Betzalzel to register me on their list and I would stay with them in the mud-hut and receive my portion of bread.

[Page 290]

Haim Zalutski, Meir Kaplan, Motl Patsanski, Motl and Dovid Weisman joined us right away.

It became clearer from day to day that we were being driven to our death. Jews from Grodno, who had been brought to Kelbasin, spoke of this very often. Many committed suicide, cutting open the veins of their arms and their legs with shaving knives. Rintzler asked the leaders of the *Judenrat* why so few were taking their own lives.

A young man from Ostrin – who was sent out with those from his *shtetl* to Treblinka and jumped off the train and came back to Kelbasin – brought back the truth. The story of the young man was thus: after the people from Ostrin were driven out of Kelbasin and were on the way to Treblinka, a Polish railroad man entered the train at the Lapy train station, and whispered into the ears of several young people the secret that they were being taken to Malkin to their death. There, he said, ovens have been built in which the Jews are burned. As a friend of the Jews, he advised them to save themselves. The young man, a blond with a non-Jewish appearance, sprang from the wagon, reached a booth of a railroad man near the train line, crawled into a pile of hay and slept through the night.

In the morning, the railroad man came to take hay for his cows and found the young man there. The young man told him the truth. The railroad man gave him bread to eat, but asked him to leave. The young man traveled during the course of several days, traveling with *goyim* (non-Jews) and arrived in Ostrin. However, he could not remain there among the *goyim*. He came back to Kelbasin through Grodno. He told the watchmen at the gate, not bad Germans, that he was coming from a work camp and they let him enter.

In a few minutes everyone knew about the young man. I ran immediately to the mud-hut, in which he was located and found a crowd around him listening to his stories. Then he asked a question, "Who has a piece of bread or a little tobacco?" As I had in my pockets both the former and the latter, from what the good Yudl Altschuler would bring me, the young man told me everything for such an important gift.

He thus told me that notices hung in every city and village, according to which everyone who pointed out a Jew would receive five kilos of sugar and everyone who would catch a Jew and bring him to the Germans would receive ten kilos. And I learned very important news from him, that there were *goyim* who gave food to Jews and I knew many *goyim* very well.

On Monday, December, 14. 1942, at eight o'clock at night, Rintzler and eight German guards entered Block No. 3, mud-hut 5, where we were located, the remaining Krynkers and Amdorers on one side and families of the *Judenrat* members on the other. Four Germans immediately stood at one door and four others by the other, to make sure that no one would run away. Rintzler, who entered on the side where the families of the *Judenrat* members were found, turned on the electricity and, holding a revolver in one hand and a blackjack in the other, pulled down women from the highest plank cots and began asking, "From where?"

[Page 291]

The first answered that she was from Sokolka; he shot her immediately. The second – from Ostrin, the third – from Grodno; thus he shot six women. The rest said that they were from Sochowola or Kusnica; he did not bother them because their *shtetlekh* had not yet been sent on a transport.

From there he went to the gate with the Germans and asked that the a*dvocat* (barrister) Fridberg of Sokolka be brought to him along with his wife and daughters. First he shot the wife, then the daughters (both beautiful women), and then him. Then he ordered that two young girls, who worked for the Germans of the *Wermacht* – one from Lunna, the barber Fatzowksi's daughter, the second from Ozary, and he shot both of them.

In the end, he left alone for Block No. 1, where the Druzgenikers were, for Frenkle's mud-hut. There he found the *advocat* Goszanski of the Grodno *Judenrat*, who had been brought to Kelbasin, dressed with a frying pan on his head and made to dance. The spectators from the mud-hut told how Rintzler went right in there and said, "*Advocat* Goszanski, come with me, quickly."

Goszanski said to him, "I will put on my furcoat."

Answered Rintzler, "You no longer need it!"

He led him to the spot near the gate where the others who had been shot lay and killed him, too.

I hid in the ruin of the remaining Jewish goods, among pillows and featherbeds.

At five in the morning, I heard Falye Lev calling me from nearby. I crawled out, because Rintzler had already left the *lager*.

Rumors immediately spread that this morning we would be taken out to the forest, 200 meters from the *lager,* and everyone would be shot on the spot, because no more transports would leave as the place where they had gone was overcrowded. I simply began pulling my hair from my head. I had the ability to escape and I had let it pass!

Jewish policemen ran around nabbing people to bury the dead. I ran to volunteer immediately. My intention was that if two Germans with guns would lead us as usual, I would run away to the forest. If they shot and hit me, that would be their luck; if not, that would be my luck.

We stationed ourselves around the dead (four men would carry two of the dead in sheets or blankets). In the distance I saw that eight Germans with machine guns were approaching us. Before they came near, I had already run away to an empty mud-hut and there, under the plank cots, I thought about how to find a way out.

A woman well-known for her daring, Mrs. Berezowski, was among the Druzgenikers in Block No. One. Her husband, a well-known Grodno merchant, had his own tar business around Oszor and Ostrin. I had been introduced to the wife a few days earlier. She told me that she had already spent 4 months in the forest, but bandits had dragged her out. They would not let her 16 year old daughter rest as far as sexual advances and that now she wanted to run away with a male. Seeing that there was a small chance of a possibility to save myself, I went to the Berezowski woman.

I explained my plans to her and the whole day we kept conferring about how we would run away from the *lager*. I had 150 dollars, she, three gold watches. We decided to approach at night the German who stood on watch by the gate and propose that for money he let us out.

[Page 292]

At nine in the evening on Tuesday, we approached the German. I remained standing a certain distance from her, as we had agreed among ourselves and she turned to the German from afar and motioned to him that he permit her to go to him to talk about something. As he asked what she needed from him, she explained that her husband worked in the Grodno Ghetto in the *Wermacht* shoe factory and she wanted to go to him.

And to the German's question, who is it that stands near her, she said to him that this one's wife, a tailor, also works for the *Wermacht*, and that he, too, wants to go to his wife. We will give him a gold watch and gold for letting us go.

The German's answer was that he cannot it. If we were caught and beaten and we revealed at which hour we had gone out, he would be shot. And he, too, had a wife and two children.

At ten o'clock the guard changed and Mrs. Berezowski tried to communicate with the German who earlier had been at the gate. He answered the same, but asked if we wanted to buy six loaves of bread, 3 kg. a loaf, for 60 dollars. We gave him the money. And in two hours, after he finished his service, he did bring us the bread, but only five loaves.

Wednesday passed quietly, Thursday, too.

On Friday, 13 wagons entered to take from the *lager* the Jewish goods left there after their owners were taken out; featherbeds, pillows, blankets, underwear, pots, pans, etc. Jewish police ran around as if poisoned, catching people for work, cleaning the *lager*, loading the wagons and, mainly, gathering together the potatoes remaining outside the *lager* and loading them. I was nabbed for the potatoes outside the *lager*. Every few hours those who were working at this were changed. At ten o'clock a car drove in from the gate of the camp.

Going back into the *lager*, I saw that Antek Moslowski was standing near the gate with a paper in his hand. He recognized me and so, as he walked, began talking to me and explaining that he had come for the wife of Yankl Shinder and that he had money for us.

I did not stop and did not answer because I would have been shot immediately for doing so. However, when I passed the gate, I ran immediately to the Lev family and explained it to them. They immediately communicated with Moslowski through the barbed wire. He explained that he had been in the Grodno Ghetto many times with Beila Walcht, who Moishel Szpic had taken out from Kelbasin right after she had been brought here. He also explained that he had given her a lot of money for Krynki Jews and that now he had come for the wife and child of Yankl Shinder.

In the Grodno Ghetto

At one in the afternoon I went out again to work loading the wagons that had come from the Grodno Ghetto. This time I decided my fate over life and death. I thus loaded the wagons and in the end I lay myself in a wagon under a featherbed. I knew whose wagon it was. Until today I do not know if the people who worked with me noticed what I had done or if they saw and kept quiet. Meanwhile, the Jews covered me with all kinds of rags.

At two o'clock the Jewish police led the wagons to the gate. The Germans asked if everything was in order; they were answered, yes. The Germans led the wagons out through the gate and gave them to the drivers from the Grodno Ghetto. At three in the afternoon they ordered the wagons to depart for Grodno.

[Page 293]

Feeling that we had already gone a kilometer, I began to move to climb out. Yudl Altshuler sprang down from wagon:

"Who is there?" – he asked.

"I, Yudl; do not make any noise!," I said to him and was already standing on the highway and was saying goodbye to him – "Yudl, stay well!" – and wanted to run away to the fields because it was already dark.

Yudl asked me where I would go. I answered him, in the direction of Krinek. He told me that he had a certificate for 2 people, and if the chiefs of the Grodno Ghetto, the assassins Vise and Streblov, were not standing at the gate, he could drive me through. Meanwhile it was already dark. Near the ghetto, Yudl went down from the wagon and asked how things were at the gate. Everyone answered that it was quiet and that the two murderers were not there.

And thus we rode through peacefully. After the gate, Yudl grabbed a Jewish policeman and asked that he take me to the bath and that I be given clean underwear. The other did everything that Yudl had asked and from the bath, he took me wherever I asked him: to Abraham Bantz in the building on Troytze Street. A good friend of mine, Leibe Adeses of Amdor, lived there. He welcomed me very well – with tea, blood sausages and bread. I slept with him.

The next morning, *Shabas*, I immediately met a good friend, Lola Shtermfeld of Amdor, and through the *Judenrat*, immediately found a place for me to sleep with Abrahaml Farasha. He found pants for me from a good friend and changed 50 dollars for 13 marks a dollar.

Shabas, in the evening, the last Jew from Kelbasin was brought to the Grodno Ghetto. All of the Krynkers became ill with typhus and I do not know what happened to them in the end, because I ran away.

The Factory-Camp

By Abraham Sofer

Translated by Gloria Berkenstat Freund

We, the remaining tanners, were led into an empty building. The walls were wet. Several of us fell on the wet cement floor and a strong cry tore out of everyone's heart.

70 people remained in the *lager* (camp) factory, several girls and women to cook and the rest – skilled workers. No children remained, except Zeidl Filipski's 2-year old daughter. He did not want to separate from his wife and child and the director was forced to agree, because Filipski was one of the best with locks (sluices) and a specialist in water management. In addition, the murderous director needed him to finish his residence.

Communication between us and "Grosman's Factory-*Lager*" was most strongly forbidden. Several "*Judenratnikes*" (members of the *Judenrat*) remained with us in the *lager*, among them the president, Yosl Galtz, and his wife. Their three children were taken out of the ghetto along with everyone.

The leather factory was surrounded by a fence and strongly guarded. The director often came in and maintained very strict discipline. The commandant of the *lager* was Yakov Kozolchik. His wife and two children also were taken out of the ghetto together with all of the Jews.

In a few days we learned that our families had been expelled to the Kelbasin *lager*, together with the Jews of the surrounding *shtetlekh*. However, it was impossible to contact those who were in the other camps. We sent several peasants to take bread and to bring greetings. It was futile; the *lager* was closed off from the surrounding world.

[Page 294]

The temperature dropped to 35 degrees. Every attempt to flee to the forest was impossible. Several young people left, taking hatchets and shovels. In about two days they returned with frozen hands and feet. We knew we would not remain long in the factory *lager*. We began to work out plans to escape, to hide in a bunker. After several consultations we found a place in the Jewish cemetery and a cement grave where the well-known lay. Only a few people knew of this. Our work had to be very conspiratorial. The initiators of this were Shepsl Kushnir and Yudl Kaplan.

Every night at around two o'clock we would bribe the policeman and tell him that we were carrying bread or other food to the *lager*. Then we would go to the cemetery, several times in pairs, and take with us what we could: dried biscuits, meat, water and other foods. There was room in the bunker for 20 people. Yakov, the commandant, also knew of this and he helped us a great deal. I went several times with Yudl Kaplan. Everything was organized that needed to be; we even prepared vessels for cooking. The grave was large, with a lot of air, and the entrance was through a headstone.

Everything was almost ready. We also permitted a woman to join us, who would prepare food. Once, when the comrades came to the spot, they found the grave emptied. We later learned that young gentiles who found our footprints in the snow had cleaned out everything. Our work, therefore, fell through and we took to a new plan: in the event that our *lager* remained in Krynki, a group of us would flee to the woods.

After six weeks, the sorrowful news reached us that all of our families had been taken away to Treblinka. Now we knew exactly what awaited us.

In the shoemaker and tailor *lager* a group prepared to escape to the woods. There, too, was plotting and studying how to hide. A few people arranged a hiding place in a boiler in the bath.

Several of us tried to go to a village and arrange with a peasant they knew for a place to hide. However, none of the peasants could and did not want to hide anyone, because the regime had threatened to shoot everyone who helped a Jew.

The new year, 1943, neared. There was no letup in the frost. The spirit of the older workers was extremely crushed. The majority of them would lay the whole night and cry. Every Friday night, Zeidl Filipski would arrange lectures on religious themes and show through numbers and "facts" that we were already near to the redemption and *Moshiekh* (the messiah) would soon come to free us. Filipski would bring examples from the Prophet Jonah, who was swallowed by a fish and *davened* (prayed) in the belly of the fish and the fish spit him out whole. On this basis, several workers would sit and recite psalms for the entire night. The young people earnestly struggled against such propaganda.

Our food was good, because we brought in all of the food that remained in the *lager*. Several women worked with the abandoned clothes, which were collected in the *Beis-Midrash* (synagogue). The better things would be sent to Germany by the ghetto-commissar. He would sell the rest to the peasants, who would come from the surrounding villages. They would stand in a row to receive our blood-splattered possessions. The girls who would work at the sorting, would, *nebek* (dejectedly), watch how their families' clothing and pillows were being sold. A group of Jews worked at the fences. Christians from the villages had already moved into several houses.

[Page 295]

The frost made it difficult to try to escape to the woods. We hoped that perhaps we would last until *Pesakh* (Passover) and then we could struggle in the woods. However, the regime authorities were not asleep: an order was issued on January 17, 1943, that Krynki must become "*Yudnrein*! (cleansed of Jews)." At night several people escaped from both camps. In the morning, the 18th, the two camps were surrounded by police and gendarmes.

From our camp, 18 men and women had escaped, among them the former president of the *Judenrat*, Yosl Galtz, and his brother Chaim-Meir, who had hidden in the boiler in the bath. The remaining escapees were: Peretz and Yashke Pruszhanski, Velvel Wolf, Yitzhak Zutz, Moishel Kagan, Abrahaml Wacht, Kushnir, Meir Gendler, Chaim Weiner, Motke Shteinsafir, Sarake Galtz, Sarake Gendler, Leah Wolf, Perl Levi, Fridke Zalkin, Mashke Kaplan and Itche Wolf. Several escaped to peasant acquaintances, some to the woods, and the remaining were later caught and shot.

Later I learned of the fate of those survivors who froze in the woods. My cousins, Peretz and Yosel Pruzhanski, were caught and tortured to death. A Russian engineer, Dimitrov, hid two girls in a room, Perl Levi and Leah Wolf – until the day of the liberation.

We, those who remained in the *lager*, were taken out to the marketplace. Sleighs waited to take us to the train, to Sokolka.

Everyone could take only one rucksack with them. Several Germans came to the courtyard of the factory and ordered everyone to give them their jewelry. If something was found on him, he would be shot.

Our murderers came to the market and set up machine guns around us. Again, our clothes were rummaged through and anything remaining there was removed. Dozens of gendarmes and Polish police accompanied us on the way. People sitting on the sleighs immediately got frozen feet; we all walked. Leaving Krynki, we were accompanied by peasants with tears in their eyes. A girl, Fanye Roitbard, left a 4-year old child who could not speak Yiddish with a Christian. The child had come with its mother from Russia and the Germans shot the mother. When we were already lined up to march, the Christian brought the young child and told him to go together with us.

In Sokolka we were hurled into dirty railroad horse cars with closed little windows; a soldier stood at each railroad car; we were forbidden to look out of the windows and the doors were bolted.

Our *shtetl* (town) was "*Yudnrein*!"

The Last Road

In the same railroad car with me were my uncle Yisroel Skowronek ("Africans") with his wife Pesha and two young sons, Lazerke and Hershele; Nyamka Skowronek and his wife – Dvoyra Manikhe's daughter; Berl, Blumka and Ruchla Zakheim; Henek Muglas and his daughter Mercha; Yisroel Kalinowitch, his wife and two children; Abrahaml Ofrimzon (Shishka's son) and his wife, son and daughter; Dodya Kirpicz, his mother and little son; Shepsl Kushnir and his son Moishele; Hershl Abramowicz; Motl Kirzhner; Yudl Kaplan and the ex-commandant of the *lager*, Yakov (Yankl) Kozolchik (Pig).

[Page 296]

Individual Jews said salms and the women cried. The remaining Jews from Sokolka were attached to our railroad cars, and all together the transport reached 1,200 people. Several were certain that we were going to Treblinka. Yakov broke out the little window and a group of young people prepared to jump. We set up a line. Shepsl Kushnir's son, Moishele, jumped first, and then Shepsl himself.

Thus one after the other they lined up along the full length of the train. A mother moved her two children to jump and she held her young son at the window, at which stood the chief initiator Yakov who helped several jump from the train. Thus jumped: Yosl and Chaim Braverman, Liebl Naliber, Hershl Abrahamowicz, Sonya Funk, Abrahaml Kleinbord, Zeidl Yakobinski, Dora Kirpicz and her little brother Zundl Kirpicz.

When I wanted to lift myself up to jump out, my aunt ran to me and with tears in her eyes begged me to travel together with them and my two cousins. She held me and begged that I not jump. Yakov himself undressed to his shirt and threw his garments out through the window. He tried to jump out through the little window, but his abnormally thick body could not go through, and all his efforts were futile. He then took out a small bottle of poison and drank it up. However, his heart was stronger than the poison – he lived and howled like a slaughtered animal. A white foam appeared on his lips, and there was no water. We rubbed the frost from the boards and thus saved him.

The railroad car was now strongly guarded and we could no longer jump. We neared Malkinia toward Treblinka. Several people began reciting Psalms. Zeidl Filipski put on his *talis* (prayer shawl) and *tefilin* (phylacteries). The hands and feet of several shook. However, the train traveled further past the Malkinia station and did not remain there. Hearts became joyful. Pious Jews argued that the recitation of Psalms had helped, and now we were being taken to work, as the director of the factory had promised.

We travel further. It is already dark. One hears a heavy sigh and the stamping of frozen feet. There is thirst. Frost is scratched from the walls with spoons and the thirst is quenched by this. The first night on the train passes. There is the torture of thirst and there is no longer any frost on the walls. People beg the guards for a little water. A little watch, a ring is given for a small pan.

On the third day, we passed a train station where several Jews and Christians cleared the snow. Several of them made a sign with their hands under the throat, shouting that we should escape – we are being taken to the slaughter! Crying breaks out with and a stronger recitation of Psalms. A shout is heard from outside that we are being taken to Auschwitz – the name of which none of us had ever heard. Is it also a Treblinka?

Night falls. Yakov orders that we burn everything we still have. Aizik Brustin ignites the first little pack of money, and after him, almost all who have something of worth. Tears run from everyone's eyes. A dreadful darkness surrounds us.

Early in the morning, Tuesday, January 21, 1942, we arrived at Auschwitz.

[Page 297]

Jumping From the Death Train and Arriving in Bialystok

The Editor

Translated by Gloria Berkenstat Freund

In a Chronicle titled "Daybook of Jewish Sorrow and Pain," which was written in the Bialystok Ghetto, according to the information of the refugees who ran here during the "*aktzias*" ("selection" actions) – there is information about people from Krynki, who jumped from the transport train to Auschwitz on January 25th, and arrived in Bialystok. The writing of the Chronicles was organized by Mordekhai Tenenboim-Tamarof, the commandant of the Jewish Fighting Organization in Bialystok, and they were hidden on the "Aryan" side of the city where they were later found with the entire "Mersik-Tenenboim Archive," after the liberation of Bialystok from Nazi paws. This Chronicle relates:

"Bialystok, Tuesday, 26th January 1943.
"Today several refugees from Sokolka and Krynki, who jumped from the train - the transport which carried out the last Jews from the Krynki Workers Camps to Auschwitz - arrived. Among the wounded were 3 Krynki girls with a young man who had been beaten by the Gestapo. The wounded were taken to the hospital."

[Page 298]

In Auschwitz

By Abraham Sofer

Translated by Gloria Berkenstat Freund

We were in Auschwitz. Everyone in the railroad cars pushed themselves to the little windows to see what happened here. The women packed their things and cried desperately. The eyes of several older Jews were unexpressive and they shouted, "May the Lord answer you on your day of distress." Zeidl Filipski stood in his *talis* (prayer shawl) and *tefilin* (phylacteries). His 2-year old child stood near him and held a *tsitse* (fringe on the prayer shawl) with a shaking hand.

Suddenly, there was a knock at the door. It was hastily thrown open and a wild cry pierced the railroad car, "Everyone, move on out! Leave the packs! Women, one side; men, the other side!"

Several young bandits stood at the door with fat clubs in their hands and beat us on our heads. When Zeidl Filipski appeared at the door, all of the clubs descended on his head and he fell in a pool of blood. Yakov stood in the first row of men wearing his only shirt. The women stood on the other side of us.

After several minutes everyone was standing one next to the other, five in a row. Five autos waited opposite us.

First, several dozen girls up to age 20 were chosen and an older murderous officer, with an enraged pair of tiger-eyes, came over to us and with his pointing finger divided us to the right and to the left, asking each of us our vocation. I stood on the right side together with Yakov and several other young ones. Immediately, we counted off several times and verified the number, and when there were 150 people present, the sorting ended.

The older ones stood on the left side. Blood ran from many heads. A group of young girls stood opposite the railroad car, all the way in the back – women with children. Among us stood Pinya Klas and his father was in the second group. The son motioned with his hand to his father that he should run from his row and stand with us. When the murderous officer turned with his back to us, the father ran over to our row.

When we started to march, the autos were already packed with women, men and children. Small, little children waved to us with their little hands and the wives of the men who had first gone with us – shouted to us with tears in their eyes and motioned to us with their hands.

We marched – into the *lager* (camp), into Birkenau.

With Krynki Jews in Birkenau

In the Birkenau *lager* in Auschwitz, we first went through the "customary procedure," - giving up our garments and emptying out the remnants of our valuables, announcements of the "laws" of the *lager*, registration, tattooing on the left arm by engraving needle (my number fell on 93886), shaving the hair, a cold, freezing shower with murderous blows, putting on ragged *lager* clothing and wooden sandals and the like.

When we stood on the street near the bath, waiting to be led to a block, we noticed in the distant woods, a tall fire which turned the surrounding sky red. And the air was filled with the smell of burned flesh. Our escorts, the beaters, also arrestees – the majority Poles, although also a few Jews among them – immediately said to us, "You do not know what that is? Burning there are your families, who were taken there today in autos!"

[Page 299]

Tears appeared in the eyes of each of us, but everyone cried quietly because crying was strictly forbidden in the *lager*.

In the morning, at twelve o'clock, several of us shared a potato with a little green grass, one plate for four men – breakfast and lunch in one. We had to eat with our hands. There was not even a drop of water. Each took a handful of dirty snow and quieted our thirst with it. It was not long before the majority of us developed diarrhea (dysentery), and going to the toilet was strictly forbidden. Only once a day, in a group, we had to empty ourselves. Immediately, people made in their pants and it became a filthy place.

At the first nightly "roll call" of the night, most of us stood with blackened eyes and some with split heads. All equally had changed in appearance. The "diarrhea" exhausted us; the air was filled with the smell of death. Everyone felt desperate and many spoke of suicide. This was the easier death; approach the electric wire of the fence and just touch it – in one second it it would be over.

Our First Victims in the "Work" Camp

On our seventh day in the *lager*, one from our block, Yasha Zelikowicz, was caught at the morning roll-call trading bread for water with a Russian prisoner of war. His name was called out during the roll call and the "block elder" along with the S.S. man "honored" him with 25 blows. His father stood in the same row and watched how they killed his son and threw him to the wall, where lay several who had perished at the wire. This was the first victim from our transport.

After two weeks, of the 150 men who had been led into the *lager* from our transport – 20 were missing. Most had gone to the wire in groups of three and four, arm in arm. In the morning after the death of Yasha Zelikowicz, when it was pitch dark, the first who went to the wire was his father, Milka Zelikowicz, taking with him a young person, Khasriel Engenradt. They fell dead from a shot to the chest, five meters from the electric wire. Again, almost all of us from the transport suffered from diarrhea. Dozens in the *lager* died every day from this plague.

The ranks of our transport group were sparser from day to day. Forty were already missing. The condition of the remaining was very bad. Every day a group went away to the "precinct," an ostensible healing center, from which few came back. When I would return from work, I would not recognize my friends. The mountain of dead near the wall grew.

Yudl Kaplan, Yeshayahu Glezer, Motl Kirzhner, Pinya Klas, Shia Shapiro and two people from Grodno would sleep together with me. Once, coming from work, I did not recognize Yudl; his face was swollen and covered in all colors – blue, yellow, green and red. At the roll call he told me what kind of day he had lived through. He did not eat after the roll call. When he received his portion of bread, he received a blow with a club on the hand and fell in the mud. I carried him into the block and laid him in the "box" (a shared place to sleep, made of cement). In two hours, he got up with a fixed expression and asked for a drink. I got off of the "box" to see if anyone had a drop of water. Returning, I found that Yudl was already dead. I lay together with him in the box the whole night. In three days, the same thing happened to Glezer.

[Page 300]

The Period of "Kanada"

The majority of us could no longer stand on our feet. At "knee-bending" many lay drawn out in the mud and no longer felt the blows of the clubs that were lowered on them. Here, the service leaders and block elders suddenly chose fifty men, who allegedly looked better, me among them, and led us to the bath. There we threw off our louse-filled garments and stood under a cold shower, not knowing what they were going to do with us. After washing ourselves, we were given clean shirts and new striped garments: pants, a blouse and a coat, and it was announced that we would work in the cleaning brigade "Canada." This "brigade" was given the name "Canada" because there was enough to eat and there as if "we lived in Canada."

In "Canada," only Eizik Tzigel and I were from our transport. The work consisted of sorting the things in the packs that the victims of the transports were forced to leave in the railway cars at the Auschwitz train station. All was thoroughly gone through; good and new garments would be sent to Germany, the remnants would go for rags. The same with the bedding.

Food that was found in the packs was given to the *lager* kitchen. Jams were taken by the S.S. men for themselves. After work everyone received some bread, under strict control. I would pour out a little tobacco into my pocket, mixed with bread crumbs and bring it into the *lager*. Among the Krynkers still alive, I divided the tobacco and bread. Entering our barracks was very strictly controlled, and the survivers waited anxiously. The eager smokers, such as Yashka Marglius and others, felt lucky when I would give them a little tobacco.

As already mentioned, I was with Eizik Tzigel, working together and sleeping together in one bed. After five days of working, he received 25 lashes for trying to carry five pieces of sugar into the *lager*. In the morning he was sent to a block, from which everyone was transported away to a place undisclosed.

Now I, among the Krynkers, remained alone. I was given a man from Grodno as a bedmate. We were good friends; however, this did not last long. Once I decided to bring a little box of sardines into the *lager* for the person in charge of the block, so that he would bring Yashka Marglius and Yehosha Shapiro to our brigade. I was searched at the gate and the sardines were found, and in the morning terrible lashes were executed on me. When my feet and hands were untied, I fainted to the ground. I no longer could go to work and my period of "Kanada" ended.

The Krynki Mutual Aid

I was taken to one of the worst and dirtiest blocks, where those returning from the "precinct" and those who were incapable of working were found.

Opposite us stood the women's *lager*. We would look from afar at how the shadows without hair, without shoes, in torn shirts moved around. It was strictly forbidden to stand near the wire and talk to the women, and the women were forbidden the same.
A group of young girls from 17 to 20 years old from our transport had entered the *lager*, but none of us knew if any of them still lived. I would often stand on the side, straining to look at the women; perhaps I would see an acquaintance.

[Page 301]

Only several dozen people remained from our transport, and their number diminished more from day to day. Several were sent away to Boba, a nearby *lager*, and one of them was taken into the *sonderkommando* (special commando – brigades of Jews working in the camps) however, we did not see him because the *sonderkommando* was separated from the surrounding *lager*. Carrying sacks of food, they would often throw bread to acquaintances, and thus our Krynker would throw some to one of us, and we would share it.

Once we succeeded in speaking through a hole which someone had chopped in the wall. From him we learned that Shlomoh Avnet - Abnet , "*der geler*" (the blond) - from our *shtetl* worked in the crematorium. He had been brought three months before us from another *shtetl*. Through the hole, I would often receive a little water and a piece of bread, too. I would wait a moment, when no one would notice and we would speak together. From him I learned precisely how the gassing and cremating of the victims was done and about the fate of our own people.

Several Polish civilians worked with us. It was forbidden to speak a word with them. Pinya Klas worked together with me on the brigade. He quickly became acquainted with a Pole and began to "trade quietly" with him – selling a shirt, a pair of civilian pants without the *lager* stripes, and so forth, which we would get from those who worked in "Canada" and in the *sonderkommando*. Pinya had a cousin, Asniel (Etniel) Leibowicz in the *sonderkommando*; he would "support" him with things. I formed a partnership with Asniel and what the Pole would bring – once a couple of eggs or what else – we would divide among us. Once, however, I was caught with five eggs in my pocket and I was punished with five nights standing in a narrow dark chimney with very little air, filled underneath with water, into which a little fluoride had been poured.

From our transport, only ten people remained in Birkenau. The master craftsman sent a group from our brigade, among us Pinya and me, to dig foundations to the ovens in the women's *lager*. We were warned that it was forbidden to speak one word with the women, even our own sisters. There we looked for the familiar face of a woman and did not find any. However, I did not lower my eyes from every passing woman: perhaps I would yet meet someone from Krynki.

Our small group again became even smaller. This time it was the end of Yehoshua Shapiro. He no longer had any strength to stand on his feet and go out to work. One day he was taken away to the crematorium.

The Krynki Girl

Here the unexpected happened to me. As on all days, I observed the passing pale, blackened women. Suddenly I saw a young girl in a torn shirt, feet bound in paper and blood running out from underneath. The head was shaved, the face small and pale. She draged a large bucket to pour out. The eyes, so familiar; was it not my school friend, Ruchla Zakheim?!

I shared my conjecture with friend Pinya. We decided to call her by name, when we went back. We both stood impatiently. And she appeared – like an unfortunate 10-year old child. I remained standing in my place in the open door. Pinya went up on the side and as she neared the barrack, he quietly called out: Ruchla! Abraham! – an answer was heard and she fell in a faint to the ground.

[Page 302]

S.S. men walked around past us. I was not supposed to move from the spot. If I had gone to her, we both would have lost our lives. I stood steadfast and I saw before me Ruchla, my friend from my sweet school years. Later in "*SKIF*" (pre-war Bundist youth organization), now, in the camp at first glance – a shadow of the always laughing Ruchla.

We decided, Pinya and I, to help her, the last surviving girl from Krynki here. I bribed my *Capo* (prison supervisor). He brought to me her arm-number and informed me of where she was located. According to her block, she had only a few more days to live. The *Capo* joined us; he carried my first few words to her – she should hold out, we would help her. He brought me back a little piece of paper from her – she wrote that she was the last remaining one from the entire transport.

She needed considerable help. First of all to have a better appearance – so she would not be one of the first candidates for going to the crematorium. We secured attire for her. We had to pay the *Capo* well for him to provide it for her. We had to pay him again to prevail on the German women who stood at the head of the *lager*, to let her out of the block. We bought them off with good cigarettes, silk stockings and other luxury articles, for which we would risk our lives carrying them to the German women.

We succeeded in bringing Ruchla to work in "Canada." Here, her situation improved; we saw her very often from afar and wrote letters. She washed dress-shirts for me so I would look clean and "be taken care of." It did not last long; as we were led from the women's *lager*. Mute and with many tears, Ruchla "accompanied" us from the site.

We announced to those from our *shtetl* in the *lager* that Ruchla Zakheim was here and that it was our duty to keep her alive as long as we ourselves had life. Pinya and I took upon ourselves the duty to do everything to save her from her present situation. I explained to the *Capo* that I had found a sister in the *lager* and that she was in danger that any day she could be "taken" in a selection. He promised me to help with protection from the German women, who stood at the head of the *lager*. We obtained and brought to the women's *lager* all that we were able to get hold of, to encourage Ruchla to feel that she was no longer alone.

The Crematoria Are Burning

The first two crematoria began to burn just before Passover. Here, at first without stop, day and night, thousands of unfortunate human souls were spit out of the chimneys. A barrack was built on the courtyard and our brigade worked there. Every day I would meet Asniel Leibowicz and Shlomoh the blond and they would tell me about the dreadful scenes that they saw near the crematorium.

In the middle of 1943, we succeeded in again working our way into "Canada." Ruchla, too, worked in "Canada's" women's brigade. Here she was considered my sister. It was strictly forbidden here, too, to speak with the women, although I succeeded in holding a short talk with Ruchla. She explained to me that all of the remaining girls who were with her had perished, until there was one other, and the last, Mercha Yaglom. Ruchla was with her in the death block, from which they were supposed to take her also to the gas chamber. Mercha was so exhausted and weakened that her strength left her and she died before they had time to take her to the crematorium.

[Page 303]

After working two months in "Canada," I became sick with typhus. I lay six weeks in the "precinct" [previously described as an "alleged healing center"] and became healthy. However, I was extremely weak and they no longer wanted to take me back in "Canada." I went to the *komande tzimere* [people who helped him recover]. However, I worked very little. Every day I would come into the *sondercommando* and receive a piece of bread from Asniel and Shlomoh. I felt terrible and could no longer go out to work; Shlomoh hid me in his bed, where I would lay until before the nighttime roll call. I would get food from him. I lay like this for two weeks.

On the first of May, we only worked until mid-day. We assembled next to Shlomoh on the box and sang workers' songs. A guard stood at the gate, who was supposed to give us a sign if the S.S. came in. Asneil would often sing Russian songs and was very joyful. Shlomoh was just the opposite. He was always lost in dreams with a quiet sad look. He would argue that we needed to free ourselves or fall as heroes in the struggle. He was always busy with plans about how to blow up the crematoria, so that there would be no more gassings.

In May 1944, Asniel Leibowicz, the other one in addition to me who remained in Birkenau from our transport, was taken away with another 200 *sondercommando* workers. They were taken to Lublin on the pretext that they would work there. However, as soon as they got off the train, they were taken to the bath. There, they were taken into another room five at a time and shot.

Let Us Blow Up the Crematoria!

Shlomoh, who now had steadfastly begun to work out a plan to blow up the crematorium, remained in the *sondercommando*. A former major, a Russian, who had been brought from Majdanek to the *sondercommando* with a group of Russians - together with Shlomoh - worked out a plan. Shlomoh confided in me that they were working on a bomb. The women who worked in the gunpowder factory would bring the gunpowder. Ignoring the fact that there were strong controls, individual women would take a little bit of gunpowder each day in their shoes and this would reach Shlomoh.

The plan called for four crematoria to be blown up all at the same moment. Then the barbed-wire would be ripped off the women's *lager* and everyone would scatter. One day crematorium number three was blown up and the German *capo* and the *obersarfuhrer* (German military rank) were thrown into the fire alive. The crematorium was crushed. Then everyone ran out on the courtyard and ran to the guard tower. Several guards were defeated with bare hands, their guns were taken, the barbed-wire was ripped off the women's *lager* and the majority escaped.

Shlomoh Avnet Killed in the Battle

The S.S. realized what was happening and raised an alarm that a battle had broken out. The majority of the brave fighters escaped. The entire courtyard was covered with red bodies, among which was found Shlomoh, shot in the stomach.

Crematorium number three no longer gassed. Shlomoh fell in the struggle for respect for the Jewish people.

At the time of Hitler's great defeat and as the Russians neared, an order was issued to evacuate our *lager* to Germany. We were taken to Shtuthof near Danzig. Here, too, the crematorium "worked," although fewer people were gassed here than in Auschwitz. Among the Poles, who were the majority here, I met one from Krynki, a former assistant policeman with the Germans. And I asked him: "Ejik Czarnyecki, you are in the *lager*, too?!" – he lowered his head and asked, "*Jeszcze zyjac?*," meaning, "You are still alive?"

[Page 304]

He related to me what had happened to those who had run away from Krynki to the woods, and how they caught those who hid in the boiler of the bath and how they were all shot in the market. When Krynki was "*Yudnrein*" (cleansed of Jews), he explained, the former ghetto commissar gathered in the *Beis Midrash* (synagogue) the clothing and underwear that the Jews had left. He, Czarnyecki, was one of the Polish policemen who stood there on guard. The ghetto commissar caught him taking out several pieces of clothing from there and, therefore, sent him to Shtutof-*lager*.

We were liberated on April 23, 1945. After a while I met my friend and fellow survivor, Ruchla Zakheim, and after many difficulties we reached Uruguay.

[Page 305]

Struggling & Wandering

(From Grodno to the Partisans)

By Feivel Wolf

Translated by Gloria Berkenstat Freund

The "Big Action" (Slaughter) in Grodno

I would leave the Grodno Ghetto every day to work in various places. Escaping was very easy, because the Jewish section foremen were the leaders and there was no special guard. The majority worked for Kaletzki of Fershtat; the firm was named "Getreider Commerce."

One day in January 1943, the cleaning of the great *shul* (synagogue) in the ghetto began. Everyone understood that there would be a transport.

One *Shabbas*, the same month, I overslept and did not go to work. If I had not overslept, I would not, as I had resolved, have come back to the ghetto. I walked around the entire day. At five in the evening I went to Lola Shternfeld. On the way a Jewish policeman caught me and demanded that I go with him – he needed me. I began to beg him to leave me because I had just come from hard labor. My talk *hut gehelfn vi a toitn bankes* (helped like cupping a dead person, i.e., was useless) and he began to pull me forcefully. Would he leave me alone? A miracle happened to me! The place was slippery and I fell with him.

A second policeman arrived during our wrestling. I thought both would take me. However, the other one motioned to the first one, "Leave him alone, the stubborn one - come!"

This policeman knew me from Lola Shternfeld's; because he had been there. I did not go to her. I ran back, because the policeman who had helped me told me that I should run away. I ran into the courtyard where I lived at Abrahaml Farasha's and hid on the roof of a shed, because people were being grabbed, just men; for what – no one knew. At twelve midnight I went into my room and felt my fingers were frost bitten.

Early in the morning we learned that the Jewish police had caught 300 men to unload coal cars at the railroad. After finishing the work, they were locked in the same cars and in two days were sent away in a transport with 5,000 more Jews.

The next day, early Monday, going to the gate was strictly forbidden. Gestapo and S.S. men surrounded the ghetto. Groups of S.S. men with machine guns stood near the barbed wire every few meters. The ghetto was quiet, a ruin. We waited to see what the night would bring. Abrahaml Farasha busied himself with something for several days in the house of his mother-in-law, Abraham Bontz's mother, and I did not attach any importance to this.

The electricity was turned on at six in the evening. Now one was sure that we were being taken to the transport because it was forbidden to turn on the electricity. At exactly eight in the evening, Wise and Streblow came in on a sled and began shooting a machine gun. They shot 12 men on the central street (on Y. L. Peretz or Troyce Street).

The show began in about fifteen minutes. Abrahaml shut off the electricity and locked up the house. I saw that everyone there was doomed. At the end he came over to me and told me to go into the bedroom with him. There under the bed we lowered ourselves to the cellar, where 20 men sat. Small children began to cry. I saw that there was no place for me there and in ten minutes I left, took a quilt from the bed and went up to the attic.

[Page 306]

The frost reached 30 degrees. Through the small attic window, I watched the Jewish policemen driving groups of men, old and young, women and small children into the *shul*. Later they were driven to the gate of the ghetto – the small children in autos and the rest on foot.

It became quiet at four o'clock in the morning. I went down from the attic to the hall. I jumped from the last step of the ladder and landed on a person's feet. This was Yosem, the pharmacist from Amdor and his son. He recognized me and we talked. A hard knock on the door interrupted our talk, "Open up, open up!"

We were quiet. Again the voice asked us to open up. His wife and mother were below in the cellar. "We can go out into the street," he said. "The transport is already full and no more are needed." I opened the door and became fearful; it was a Jewish policeman.

"Do not be afraid, it will be quiet until night!" he told us. And at nine o'clock Wise would talk to us and the *Judenrat* about what would happen next.

Escaping from Grodno

Right at the start of the day I went out into the street to seek advice on how to escape. Immediately I met Dovid Sisken, who promised me great luck. He, one of his sons and his sister-in-law, all four of us, would go to the village of Simerenke, where a sister-in-law lived who had converted. For money, a place for him to leave was ready - through a house that had an exit on one side out of the ghetto on Dominikanska Street, and on the other side where the Christians lived. However, I didn't believe that I could depend upon him and in a few hours I went away seeking another way. Sarnacki of the *Judenrat* still saved his pride by slapping people in the middle of the street.

Before long, I encountered Yankl, Ruchka's son, Chaim Lipman, Berl, Basha's son, Motl and Dovid Weisman and one of the Bukhs – all of Amdor. And all were looking for a way to flee together.

The night passed. Jewish police again grabbed people, street by street, for the transport. We all, seven men, isolated ourselves at the Kosmane's on Vilenski Alley. We had hatchets, knives, and iron bars. If the Jewish police took us, we would put up resistance. Yankl, Ruchka's son and Chaim Lipman went into the Kosmane's cellar. The other five, up to the attic.

It was quiet all of Tuesday. However, when it got dark, people were again caught for the transport.

All seven of us spent the night of Tuesday into Wednesday sitting in Kosmane's cellar. On Wednesday, the day was again quiet. When it got dark, again there were seizures. On the night of Wednesday to Thursday, the Jewish police were looking for ways to save themselves, because at the train, Wise had thrown many policemen in the railroad cars and sent them away together with all of the Jews. The night of Wednesday to Thursday, all seven of us did not leave each other in the Kosmane's courtyard, because two young Grodno men had promised us that they would lead us out of the ghetto.

At four in the morning a handsome, daring Jewish policeman approached us, not from Grodno, but from Plotzk – and asked, "Who can take me with them? I will lead all of you out of the ghetto."

[Page 307]

Yankl, Ruchka's son said: "I can." He knew a widow near Skidl, who loved him. And he had previously stayed with her for three months. The policeman thought this was possible and asked us to be prepared, and at six in the morning he would lead us out.

We all shaved, in order to look human on the Aryan side and at exactly six we left. The policeman first, I second, Chaim Lipman third. It did not even take a minute and we were on the other side of the barbed wire.

Afterward, we crawled through a hole not far from the bridge on Vilenske Alley.

With several large strides we were on Dominikanska, and from there we went quickly through Huvera Street to Brigidske, and in ten minutes we were at the Slabodker Market. From there we took the Skidler highway out of the city.

On the way we encountered gentiles who carried shipments of wheat, cattle, pigs and sheep to Grodno, and looked at us like wolves. Yankl, Ruchka's son, and the policeman fled to the left of the highway, and we, six men, to the right.

We reached Nieme through Raves, where a village that none of us knew the name of, stood on the other bank (later we learned that it was named Szydowszczyane). It was risky to cross the river because it was not frozen everywhere. I broke a small tree, made a long stick and with it in my hand, I went first, step by step; cautiously, we went this way, one 10 meters from the next, and with each thrust at the ice, I thought I was under it. The gentiles came out of their houses to look. We all thought they would grab us and take us to the Germans. However, when we were across, they scattered among the houses.

Wandering - Homeless

From there, we went through forests and fields, arriving at the Zarubiczer colonists in the evening. Each of us had left something there - someone a cow, someone a wagon, someone furniture and someone ordinary things. None of them allowed us into their homes. Motl Weisman received half a loaf of bread and onions from his colonist.

All of the gentiles closed their doors in the Zarubiczer village and did not let us in. We began to go to farmhouses to try to get something to eat. Maybe something could be found in the stables. In one of the farmhouses we disbanded. Lipman and I kissed and I left for Krynek. Thus began my long wanderings. I spent the night in a barn, but did not spend the day there.

In a few days, during the evening, I arrived in Kowali, 2 kilometers from Spodville, 9 kilometers from Krynek. The gentiles there were White Russians, strong patriots of communism, who never bothered any Jews. Many suffered with the Germans, who shot their young, cultured and class-conscious people. There I breathed easier. My intention was to learn what was happening to the surviving Jews of Krynek and if I could go to them and remain until the summer.

I decided to go to Zina Elizorowicz, the wife of the village magistrate Aleksander Elizorowicz, one of the best people in that area, who had to hide from the Germans. Zina gave me a very friendly welcome, fed me well, let me dry out my wet things and showed me a stable where I could rest for a few days. Secondly, she would go to Krynek to *Pani* (Mrs.) Roitberg, her best friend, and see her husband there and tell me what was happening there.

[Page 308]

The information that I received through her after a few days was that at the beginning of the week, early Sunday, 200 Jews were taken away by foot to Sokolka. She learned nothing of my brother, Itshke. Her friend *Pani* Roitberg, who was to come to her in the village at the last minute, as had been agreed, did not have time to flee.

Zina further explained that three Jewish young men, Peretz Pruszanksi, his brother and another man, fled to the barn of a gentile from Krynek. The gentile noticed them - pretended that he did not - and betrayed them to the Germans. While they were being led out of the barn, the gentile asked that he be given their boots, and they were led barefoot over the snow to the Christian Black Hundred (a Russian anti-Semitic, conservative, nationalist group founded at the beginning of the 20th Century) and were shot there.

I met a second good friend in Kowali, Zina Zamirowski, who warned me that, for God's sake, I should hide and not entrust my life to anyone in the village. Several from the village itself, she said, who are hiding Jews here, *lekn oif nisht kein honik* (do not lick honey – i.e., could not be trusted).

Incidentally, she told me a story about a person from Krynki, Khatzkl "*Telya*," who let himself be convinced by the Germans that they would make him a non-Jew. And he worked with them and revealed all of the secrets he knew of what was happening among the Jews. Last Thursday, he was told to put on good clothes, and the peasants who came to the market were told to watch, so that they could see him being led to the church to convert. He was converted at the Polish cemetery.

In short, I had to escape from Kowali, too, and here first began my actual wandering. There is not enough space here to write it all – I will be satisfied with telling something about the more remarkable "lodgings" and experiences.

One of the subsequent places to which fate brought me was to Aleks Antoshewicz, 2 kilometers from Spodville, from whom I hoped to learn a little about my brother Itshke who remained in the Krynki Ghetto. This Aleks had been friends with Iser Zak and Hershl Dworetskin of Groise-Brestowic for years and prepared in a barn, under some wheat, a pit to hide them. They actually fled from the Wolkowisker *lager* and went straight to Aleks. However, because they were careless, they fell in to the hands of the Germans and were brought to Klein-Brestowic.

Today, how great was my surprise as it was revealed that my brother Itshke was alive and had been hidden by Aleks in the pit. I was so moved by my meeting with him, Itshke looked very different from me – fresh and well dressed.

I could not stay with the commendable and friendly Aleks and I remained for a time nearby. My brother Itshke was forced to leave the place because a "*parobik*" (a hired agricultural worker) worked there. Incidentally, he was not on friendly terms with his boss, and had threatened to teach him a lesson for hiding Jews. Therefore, Itshke went to a widow, Yeruliczykhe, in Spodville.

Our situation in Spodville was terrible, too, although only a few people knew where we were hiding. The Christian who had bought our house from the Germans sniffed and searched for where we were hidden in order to catch us and give us to the Germans.

On the first of March, we spent the entire day in the field between rocks 2 kilometers from Aleks's. That Christian discovered us here. He explained that he had gone to the woods searching for stumps to dig up for heating and did not mean, God forbid, to do anything bad to us.

[Page 309]

The next morning, 8 Germans and 4 Polish policemen ransacked Aleks's house, the stable and barn; they were looking for us there. The same night we went to Kowali and hid in the stable of a good gentile. However, we could not remain there for long.

A few days later, gentiles, who were our good friends, told us that the mood toward us was very bad. Four young gentiles from Spodville took the opportunity to come with guns at night to rob the local colonists, ostensibly speaking Yiddish among themselves and calling each other by our names. They even raped several young, pretty gentile girls – on our account, because the victims thought this was our work. It was demanded of the Spodville magistrate that he give us up. Our friends advised us to go somewhere else until the crowd calmed itself. Therefore, we left at the end of March for Firowszczic with a good gentile, Szmigin.

At night, he showed us the direction to go where, in the nearby bushes in the swamp, we would meet five Russians, who were hiding from the Germans. Perhaps they would take us in. We went there, walked around and, at first, did not notice any people. Then my brother, who had very good hearing, heard the sound of coughing. From that we guessed they were in a hut of hay, and that is where a group of bandits was found. One of them crawled out and began questioning us; who are we?, who knows us?, and who do we know? And we told them that we were Jews; and he asked if we knew Beilya of Podbyaiki. When it was shown that we did know her; he called her out to us. We began to speak Yiddish; but he did not let us continue because suspicion could be aroused among the Germans and the local neighbors that Jews could be found here and that would bring raids.

Immediately the remaining five bandits came out against us and with guns in their hands demanded that we leave the area. Nevertheless, they permitted us to stay there for several days.

During the same week, the partisans (civilian resistance fighters) caught two Germans in Olekszic. They slaughtered them with bayonets and threw them under a bridge. The local gentiles ordered the bandits to leave the area for several days because raids were expected. My brother and I, left for the Kowalker Forest.

In the evening of the first day of the Russian Easter (Passover), we arrived in the village of Badsziki and went into a house, where we were taken in with extraordinary hospitality and were well treated. We were invited to in while we were in the area, and a razor was brought for us to shave. We really wondered about this. In the morning we learned what had led to this exceptional hospitality.

Two gentiles had driven into Grodno and met a German. One gentile had taken off his hat for him; the second, however, who sat in the back bundled up in a hood, did not. The German ran to the wagon and slapped him. However, it was not a person, but a covered up slaughtered pig. The gentile took out a revolver and shot the German and escaped with the wagon and the pig.

Therefore, the Germans took twenty-five men, Polish intellectuals including doctors, teachers and priests, from Grodno to be held until the guilty party could be found. They declared that if in the course of 24 hours the guilty one did not come forward they would be shot. And the men were, indeed, killed.

[Page 310]

The Poles had begun to get a taste of Hitler's rule. We, too, had already begun to feel it during our search in the local villages.

In seven days we went back to the swamp. We had enough there to sustain us. The bandits all wanted to live with Beilya. She, again, lived only with one of them, and he would come to eat with us every day. Therefore, the rest had complaints about us.

First I would visit someone in a village and this person would not want to give me any bread. I would warn him that when the Germans left, I would not forget, and that he should take that into consideration. And such a warning would help.

In July 1943, the bandits left to get food and on the way met regular partisans and later left with them. They did not want to take us with them. Itshke and I left for the Spodville area to hide in the fields, and Beilya stayed alone in the swamp. Later the bandits again returned there and summoned us and promised that they would soon leave with the partisans and would take us with them.

In the end they left on a beautiful Sunday and did not take us with them. In the evening, Itshke, Beilya and I, crawled into a stall and went to sleep. During the evening I woke up. Beilya was not there. Suddenly I heard a shout and spasms. I woke up Itshke and we left. We saw that Beilya lay drawn out on the ground and that her bandit was choking her and hitting her over the head. We tried to save her; he began to shout to his bandits and warned them that we were speaking Yiddish. Talking to him did not help. In the end he told her to go with him. She wanted to take her things, but he yelled out that she no longer needs things. She sobbed and he dragged her away with him.

We both immediately fled the spot and hid for the entire day among the bushes. At night we went out in the direction of Spodville. First the bandit sprang out from under a bush with a gun in his hand and demanded that we raise our hands. However, he did not bother us and to our question of where Beilya was – he had dragged her away at night – he claimed that he later fell asleep and she had run away.

We went on our way and before daybreak arrived between Badszike and Kowali in the field of *Tiotke* (Auntie) Zamirowski.

The entire time, my brother had carried around the idea of going to Bialystok, because there were still 30,000 Jews there. We told this idea to the *Tiotke*. She was truly against it. However, my brother was deeply bothered by the fact that we had to hide from the Russians. And we could no longer hide in their area. As a result *Tiotke*'s son went out riding among the gentiles. They often came from Bialystok to find out what was happening among the Jews. He returned with good news, that the work was not difficult and that they explained that the Germans would no longer bother them.

My Brother Leaves

The *Tiotke*'s son brought us a razor, a good jacket and a hat from the house, and my brother and I said goodbye and kissed and he left for Bialystok. He promised me that if it was peaceful there, he would let me know, and that he himself would come back to take me there. It was Tuesday, August 10, 1943.

[Page 311]

Around August 20th, the *Tiotke* berated me for permitting Itshke to go to Bialystok. The liquidation of the Bialystok Ghetto began on the 16th. The Jews had staged a rebellion and the gentile wagons were not permitted to go into Bialystok. From day to day we waited for Itshke; perhaps he would save himself. However, he never came.

Until late in the autumn I would hide in the fields among the peas, stones and potatoes. Three times a week I would come to Aunt Zamirowski and take food from her. It began to snow and I walked around barefoot and had great difficulties. I could not remain in the barns because of the raids. Again I went to the swamp and there I met three young gentiles from Kowali and we stayed with them. Later I met one of the bandits, who we had been with earlier. This one happened to be one of the good ones, and he had wanted to take us with them to the partisans. He promised me that they would soon arrive with their commander and then I would go with them.

I Join the Partisans

A considerable amount of time passed. His commander agreed on March 16, 1944, to take me with them, if I would be the leader. They tested me and were persuaded that I really did know every place in that area. First, the commander, a 22-year old gentile, talked with me and, incidentally, asked me, where had I hidden my gold? All Jews are rich! I had to explain to him that I was not from the rich; that I came from a nearby village. I told him the truth about which gentile was holding my things and that he would not give them back to me. And we took many times their worth from him and I became rich with a pair of boots on my feets and a complete set of clothes on my back.

(Feivel Wolf)
Decorated Krynki Rebel

I went with them to an *aktsia* (action) to blow up the Baranowicz-Bialystok rail line and I helped them locate an alcohol factory not far from Spodville and we blew it up along with the Germans. Nevertheless, the partisans again left me alone, with the explanation that they were going to an area where Jews were hated and when they returned on March 24th, they would take me with them to the Lipieszan Plain. I lamented this greatly after I had helped them so much.

And after eight days they came back and took me with them.

[Page 312]

Krynki Partisans

The Editor

Translated by Gloria Berkenstat Freund

A group of young people, the majority from Krynki and the rest from surrounding towns, who after the liquidation of their cozy communities found a temporary place of refuge in the then "calm" Bialystok ghetto. They were the first to leave from this ghetto and go to the forests, in December 1942, to lead partisan activities against the German murderers. Their commander was the Krinker Moshe Slapak ("Maxim" was his partisan name). He had served in the military and had seen action.

"The group's base, that consisted of 17 to 30 people, was in Lipovy-Most, fifteen kilometers east of Krynki." This is from the book "*Sefer HaPartizanim HaYehudim*" ["Book of Jewish Partisans"] (about the Jewish partisans, Volume One, Published by "Workman's Publishing House" with the help of "Yad Vashem", in Rehavia, 1958). "They prepared mud huts for about forty people and they were even better armed than most of the other partisan groups when they started their activities.

During its short existence, the entire united group managed to carry out several daring raids. They attacked several small police stations in the area and managed to disperse several German guard posts and to take weapons from their sentries."

"Maxim" chose to enlarge his group and lead the negotiations and organized another company to leave the Bialystok ghetto for the forest. But just then, at the end of January 1943, the Germans surrounded the base of "Maxim's" group. A battle broke out in which the numerically superior and better armed Germans were forced to retreat, dragging with them six dead and a number of wounded. One partisan also managed to take the rifles of the dead Germans.

"But it was clear that the Germans would come back with a larger force and they had to abandon the base," continues the "*Sefer HaPartizanim HaYehudim*" [The Book of Jewish Partisans]. Meanwhile it appeared that the commander, "Maxim," was severely wounded and would not be able to go. In order not to be a burden to his comrades, "Maxim" shot himself.

"The news about this battle spread throughout the whole area and made a great impression on the peasants. Secretly they would tell one another that "magnificent" strong Jewish partisans were active in the area. The sighting of a Jewish armed partisan in a village became commonplace and this helped other Jewish companies to form in the forest. But the "Krinker" group had ceased to exist independently after four of its youngsters were burned alive by the Nazis during a raid on a village."

The participants that we know of in "Maxim's" partisan group, besides himself were the following Krynki young men. Moshe Mulye Nisht (a son of Shlama Feyvel), Mulye Weiner (a son of Moshe'ke Shmuel "Americaner"), Mulye Bashevkin (a grandson of Naranishtik), Yudel Levin, Nyanye Rabinovitch (a son of Leybl Rabinovitch) and Moshe Weiner.

Of the few who survived some, including Mulye Nisht, joined another company with which "Maxim" negotiated. In February 1943 they left for the Suprasler forests and the Izover Massif.

[Page 313]

"Not concerned about failure," writes Moshe Kachanovitch in his book about the Jewish partisans in Eastern Europe, published in 1954, "more groups of young men and women came to the Suprasler forest from the Bialystok ghetto and from surrounding towns. In the Summer 1943, they all got together and created the Jewish "detachment" *Foroys*" [In Advance], at the head of which was the commander "Sasha" (Yeshy or Yonah Sokhatchevski) and the Krinker Rivka Shinder-Voyskovska who was one of the organizers of the uprising in the Bialystok ghetto, as "commissar" of the brigade."

The especially difficult conditions in the area, especially cruel in winter and the lack of weapons, made their activities very difficult and caused great losses. Commander Sokhatchevski was killed and a dumdum bullet badly wounded Rivka Shinder-Viskovska during a battle with the Germans in 1944. Her wounds were deep and the inside of her hand was smashed. Because of the terrible conditions, her wounds became infected and she was in danger of being poisoned.

A Soviet airplane quickly evacuated her and she was taken to a Moscow hospital where she was laid up for eight months. She was presented with a lot of military decorations by both the Russian and Polish military leadership.

"Not taking into consideration the heavy losses,"it is further told in "*Sefer HaPartizanim HaYehudim,*" the "Foroys" detachment carried out an important raid under the leadership of the Krynki partisan Abrahmel Krutsevski (Lipe's). The echo of this raid resounded far and wide. They blew up the electric works in Krynki. This lightening strike was precisely prepared in great detail. The needed information was delivered by the young women of the Bialystok Anti-Fascist League. The German guards at the electric works were astounded by the sudden attack. They threw down their weapons and tried to run away but the road was blocked. The electric station was destroyed entirely. They took weapons from the Germans and anyone who put up a fight was killed. The partisans managed to leave the shtetl in peace and in the dark, except for Abrahamel Krutsevski who was killed during the explosion.

"The next day large signs were hung in the streets of Bialystok and in the towns and villages in the area about the "crime" that happened the night before in Krynki."

More about Moshe Slapak and his Krynki partisan group[1]

Shmuel Geler

A son from a middle class family, a graduate of the "*Tarbut* School" [Zionist Hebrew school], Moshe Slapak joined the ranks of the Communist youth at the age of about sixteen. At the same time he studied by himself and was deep into the works of Marxist and Communist theory. He spread their belief among the Krynki youth with great enthusiasm. In secret clubs in "Masuvkes" in the Sholker forest, he taught Communist thought and propagandized their efforts.

[Page 314]

Just like a lot of others, Slapak truly believed that these ideas would save the world from oppression, exploitation and need. With time Moshe Slapak's ideas spread near and far in the region and led him to the poor White Russian villages where he distributed his literature and organized secret cells. He took part in the Party district meetings in Grodno and Bialystok.

His activities were not hidden from the watchful eyes of the Polish "defensive." Slapak had to leave Krinik and live "underground." He wandered around with false papers, hiding out in Grodno, Bialystok and other places. Despite the threat of danger he continued his Communist activities.

In 1930 he was arrested in Vilna during a surprise raid on the Communists and was tortured in the cellar of the Police secret police. Despite being tortured Slapak did not break and did not give up his comrades. According to the verdict he was sentenced to six years in Lukishker prison and after his release he returned to Krinik. Although in terrible physical shape, he still believed in Communism for which he had given up his best years.

In 1939, with the arrival of the Russian army, Slapak lead a union of Krynki partisans and was very active in Communist communal life. But with time the Soviet rulers demoted him. Their reason was that the Polish Communist Party was full of Trotskyites and provocateurs. They no longer had confidence in the loyal, faithful Communist – Slapak.

At the outbreak of the German-Russian war in 1941, Slapak, together with a group of Krynki young people successfully escaped to the Bialystok ghetto. He was in the underground movement and led a bitter dispute concerning the way to fight against the Nazi murderers. The majority felt it should be carried out in the ghetto. The Krinkers, with Slapak and Rivka Shinder at the head, thought that they should flee to the forest and there, together with the Russian partisans, fight again the cruel Nazis.

Slapak left the Bialystok ghetto leading twenty people (mostly Krinkers) in December 1942. His headquarters was located in an ideal, strong, well-guarded bunker in the Lipovy-Most forest.

The Krynki group was disciplined and took only bread, potatoes and necessities from the peasants in the area. Slapak had issued a strong order not to steal anything. To make it look like they were Russians, the group was dressed as Red Army soldiers and carried Russian weapons, but the peasants knew that they were Jews.

As soon as the Krinkers were organized in the forest, Moshe Slapak sent two armed messengers to Bialystok so that they would lead Jews from the ghetto to the forest. When the Suprasler partisan group arrived, Slapak first of all supplied them with food and then posted three of his fighters to watch and protect their bunker.

Slapak sought to make contact with Russian partisans and he was successful in establishing contact with partisan commander "Alexander," a Russian officer. Slapak planned to get more Jews from the ghetto to enlarge his group and take revenge on the bestial Nazis.

[Page 315]

Peasants worked at felling trees in the area of Slapak's base. The tracks in the snow showed that partisans were hiding in the area. On the 10th of February 1943 the guards arrived on the run and said that a group of civilians with arms were entering the forest. There were about fifteen armed people at the base. (The rest were on various missions.) Over two hundred armed "Vlasovtses" (Veisgvardeyshe Russian Black Hundreds, lead by General Vlasov), local policemen and Germans opened fire from all sides. Slapak with his small number of fighters took up the uneven battle. The shooting lasted several hours. Moshe Slapak was badly wounded in the stomach and died in the hands of his own Krynki fighters when they had carried him into the bunker. Three other fighters fell as well.

Ten Germans and their helpers paid with their lives for the attack. This was the first fight with the Germans in the Bialystok forest.

After the losses of the first fight, the group dispersed. Some went to other partisan groups and most gave up their lives fighting the Nazis.

Partisans and Krynki fighters
Jews and their unity

Besides the above mentioned Krinkers from our cozy shtetl who were active in partisan ranks, listed below are the names of those from our shtetl who served as Jewish partisans. These are the people that we know of:

1. **Beyl'ke Shuster-Greenstein** who together with her husband, turned up in Minsk after they fled Krynki during the retreat of the Russian army. While in the Minsk ghetto, they came in contact with Russian partisans who were active in the Staroseler forest in 1942 and joined their ranks. Beyl'ke escaped and also excelled.
2. **Feyvel Wolf** escaped from Kelbasin camp and later, after wandering for a long time, turned up in the Spring of 1944 in a Russian partisan group that was active in the forest.
3. **Abrahamel Soyfer** fled from Krynki to the east during the retreat of the Red Army. He was captured by the Germans along with Soviet soldiers and succeeded in escaping. While wandering in the forest in 1941, he met up with a Russian partisan group and joined them. He had carried out a secret mission in the Krynki ghetto. The Germans captured him as he was leaving the ghetto with a package of medicine for the partisans. He was "interrogated" and should have died, but thanks to Jankel Kozoltchik, the commandant of the Jewish "ordenungs-dienst," he was saved.
4. **Shmuel Geller**, when the Red Army started the Second World War, was in the eastern part of Poland and traveled at first to Ivye and later to Lida. He fled the Lida ghetto in 1943 with a group of Jews and went to the partisans in the Galiboki forest. He was a partisan in the Kalinin Detachment, Kirov Brigade until liberation in June 1944.
5. **Shlama Avnet** (Avnet "the blond") was in Aushwitz death camp in 1944 and planned to blow up the crematoria. He was killed carrying out the mission.

[Page 316]

A Krinker "organizes" a Passover Seder in a German concentration camp[2]

At the beginning of 1943 Jews from the Krakow ghetto had to move to a larger camp in the town of Plaszow that had been prepared on the land of its destroyed Jewish cemetery. The more active and wealthy Jews who were employed in the surrounding factories prepared to arrange their own camps in their factories. The Jews helped considerably with money for the expenses of building material, and after a long, hard workday they also labored overtime to build the barracks. This was how two such camps were put up. One of them was for "*kabelverk*" [cable work].

These camps were ruled by the so-called "verkshutz" [security]. It was made up mainly of German people who turned a blind eye to much of the social and cultural life. So there were celebrations Friday night and on various Jewish holidays in the "cable factory."

The spirit of the celebrations was Moshe Smuelovitch, may his memory be blessed, who came from Krynki. Until the war broke out he was a teacher of Jewish subjects in the Krakow Hebrew High School named for Dr. Chaim Hilfstein. He was very well liked by the students and popular in the city. As proposed by Dr. Hilfstein, who at the time of the occupation was chairman of the "Jewish Social Self-Help," Professor Shmuelovitch was appointed head of the distribution of medications and food that was sent to help the camp.

This made it possible for him to move around the camp, stay in touch with prisoners and organize all kinds of gatherings. From these the Seder night was especially remembered. It was organized in a women's barrack and there was a table covered with matzahs and wine. Professor Shmuelovitch then carried on a deep comparison between the difficult afflictions that Pharoah put on the Jews in Egypt and the situation of the prisoners in the camps.

At the end of 1944, the prisoners were sent to other camps. Moshe Shmulovitch was killed on the 22nd of January 1945 in Guzen, when after "disinfecting" the naked prisoners were held for several hours in the freezing cold. His fifteen-year-old only son Uri, who was with him in the cable camp, was a survivor and arrived in Israel with a group of child immigrants. He later graduated from Haifa Polytechnical and is currently an engineer at the Weizman Istitute in Rehovot.

Exhumation of the martyrs who were murdered during the slaughter of Passover Eve, 1943

[Page 317]

Exhumation of the Krynki martyrs[3]

By Shmuel Wolf and Heschel Eizen
(one of the *shoyhet's* [ritual slaughterer] sons)

Translated by Gloria Berkenstat Freund

Due to the initiative of fellow Krinkers in Bialystok, the help of the Jewish District committee and financial aid from the Krinker *landsmanschaft* [association of fellow townspeople] in America the exhumation took place. A brigade of Jewish workers, under the leadership of Krinker Shmuel Wolf and Heschel Eizen, began the exhumation of the martyrs on the 10th of December 1947. The two mass graves were on Shmerl the *Kotler's* [boilermaker, teakettle maker] square, on *Bod Gesl* [Bath Lane] in Krynki which had become a place to throw garbage.

This is where they were shot, Friday Passover Eve 1943, during the round up of old people in the ghetto. Thirty-nine of the nicest and most religious Jews in the shtetl headed by the Hasidic rabbi.

They had dug down a meter when they saw two rows of dead bodies. In the first row there were fifteen people and in the second, nineteen. All of them were dressed in their clothes with the yellow patch. Some had Hasidic skullcaps on their heads, some with eye glasses. The Hasidic rabbi was recognized due to his long *kapote* [long, black coat worn by orthodox Jews] and skullcap. Lying in the grave with the thirty-four bodies were two older children.

About three meters on the side, they found the second grave where five women lay separately.

The funeral was held Thursday, 27 Kislev 5707 – the 11th of December 1947 at half past two in the afternoon at the Jewish cemetery in Krynki.

[Page 318]

The roster of the victims. The victims of the bloody Passover-eve

Of the thirty-nine victims of the bloody Passover-eve who were exhumed it was possible, due to volunteers from several communities and lists, to put together the following list of thirty-three names and some nicknames.

The twenty-eight men

1. *Reb* [Mr., or term of respect] Shmuel Lev, the Hasidic rabbi ("the *geler*") [blond]
2. *Dayan* [Judge in the Jewish court] *Reb* Leyb (Leybke) Segal
3. Heykel Alian (owner of a restaurant)
4. Moshe Alekshitzer
5. Heschel Okun ("Heschel the *Meshores*") [Servant]
6. Sender Aronovitch ("Sender the *Pupeks*") [navels, gizzards]
7. Hershel Aronovitch (one of Sender's sons)
8. Meir Blokh (Meir "mantzes") [little bits]
9. Abraham Brevdeh (a Hasid, manager of the "*Hakhnoses Orkhim*") [Sabbath shelter for poor wanderers]
10. Pinie Gendler (Pinie Munie Feygel Yehushe's)
11. Velvel Veinach (the *Valker*) [preparer]
12. Benjamin Veyrach (Naome Ide's)
13. Abraham Lopate (Abrahmke "drales")
14. Moshe Lapate
15. Mosheke Lev ("*maziks*" [mischievous, clever, daring] Chana the baker's husband)
16. Motke Levin (the tailor, "the *horbultchik*") [hunchback]
17. Shmuel Levin (Munie Khsrial's, a sexton in the synagogue)

18. Muntchik Wolf (the blacksmith)
19. Jankel Wolf (Aaron's son, Muntchik the blacksmith's grandson)
20. Natanovitch
21. Henoch Nakdiman (one of the sons of Hertzke from the leather factory)
22. Mones Potchevutski (a veneer storekeeper)
23. Alter Kaplan ("the Hon") [rooster]
24. Monie Yakov Kaplan (a leather manufacturer)
25. Daniel Kaganovitch ("the Hoykher") [tall]
26. Motl Kravetski (Shmuel and Bashke Spodviler's son)
27. Rabkin
28. Sender Shafir.

The five women

1. Eylin (old Mendel's wife)
2. Chana Alekshitser
3. Okun (Heschel Okun's mother
4. Shoshke Lascher (Shoshke Rachel Matske's, the egg dealer)
5. Feygel Nakdiman (Israel Hertzk's wife)

On the Ruins of Jewish Krynki

My Shtetl, Krynki

by Sarah Fel-Yelin

Translated by Gloria Berkenstat Freund

My little shtetl Krinik, an image in memory –
Hardly dimmed in the mist of years;
My father and brothers, home and my garden –
Is there still a trace remaining there now?

Gray years of destruction and war,
With a slaughterer's knife they tattered our nation;
In ashes somewhere the family remains,
Never gathered from the flame of the Nazi animals.

I spun a thread of sorrow and hope,
In search of names of dear ones, not found;
Still further and further the search renews
Among the liberated remnants of hell.

And I am back in the shtetl
The destruction, the bleak depressing sight;
At the market place – a ruin with scraps,
In the obliterated little streets my eyes search.

There is the well, the trees, the house,
I yell with a quivering voice:
"The trees!…My father on the day –

of my birth –
Planted five trees sixty years ago!"

And here is the house, the balcony, the garden,
A strange family lives there now;
As if feverishly I touch a board, a stone –
As if by an open grave I am choked with sobs.

They stand there without words, the Polish neighbors –
"Yes, yes, they did not spare anyone,
Troubles and terror also boiled up for us,
But the lot of the Jews was horrible".

[Page 320]

In my heart hammers beat, my heart bleeds,
I think I feel my father wherever I turn,
In the smell of the air – his blood, his tears,
In every little stone and every grain of sand, he is.

As if from a funeral, I look back
At my home and at the green trees:
At a shtetl with Jews, factories and stores,
Remains at the end an illustrious name.

The death of Krinik is written in the record,
Its fighting spirit remains its legacy;
Its heroic stand until the last day, to the bitter end,
The courage of our martyrs lies heavy
On the scales.

My little shtetl Krinik, an image in memories –
Bloody destruction, terrifying years;
Of our nearest and loved ones nothing remains,
Only a family gravestone: five green trees.

Footnotes:

1.   The details about Moshe Slapak from the Bialystok ghetto and from the forest where given by partisan "Leon" from the Suprasler partisan group
2.   From Dr. Michael Weichert's memoirs.
3.   From documents at the Jewish Historical Institute in Warsaw

[Page 319]

Translator's note:

The Hebrew section by Baruch Niv (Bendet Nisht) on 319 is equivalent with the Yiddish section on 323. Therefore, it is not being translated.

Entrance to Krynki from Sokolka

The Kavkaz Beis Midrash, today a movie theater

The destroyed Great Synagogue, 1967

[Page 321]

With the Krynkers – on the Way to Israel

by Arnold Rozenfeld

Translated by Jerrold Landau

Years passed. The bitter fate summoned me to Italy after the war, on my long journey to the Land of Israel. I began to work as the principal of a large school in the city of Cremona, not far from Milan. To my great joy, I found the Polonski sisters from Krynki there. I hired one of them as a teacher in my school. After I returned from Russia, the financial situation of my family was not great. Nevertheless, I did not complain about my fate, and I did not request help even from my relatives. However, the Polonski sisters were inspired and wrote to the friends in the United States. Then, Krynki natives and my former students, sent help. I will never forget this!

Dearer than everything, however, was my emotional meeting with my dear friend Bendet Nisht in Milan. I stood in front of the door of one of the offices of the camp of Jews there, and I suddenly noticed that the name of the high officer who was serving the people was Bendet Nisht. There were no bounds to our joy. Through his efforts, I was invited to be the principal of the high school in Rome, or to supervise the Hebrew schools of the central committee of Jewish camps in Italy. However, my intention was to make aliya to the Land of Israel, and not to delay and accept good positions in the Diaspora.

Krynki natives are my good friends to this day, and my joy is great when I meet one of them.

Grodno Street, 1967. The current police station is on the left.

After the Holocaust

[Page 322]

On the Ruins of Jewish Krinek

By Beylke Shuster-Greenstein

Translated by Judie Goldstein

As a remnant of my entire family only I remain. It is unbelievable that I am alone, but it is so. On leaving the forest, in 1944, I immediately set out for Krinek to see if perhaps I would find somebody there.

On the road to the shtetl were military personnel with rifles, wearing badges of the detachment I had fought with. They told me about the report from the border patrol, that there were no Jews left in Krinek and it was dangerous to go there because the "*A.K.A.*" [Armej Krajowa – Polish Nationalistic anti-Semitic partisans] was on the rampage there. The couple of Jews who survived were in Brestovitz. I soon traveled there and met Herschel Roitbord and Pearl Levi, Jankel the *Klorn's* daughter. I hear from them, for the first time, about the sad end of my family and of the whole shtetl.

"Not anymore to Krinek!" concluded Pearl.

But still I could not bear the thought that I was finished with this. And so with the help of fellow Krinkers and newspapers, I found an aunt who lives in Argentina. Beside myself, she is the only member of our entire family that once numbered more than a hundred.

The memorial book should, for our children and us, remain a living memorial.

On the Cemetery of Our Hometown

Sarah Fel-Yelin

1960, forty years after I had left Poland, I returned to my hometown.

A shtetl – a cemetery, a ruin, Jewish Krinik is no more! The round market place stands naked – no more stores, the gates or the houses around it. Here and there houses remain, they are gray, shrunken, buried in the earth. I find Plantanske, recognizable because of the five trees my father planted at my birth. I recognize the well that now stands dry against the square where Boruch *khokhem's* [wise] house was.

I stand there thinking. With a sea of tears in my eyes, I look at my house. None of my dear ones are here. A woman comes out, feels uncomfortable, frightened. Perhaps she thinks that I have come after my inheritance? A second neighbor comes outside. We shake hands. His name is Michal Tzarevitch. Yes, certainly he knows Eli the tinsmith and his family…

1967 – Tepershe Street (Plantanske) in the snow

[Page 323]

Where and how – nobody knows anything: "It was terrible…Nobody's life was safe, if they spoke a word to a Jew…" He wonders: - "Are you Eli's daughter – the small blond young lady?"

We go to the cemetery. Even the dead were not spared by the Nazi animals. The gravestones have been knocked down and the fence is broken. Edward Pogoda, a director of a larger enterprise in Bialystok, my former pupil from Krynki, had brought me to the shtetl. "When the Red Army opened the train cars and begged the Jews to save themselves, a lot of them answered, 'We will manage.'"

"Yes: I know about this," my father wrote me. "I did not want to abandon my home. We have already lived under the Germans once."

Krinik – the little shtetl – has become a cluster of houses without one Jew, but Krinkers are now everywhere. I travel around the United States – meet a fellow Krinker here and there; in Poland I met several Krinkers – Rivka Shinder, a former partisan captain with a dumdum bullet shot into her arm, an important person in Poland, and also others.

Let us, Krinkers, from everywhere recognize and understand that all of us together carried from our shtetl an important inheritance – the tradition of justice and self-sacrifice; the tradition of together in life and combat!

On Our Ruins

Boruch (Bendet) Nisht

Coming to Israel in 1933, I immediately went back to Poland to finish my mission of organizing "illegal" immigration from there and later from all of Europe.

First of all I went to Krynki to see my family, friends and to visit the shtetl that was so dear to my heart. I was born and bred in Krinek, studied there and was a member of institutions there.

And I made *aliyah* [immigrated to Israel] in 1935, leaving Poland forever – I felt that I had to say farewell to my cozy shtetl, because who knew if I would ever see Krynki again. In the summer of 1939, I had to be in Poland again and visited Krynki. Then the bleak war broke out there and like all the Jewish communities, our Krinek was wiped out.

Soon after the war I traveled to Italy as an emissary for the Jewish Agency – to rescue Jews, the remnant from Europe, to bring them help and restore immigration to Israel. I was aware that there were several Krinker survivors in Italy. I started to search for them in order to do something for them. And so I found Ayzik and Motl Brustin in a camp in southern Italy, Lola Wolf in Rome, Shaya-Leyb Nisht's daughter and family – in a northern camp. I learned from them more precisely what had happened in our Krinek.

In 1945

Late, in 1949, I was appointed Israeli Consul in Warsaw. I threw myself into my work, diplomatic and consular, especially concerning immigration to Israel. At the time a small exit door was open for Jews from Poland and for me it was a great and rare honor to give out the first Israeli visas, to our brothers, at the legation in Warsaw. It was from there, in past years, that I secretly dispatched pioneers to Israel.

[Page 324]

But no matter how busy I was with my specialized activities, Krinkers were constantly on my mind. I had to go there to see what was happening there and perhaps still find one of ours.

I was advised not to travel by train because gangs of Fascists, who were on the rampage, were killing Jews on trains – allegedly as "Communists who had seized control of the government in Poland." I drove my car directly to Bialystok. The road from Warsaw went quickly. The highways were empty, no cars, not even a wagon. It was as if everything had died out. In Bialystok a lot of streets were in ruins, torn up; traces of the Nazi animals were visible in the large mass grave of the cruelly murdered Jews of the city, an atrocity that has become prominent.

First of all I went to the Jewish Committee, the head of which I was given to understand, was a Krinker, from the Petritser family. I met him and we talked; I felt he was weighing his words carefully as he was an official in a Communist country and limited in what he could talk about and perhaps even think.

There were very few Jews in Bialystok, remnants of the surrounding towns, where it is now impossible to stay – as the solitary, miraculous survivor. I learned from Petritser that there was a Krinker in the local old people's home – Adinak's wife. I went to visit her, thinking perhaps I could help her with something. Except for meeting her, there was no pleasure in our encounter.

I continued on my way to Krinek. The road was empty. I drove quickly. There was a policeman with me in civilian clothes. The district police commandant told him to accompany me.

"*Ot in shoyn Sokolke*" ["Here in Sokole already"] – do you remember the tune? I must see it up close, not just drive through. We got out, searched for a restaurant and found only a gentile inn, not a Jew to be had. The city was hardly damaged. But two houses had fallen, Kantor's and Kapeliushnik's, where Krinkers would stay overnight or wait for the bus to or from Krinek. Sokolke, the effervescent Jewish city with its Jewish laborers, artisans, storekeepers, merchants and leather factories – all of it perished in the Holocaust.

I traveled further. The villages rushed past; Sloike, Sudzialove, Ostrove, and we reached Krynki. Coming from the mountain it was close at hand. It did not appear as it was. There were less houses, it felt as if there was nothing moving in the fields and near the highway it was empty, dead – Krynki!

The Sokolker gentile street with its small houses rushed by. Here was the market. It seemed as if Ozsheshkove (Heykel's) Street had disappeared – everything burned. On the market place – there were no more round stores, no more firemen's shed. A lot of houses have fallen down – Mordchailevitch's, Chatzkel the *Shenker's* [tavern keeper's] and all around it was empty.

The *Potcht* [post office] Street was empty, not one house until Kleyne's Street (Vonske). Where is Zezmer's house, where is the "*benkl*" [small bench], where are the houses I knew so well, where did my childhood years go? No more Jankel and Shmuel Vine's (Fink's), Mordchai Terkel's houses, the house where the Tikotskis lived – everything is destroyed.

Going further: streets, lanes – half and entirely burned. "Kavkaz" – almost clean of houses, Kastsiol Street half burned down, Garbarske – in ruins; of the school – a singed skeleton. From the large *besmedresh* [synagogue] with the boarded up windows and doors – hit a melancholy note. Only the non-Jewish streets are whole.

There is not one Jew in the whole shtetl. Several of our Krinkers came here to visit soon after the war and then left. Krinek is "free of Jews". Gentile live in the still habitable houses that previously belonged to Jews.

[Page 325]

I drove my car to Yanek Laputch's, the shtetl photographer. He recognized me immediately, found a couple of my old photographs and told me about himself and his late wife Malka "the converted Jewess." We spoke in Yiddish and he winked at my escort, the policeman, and presented me with a question, whether "the uncircumcised understands the language?" and concluded: " Yes, yes, no lady – it is sad, very bad now, to have lived a life among Jews and now I must die among gentiles"…

The Krynki cemetery, soon after
"liberation" visit of Lola Wolf-Reznick

I visited the cemetery. The gravestones are sinking. The mass grave, in which our Krinkers, who gathered and visited after the war from various places, and the exhumed corpses of those murdered by the Nazi animals at the beginning of their invasion, does not have a gravestone. The grave has begun to sink and has the appearance of a large pit. The government watchman for the cemetery expressed a wish, if I could give him some money he would be able to better tend to the cemetery and bring some order to this holy place.

In general, gentile acquaintances that I met in Krinek during my visits in 1950 and 1951 – turned out to be friends of the Jews and righteous men. A lot were afraid to speak to me when they saw the police guards who accompanied me, especially in 1951 when secrets agents dogged my every step. That time I was absolutely sure that I would never see our Krinek again.

My last visit

But "*a mentsch trakht un got lakht*" [man plans and god laughs]. Sixteen years later, in 1967, I was once again in Poland as part of an Israeli delegation to unveil a monument in memory of those murdered in Auschwitz.

Although our itinerary was over full and the deadline on our visas did not allow for any free time in Poland, I decided to escape to Krinek and see what was happening there and take some photographs.

From Warsaw to Bialystok the Israelis traveled together by train. But to go to Krinek I had no alternative but to travel there by taxi. The young Polish driver insisted on driving through Suprasl: "It is closer," he claimed. True, but it is a forest road where you do not see a soul.

[Page 326]

Now it is very difficult to recognize our hometown that lies next to the Russian border and where outsiders are not important; and such a person has now arrived – He is suspicious and nobody dares to speak to him.

1967 – at the square at the market place – now a city garden (photographed on a snowy day)

I went directly to the police and simply told them about my visit and that I wanted to take several photographs. The Chief of Police wondered a little at my audacity to come to a border town without written permission and wanting to take photographs. But after a short chat and with the help of a bottle of liquor that a gentile, Krynki acquaintance had brought with him everything was kosher. The chief was honored and he showed me the city, as if he were its founder.

The market place is now a city garden. "It is just in the process of being prepared." – he told us. After this "major" change he showed me the "Kavkaz" *besmedresh* [synagogue]. "That," he arrogantly emphasized, "is now the movie theater where they have good movies every week." "Yente's" *besmedresh*, for many years a part of the Hebrew school, was located on the second floor, and is now a food cooperative and a warehouse for flour, sugar and other products. By the way, at the cooperative I recognized Guttseit's daughter (a "half" German was at that time in Krinek) and she was surprised that I was still alive. The large Synagogue, rebuilt, is now the post office. There is nothing left of the other synagogues and houses of study.

The beautiful effervescent center of cultural and social activity, Krynki, is now a large, quiet village where men pass the time drinking booze...Krynki, our Jewish hometown, has been destroyed and cut down together with our martyrs. May their memories be blessed!

A light snow began to blow in the wind when I took the photographs, but everything was misty, every my eyes. My last visit to Krynki was complete.

> On tne hillstands a tree
> Looking down at
> The small town, there, in the valley –
> Together they were slaughtered, destroyed.

> (from Song of the Jewish people).

Leaving Krynki

[Page 327]

1967 – the ruins of the large synagogue

The large synagogue, rebuilt – today a post office

"Kavkaz" besmedresh (now a movie theater)

Besmedresh "Yente's" – now a food cooperative

1967 – the former market place,
in the background – the ruins of the large synagogue

[Pages 328-332]

Necrology

Transliterated by Jim Yarin

Edited by Jerrold Landau

We will remember the Jews of Krynki by family, from street to street and from house to house.

Note from Jerrold Landau: The original necrology was organized by street. The list of names on each street were likely meant to represent the order of the houses on the street. The translation is set up with all the names alphabetized in English. The streets have been included in the fourth column, however the ordering of the names per street could not be preserved. The following are the streets listed in the necrology, by page (the last street per page flows onto the following page):

Page 328: On the market, Poczta Gasse, Szmole Gesl (Wanska), Tepersze (Potters) Gasse,
Page 329: Bialystoker Gasse, Sokolker Gasse, Kavkaz.
Page 330: Zobie Gasse, Bod (Bath) Gesl, Garbarske (Tanners) Gasse, Continuation of Garbarske Gasse (from the left side of the market).
Page 331: Paretszer Gasse, Rynkowe Gasse, Gmine Gasse, Szislewice Gasse, Czerkowe Gasse.
Page 332: Mil Gasse, Hassidim or Paltiel's Gasse (Grochowa).

The name spelling style used by the original transliterator was generally phonetic. When editing, I preserved the phonetic style, and did not render the surnames into Polish style. At times, you will find more than one entry for a specific name. This likely represents both a residential and a business location for the individual (in fact, many such cases have one of the locations listed as "on the market." The possessive style names in some entries represent the common nicknaming style of that period, whereby a person may have been given the nickname based on a spouse or parent in the possessive form.

Last Name	First Name	Occupation / Other info / Nickname or Possessive Name	Street
	Chaim Velvel	from Wolka	Hassidim or Paltiel's Gasse (Grochowa)
	Efraim Leib	the Shamash	Poczta Gasse
	Eidel	the Dybbuk	Sokolker Gasse
	Elkonah	the shoemaker	Gmine Gasse
	Kalman	of the Courtyard	Szislewice Gasse
	Shlomo	the Yellow	Czerkowe Gasse
	Teme	the woman glazier	Mil Gasse
	Tzipke	the market sitter (i.e. the woman tending to her stall in the market)	Gmine Gasse
Aberstein	Itsche		Tepersze (Potters) Gasse
Aberstein	Chaim	roofer	Tepersze (Potters) Gasse
Aberstein	Hershel		Tepersze (Potters) Gasse
Abramowitz	Moshe		On the market
Adin	Binyamin		Tepersze (Potters) Gasse
Adinak	Motke		Continuation of Garbarske Gasse
Ahon	Heshel	Heshel the Shamash	Tepersze (Potters) Gasse
Ahron	Reuven		Bialystoker Gasse
Ahronowitz	Bashe		Garbarske (Tanners) Gasse
Ahronowitz	Hershel	Pupke's	Garbarske (Tanners) Gasse
Ahronowitz	Leibke		Garbarske (Tanners) Gasse
Ahronowitz	Sender		Garbarske (Tanners) Gasse
Ahrontshik	Chaim Yosel		Garbarske (Tanners) Gasse
Alta		Baker lady	On the market
Alta		Meirem's (Meirem's wife)	On the market
Antstein	(Karishl)		Tepersze (Potters) Gasse
Antzis	Berl		Poczta Gasse
Antzis	Hershel		On the market
Anushewitz	Paltiel		Hassidim or Paltiel's Gasse (Grochowa)
Ash	Yudel	in-law of Dralies	Bialystoker Gasse
Ash	Yudel		Szmole Gesl (Wanska)

Augustowski	Henya	Lantse's	Sokolker Gasse
Ayan		family (the mill)	Mil Gasse
Ayan	Alter		Poczta Gasse
Ayan	Chaim		Bialystoker Gasse
Ayan	Niamka		Poczta Gasse
Ayan	Zelig	Zelig Posziak	Tepersze (Potters) Gasse
Aychnboim	Ahron	son-in-law of Tursky	Bialystoker Gasse
Aylin	Alter		Czerkowe Gasse
Aylin	Itshka		Paretszer Gasse
Aylin	Zecharya		Paretszer Gasse
Bakstein	David		Kavkaz
Baraban	Cheikel	the Mitse's	Gmine Gasse
Bardlas	Leime		Rynkowe Gasse
Bas	Moshe		Garbarske (Tanners) Gasse
Bas	Pinya		Sokolker Gasse
Bekelman	Eliahu		Gmine Gasse
Berkowitz	Chana		On the market
Bezdush	Alte		Zobie Gasse
Bialystoker	Ayde		Rynkowe Gasse
Biegon	Feivel		Continuation of Garbarske Gasse
Blaustein	Meyer	from Syulk	Mil Gasse
Bloch		shoemaker	On the market
Bloch	Eli		Bialystoker Gasse
Bloch	Meyer	Mantshe's	Mil Gasse
Bloch	Shmuel Hertzel	Katshka's ["Ducks"]	Bialystoker Gasse
Blumenthal	Hershel		Gmine Gasse
Blyacher	Leibe		Paretszer Gasse
Blyacher	Nachum		Paretszer Gasse
Blyacher	Tyba		Tepersze (Potters) Gasse
Blyacher	Yehuda		Tepersze (Potters) Gasse
Bogotilski	Dodel		Szislewice Gasse
Bolshon	Asne		Rynkowe Gasse
Bolshon	David Leib		Rynkowe Gasse

Bolshon	Niome		Rynkowe Gasse
Bolshon	Zeidke		Czerkowe Gasse
Borowski	Gedalyahu		Rynkowe Gasse
Borowski	Hershel		Rynkowe Gasse
Borowski	Pinye		Rynkowe Gasse
Braverman	Moshe		Kavkaz
Braverman	Yehoshua		Hassidim or Paltiel's Gasse (Grochowa)
Brenner	Boris		Bialystoker Gasse
Brenner	Chaim		Bialystoker Gasse
Brewde			Hassidim or Paltiel's Gasse (Grochowa)
Brewde	Berl		Gmine Gasse
Browde	Avraham		Bialystoker Gasse
Browde			On the market
Brustin	Shimon		Continuation of Garbarske Gasse
Buki	Shimon	the baker	Garbarske (Tanners) Gasse
Bunem	Yosel		Continuation of Garbarske Gasse
Bushnyak	Shimon	Tsinge's	Gmine Gasse
Charu	Iser		Sokolker Gasse
Charu	Mikhel		Gmine Gasse
Chashkes			Gmine Gasse
Chashkes	Babke	Tsinge's	Gmine Gasse
Chashkes	Idel		Tepersze (Potters) Gasse
Chasid	Yosel	Yose Motshke's	Tepersze (Potters) Gasse
Chasid	Shlomo		Mil Gasse
Chatskel	Sarah		On the market
Chatskel	Shimon Yoel		Rynkowe Gasse
Chatskel	Yosel	Mashelne's	Kavkaz
Chirik			Hassidim or Paltiel's Gasse (Grochowa)
Chirik	Yehoshua		Continuation of Garbarske Gasse
Chover	Noach		Gmine Gasse

Chust		Latata's	Bod (Bath) Gesl
Dande			Kavkaz
Dines		the tinsmith	Gmine Gasse
Ditkowski	Avraham		Mil Gasse
Dobrymisl			Mil Gasse
Draznin	David		Paretszer Gasse
Dreishpil	Yonah		Kruszyniany
Dreizik	Chana		Tepersze (Potters) Gasse
Dreizik	Mordecai		Zobie Gasse
Dreizik	Sheika		Bialystoker Gasse
Dreizik	Moshka		Sokolker Gasse
Dubinski			Gmine Gasse
Dubinski	Henech		Garbarske (Tanners) Gasse
Dubinski	Miklah		Tepersze (Potters) Gasse
Dubinski	Nachum		Garbarske (Tanners) Gasse
Dubinski	Yisroel		Bod (Bath) Gesl
Dule	Max	Feldsher/field barber-surgeon	Hassidim or Paltiel's Gasse (Grochowa)
Eframzon	Moshe		On the market
Efron	Rochel		Zobie Gasse
Efron	Tsirl		Zobie Gasse
Eizen	Michel	the Shochet / ritual slaughterer	Bialystoker Gasse
Eizenshmidt	Yankel Shmuel		Continuation of Garbarske Gasse
Eizenshmidt	Yudel		Czerkowe Gasse
Ekstein	Chaim	the carpenter	Kavkaz
Epstein			Zobie Gasse
Epstein	(Mantifuzl) Mendel		Sokolker Gasse
Fal	Eli	Eli the tinsmith	Tepersze (Potters) Gasse
Falk	Dina		Bialystoker Gasse
Farber		Moshe Hershel	Mil Gasse
Farber	Alter		Garbarske (Tanners) Gasse
Farber	Beirach		Kavkaz
Farber	Dvorah	from the rickshaws	Poczta Gasse

Farber	Chilke	the bath attendant	Bod (Bath) Gesl
Farber	Mordecai	Chabad	Mil Gasse
Farber	Yekutiel		Bod (Bath) Gesl
Feidler	Ester	Ester Arye's	Tepersze (Potters) Gasse
Feinberg	Tsile		Continuation of Garbarske Gasse
Filipski	Zeidel		Gmine Gasse
Fink		of Halickie	Tepersze (Potters) Gasse
Fink	Gershon		Continuation of Garbarske Gasse
Fink	Meyer Leib		Garbarske (Tanners) Gasse
Fink	Yaakov	Meir Teibe's	Garbarske (Tanners) Gasse
Fridman	Leizer	from Gabyut	Mil Gasse
Fridman	Avrahamel		Tepersze (Potters) Gasse
Furman	Avrahamel		Szmole Gesl (Wanska)
Furman	Elke		Kavkaz
Furman	Leizer Yankel	Shwester = sister	Kavkaz
Furman	Motke		Szmole Gesl (Wanska)
Furman	Simcha		Gmine Gasse
Furye	Abrahamel		On the market
Furye	Wichna		Poczta Gasse
Gabay	Moshe		Bialystoker Gasse
Gabay	Hershel	Gabaytshek	Garbarske (Tanners) Gasse
Gabay	Moshel		Garbarske (Tanners) Gasse
Gabay	Yisroel	The melamed – teacher of children	Gmine Gasse
Gabay	Yoske		Poczta Gasse
Galinski			On the market
Garborwski	Avrahamel		Paretszer Gasse
Garber	Batshe		On the market
Garber	Moshe		Bod (Bath) Gesl
Garber	Moshe		Mil Gasse
Garber	Moshke		Garbarske (Tanners) Gasse
Garber	Yankel	Matise's	Garbarske (Tanners) Gasse
Gel		family	Mil Gasse

Geler	Chaim Sheime	Maznik	Continuation of Garbarske Gasse
Gendler			Szmole Gesl (Wanska)
Gendler	Chana		Tepersze (Potters) Gasse
Gendler	Todel		Sokolker Gasse
Gendler	Pini	Feigel Yeshiya's	Mil Gasse
Gendler	Yosel	Fante's	Continuation of Garbarske Gasse
Gertskes			Gmine Gasse
Gilule	Leizer		Continuation of Garbarske Gasse
Gipsman	Tehila	the seamstress	Gmine Gasse
Glazer	Mordecai Eli		Szislewice Gasse
Glazer	Sheye		Szislewice Gasse
Gobinski		Ahrtshik	Bialystoker Gasse
Gobinski	Ezra	the carpenter	Bialystoker Gasse
Gobinski	Zidka		Poczta Gasse
Goland	Gotlieb		On the market
Goland	Gotlieb		Bod (Bath) Gesl
Goldin	Itshke		Garbarske (Tanners) Gasse
Goldschmid	Shalom	Tolya	Bialystoker Gasse
Golinski			Tepersze (Potters) Gasse
Goltz			Szmole Gesl (Wanska)
Goltz	Nachke		Zobie Gasse
Goltz	Yosel		On the market
Golub	Chaim		Garbarske (Tanners) Gasse
Golub	Mashke	Asher Shaya's	Czerkowe Gasse
Golub	Shimon		Garbarske (Tanners) Gasse
Golub	Tevel		Garbarske (Tanners) Gasse
Gordon		Margatkas	Tepersze (Potters) Gasse
Goz	Shmuel Iser		Poczta Gasse
Gozshanski	Dovka	Moshe Kreina's	Bialystoker Gasse
Gozshanski	Mordecai Sholom		Rynkowe Gasse
Gozshanski	Yankel		Rynkowe Gasse
Greenblatt	Leibel		Bialystoker Gasse

Grodski	Mordecai Shimon		Bialystoker Gasse
Grodzitski	Shemaya		Garbarske (Tanners) Gasse
Grossman			Mil Gasse
Grossman	Hershel		Gmine Gasse
Grossman	Yankel		Gmine Gasse
Gurewits	Itshke		Mil Gasse
Gurewits	Noteh		Garbarske (Tanners) Gasse
Harkavi	Alter	the locksmith	Kavkaz
Harkavi	Gedliahu	the tailor	Sokolker Gasse
Hendritsicha			Szmole Gesl (Wanska)
Herbarem	Gedliahu		Bialystoker Gasse
Herbarem	Avraham		Szislewice Gasse
Jocawitzki			On the market
Kagan	Moshe	Pinchase's	Garbarske (Tanners) Gasse
Kagan	Moshe		Continuation of Garbarske Gasse
Kagan	Pinchas		Bod (Bath) Gesl
Kagan	Tuvyah		Continuation of Garbarske Gasse
Kagan	Yosef		Paretszer Gasse
Kaganowitz	Avrahamel		Szmole Gesl (Wanska)
Kaganowitz	Daniel		Szmole Gesl (Wanska)
Kaganowitz	Daniel		Tepersze (Potters) Gasse
Kaganowitz	Yosel		Gmine Gasse
Kalinowitsh	Yisroel		Garbarske (Tanners) Gasse
Kalmanowitz	Betzalel		Sokolker Gasse
Kalmanowitz	Tzolke	(JL note: Tzolke is a diminutive of Betzalel)	Szmole Gesl (Wanska)
Kaminski	Zeidke		Zobie Gasse
Kantor			Poczta Gasse
Kantor	Avrahamel		Mil Gasse
Kapeloshnik	Nechemya		Hassidim or Paltiel's Gasse (Grochowa)
Kaplan		Kapitsa	Paretszer Gasse
Kaplan	Alter		On the market

Kaplan	Alter	Meir Abba's	Sokolker Gasse
Kaplan	Binyamin Yankel		Mil Gasse
Kaplan	Chaim Zelig		Mil Gasse
Kaplan	Eber		Sokolker Gasse
Kaplan	Eli	Kirbes = pumpkin	Sokolker Gasse
Kaplan	Malkah	the glazier lady	Sokolker Gasse
Kaplan	Meyer	Feiga Mara	Sokolker Gasse
Kaplan	Nioma	Froida's	Sokolker Gasse
Kaplan	Reuben	Froida's	Sokolker Gasse
Kaplan	Yisroel Berl		Zobie Gasse
Kaplan	Yoel Hershel		On the market
Katz		Futke's	Hassidim or Paltiel's Gasse (Grochowa)
Katz	Zalman	the tinsmith	Bialystoker Gasse
Kirpitsh	Avrahamke	from Pyetrashevich	Mil Gasse
Kirpitsh	Henech		Tepersze (Potters) Gasse
Kirpitsh	Moshe		Tepersze (Potters) Gasse
Kirpitsh	Zawel		Rynkowe Gasse
Kirzshner		Alter Hershke's	Gmine Gasse
Kirzshner	Alter	Zshuzshe's	Kavkaz
Kirzshner	David Shlomo		Sokolker Gasse
Kirzshner	Yeshayahu		Continuation of Garbarske Gasse
Kirzshner	Zeidke	of Wólka	Rynkowe Gasse
Klas			Rynkowe Gasse
Klas	Meyer		Paretszer Gasse
Klas	Moshke	Shimshke's	Garbarske (Tanners) Gasse
Kleinbort			Gmine Gasse
Knishinski	Yoske	Nachum Anshel's	Garbarske (Tanners) Gasse
Kobrinski	Yosel	Holinkerke's	Paretszer Gasse
Kolodner	Abrahamshik		On the market
Kolodner	Yisrael		On the market
Konchewiski			Tepersze (Potters) Gasse
Konchewiski	Tevel		Garbarske (Tanners) Gasse

Kopel	Chaim Gedalia		Szmole Gesl (Wanska)
Kopel	Chaim Gedalia		Sokolker Gasse
Kopel	Meyer Yeshiye		Garbarske (Tanners) Gasse
Kopel	Velvel	from Ozierany	Gmine Gasse
Kopel	Yankel	(Mottel Avrahamchik)	Szmole Gesl (Wanska)
Kopiche	Meyer		Paretszer Gasse
Kopiche	Yankel		Gmine Gasse
Korngold	Berl		Hassidim or Paltiel's Gasse (Grochowa)
Kotlyer	Betzalel		Rynkowe Gasse
Kotlyer	Hershel		Rynkowe Gasse
Kotlyer	Yosel		Rynkowe Gasse
Kotlyer	Zalman		Rynkowe Gasse
Kozlowski		From Lopinice	Gmine Gasse
Kozoltshik	Baruch	Milb	Kavkaz
Kozoltshik		Milbe's	Zobie Gasse
Kozoltshik	Yisrael	Tutsh	Kavkaz
Krawtshik		Kadelak	Paretszer Gasse
Kreingel	Mendel	The artisan's	Garbarske (Tanners) Gasse
Kreingel	Shlomo	the artisan	Bod (Bath) Gesl
Krinski	Betzalel	the melamed / teacher	Bialystoker Gasse
Krinski	Tzolke	the melamed / teacher (JL note, Tzolke is a nickname for Betzalel)	Kavkaz
Kruglyak	Shmuel		Paretszer Gasse
Krutshewski	Hershel	Lipa's	Bialystoker Gasse
Krutshewski	David		Paretszer Gasse
Krutshewski	Shmayke		Continuation of Garbarske Gasse
Krutshewski	Teibe		Paretszer Gasse
Kugel	Alter		Continuation of Garbarske Gasse
Kugel	Leizer		Rynkowe Gasse
Kushner	Iser	the butcher	Gmine Gasse
Kushner	Lishka		Bialystoker Gasse
Kushner	Shepsel		Gmine Gasse

Lapata			Szislewice Gasse
Lapata	Meirim		Tepersze (Potters) Gasse
Lapata	Nysel	Droles	Tepersze (Potters) Gasse
Lapata	Sheina	The Dralie's	Bialystoker Gasse
Lapata	Yitzchak		Bialystoker Gasse
Lash	Velvel		Gmine Gasse
Lasher	Yakov		Bod (Bath) Gesl
Lawler	Chaim Mordecai		Garbarske (Tanners) Gasse
Lawler	Shmayke		Mil Gasse
Leibowitz	Artshik		Paretszer Gasse
Levin	Chaim Moshe	Zamilok / zamler=collector	Bialystoker Gasse
Levin	Eli	The Zoeler	Tepersze (Potters) Gasse
Levin	Feivel		Szislewice Gasse
Levin	Mikhel	Mikhel Munya's	Sokolker Gasse
Levin	Mordecai	Harbolshik the tailor	Tepersze (Potters) Gasse
Levin	Moshe Ber		Mil Gasse
Levin	Nachum	Nachum Captain	Tepersze (Potters) Gasse
Levin	Nachum	from Skidel	Mil Gasse
Levin	Welly Masha		Tepersze (Potters) Gasse
Lew		lady baker	Szislewice Gasse
Lew		the Lyalke = doll	Mil Gasse
Lew	Henya		Kruszyniany
Lew	Hershel	Yachsan = person of privilege	Bod (Bath) Gesl
Lew	Mordecai	from Kruszyniany	Hassidim or Paltiel's Gasse (Grochowa)
Lew		the Hassidic rabbinical teacher	Hassidim or Paltiel's Gasse (Grochowa)
Lew	Sheime		Kruszyniany
Lew	Yankel	Bertshikowe's	Garbarske (Tanners) Gasse
Lew	Yonah	the smith	Mil Gasse
Lew	Yisrael	shoemaker	Tepersze (Potters) Gasse
Lew	Yonah	the smith	Mil Gasse
Lewski	Shmuel	tenor	Continuation of Garbarske Gasse
Lichtenstein		Dr.	Garbarske (Tanners) Gasse

Lider	Chaya Sara		Czerkowe Gasse
Lider	Abrahamel		On the market
Lider	Efraim		Sokolker Gasse
Lider	Mordechai		Sokolker Gasse
Lider	Motel		Mil Gasse
Lider	Shaya		On the market
Lipshits	David	Kasriel's	Bialystoker Gasse
Lipshits	Hershel	Kasriel's	Bod (Bath) Gesl
Lipshitz	Sheike		Szislewice Gasse
Lipunski	Motel		Mil Gasse
Listokin	Aizik Leib		Gmine Gasse
Listokin	Chaim		Poczta Gasse
Listokin	Fishka		Bialystoker Gasse
Listokin	Zidke	of Wolka	Zobie Gasse
Lobendik	Avrahamke	The Farchrenter (arrogant one)	Szmole Gesl (Wanska)
Lobendik	Hershel		Tepersze (Potters) Gasse
Lobendik	Yerucham		Sokolker Gasse
Loginski			On the market
Losh	Velvel		On the market
Losh	Zalman		On the market
Lozowski	Chaim	the shoemaker	Bialystoker Gasse
Lozowski	Michel		On the market
Lozowski	Michael		Mil Gasse
Lublinski			Szislewice Gasse
Lupamsh	Feivel		Gmine Gasse
Manicher		Mandelech	Kavkaz
Marantz	Freidel		On the market
Margolis			On the market
Margolis	Hershel		Hassidim or Paltiel's Gasse (Grochowa)
Margolis	Velvel	Moshele's	Continuation of Garbarske Gasse
Meister	Shepe		Szmole Gesl (Wanska)
Mendelewitz	Lishka		Bialystoker Gasse

Mendelewitz	Yosel		Bialystoker Gasse
Meyerowitz	Zelig	Wentsel	Continuation of Garbarske Gasse
Mikhlis	Betzalel		Hassidim or Paltiel's Gasse (Grochowa)
Miller	Benyamin	lZyama der Beder (bathhouse manager)	Tepersze (Potters) Gasse
Miller	Cheikel		Szmole Gesl (Wanska)
Mirowski		Dental technician	Bialystoker Gasse
Mishkowsky	Avraham		Hassidim or Paltiel's Gasse (Grochowa)
Monachas	Yisrael		Poczta Gasse
Mordchilewitz			Poczta Gasse
Mordchilewitz			Tepersze (Potters) Gasse
Mordchilewitz	Avraham		On the market
Morein	Ahron	of the Hores	Tepersze (Potters) Gasse
Morein	Moshe		Tepersze (Potters) Gasse
Morein	Moshe		Mil Gasse
Morein	Moshel		Continuation of Garbarske Gasse
Morgenstern	Chaim	the shochet: ritual slaughterer	Bialystoker Gasse
Mostowlianski	Yosel		On the market
Mostowlianski	Yosel		Bialystoker Gasse
Musaf	Berl		Kavkaz
Nakdimon	Berl		Gmine Gasse
Nakdimon	Yisrael		Gmine Gasse
Neiman			Mil Gasse
Neiman	Eizik		Mil Gasse
Neiman	Meir Abba		Gmine Gasse
Neiman	Mikhel	Lontse's	Kavkaz
Neiman	Mosheheke	Lontse's	Continuation of Garbarske Gasse
Neiman	Nyanka	Lontse's	Sokolker Gasse
Niewyazshski	Pinye		Continuation of Garbarske Gasse
Nisht		family	Bialystoker Gasse
Nisht	Henech		Poczta Gasse

Nishe	Shlomo Feivel		Poczta Gasse
Noliber	Shmuel	Shmuel Katshka's	Tepersze (Potters) Gasse
Noliber	Leibke		Szislewice Gasse
Noliber	Velvel	Katshka's	Tepersze (Potters) Gasse
Notes	Yosel		Garbarske (Tanners) Gasse
Notowits	Meyer Yonah		Gmine Gasse
Nowik			Sokolker Gasse
Nowik	Avrahame	the dark	Garbarske (Tanners) Gasse
Nowik	Beile	confectionary	On the market
Nowik	Yankel		Poczta Gasse
Ogushewitz	Paltiel		Hassidim or Paltiel's Gasse (Grochowa)
Okun	Shmuel	Shmutke's	Garbarske (Tanners) Gasse
Olean	Cheikel	restauranteur	On the market
Olean	Cheikel		Sokolker Gasse
Olean	Meyer		On the market
Olken	Shmuel		Bialystoker Gasse
Orinak	Sheika		Sokolker Gasse
Ostrinski	Eizik		Continuation of Garbarske Gasse
Ostrinski	Shimon		Bod (Bath) Gesl
Ostrinski	Tevel		Bialystoker Gasse
Ostrinski	Yechiel		Szislewice Gasse
Ostrinski	Zalman		Paretszer Gasse
Oynustawski	Henia	Lantse's	Sokolker Gasse
Pat	Ahron	Smatnik	Zobie Gasse
Pat	Moshe		Zobie Gasse
Peteritser	Chana Rishke		Gmine Gasse
Piper	David		Sokolker Gasse
Pohulyanker	Fishel		Garbarske (Tanners) Gasse
Pohulyanker	Zlatke		Garbarske (Tanners) Gasse
Polanski			Szmole Gesl (Wanska)
Potshabutski			Poczta Gasse
Potshabutski			Szmole Gesl (Wanska)

Potshabutski	Anshel		Bod (Bath) Gesl
Pruzanski	Chaim Asher		Sokolker Gasse
Pruzanski	Chaim Gershon		Continuation of Garbarske Gasse
Pruzanski	Feivel		Szislewice Gasse
Pruzanski	Eizik (Jack)		Garbarske (Tanners) Gasse
Pruzanski	Mishke	Chaim Asher	Paretszer Gasse
Pruzanski	Moshe Vevke		Continuation of Garbarske Gasse
Pruzanski	Yisroel	Chaim Asher's	Continuation of Garbarske Gasse
Rabinowitz	Feivel		Continuation of Garbarske Gasse
Rachkin	Shmuel Yitzchak		Tepersze (Potters) Gasse
Rosyanski	Yankel David		Paretszer Gasse
Rotbort	Monia		Poczta Gasse
Rubenstein		sisters	Poczta Gasse
Rubenstein	Abrahamel		Szmole Gesl (Wanska)
Rubenstein	David		Sokolker Gasse
Rubenstein	Leibel		Sokolker Gasse
Rubenstein	Malka		Garbarske (Tanners) Gasse
Rubenstein	Yasha	cabinet maker / carpenter	Sokolker Gasse
Rubenstein	Yechiel	Karmiz	Continuation of Garbarske Gasse
Rudi	Avraham Shmuel		Bod (Bath) Gesl
Rudi	Efraim Eli		Czerkowe Gasse
Sapir	Yisroel		Kruszyniany
Sapirstein	Merke		On the market
Sapirstein	Moshel		On the market
Sapirstein	Yekutiel		On the market
Sapirstein	Yekutiel		Tepersze (Potters) Gasse
Segal	Leibke		Szislewice Gasse
Segalowitz	Moshe Ahron		On the market
Shachnes		Noach Keila's	Zobie Gasse
Shafir	Hinde	Alyote's	Garbarske (Tanners) Gasse

Shafir	Sender		Garbarske (Tanners) Gasse
Shapiro	Abba		Sokolker Gasse
Shein	Asher		Rynkowe Gasse
Shein	Mashke		Szislewice Gasse
Shein	Noske	the lathe turner	Mil Gasse
Sheinberg	David		Szislewice Gasse
Sheinberg	Efraim		On the market
Sheinberg	Miriam	Efroytshik's: (i.e. Efraim's wife)	On the market
Sheinman	Feivel	Bobitse's	Garbarske (Tanners) Gasse
Shimer		from Grajewo	Gmine Gasse
Shinder	Arka		Sokolker Gasse
Shinder	Chaim Eli		Czerkowe Gasse
Shinder	Sender		Sokolker Gasse
Shinder	Yankel		Gmine Gasse
Shishlitsan			Gmine Gasse
Shishlitsan	Alter		Zobie Gasse
Shishlitsan	Eli		Sokolker Gasse
Shmidt	Berl	Komiteitser	Garbarske (Tanners) Gasse
Shmidt	Ozer		Sokolker Gasse
Shmulewitz	Kalman		On the market
Shmulewitz			Czerkowe Gasse
Shneider		Family Zshuzshe's	Zobie Gasse
Shneider		Podrip	Paretszer Gasse
Shneider	Shaya		Kavkaz
Shneider	Tsale		Kavkaz
Shneider	Yudke	wagon driver	Kavkaz
Shogom	Alter		Tepersze (Potters) Gasse
Sholochowitz			On the market
Sholochowitz			Mil Gasse
Sholochowitz	Ozer		Tepersze (Potters) Gasse
Shoshanski	Pinie	the Chochom's (son of the wise man)	Szmole Gesl (Wanska)
Shturmak		Gimzshe's	Gmine Gasse
Shturmak		the lathe turner	Szislewice Gasse

Shturmak	Alter		Czerkowe Gasse
Shturmak	Alter		Mil Gasse
Shturmak	Avrahamel		Paretszer Gasse
Shturmak	Beile Feigel		Czerkowe Gasse
Shturmak	Motel		Paretszer Gasse
Shulruf	Shmaryahu	Shmerl from Kotly	Hassidim or Paltiel's Gasse (Grochowa)
Shushan	Berl		Kavkaz
Shuster	Abke		Bod (Bath) Gesl
Shuster	Peretz		Poczta Gasse
Shuster	Gedliahu		Tepersze (Potters) Gasse
Shuster	Itzik		Szmole Gesl (Wanska)
Shuster	Moshe		Gmine Gasse
Shuster	Moshel		Garbarske (Tanners) Gasse
Shuster	Tevel		Garbarske (Tanners) Gasse
Shuster	Yankel	Abke's	Garbarske (Tanners) Gasse
Shuster	Yisroel		Gmine Gasse
Shuster	Yisroel	Volove	Mil Gasse
Shweitzer	Berl		Szmole Gesl (Wanska)
Shweitzer	Chaim Ahron		Szmole Gesl (Wanska)
Shweitzer	Shlomo Chona		Sokolker Gasse
Shweitzer	Shmuel Chona		Szmole Gesl (Wanska)
Sikorski			Mil Gasse
Sirota	Avrahamel		Kavkaz
Sirota	Yisroel	Elisha's	Kavkaz
Skowronek	Moshe	Africaners	Paretszer Gasse
Skowronek	Moshe	the Africaner: from Africa	Gmine Gasse
Slapak	Beilke		Hassidim or Paltiel's Gasse (Grochowa)
Slapak	Moshe		Gmine Gasse
Slapak	Moshke		Kavkaz
Slapak	Yitzchak		Sokolker Gasse
Slowr	Leibka		Sokolker Gasse
Slowr	Sholmo		Sokolker Gasse

Sofer	David	Dyodia the baker	Sokolker Gasse
Sofer	Sender		On the market
Sofer	Sender		Czerkowe Gasse
Sofer	Yisrael		Sokolker Gasse
Sofer/Safer	Yisroel		Hassidim or Paltiel's Gasse (Grochowa)
Stamblier	Nonie		Gmine Gasse
Stein	Eliezer		Bialystoker Gasse
Steinsaper	Henech		Poczta Gasse
Steinsaper	Motke		Bialystoker Gasse
Stolarski	Baruch		Mil Gasse
Stolarski	Binyamin	Ozshorske's	Paretszer Gasse
Stolarski	Efraim		Kavkaz
Stolarski	Itsel		Czerkowe Gasse
Stolarski	Zelig	Ozshorske's	Kavkaz
Stolarski	Zelig Yosel		Czerkowe Gasse
Stotski	Karpel		Garbarske (Tanners) Gasse
Stotski	Yakov Yeshiye		Garbarske (Tanners) Gasse
Suraski	Baruch		Bod (Bath) Gesl
Suruk	A		Poczta Gasse
Talkowski	Velvel	of Plante	Tepersze (Potters) Gasse
Tarlowski	Abba		Continuation of Garbarske Gasse
Tarlowski	Baruch		Continuation of Garbarske Gasse
Tarlowski	Dobe Chana		Continuation of Garbarske Gasse
Tarlowski	Motel		Continuation of Garbarske Gasse
Temkin	Yankel		Kavkaz
Terkel	Avrahamel		Tepersze (Potters) Gasse
Terkel	Motke		Poczta Gasse
Tewel	Berl		Szmole Gesl (Wanska)
Tewel	Yankel		Szmole Gesl (Wanska)
Toltshes	Lozer	Golye's	Mil Gasse

Trashtshon	Moshe		Tepersze (Potters) Gasse
Trashtshon	Tevel		Tepersze (Potters) Gasse
Tseshler			Gmine Gasse
Tseshler	Yankel		On the market
Tsifer	Beirach	Naser Arbeiter = worker of wet objects (a type of textile work)	Bod (Bath) Gesl
Tsigel	Eli Chaim	the painter	Gmine Gasse
Tsimerman			Gmine Gasse
Tsemachowski	Chaim	from Nowy Dwór	Hassidim or Paltiel's Gasse (Grochowa)
Tultses	Golya		Mil Gasse
Turski			On the market
Turski			Hassidim or Paltiel's Gasse (Grochowa)
Wein	Fishel		Poczta Gasse
Wein	Sender		Poczta Gasse
Wein	Shmuel		Poczta Gasse
Weiner	Dudi	Yididka's	Kavkaz
Weiner	Eizik		Tepersze (Potters) Gasse
Weiner	Eli	Meir Fishel's	Gmine Gasse
Weiner	Moshel		Poczta Gasse
Weiner	Moshehke	Amerikaner	Continuation of Garbarske Gasse
Weiner	Motye		Rynkowe Gasse
Weiner	Velvel		Paretszer Gasse
Weiner	Yankel		Continuation of Garbarske Gasse
Weiner	Yankel	Chozsheike's	Bod (Bath) Gesl
Weiner	Yishayahu	Yididka's	Kavkaz
Weiner	Yudel	Zshidak	Continuation of Garbarske Gasse
Weinrach	Shye		Mil Gasse
Weinstein			On the market
Weirach	Meyer	Tsygele = goat	Zobie Gasse
Wrirach	Yehosha	rope maker	Bialystoker Gasse
Wilenski	Shlomo	of Bytyñ	Paretszer Gasse

Wilenski	Yehuda		Mil Gasse
Wilenski	Zelig		On the market
Wilenski	Zelig		Bialystoker Gasse
Winograd	Berl	the geler: blond one	Continuation of Garbarske Gasse
Wisok	David	the blind baker	Mil Gasse
Wolf	Abke		Garbarske (Tanners) Gasse
Wolf	Ahron	Ahron Montishke's	Tepersze (Potters) Gasse
Wolf	Ahron		Garbarske (Tanners) Gasse
Wolf	Muntshik		Garbarske (Tanners) Gasse
Wolf	Yankel	Spodwiler	Continuation of Garbarske Gasse
Wolf	Zalman Nisel		Garbarske (Tanners) Gasse
Wolfowitz		Moshe Kreine's	Kavkaz
Wolinski	Yitzchak	Ozieranyer	Bialystoker Gasse
Wolkow	Itshe	Gronem	Kavkaz
Wollman	David	David Lokyar	Tepersze (Potters) Gasse
Wordbeiytshik	Tsharne		Zobie Gasse
Worobeiytshik	Shlomo		Garbarske (Tanners) Gasse
Wosilski	Yeshayahu		Sokolker Gasse
Yaglom	Henech		Tepersze (Potters) Gasse
Yaglom		From the mill	Bialystoker Gasse
Yarida	Moshe Mendel		Poczta Gasse
Yarushewski	Yisroel		Szislewice Gasse
Yasem/Yosem		pharmacist	On the market
Yasem/Osem	Itschke		Paretszer Gasse
Yasem	Leizer	Malach hamavet (angel of death)	Continuation of Garbarske Gasse
Yasem	Moshe	From Olekshits	Gmine Gasse
Yatwetski			Szislewice Gasse
Yellin	Berl	shoemaker	Tepersze (Potters) Gasse
Yisroel	David		Rynkowe Gasse
Yoches	Fishka		Kavkaz
Yoches	Meir	Fishka	Kavkaz

Yudzik	Yudel		Continuation of Garbarske Gasse
Yozelewitz	Chatzkel		Bod (Bath) Gesl
Zak		family	Mil Gasse
Zakheim	Berl		Gmine Gasse
Zaleski	Moshe		Hassidim or Paltiel's Gasse (Grochowa)
Zaleski	Zeidel		Hassidim or Paltiel's Gasse (Grochowa)
Zalkin	Moshe		Sokolker Gasse
Zalkind	Melech		Bod (Bath) Gesl
Zaltsberg			Kavkaz
Zalutski	Chaim		Continuation of Garbarske Gasse
Zalutski	Yisroel		Continuation of Garbarske Gasse
Zazdra			On the market
Zditowiski	Baruch Mordechai		Szmole Gesl (Wanska)
Zditowiski	Pesach	from Osnar	Mil Gasse
Zelikowits			Szislewice Gasse
Zevin	Chatzkel		Gmine Gasse
Zevin	Moshe-Ahron		Szislewice Gasse
Zevin	Yitzchak	Moshe Ahron's	Continuation of Garbarske Gasse
Ziskind			Sokolker Gasse
Zubatz	Itsha		Szmole Gesl (Wanska)
Zubowski		the Tkoczes	Bialystoker Gasse
Zubowski	Shabtai		Szislewice Gasse

[Page 333]

They Fell for the Defense of Israel's Birth
An Eternal Praise for Their Memories!

Translated by Benjamin Kamm

Yisrael Korngold z"l

Yisrael Korngold, son of Khayim Korngold, was born in Krynki on February 2, 1883.

As a member of *Poalei-Tsion* [the Workers of Zion], he made aliyah to Israel in 1908, and worked in Judean settlements with a number of friends living in Komonah. Some time later, he moved to the Galilee with the original workers at Khavat-Kinneret. From there he went to Sigrah and was a guard on the Shava farm. At the same time he served as secretary for the Galilean branch of the *Poalei-Tsion* party.

On Passover eve 1909, a Christian Arab from the nearby village Kfar Kanah tried to rob a Jew traveling from Sigrah. The Jew, trying to defend himself, shot the attacker and killed him. The villagers of Kfar Kanah, hoping to avenge the blood of their fellow, ambushed Korngold near his settlement's cemetery. After trying to convince him to fight with them, with no luck, they fatally shot him. This happened on the seventh day of Passover, April 12, 1909.

The writer Rabbi Binyamin Hamanoakh, who worked with Korngold on Kinneret, wrote of him: "Yisrael Korngold was a man with no illusions. He came to Israel after his temple had been destroyed in Russia. He was a man of character, solid as though made of an iron body and iron spirit. He was organized but without excesses. He never offended nor did he sarcastic anyone. He loved books, literature and language, and read at every available moment."

When the news of his death was made known to the Zionists of Krynki, they eternalized his memory by inscribing him in the *Sefer Hazahav* [Golden Book] of the *Keren Kayemet L'Yisrael* [Jewish National Fund].

Korngold's remains, among the first graves of the Jewish Guard in Israel, are buried today in Tel Chai, in the cemetery of the Hashomer [movement].

Tuvia Gendler z"l

Tuvia Gendler, son of Tsvi and Tsiporah Gendler, was born in Krynki in 1914, and received his Zionist education in the *Tarbut* [Culture] Hebrew School. As a teenager he was a member of *Hechaluts Hatsa'ir* [The Young Pioneer]. He made aliyah to Israel with his parents in 1930, and worked in Sirogin as a driver and copier. He was a sportsman and a member or the referees association for soccer and a volunteer firefighter in Tel Aviv. He was a hard worker his entire life, loyal and modest in all of his dealings.

During World War II he served in the British army, fighting in Africa and Greece. In Greece, the Germans captured him. Even though the four years of his captivity weakened his body, he reenlisted in the *Tsahal* [Israel Defense Force]. First he served in the artillery corps, and then was moved to medical service with the rank of Sergeant. He was killed in a traffic accident in Haifa at the end of his service on November 5,1948. On that day he was brought to eternal rest in the cemetery at Nakhalat Yitskhak.

Tuvia Gendler

[Page 334]

Yehuda Zhack z"l

Yeduha Zhack the son of Yitskhak and Freida Zhack of Krynki was born during Hannukah on November 30, 1926 in Geva in the Jezreel Valley.

Yehuda Zhack

When he was five years old, his family moved to Tel Aviv, where he studied in the school for workers' children. From his youth he was eager to help with his mother's work. He excelled in his studies, and was especially talented in technology and mathematics. When he finished his primary education, his parents expected him to learn a trade, but the principal of his school got him a scholarship so that he could continue his studies in high school. There he took college mathematics and physics courses. His concise essays excelled in clarity, thought, and completeness of expression. In his final year he organized the *Shedemah* group with his friends from the *Hanoar Ha'oved* [The Working Youth] movement, with his intention being to join the group and help them fulfill their goals as *chalutzim* [pioneers]. The group later settled in Revivim.

While the group was hiding in his parent's house, and even though he was well known in the Gadna, their leader forbid him from participating in any of their activities. They believed that if the British or secret police had captured him they would have included his house in subsequent searches. His friends, who participated in the group, called him a coward for apparently shirking his role. However, he decided to bear the insult without justifying himself, so that he would not reveal the secret hideaway.

He studied at the *Technion* in Haifa after finishing high school. He completed the compulsory year of security service as a guard, and while studying at the *Technion* he was a private in the Students' Regiment of the Haganah.

Early in 1948 he volunteered for an infantry unit in Haifa, and took part in battle activities in and around the city. His first course was in armory, and he completed it with excellence, and was appointed the regiment's traveling arms repairer for the platoon camping near Haifa. Because of a shortage of fighters, he joined the platoon's battle operations. And later he joined in the movement to free western Galilee. On the front line while capturing Akko, he volunteered for the regiment's storming unit. In the morning of May 17, 1948, as he was returning a sniper's fire, he lay low with his friends on the roof of a tall house opposite the wall of the old city. Yehuda cautioned the machine gunner lying beside him not to stand up. But he himself was not careful and was wounded by a bullet which struck his steel helmet, and he took it home as a souvenir. Subsequently, while he was attempting to lift an abandoned machine gun onto a wall, he was struck in the head by a bullet and died.

He was brought to eternal rest in the cemetery in Nachalat-Yitskhak in Tel Aviv on May 19, 1948.

Nakhum Nisht z"l

Nakhum Nisht son of Barukh-Bendet and Rakhel Nisht was born on December 29, 1921, in Krynki, where he studied in the *Tarbut* Hebrew school. He made aliyah to Israel in 1934, to his relatives in Kvutsat Geva, and continued his studies at school there in *Eyn Charod.* With their completion, he entered the workforce in Geva.

Nakhum Nisht

[Page 335]

He was active in the Field Corps during World War II, enlisted in the British army and served in the Drivers Corps of the *Shemidi* camp. "I'm not doing this for the English," he explained, "and it is better that I should regret what I have done than not to enlist." He wanted to fight, but he was destined for monotonous, agonizing days in the desert. He struggled with himself to avoid becoming a "soldier" in his manners and speech, and not lapse into card games. He even struggled with his tendency to watch the games. In the desert, he tried to keep himself busy with cultural activities. He prepared a masquerade for Passover, often read the Bible, dreamed of his studies and especially enjoyed listening to music. He was also interested in sports, and was eager for any news that came from Israel, especially about the various political parties. Every scenic view that he saw reminded him of the homeland.

Even though he was a loner and didn't talk about himself, he regularly wrote home. He was very emotional, yet shy. Because he had upset his father in his youth, he often imagined that he was insulting other people. He tried not to bother his colleagues.

He served in such places as Libya, Tripoli, and Italy. In an accident in Benghazi, he suffered severe wounds and lay in a hospital for six months. Yet refused to be released from the army and sought a medical examination to prove his health. "The war is not yet over," he asserted, and remained in the army an additional year. He was angry that volunteering for the brigades was not as rapid as he expected. In his soul he remained a man of creation, and not of war. The destruction in Greece depressed his spirit. "How many men's lives were lost in this wilderness with no value?" he complained. "How many millions were invested in this, which could have been helpful to both sides?"

In a later period, when he saw the Mandate government's relationship to the Jews, he could no longer serve in the British army. In June 1946, during the investigations, detentions and destruction in Yagur and other places, he informed his commander that if he was not released, he would not be responsible for his actions. When he was discharged, he returned to Kvutsat Geva, and was received as a member. He rejected the suggestion that he move to the city as a clerk, because "there is a more immediate need for agriculturalists," and did not seek a comfortable or easy life. He was a man of obligation, fulfilling the dreams of his body and soul.

When the War of Independence broke out, he enlisted in the Field Corps, and refused to go for a Sergeant's course, explaining that there was a need for good privates. He wrote to his father "after working and guarding in the Kvutsa, I am going to other places. If my letters are delayed, don't worry."

He died March 19, 1948, in battle on the Gilboa [mountain] across from the Sollel-Bone quarry. He was among the first injured, but in his usual way he did not leave his position, saying, "I can still fight." He continued until he collapsed.

He was buried in the Geva cemetery.

Ya'ir Friedman z"l

Ya'ir Friedman the son of David and Miriam Friedman was born on December 12, 1930 in Ramat Hasharon to his hard working parents from Krynki. He grew and was educated in the spirit of labor. He was one of the excellent students in the public school, and after that in the *Tichon Khadash* [New High School] in Tel Aviv. A member of the Gadna, he was counted among the Field Corps in the Sharon district.

Ya'ir Friedman

He was drafted into service in a company of one of his regiment's brigades. Although he was his parents' only son, he rejected the associated privileges, instead asking to join a fighting unit. He participated in battles in Arabic Kfar-Saba and Latrun, in addition to the capture of Kakun, Migdal Tsedek and Rosh HaAyin.

He fell in the heavy fighting that was conducted face to face by Kula on July 17, 1948, and was buried in the cemetery in Netanya.

[Page 336]

Yitskhak Khefer z"l

Yitskhak Khefer (Litvak) son of Nakhum and Sarah (the daughter of Binyamin Ya'akov and Rakhel Kaplan from Krynki) was born in the village of Vitkin in August 1936 to agricultural parents from among the village's founders.

Yitskhak Khefer

He went to school there completing school. He was active in the life of the village, especially in cultural matters. He wrote poems and drew sketches for his friends in the community and was beloved by all. He enlisted into the army's air force and was involved in cultural and entertainment activities. He was among the first *Mister* [a class of IDF plane] pilots, and when he finished his service, he reenlisted in the army as a pilot. He participated in the Sinai campaign. He died on March 10, 1958 during a military mission, and was buried in the military section of the cemetery in Kfar Vitkin.

[Page 338]

Monument On The Field Of Ashes At Treblinka

Translations by Judie Goldstein

A cemetery without any bodies, rocks for grave stone,s no bones.

[Page 339]

Perpetuating And Remembering

A symbolic grave stone for the Krynki Martyrs,
at a Yizkor [Memorial] gathering of the Krynkers in Israel

[Page 340]

Krynker Yizkor Committee
that is made up of
Krynker Relief Committee And Krynker Youth Circle

~~~~~~~~~~~~~~~~~~~~~~~~~~~~~~~~~~~~

Dear Fellow Krynkers:
We call you to honor the memory of our Krynker Martyrs at the 12th Yahrzeit that is upcoming
Sunday, the 14th November, 2 o'clock P.M.

At **Adelphi Hall, 74 5th Avenue,** between 13th and 14th Street, New York, **Room 10B.**

At this year's Yizkor gathering we have a very distinguished Krynker guest, **Bendet Nisht** (now he calls himself **Baruch Niv**).

Bendet Nisht came from Israel in order to be at our yearly Yizkor gathering.

Bendet Nisht, besides working for world Jewry became well known by serving the Israeli government as Israeli Consul to Poland and Romania.

As Consul in Poland he had the possibility of going to our shtetl Krynik three times. **Bendet Nisht** will be at the Yizkor gathering to tell us what he saw and heard in Krynik. He will also bring personal greetings from all the Krynkers in Israel, to the relatives and acquaintances.

Bendet Nisht
(Baruch Niv)

At the Yizkor gathering people will speak about the plantation project our memorial in Israel.

This year large Yizkor gatherings have also been organized in Chicago and Los Angeles and **Bendet Nisht** will also make appearances there.

We urge you to come to the gathering and to honor our Krynker martyrs in a worthy manner.

Be on time! You will be able to see the "movies" from previous years' Yizkor gatherings and from Tursky's banquet. The "movies" of this year's gathering will be shown next year.

Krinker Yizkor Committee, Krynker Relief Committee, Krynker Youth Circle

Krinker Memorial Fund
c/o Nota Koslowksy
41 Union Square, New York 3, N.Y.
Tel. AL5-5787

Lois Shein (Leibke Noske's)
Nota Koslowsky
Itche Novi

[Page 341]

Krynker Yizkor Committee presenting a check to build
A Children's house in Kibbutz Rosh Hanikra, Israel

From right, sitting: Yekutiel Tursky, Lois Shein, Baruch Niv, Israel Stolarsky, Irving Novik, Yitzhak Farber
Standing: Eli Levin, Aba Blok, Florence Friedman, Zaydl Kaplan, Mayer Bloch, Ester Schneiderman, Jankel
Kirschner

The Chairwoman of the Union of Krynker Landslayt in Los Angeles, Sophie Berger,
presents a check to the representatives of the "Histadrut Campaign" in America

[Page 342]

This Is How We Began

Trees · Candles for the departed
In memory of our martyrs

The shocking Second World War came to an end. Individual Krynker survivors arrived in Israel and brought news of our hometown – terrible. Everyone was murdered, exterminated by the Nazi animals and their helpers among the Polish population. We were shaken even though we already knew about the situation of our brothers and sisters.

The Jewish settlement in Israel decided to propose a forest of six million trees in memory of our devoured brothers in Europe. We, Krynkers in Israel, as well as throughout the world, planted in *Yaar HaKdoshim* [Martyrs' Forest] up to two thousand trees in the "Krynker small forest" in memory and in the names of our annihilated townspeople.

Krynker landslayt from America, Argentina, Israel, etc. planting the "Krynker small forest" at the "Martyrs' Forest"

[Page 343]

Plaque about the building of the children's house

A Children's House In The Name Of Our Murdered Community

The Krynker Committeee in Israel had the idea to perpetuate the memory of our community with an institutional monument that would carry its name and at the same time serve as a point of renewal and vibrant life.

After much deliberation, we accepted the proposal of the general workers' organization *"Histadrut"* [The Jewish Agency] in Israel to build a children's house in a newly settled *kibbutz,* Rosh Hanikrah, located at the Lebanonese border. The kibbutz was being settled by young immigrant survivors, who had just arrived from refugee camps in Europe. There were already a few children there, but without a specially maintained building for them.

With *"Histadrut's"* help and the Krynker landsmanshaften in New York, Chicago, Los Angeles and Israel the children's house was built at the kibbutz and it is now full of happiness and high spirits.

[Page 344]

The children's house building

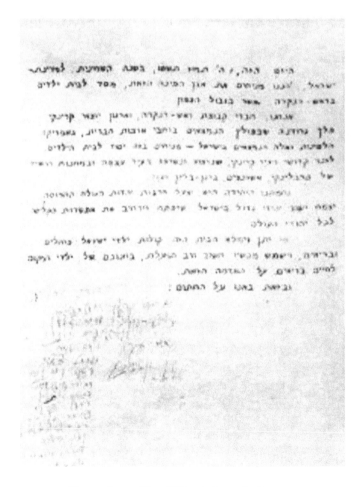

*Cornerstone of the children's house in the name
of the Krynki martyrs, in Kibbutz Rosh Hanikra*

[Page 345]

In the name of Kryinkers, says B. Niv (Nisht)
The opening ceremony speaker

Mordchai Vilensky, Sheyma Kaplan
and Baruch Niv, unveiling the plaque

Krynker guests with the Kibbutz children

With the work associates

[Page 346]

Our Written Grave Stone

To perpetuate the memory of our annihilated Jewish community we planted trees in the name of those murdered on "Yaar HaKdoshim" [Martyrs' Mount] and built the children's house in Kibbutz Rosh Hanikra. However we still were not satisfied.

We took on a third task to erect for our Jewish hometown a written memorial that would be sent to every Krynker family and individual Jews wherever they were in the world, to their homes. That is the Yizkor Book that you see before your eyes.

Below is an extract from the "brochure" which was published about three years ago as an indication of the content for the projected "Pinkus Krynki".

Table of Contents of "Pinkus Krynki"

[Page 347]

A Memorial Book about the Destruction of Krynik

"*Krynik in Khurbn*" (Holocaust in Krynik)

A memorial book, by Abraham Soifer a Krynker survivor, was published in 1948 by the Krynker Relief Union of Uruguay and Argentina.

The book, 269 pages, printed in Montevideo is illustrated and contains a map of Krynik on which the ghetto limits are drawn.

The author dedicates the opening chapter to "young memories of a dear time in the past," describing life in the shtetl until the outbreak of the Second World War. Then he goes on to events in Krynki from the beginning of the war and describes life in the shtetl under the Red Army until the sudden attack by the Germans in June 1941. Then Soifer describes his flight from home to the East, his joining a Russian partisan group and his perilous return during his mission to Krynki.

Here he first describes what he found, saw and lived through in the ghetto and the destruction of the community. Soifer further describes his survival with the remnant in the work camp where the Nazis, after forcing out the Jews from Krynik, "employed" slaves to do the work of Hitler's war machine. These were a couple of hundred Jewish tradesmen and from there they were taken on their last journey to Auschwitz.

In the rest of the book A. Soifer tells what happened and the suffering he saw and endured in the "king of demons" destruction in the extermination camps and what he and other Krynkers experienced. They all displayed valor and were heroic and generously helped to fight these evil men and even took part in the plan to blow up the crematoria.

We have taken excerpts from "*Krynik in Khurbn*" and put them in our Yizkor Book.

[Page 348]

Memorial plaque in the "Holocaust Chamber"
at "Har Zion", Jerusalem

Memorial Service For the Krynker Martyrs

Memorial service at the memorial monument. At the cemetery in Buenos Aires, Argentina

Memorial service in Tel-Aviv

[Page 349]

Chairmanship of the Memorial service
Montevideo, Uruguay

Memorial service in Montevideo

[Page 350]

Krynkers Around The World

Translated by Judie Goldstein

Krynker gathering in Israel (first half)

Krynker gathering in Israel (second half)

Gathering of Krynkers in Israel 1964 with a foreign guest

[Page 351]

Krynker Relief Committee, New York, 1918

From right sitting: Boruch Sanders, Abe Kaplan, Meyer Blok, Lois Shine, Irving Novak, Kutiel Tursky, Morris Brudovsky, Florence Friedman, Sam Leibovitch.
Standing: Abe Blok, William Levin, Motl Kugel, Sarah Gabai, Mayer Falk, Saul Gordon, Jacob Kirzhner, Berl Zakon

Former Krynkers active in Chicago

[Page 352]

Fellow Krynkers committee in Los Angeles

1963 Fellow Krynkers committee in Buenos Aires

[Page 353]

Active members of the Krynker Landsmanschaft in Montevideo

Active members of the Krynker Landsmanschaft in Buenos Aires

Gathering of Krynker in Montevideo with the participation of Bendet Nisht (B. Niv)

[Page 354]

With Yosie Drayzik the only Krynker in Porto Alegra, Brazil

Meeting of the former Krynkers committee in Montevideo

Gathering of former Krynkers in Melbourne, Australia, 1968
Standing from left to right: Shimon Mordech (Mordchelewiec), Yankel Lieberman, Tevl Pruz'ansky, Mrs.
Mintz, Yehazkel Mintz, Mrs. Pruz'ansky, Hershel Mintz, Fanny Garkovy-Fink, Grokovy, Fanny Smom-Pruz'ansky.
Sitting from left to right: Mrs. Pruz'ansky (Gershon Pruz'ansky's widow), Israel Tzukert, Fanny Liberman-Fink,
Bendet Nisht (Baruch Niv, Israel), Lana Tzukers (Lev), Abraham Tzukert, Mrs. Mintz
Sitting first row: Mrs. Mordech, Mrs. Shimon, Gdalia Rubinstein

[Pages 355-357]

Note: List of photos. This has not been translated.

[Pages 358-359]

Note: List of authors. This has not been translated.

[Pages 359-360]

Translator's note: The Hebrew section by Dov Rabin on pages 359-360 is equivalent with the Yiddish section on pages 361-362.

[Page 361]

The Final Word

Translated by Judie Goldstein

Many years ago I began collecting material about Jewish Krynki in regard to a Yad Vashem project to investigate the history of the Jewish communities in Grodno Province and their destruction. Later, with the thought of publishing a Krynker Yizkor Book, I informed my good friend, since the beginning of the "HeHalutz" movement in Grodno District Bendet Nisht (Baruch Niv), during an accidental meeting.

He told me about a group of Krynkers, of which he was one, that meets periodically to gather memories of the hometown and jot them down as possible material for a projected Yizkor Book, and they "correct" each other in order to be as factual as possible. I encouraged Bendet and thought that that this was a good way in which to gather material for a memorial book.

Bendet asked me if I would agree to join them in preparing the book that the Krynkers planned to publish. I answered that I was prepared to "discuss" the matter further, but the main point was that the Krynkers would have to create this book on their own.

I might be interested if this were a fitting memorial and dealt specifically with the Krynker community, according to my concept and the research material that I had gathered during a previous search (in the Spring of 1920 to organize a first Pioneer *aliyah* to Israel).

In the meantime they should gather necessary documents and other material, especially about the Holocaust.

Two lovely years passed and I was invited to "interpret meanings" with the initiators of the "*Pinkus*". These meetings convinced me that these people were serious and they had the right material to publish a book. We thoroughly discussed the situation and in good faith and mutual understanding resolved the following points.

    a.   The aim of the "*Pinkus Krynki*" is to be a monument and eternal memorial, a real legacy by the ex-Krynkers in Israel and their descendants for generations.

    b.   The "*Pinkus*" is to be an authentic witness of the Holocaust and destruction of Jewish Krynki, with special emphasis on heroic acts, active and passive, that accompanied the annihilation. In order to meet the last wishes of our destroyed people, it should be told and written "for the world" so they will understand what these people were put through and how they were exterminated.

    c.   The "*Pinkus*" should also contain the history of the Jewish community in Krynki to the extent that documentation is available. The plan and contents of the "*Pinkus*" should be objective and the articles and facts should be precisely established.

[Page 362]

    a.   The "*Pinkus*" should mainly reflect the life of the Krynker community in its last year - all aspects of the community and especially its special characteristics.

b.   The purpose of the "*Pinkus*" is to perpetuate the community as a whole and not to serve as private family memorials. It is important to remember that the "*Pinkus*" is a monument for those who are no longer among the living and that it be consistent.

It is on this basis that the soul of the book, "*Pinkus Krynki,*" that lies before you, was built, even though we could not obtain all the information we wanted.

For instance, we were short on historical facts and even statistics (about the Krynki population, for example). The Krynker *Landslayt* organization in Israel turned to the Krynki municipal government and to the Jewish Historical Institute in Warsaw and begged for help in finding these facts and to have them sent to us. But it did not help.

We had to make do with the material that was readily available and set up, for instance, only sporadic historic chapters and thinly spread bits and pieces. But we brought the "substance" to the "*Pinkus*" - which you can read for yourself and which we already wrote about in the introduction.

The "*Pinkus*" was produced entirely by Krynker *landslayt*, through their brotherly cooperation and warm response in writing for the book, several due to their memories and cleverness, others by gathering material together, including photographs, etc.

In the end, I feel it is necessary - my duty to mention and praise all those dear volunteers who organized the "*Pinkus*" in general, from the book committee and my editorial colleagues and especially the man who spear-headed the project Bendet Nisht-Niv. Despite the obstacles, he persevered through the years and being a "man who does what he says" and who "completes his projects" he brought the "*Pinkus Krynki*" to press.

He deserves our heartfelt thanks!

Dov Rubin
Jerusalem, 15 *Shevat* [January] 5730 [1970]

[Pages 363-367]

Aid Index of Topics*

From the history of Jews in Krynki until the Nazi invasion in 1941 (ordered by the aleph beit)

Translated by Jerrold Landau

Note to the Reader: Pages 369 - 378 (original pages 363 – 367) are only printed / useful to scholars who are reading this English book to get information that is in the original "Pinkas Krynki" Yizkor book.
        * Of specific topics that are not noted as unique headings, and are not included in the center [i.e. the table of contents]

> *Translator's note:* The Hebrew index is on pages 363-364, and the Yiddish index is on page 365-366. The original was alphabetized according to the Hebrew / Yiddish alphabet. The translation has been alphabetized in accordance with the English. The Hebrew and Yiddish indices largely match, but have some discrepancies. Where the Hebrew and Yiddish match, I have placed an asterisk in the Yiddish page column. Where the entries match, but the pages differ, I have placed page numbers in both columns. Where an entry occurs in Hebrew but not in Yiddish, or vice versa, the column in for which the entry was not present was left blank. A spot check of the page numbers indicates that the original indexing may not have been completely accurate. Furthermore, the translation may indicate page breaks somewhat different than the original (i.e., the indication of a page break was often bumped to a paragraph end). This will result in the possibility of one-page discrepancies in the indexing.

* Page Numbers refer to original book

[Page 368]

Two Years of Soviet Rule 1939-1941
(in chronological order)

Translator's note: the Hebrew and Yiddish versions of this small chronology are equivalent.

Jews greet the Red Army (1939)	231
Refugees from Poland (Biezences)	234
Exile to the interior of Russia	232
Trotskyites	229
Soviet regime – means a permanent prison	232
Survival due to exile	234

Destruction and Bravery
(in chronological order)

Translator's note: Hebrew is 367-368, and Yiddish is 368-369. The vast majority of entries were equivalent in Hebrew and Yiddish, but there were few that did not have a matching entry. As in the index of topics, an asterisk in the Yiddish page column indicates that the same page numbers were listed in the Hebrew and Yiddish sections.

	Page in the Hebrew index	Page in the Yiddish index
Setting the *Beis Midrash* on fire	275	*
Poles, former Communists, threaten our lives	251	266
Removing one's hat and greeting every German	238	266
Whippings, beatings, thrashings	241	266
"Neighbors" rejoice over the confinement of Jews to a ghetto	239	266
Recital of Psalms shall save us	229, 232, 254, 296, 298	*
We will somehow manage, even now	323	
Waiting until Amalek received the final end of Haman – claim those opposed to revolt	275	*
A proof from the prophet Jonah that we should pray in the innards of the fish and we will be saved	250, 294	294
Four housewives next to once chimney	239, 273	*
Communal kitchen set up in the ghetto	243	*
An exemplary hospital and infirmary created in the ghetto	243, 270, 273	*
Forcing Jewish workers to go naked into a muddy stream and throw mud at each other	241	*

Aktion to rape Jewish girls	242	*
Jewish holidays designated for murder	242	*
Baking of Passover matzos in secret	125, 242	242
The murderers sing "When Jewish blood drips from the blade of the knife, the war goes better"	242, 282	242
Mosheke Lew (the baker) fights with the murderers	242, 270, 282	*
Clandestine radio receiver placed in a barrel	243, 274	*
To fight with the Nazis in the ghetto or forests?	314	*
"Neighbors" invited to the celebration of the deportation of the Jews	244, 275	275
Friendship with the Christian side decisively terminates	272	*
Gentile partisans take everything from a Jew who encountered them in the forest, and send him back to the ghetto	243, 274	274
Shkotzim [derogatory term for gentiles] pillage in the Jewish areas	309	*
An apostate informer gets "The World To Come"	308	*
German captains burst out laughing and photograph the atrocities during the liquidation of the ghetto	244, 276	276
The Christians rejoice – Now we will be freed of the *zhyds*, and will even inherit them	267	*
"General" sale of the belongings of the Jews, and the Nazis arrange what is left	244, 295	*
"You they will still have for a few days!"		271
"And let our eyes witness Your return to Zion in mercy" in the *Shmone Esrei* that was interrupted in the middle	251, 252	
"Natural death camp" for members of 21 communities	245, 277	*
Torments in attending to the call of nature	279, 299	*
Suicide in Kelbasin	248	*
"Why are so few dying here?"	247, 290	290
The chief slaughterer "intelligent" and a coward	245, 278	*
The wild beast (bloodhound) of Kelbasin	245, 278	*
A hiding place in a bathhouse tank	249, 250, 258, 294, 295, 304	*
Price for a Jew: 5 kilograms of sugar for showing where one is, 10-20 kilograms for turning him in to the Germans	290	*
Ukrainian gendarmes and their wickedness	253	*
A Polish woman says to my wife "Give me your felt boots, as soon you will no longer have a need for them!"	251	*

[Page 369]

Index of Places
Villages and streams in the Krynki area

***Page number listed refer to original book page numbers, not this English translation ***

Places to which the Jews of Krynki
maintained regular connections

Grodno	25, 27-29, 31, 33-35, 38, 39, 51, 52, 54, 56-61, 69, 72, 73, 75-78, 81-86, 88, 90, 92, 94, 95, 107, 109, 115, 133, 138, 140, 159, 167, 168, 177, 203, 204 229, 232, 245, 248, 249, 251, 265, 277, 284, 285, 290, 291, 305-307, 30, 314
Dąbrowa	50, 85, 245, 277, 285
Holinka	60, 205, 245, 277
Harodok	30, 41, 75, 77, 109, 117, 199
Nowy Dwór	47, 50, 245, 248, 277, 286, 287
Supraśl	259, 313, 314, 321, 326
Sokółka	29, 35, 38, 59, 76, 81, 93, 109, 115, 129, 136, 222, 233, 242, 245, 246, 250, 254, 255, 272, 277, 296, 297, 308, 319, 324
Sidra	79, 245, 277
Kozienice	29, 35, 38, 84, 90, 245, 277, 284, 285, 291
Kruszyniany	25, 31, 52, 61, 81

Camps in which the martyrs of Krynki were tortured and murdered

Auschwitz	286, 296, 297-304
Birkenau	298, 391, 303
Kelbasin	244-249, 251, 260, 272, 286, 288-293, 294, 315
Treblinka	251, 254, 25, 288, 290, 294, 296

[Page 370]

In Conclusion

The Editors

Translated by Judie Goldstein

With the conclusion of the *"Pinkus Krynki"*, we would like to express our thanks to all of those who contributed articles, photos, maps, etc to the publication of the Yizkor Book; and to those who put together the list of Jews in Krynki; and our landsman Abraham Soifer who allowed us to use and translate parts of his book *"Krynik in Hurbn"* [Disaster in Krynki] and his publishers the Krynker *landslayt* in Uruguay and Argentina; our friend Emil Sola who skillfully published the *"Pinkus"* and especially for creating the jacket and the book binding, as well as the printing and his workers.

And a special thanks to the artist Mrs. Nuta Kozlowsky (Chicago) who furnished the sketches of the Holocaust for the *"Pinkus"*.

Praise all of them.

[Page 371]

After the Book was Completed

Translated by Judie Goldstein

The following pages contain details and photographs that for various reasons were not included in the book.

More Names Of Krynker Fighters Who Perished

After the text of our *"Pinkus"* was printed, we became aware of more names of Krynker fighters who perished (published in *"Lexicon HaGbura"*, Part 2 of Volume 1, published by "Yad Vashem", Jerusalem, 1969.

1.   Lev Mashal, son of Tuvia and Feyga, Born 1911 in Krynki, lived and worked in Bialystok, a member of the Underground, fell during the uprising, August 1943. Details supplied by Geler.
2.   Kolia and wife, from Krynki, belong to the Underground in Bialystok ghetto, perished August 1943.

[Page 372]

Personalities

Translated by Judie Goldstein

Wolf Weiner
(Velvel der Stoler
[the carpenter])
Former alderman
and Vice-Mayor
in Krynki

David Gotlieb
Leader of the Krynker
"Bund" and was
Vice-Mayor in Krynki

Jakob Mordchilevitch
Through his efforts
the synagogue was
rebuilt after the fire

Organized Community Events

"Tarbut" School Classes

Bund" activists in Krynki

The Drama Circle
[Written on the right hand photo: Krynki Drama Circle June 1939]

[Page 373]

Krynki Today ... (April 1967)

The market place and the Orthodox Church

The market place

The market place today a city park

[Pages 374-375]

[Page 376]

The town, the Holocaust, and the revolt in the eyes of Krynki

Supplementary Material

(Not included in the Yizkor book)

Synagogues in Krynki

(* Click on the photographs to enlarge)

**The photos are courtesy of Krzysztof Schabowicz <schaby@neostrada.pl>,
who granted permission to display them in this project.**

*Four views of the 19th century "Kaukaski" synagogue.
It still stands on the market square at Gorna Street, and is now used as a movie theater.*

*Four views of a Chassidic synagogue on Grochowa Street,
probably built in the 19th century. The building is now a warehouse.*

Cemetery in Krynki

**The photos are courtesy of Krzysztof Schabowicz <schaby@neostrada.pl>,
who granted permission to display them in this project.**

The oldest identified matzeva are from the middle of the 18th century

You Tube video from Krynki, Poland

Link & translation provided by Robin Koerner

A local historian is giving a tour of the town to local high school students in Polish – you can see some of what is left of the Jewish life that once flourished there.

My nephew's fiancée translated the conversation for me (see below) which tells a little about the Jewish history & other info on the town. Just thought it was interesting & wanted to share it with you. The video was sent to me by another "landsman" and Facebook friend of mine, Diane Fisher who lives in San Francisco – her grandfather is from this town also.

"Żyjemy Razem". Krynki 2010

We live Together. Workshop. Krynki 2010. Warsztaty wielokulturowe. Zobacz film
http://www.youtube.com/watch?v=a2b--XbG_go">http://www.youtube.com/watch?v=a2b--XbG_go

---

Children introducing themselves by name, they are all students of the local school/youth organization in Krynki.

Interview between boy in black & white coat and local historian:

Boy: What is the name of the building we're standing in front of and when was it built?

Historian: The building in front of us is the Beth Midrash (study hall) and it was built in the 19th century. We are in a section of town called "Caucasian." Where does it get this name? During the late 19th to early 20th century the leather industry was prominent here and all the raw leather was imported from Caucasia (a mountainous region in Siberia). This name was adopted by the Jewish people working and living here and it is also what the synagogue was named.

Interview between young girl and historian

Girl: May I ask you who built the doors we're standing in front of and when were they built?

Historian: This building is from the pre-war era. A Jewish family lived in this building prior to the war and the doors were likely crafter by a Jewish carpenter. What do they symbolize? The ornaments on these doors, the head of a lion, palm leaves, grapes are all common symbolic items seen throughout Judiasm. I believe these doors are also from the pre-war.

Next interview

Girl: Ms. Cecilia, how and when was this building constructed?

Historian: This is the church of Krynki, built from 1907-1912 in the Neo-gothic style during a project created by a well-known architect of the late 19th and early 20th century Stefan Syzller.

Next interview

Girl: What are these ruins?

Historian: These are the ruins of the largest synagogue in Krynka which was called "the Great Synagogue." It was built in the late 18th century, it was several stories tall with elaborate decoration inside. The building was destroyed in 1944 as the last of the German army was fleeing Krynki. The ruins stood in the same condition until the 1970s when they were burnt down completely, leaving only these walls behind.

Next interview

Girl: Who did this beautiful house belong to, was there anything interesting that happened here?

Historian: This is a very characteristic building that is seen all over Krynki. It is made of light-colored brick, with a very decorative balcony and a distinct Star-of-David within the brickwork at each corner of the house.

Next interview

Girl: Ms. Cecilia, what year was our parish church built?

Historian: The construction took place between 1864-1868 and it is the first brick and mortar Orthodox Christian house of worship in Krynki. Prior to that there were 2-3 wooden churches before a larger group of Christians moved into the area and built this.

Next interview

Girl: I know that this is a synagogue but does it have any special meaning?

Historian: This synagogue belonged to the Chasidic Jews of Slonimski, it is also from the 19th century. As you can see it is a brick building which once was beautifully decorated however is now falling apart. It is also known as the Jewtes Beth Midrash because the founder of this synagogue was Jewta Rotawoloska Waltham (?).

Historian: Krynki is located in a very geographically interesting area of Poland, as well in an interesting area of Europe for several reasons. It was a highly diverse area both culturally and religiously people whose footprints can be seen to this day. Also the layout of the town itself is very original in that there is a central, six-sided central market with 12 roads coming off of it. It is one of only two places in the world built this way, the other being Paris whose central market was constructed 100 years after the one in Krynki was built.

Message scrolling at end: After this original documentary was filmed, several others have created similar films, texts and works of art inspired by the students of the local Krynki school.

NAME INDEX

C

D

E

Lightning Source UK Ltd.
Milton Keynes UK
UKHW032242060223
416580UK00007B/674